WARSHIP 2008

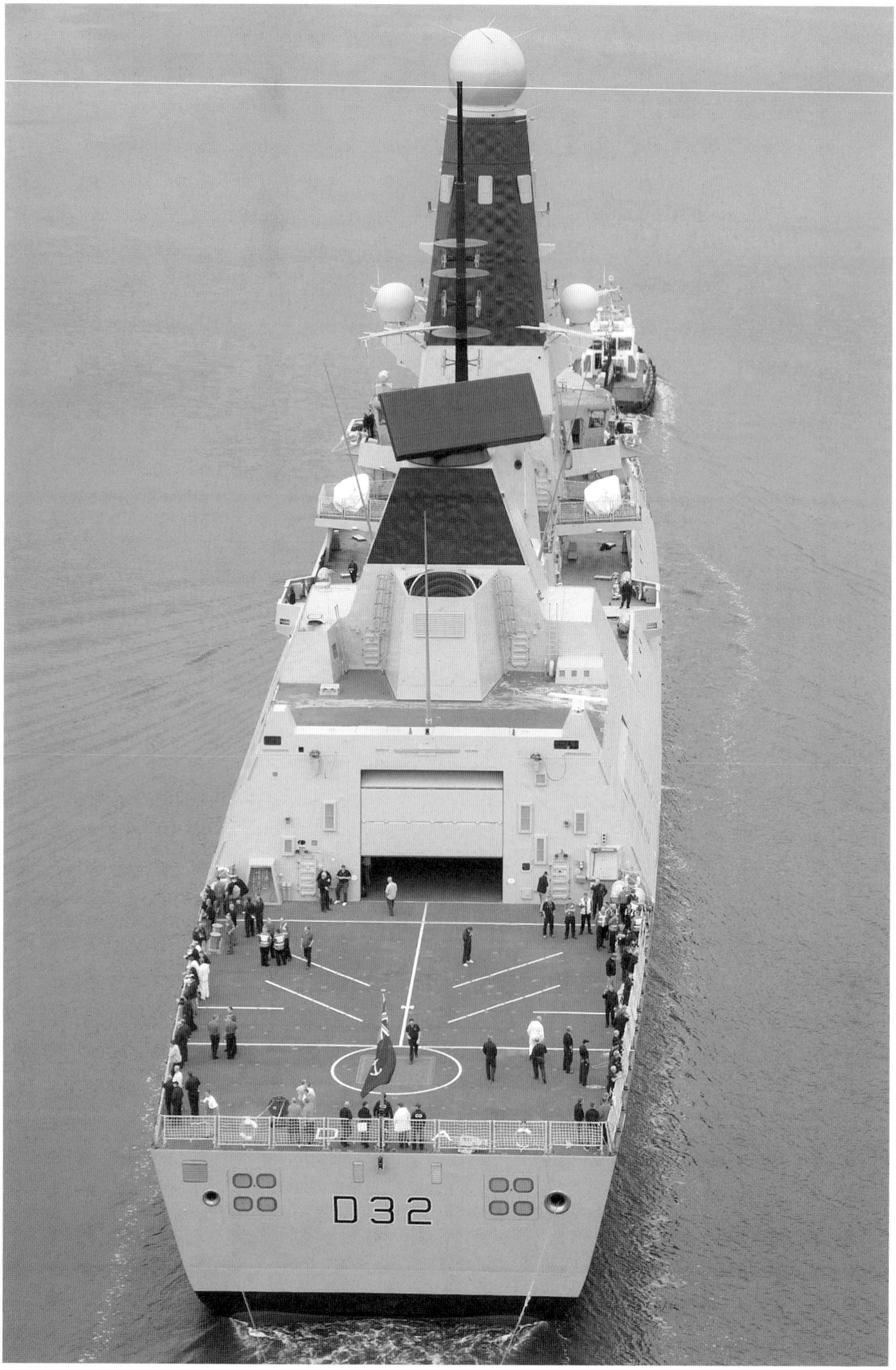
D32

WARSHIP **2008**

Founding Editor: Antony Preston

Editor: John Jordan
Assistant Editor: Stephen Dent

CONWAY

Frontispiece:
The first British Type 45 destroyer, HMS Daring, passes under the Erskine Bridge on her return from successful initial sea trials on 14 August 2007. (Conrad Waters)

Conway offers *Warship* readers the opportunity to guarantee that they will receive their copy of the annual. This publication is available as an annual direct subscription from Conway at a pre-publication offer price. To receive further details, or to reserve your copy, please email:-
orders@anovabooks.com You will also have the opportunity to register for email updates, book news and special offers.

The team at the *Warship* annual always welcome contributions and comments from readers, so if you are interested in writing for us, or simply want to express your views about current or future issues, please contact us at our postal/email address:-

JOHN JORDAN
Editor *Warship*
Conway
10 Southcombe Street,
London W14 0RA

email: warship@anovabooks.com

© Conway 2008

First published in Great Britain in 2008 by Conway,
an imprint of Anova Books,
10 Southcombe Street, London, W14 0RA
www.conwaymaritime.com
Tel. +44 (0)20 7605 1400   Fax. +44 (0)20 7605 1401

All rights reserved. No part of this publication may be reproduced, stored in a retrieval system, or transmitted in any form or by any means, electronic, mechanical, photocopying, recording or otherwise, without the prior permission of the publisher.

British Library Cataloguing in Publication Data
A record of this title is available on request from the British Library.

ISBN: 978 1 84486 062 3

Printed and bound by Times Publishing, Malaysia.

CONTENTS

Editorial 7

FEATURE ARTICLES

Hôshô: The first aircraft carrier of the Imperial Japanese Navy 9
Kathrin Milanovich describes Japan's first aircraft carrier, the design process and subsequent modifications, and corrects a number of errors about the ship which have found their way into published sources.

The Action off Calabria and the Myth of Moral Ascendancy 26
Vincent P. O'Hara examines the Action off Calabria and the claims that it was instrumental in the Royal Navy establishing a psychological advantage over the Italian Regia Marina in the Mediterranean in 1940.

Diminishing Returns: Small Battleship Designs, 1919-1953 40
Stephen McLaughlin describes a number of designs for battleships of reduced size, the result of political and economic pressure, none of which ever got beyond the drawing board.

Imperial Japanese Minelayers *Itsukushima, Okinoshima, and Tsugaru* 52
Hans Lengerer takes a detailed look at three purpose-built cruiser minelayers.

The Odyssey of Von Spee and the East Asiatic Squadron, 1914 67
Philippe Caresse looks at the origins and formation of the German East Asiatic Squadron and its passage across the Pacific Ocean in 1914 to its final defeat and extermination at the Falklands.

Italian Fast Coastal Forces: Development, Doctrine and Campaigns, 1914-1986. 85
Part One: From the Beginning to 1934
Erminio Bagnasco, **Enrico Cernuschi** and **Vincent P. O'Hara** trace the development of the Italian MAS boat from its conception to the interwar period.

The Soviet Project 7/7U Destroyers 99
Vladimir Yakubov and **Richard Worth** tell the story of the workhorses of the Soviet Navy during the Second World War: the Project 7 and Project 7U classes of destroyer.

The Cruiser *De Grasse* 115
John Jordan and **Bruno Gire** recount the story of a ship which was ordered in 1938, had its construction suspended in June 1940 when 28% complete, was launched postwar to clear the slipway, and was eventually completed as the prototype of a new series of French anti-aircraft cruisers.

First Class Cruisers: Part Three 136
Chris Ware provides the long-awaited final part of a trilogy of articles, examining the development of the Royal Navy's First Class cruisers from the turn of the century and concluding with a study of operations in the First World War.

Continued overleaf...

REVIEW SECTION

Warship Notes 146
Stephen Dent: HMS *Furious*.
Jean Hood: The Mystery of the SS *Castor*.
William G Crawford: The bombing of HMS *Iron Duke*, October 1939.
John Jordan: The Fonds Potsdam.
Hans Lengerer: The Mihogaseki Incident.
Ian Sturton and **Stephen Dent:** The Victorian gunboat *Handy*.
A's & A's: Armed Merchant Ships 1885 • IJN Kana scripts • Yugoslav Destroyer *Split* • Brennan Torpedo • Mystery Gunboats

Navies in Review 2008 162
Conrad Waters provides an overview of the year's naval developments, construction and procurement.

Reviews 180
Churchill's Navy • Attack from the Sea • The Banzai Hunters • Changing Course • *Nelson* to *Vanguard* • No Higher Honor: Saving the USS *Samuel B. Roberts* in the Persian Gulf • Aircraft Carriers • River-class Frigates and the Battle of the Atlantic • Six Frigates • Send a Gunboat • The Battle of Jutland • Crisis at Sea: the United States Navy in European Waters in World War I • HMS *Endurance*, the Red Plum • Hitler, Dönitz and the Baltic Sea • From Mahan to Pearl Harbor • Liberty: The Ships that Won the War • The Second Attack on Pearl Harbor • The Way of the Ship in the Midst of the Sea • Lamentable Intelligence from the Admiralty: the Sinking of HMS *Vanguard* in 1875 • Admiralty Salvage in Peace and War 1906-2006 • Tigris Gunboats: The Forgotten War in Iraq 1914-17 • British Warship Losses in the Ironclad Era, 1860-1919 • Contributions to the History of Imperial Japanese Warships • Lessons Not Learned: The U.S. Navy's Status Quo Culture • USS *Ranger*: The Navy's First Flattop from Keel to Mast • The US Navy against the Axis: Surface Combat 1941-45 • The U-Boat Century • Japanese Warships at War • Come Hell & High Water • HMS *Fearless*: The Mighty Lion • Aircraft Carriers at War • Ever the Apprentice

Warship Gallery 198
Glenn Pettit introduces a previously unpublished collection of photographs taken during and immediately after the Great War by a New Zealander, W J Connors. **Jeffrey Charles** writes about the little-known Rhine Patrol Flotilla and the ML's in which Connors served.

CELEBRATE THE 30TH VOLUME OF *WARSHIP* WITH SOME VERY SPECIAL OFFERS FROM CONWAY

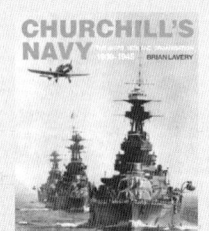

Churchill's Navy
£40 £30
ISBN 9781844860357

Submarine
£20 £15
ISBN 9781844860463

Conway's War at Sea in Photographs £25 £15
ISBN 9781844860456

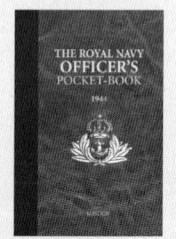

Royal Navy Officers Pocket-Book £6.99 £5
ISBN 9781844860548

UK Postage: £1.50 per book | Overseas Postage: £3.00 per book
By phone: Telephone our distributors HarperCollins on 0870 787 1613 and quote reference CH898
By post: Mail order, HarperCollins Distribution, Campsie View, Westerhill Road, Bishopbiggs, Glasgow, G64 2QT
Cheques in UK Sterling made payable to HarperCollins Distribution.
Postage must be added as per above. All orders to quote reference code, full postal address and telephone number.

EDITORIAL

The readers' response to *Warship 2007*, both verbal and written, has been particularly pleasing. We are receiving an increasing number of comments (mostly favourable) on the feature articles and 'notes' published, and a number of readers have written in with corrections and further information which we are publishing under A's and A's in this year's annual.

Whilst many of the names of our contributors this year will be familiar to readers of *Warship*, we are continuing our efforts to secure a broader base of authors. Among the newcomers this year we welcome Richard Worth, Vladimir Yakubov and Bruno Gire. Vladimir should have been credited alongside his customary collaborator Richard Worth for the detailed captions of Soviet warship photos published in last year's Gallery; unfortunately, due to an editorial error, his name was omitted. We are aiming to set this right this year with the publication of a first feature article by both authors on the Soviet destroyers of the Project 7/7U classes. It is hoped that this will be the first of many.

Bruno Gire, by day a technology teacher in a French secondary school, is also a first-rate graphic artist who has been conducting research in a newly-available section of the French official archives dubbed the Fonds Potsdam. Repatriated in the early 1990s after the fall of the Berlin Wall, the archive in question comprises documents removed from France by the Germans after June 1940 and subsequently captured by the Russians (see the Editor's fuller account in this year's 'Warship Notes'). The archive has since been reclassified and the documentation is now being made available to researchers. The Germans were primarily interested in the latest French designs, so much of the new information concerns the ships under construction at the time of the Armistice. Bruno Gire has been given privileged access to the official plans of the cruisers of the *De Grasse* class and has used these as the basis of line drawings which illustrate his collaborative article with the Editor on the name-ship of the class, the construction of which was suspended during the war. De Grasse would subsequently be completed to a modified design as an anti-aircraft cruiser, and would end her active service life as a command ship for the French nuclear tests in the Pacific.

Philippe Caresse made his *Warship* début last year with his article on the loss of the battleship *Iéna*. This year he turns his attention to the German East Asiatic Squadron of von Spee, and in particular the two ships at its core, the élite armoured cruisers *Scharnhorst* and *Gneisenau*. Philippe's focus on the peregrinations of the squadron prior to engaging Cradock's ships in the Battle of Coronel serves to highlight some little-known episodes such as the attack on Tahiti. The logistical problems experienced by von Spee's ships while operating in the broad expanses of the Pacific Ocean, far from their base at Tsingtao on mainland China, feature prominently in the author's account.

From the same historical period we are pleased to be able to publish the last part of 'First Class Cruisers' by Chris Ware. The first two parts appeared in *Warship 2000-2001* and *Warship 2001-2002* respectively and were co-authored with the late David Topliss. Those readers who have written in will be pleased to know that Chris has now been able to complete the series. Part Three covers the last and most impressive classes of armoured cruiser built for the Royal Navy: the *Hampshire*, *Duke of Edinburgh*, *Warrior* and *Minotaur* classes. The author rounds off his coverage of the technical aspects of these designs with some important questions – and some interesting conclusions – about the operational value of the RN armoured cruisers during the First World War.

This year's annual sees two articles on the Imperial Japanese Navy. Kathrin Milanovich writes about Japan's first purpose-built carrier, *Hôshô*. Influenced by the contemporary British *Hermes*, *Hôshô* was nevertheless a typically idiosyncratic Japanese design, with separate hangars for bombers and fighters each served by its own lift atop a cruiser hull capable of 25 knots. Other innovations included hinged funnel uptakes and retractable 8cm HA mountings on the flight deck.

Our second article on the IJN is contributed by established author Hans Lengerer, who writes about the purpose-built cruiser minelayers of the interwar period. The Japanese, who had converted two elderly armoured cruisers into minelayers during the years 1917-23, insisted during the London Conference of 1930 that these ships should be replaced by modern units displacing up to 5000 tons. Having completed a cruiser minelayer of moderate displacement, *Itsukushima*, during the late 1920s, the IJN embarked on the construction of two larger ships, *Okinoshima* and *Tsugaru*, during the 1930s as replacements for the elderly *Aso* and *Tokiwa*. All three ships were noteworthy for their use of multiple internal mine tracks and for their impressive mine capacity.

The Mediterranean theatre also features prominently in this year's annual. In the first of two articles on the MAS boats of the Italian Navy Erminio Bagnasco, Enrico Cernushchi and Vincent O'Hara look at the early origins of the type and the remarkable successes achieved by the Regia Marina's 'mosquito fleet' against the navy of Austria-Hungary in the narrow waters of the Adriatic during the First World War; these culminated in the sinking of the dreadnought battleship *Szent István* in June 1918. The article concludes with the technological developments which followed the Great War, and in particular the quest for high speed and improved seaworthiness which would again make the MAS boats a force to be reckoned with during the Second World War.

Vincent O'Hara is also the sole author of an article on

The Russian armoured cruiser Riurik *passes the ships of the British Second Cruiser Squadron at anchor during the Fleet Review of 1909. The last and most powerful of the armoured cruisers built in Britain, Riurik had completed at Vickers, Barrow, the previous year, and when the Review took place in early August had only just undergone further modifications which included a new pole foremast. The photo shows her passing under the stern of the Warrior-class cruiser Natal (two white bands on funnels 1 & 4), which was likewise built by Vickers, and to the right of her bow can be seen Natal's sister Achilles (no funnel bands). A third (unidentified) ship of the class can be seen beyond Natal. This last generation of armoured cruisers is the focus of Chris Ware's article 'First Class Cruisers' on p.136 of this year's annual.* (CPL)

the Action off Calabria of July 1940, in which the Regia Marina squared up for the first time against the British Mediterranean Fleet. This inconclusive battle, which as the author points out was characterised by the tentative manoeuvring of both sides and a reluctance by Admirals Campioni and Cunningham to force a conclusion, has been widely interpreted by British military historians as establishing a 'moral ascendancy' of the Royal Navy over the Italian Fleet which would dictate the course of the naval war in the Mediterranean during the following 18 months. The author argues that these claims are unsupported by the facts, and derive from the subsequent self-serving proclamations of Cunningham and Churchill.

Stephen McLaughlin has acquired a reputation for thoughtful analysis and reflection. In this year's article, 'Diminishing Returns', he looks at the proposals for small battleships advanced during the interwar period, when all the major navies – or, perhaps more accurately, the politicians in their respective countries – were looking to reverse the trend towards ever-bigger, more powerful and more costly ships. In the event none of these designs was successful, in part because it proved so difficult to scale down the capabilities of existing battleships to fit into a smaller hull, but also because advances in technology and the increasing threat from the air meant that there was now more and more equipment to be fitted in. Despite these failures, both the British and the Soviets seriously considered new small battleships following the Second World War – although by this time 'small' was a relative term.

Besides the usual A's and A's and the item on the Fonds Potsdam already mentioned, this year's 'Warship Notes' include an account by Hans Lengerer of the Mihogaseki incident of 1927, when in the course of night manoeuvres two destroyers were sunk and two light cruisers seriously damaged and a series of previously unpublished photographs of the bombing of HMS *Iron Duke* at Scapa Flow 17 October 1939. Assistant Editor Stephen Dent and Ian Sturton also contribute a pictorial feature on the Victorian gunboat *Handy*, currently lying in Pound's Yard, Portsmouth.

Two years ago one of our New Zealand subscribers, Glenn Pettit, contacted me to say that he was in possession of a collection of photographs belonging to a former RNVR officer of the First World War, Lieutenant W J Connors. Connors saw considerable action during 1917-18 with the ML's, the US Elco-built Motor Launches, and subsequently served postwar with the Rhine Patrol Flotilla, a key element in the Allied force of occupation. The photos are remarkable and form the focus of this year's 'Warship Gallery', with a brief biographical portrait of Connors supplied by Glenn Pettit and a detailed account of ML operations on the Rhine by Jeffrey Charles, a noted specialist.

We hope you will enjoy this year's *Warship* as much as we have enjoyed putting it together. The future is bright, with many of the feature articles for 2009 and 2010 already scheduled. These will include: Britain's postwar submarine strategy; the floatplane conversion of the IJN battleships *Ise* and *Hyuga*; the cost and logistical implications of the Victorian Navy's changeover from sail to steam; the building of the battlecruiser *Repulse*; weather losses of destroyers during the Second World War; the Soviet cruisers of the *Kirov* class; and the British cruisers of the *Fiji* class. A number of these articles will be by authors new to *Warship*.

John Jordan

HÔSHÔ:

The First Aircraft Carrier of the Imperial Japanese Navy

Kathrin Milanovich describes the design process of Japan's first aircraft carrier, details the modifications which subsequently were found necessary, and corrects a number of errors about this ship which have found their way into published reference sources.

The aircraft carrier, Hôshô was designed against a background of the IJN's own experience with seaplane tenders but also with reference to contemporary British carrier conversions (*Campania*, *Argus*, *Furious* and *Eagle*) and the purpose-designed carrier *Hermes*. This was the IJN's first attempt at carrier design at a time when arrangements for operating and handling aircraft were in their infancy. The aircraft of the period were light, small and slow and at an early stage of development; their tactical value was yet to be confirmed and each model would be quickly superseded by more advanced types. Nevertheless Hôshô was designed with the operation of current aircraft in mind, and little consideration was given to the possible characteristics of future carrier-based aircraft because nobody could foresee their rapid progress.

The hull had the general lines of a large cruiser, and data on *Hermes* (supplied by Japan's famous, progressive but ill-fated naval architect Fujimoto Kikuo) influenced the decision to restrict propulsive power to that required for a maximum speed of 25kts. However, unlike *Hermes* a split-level hangar was adopted, with a shallow section forward for fighters and a deeper hangar for attack planes aft located at the level of the upper deck. The two sections of the hangar were separated by a transverse passageway. The ship was completed with a full-length flight deck and a small island topped by a tripod mast to starboard. The island was located well forward, and there were three hinged funnels abaft the island and a folding aircraft crane at its forward end. The first landings and take-offs from the flight deck took place on 22 February 1923, two months after Hôshô's completion at the Yokosuka Navy Yard. These and subsequent trials would result in conversion to a flush-deck configuration, the island being seen as an obstruction by the pilots; at the same time the sloped part of the flight deck was remodelled.

After that Hôshô was assigned to the fleet but also used as an experimental ship for aviation equipment. Many different types of arrester gear and crash barrier types were trialled. Arrester gear included the British longitudinal wire system, the French transverse Fieux system, the Japanese

Port beam view of Hôshô at 6/10 full speed, 4 December 1922. (Hans Lengerer collection)

Kayaba and finally the Kure system, while crash barriers were first of the British type and were then changed to the Japanese Kugisho series. During this time *Hôshô* participated in operations connected with the Shanghai Incident, and later also in the early phase of the China War.

Stability and strength were improved after the *Tomozuru* and Fourth Fleet Incidents, and efforts continued to modernise her aviation equipment. However, the development of carrier-borne aircraft was so rapid that she could not keep pace. With her operational value limited to carrying mainly outdated fighters she was used as a direct escort ship for the battle force until the middle of 1942, and subsequently as a training carrier for new pilots. When heavier and faster aircraft types entered service her flight deck was extended fore and aft, length increasing from 165.25m to 180.80m. In this condition stability deteriorated to such an extent that ocean navigation was prohibited and restrictions were placed even on her operations in the Inland Sea. *Hôshô* survived the war as one of the few operational vessels of the IJN. She was subsequently converted and used as a repatriation transport until August 1946. Scrapping was begun in September and completed after eight months.

From a technical point of view her characteristic features may be summarised as: (1) 'skeleton floor' framing with double bottom, (2) first adoption of Sperry gyro stabiliser system in a large ship, (3) hinged funnels lowered outboard when conducting flight operations, (4) flight deck sharply sloped down at the bow, (5) an unusual (and unsuccessful) hangar arrangement, and (6) conversion from island to flush-deck carrier. She contributed much to the training of carrier pilots, testing of aviation equipment and the tactical use of the aircraft carrier in the course of her operations with the fleet. Her career was nevertheless that of an experimental carrier rather than an operational one.

The primary focus of this article is on the genesis, first landing test series and subsequent conversion; later revisions and modifications made to the ship in later years receive more limited coverage.

Background of the Design

Operational experience with *Wakamiya Maru* both in war and exercises revealed the biggest defect of the first generation of seaplane carriers: dependence upon weather conditions for air operations; and the need to hove to during the time-consuming process of launching and retrieving seaplanes, hence an inability to accompany the fleet. This led to a requirement for a ship capable of operating planes in all weathers and with sufficient speed and seaworthiness to accompany the fleet. Reports submitted by Lt-Cdr Kaneko Yôzô early in 1915, after the Tsingtao operation, and Lt-Cdr Kuwahara Torao two years later (after three months aboard on *Wakamiya* when the ship was assigned to the First Fleet in the autumn of 1916) highlighted grave shortcomings and suggested the need for a ship operating wheeled aircraft which could land on. At first the Navy General Staff (NGS) was impressed by the actions of the British seaplanes in the European theatre. However, the reports of the Japanese naval officers detached to Britain confirmed the opinions expressed by Kaneko and Kuwahara.

When the NGS oped for the construction of an aircraft carrying ship a new building programme was prepared as a response to the US Navy's massive 'Three-Year Plan' of 1916. This 'Eight-Six Fleet Replenishment Programme' was authorised by the 40th Diet session (22 December 1917 – 26 March 1918) and was sanctioned by the Emperor on 22 March. Among the 86 ships in the pro-

Table 1: CHANGE OF NGS REQUIREMENTS (EXTRACTS)

	1918	1919
Displacement:	about 10,000tons	
Speed:	30knots	
Range:	8,000nm at 12knots	
Armament:	eight 14cm LA, four 8cm HA, four searchlights	12cm HA in place of 8cm if possible.
Cost:	Yen 7,000,000	
Design:	Modelled on British *Furious* and *Campania* to speed construction.	
Aircraft:	Short torpedo bomber: 16 (+6)	Torpedo bomber 16 (+16)
	Sopwith fighter:18 (+8)	Fighter/Recce: 16 (+16)
	or	
	Short torpedo bomber: 6 (+6)	
	Yokoshô reconnaissance: 6 (+6)	
	Sopwith fighter: 10 (+10)	
	or	
	as above but only 3 (+3) Short TB	
Aviation arrangements and equipment:	Small fighters to take off from the forward hangar and land on the water.	Separate take-off and landing decks. Fitting of workshops.
	Large aircraft to be stored in the after hangar and take off from the sea.	Special magazines for bombs and torpedoes. Torpedo adjustment and maintenance workshop.
	Take-off deck to have a slope of 2°; length 69m; width: 18.3m (max.) to 4.9m (min.).	Spacious accommodation.

gramme were six 'special service' ships (*Tokumukan*). Five were completed as tankers of the *Shiretoko* class but the sixth ship, for which Yen 1,200,000 was allocated in Japanese Fiscal Year (JFY) 1918, became the first carrier in the world to be designed from the keel up and the first to be completed: *Hôshô*. Because the classification 'aircraft carrier' did not exist, construction was prepared under the term 'No.7 Special Service Ship'.

Change from Seaplane Tender to Aircraft Carrier

The basic design was drawn up by a team in the corresponding section of the Navy Technical Department (NTD) under the direction of Lt-Cdr Taji Yasuji (Hiraga Yuzuru's favourite disciple who studied in Britain before Fujimoto Kikuo) and Cdr Kawai Teiji (who returned from his study in Britain when the First World War broke out). However, there were no fixed views regarding the arrangement and shape of the flight deck, nor on take-off and landing fittings nor on the arrangement and fitting of hangars and aircraft lifts. In particular there was considerable uncertainty regarding the aircraft to be embarked, which constituted the main weapon of the new ship; new types appeared every year with marked differences compared to their predecessors, thus requiring changes. The design was initially to be based on the British *Campania*, which had been described in Fujimoto's report from Britain. The first sketch design therefore featured only a take-off deck, and the requirements of the NGS were limited to the armament: (1) aircraft: 16 (+16) bombers, 8 (+8) reconnaissance planes, 8 + (+8) fighters and (2) guns: four/eight 14cm low-angle guns and four HA guns.

In 1918 the '8-8 Fleet Completion Program' was drawn up. In connection to the requirement for further two aircraft carriers (*Shôkaku* and another unnamed ship) the NGS specified its requirements (see Table 1) after considering new reports about *Campania* and *Furious* (before conversion) and the Fundamental Design Section responded with the design of a seaplane carrier with a take-off deck forward, bridge and funnels directly behind it amidships and a hangar for large planes aft (in effect a Japanese version of *Furious*). Meanwhile Lt-Cdr Kuwahara had participated as an observer in the landing trials on the converted *Furious* and also inspected *Argus* in the last month of the war. His reports, information about *Eagle* and *Hermes* (by then-Captain Yamamoto Eisuke, naval attaché in Britain), and later also lectures about these ships resulted in a change of requirements from seaplane carrier to aircraft carrier in April 1919 (see Table 1) and subsequently the complete revision of the design. The flight deck was no longer divided into two by the superstructure but changed to a through deck extending the whole length of the ship. The funnels were now arranged as on completion, but there was a pole mast on the island bridge in place of the later tripod. The basic design was completed in December 1919.

Construction

Construction was due to be allocated to the Yokosuka Navy Yard, but following a report from the latter dated 10 November the Navy Ministry decided that the hull would be built up to the launching stage by the Asano Shipbuilding Co. at Tsurumi (near Tôkyô), the order being placed on 30 March 1920. At the same time it was informally indicated that the hulls for two further carriers, with a displacement of around 13,000 tons, would also be built by this shipyard.

Asano Shipbuilding Co. had been founded by Asano Soichirô in 1917 and completed in 1918 as a major shipyard for mercantile construction. However, following the end of the First World War orders for ships were reduced dramatically and this shipyard appears to have been selected as a reserve for warship construction. Geography also played an important role, as the Yokosuka Air Group and the Yokosuka Air Weapon Division were the centres of naval aviation.

The keel was laid on 16 December 1920 and the launching ceremony took place on 13 November 1921. On the same day, *Hôshô* was transferred from 'special service' ship to the register of 'aircraft carrier' as the third ship after *Wakamiya* (1 April 1920) and *Shôkaku* (3 March 1921). The hull was handed over to the Navy on 10 January 1922 and towed to Yokosuka N.Y. for fitting-out work, which was undertaken in co-operation with about 300 workers dispatched from the Asano Co. At that time it was anticipated that the scheduled completion date could not be met (*Hôshô* was 65.5% complete in March 1922), so it was put back to December 1922. Repeated changes to the orig-

An aerial view of Hôshô taken in December 1922. Note the open lift wells and the crane on the flight deck forward of the bridge. (Hans Lengerer collection)

WARSHIP 2008

Profile and Plan Views 1922. (Drawings by Michael Wünschmann, 1982)

inal design had already delayed construction prior to launch, and the reasons for the new delay were:

– modifications to the flight deck, island, mast, etc.;
– late delivery of the gyro stabiliser system from Sperry Co. (it would not be available before mid-March);
– trials with the arrester gear were still continuing;
– the 200-ton floating crane at the Yokosuka N.Y. would be in use during May for the change of battleship *Nagato*'s main guns.

The boilers were installed in early February; the main engines followed two months later. The armament was installed in May and the preliminary trials took place in late of October, together with the gunnery trials. The official trials took place 1-20 November and ended with the final trial of the gyro stabiliser on 5 December. *Hôshô* was commissioned as the world's first purpose-built carrier on 27 December 1922 (*Hermes* had been laid down earlier in June 1918 and also launched earlier in September 1919, but was not completed until July 1923).

Description of the Ship

Hôshô was a small ship with a displacement of 7,470 tons standard and 9,494 tons normal. The hull followed the general lines of cruisers designed for the '8-8 Fleet', and had a similar bow and stern configuration. The only unusual feature of its construction was the skeleton floor, a unique double bottom system patented by Lt-Cdr Taji designed to provide sufficient lateral strength with comparatively light weight.

The flight deck was on a single level and extended over the whole length of the ship (168.25m) with a maximum width of 22.6m from about the mid-point to near the after end. The wedge-shaped fore part (about one-sixth of total length) was inclined downwards at 5° to assist the acceleration of the aircraft at take-off. This section was supported by posts resting upon the foundations of the upper deck (used as anchor deck), the front wall of the forward hangar being located around the beginning of the slope. The after end was slightly narrower than maximum beam and rounded downwards for about 1m to facilitate the approach and touch down of landing aircraft.

The construction of an effective arrester gear system proved to be the most difficult issue to resolve, and Japanese technology of the period was not up to the task. About fifteen different designs of landing equipment were trialled before the eventual adoption of the longitudinal wire system. This latter system was imported from Britain following a study by Lt-Cdr Kaneko, who had been dispatched to the USA and Britain in September 1916 and had observed several trials at the British Test Station on the Isle of Grain. Kaneko had also boarded *Campania* and observed landing and take-off tests with *Furious*.

A small bridge structure with a tripod mast similar to that of the light cruiser *Tenryu* was placed to starboard of the flight deck well forward. The compass bridge had originally been designed without a canvas roof and screen; however, both would be adopted, together with an increase in floor area to obtain more space for the movable 2.5-metre base rangefinder and the tripod mast. The latter had replaced the original pole mast in order to obtain a more stable platform for the mounting of a fire control system then at the testing stage. Forward of the bridge was a collapsible crane for loading aircraft into the forward hangar. Immediately abaft the bridge and also to starboard were three hinged funnels which were normally in the upright position but tilted 90° to the horizontal position during flight operations to keep exhaust gases clear of the flight deck. This was also a feature of the US Navy's *Langley* and the later *Ranger*, but these were the only other ships to adopt this system. The funnels were not placed outside the contours of the hull, so the flight deck had to be cut out to accommodate them. This, together with the reduction in the width of the flight deck forward reduced the 'free area' available for flying operations.

The arrangement of the hangars was quite different to that adopted for later carriers and would not be repeated. The division of the hangar into forward and after sections by an open transverse passageway abaft of amidships was a characteristic feature, and the split level of the hangar deck was arguably the greatest defect of the design. The forward hangar was placed on the forecastle deck that ended at the position of the passageway; it was narrow, with a relatively low deck-height, and could be used only for small aircraft such as fighters. Open galleries to either side of the forward hangar accommodated the boiler uptakes, the after 14cm guns, and the ship's boats, of which there were six to port but only two to starboard. There was a single communicating door between the hangars which was used for the transport of aircraft engines from fore to aft in order to be refitted and adjusted, transit being made via the passageway. From the passageway to Frame 127.5 a broader and deeper

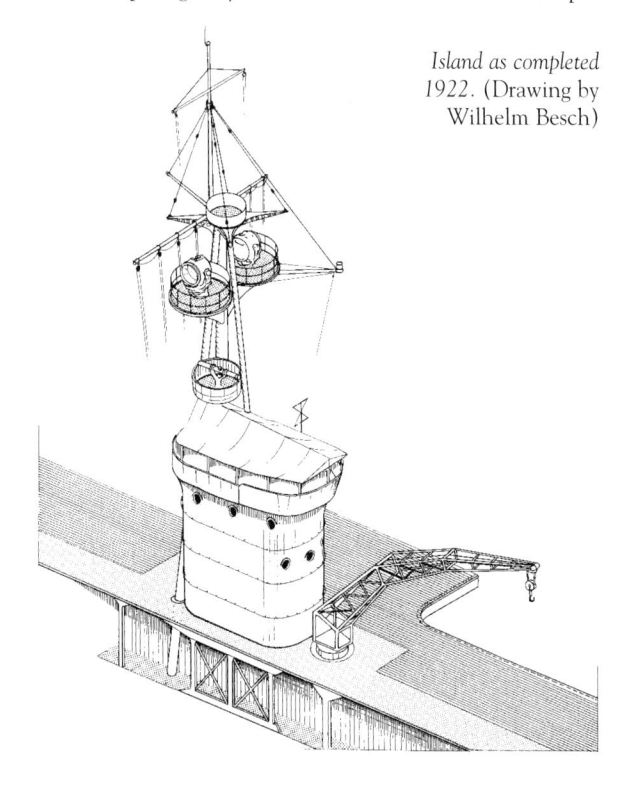

Island as completed 1922. (Drawing by Wilhelm Besch)

WARSHIP 2008

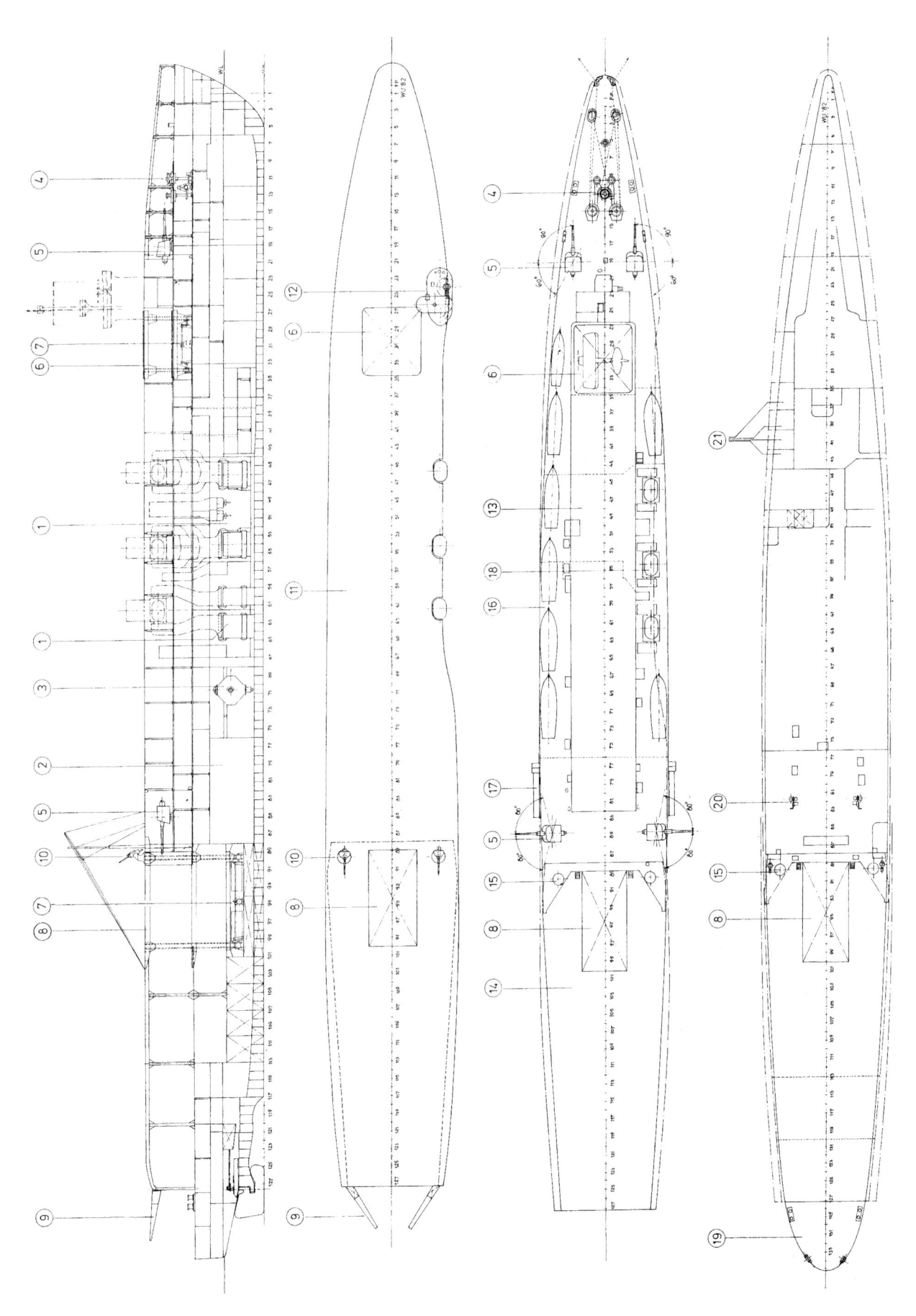

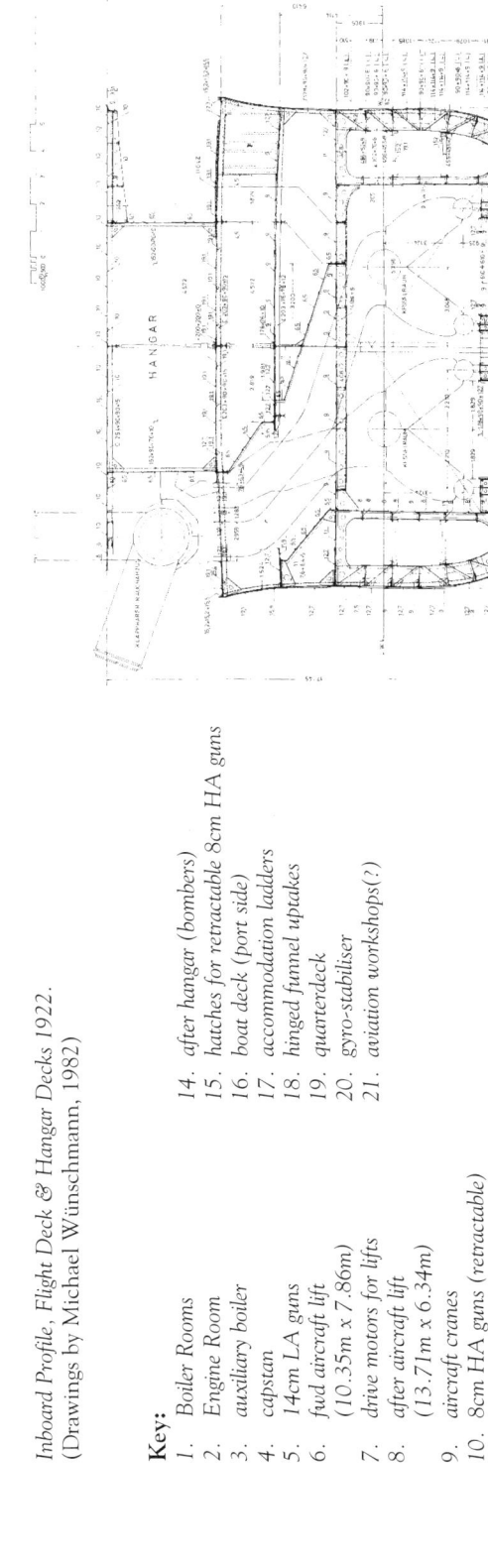

hangar extending the full width of the hull with its floor at the level of the upper deck was designed to accommodate large aircraft types, reserve planes, spare parts and repair shops. From Frame 127.5 to the stern the 'free' area of the upper deck was mainly used for berthing functions.

The forward hangar could accommodate nine small aircraft, and the after hangar six large large bombers and six reserve planes. Aircraft lifts were located at the forward end of each of the hangars; the forward lift measured 10.35m x 7.86m, and the after lift 13.71m x 6.34m. There is evidence to suggest that the dimensions of this hangar, particularly height, were selected with a view to stowing Mitsubishi's Type 10 torpedo bomber (one of the three Type 10 models designed by a British team headed by H. Smith), which as a triplane had a height of 4.46m. However, this aircraft proved unsuited to carrier operations and had to be replaced by the Type 13 torpedo bomber.

Because *Hôshô* was a small ship the fitting of a Sperry gyro stabiliser was considered necessary to reduce rolling and to obtain a stable platform for take-off and landing. The system was mounted in a compartment between the engine rooms (ER) and the boiler rooms (BR), and was calibrated by technicians of the Sperry Co. in company with IJN personnel (Dr. Sperry subsequently went to Japan and delivered a lecture as a guest of the Japanese Shipbuilder Society). The operation of the gyro stabilisation system was initially problematic due to poorly-trained personnel; it would be some years before the theoretical benefits would be fully realised.

The propulsion system consisted of two Parsons impulse/reaction geared turbine sets, each with HP and LP turbines in parallel driving a single shaft via reduction gearing. Designed horsepower was 30,000shp on two shafts to give a speed of 25kts. Steam was supplied by eight Kampon Type B watertube boilers with superheated steam operating at 138°C and 18.3kg/cm^2 pressure. Four of the boilers were oil-fired, the others employed mixed firing; the former were located in BR no.1, the latter in BR nos. 2 and 3. The first and second funnels served the oil-fired boilers, the third the boilers with mixed firing. On her trials off Tateyama on 30 November 1922 *Hôshô* attained 26.66kts at a displacement of 9,510 tons with 31,117shp. Range was 8,680nm at 12kts and she carried 2,700 tons of fuel oil and 940 tons of coal, an extraordinarily large bunkerage for such a small ship.

Opinions about the operational use of carriers differed widely, and the installation of low-angle guns for defence against light surface forces was considered necessary. The four 3rd Year Type 14cm/50 guns were located at forecastle deck level beneath the inclined part of the flight deck forward just forward of the after hangar. For defence against air attacks two 3rd Year Type 8cm/40 HA guns in disappearing mountings were located on either side of the forward edge of the after aircraft lift.

Landing Trials

Hôshô was commissioned with most of her aviation equipment incomplete, so landing trials had to wait until late February 1923. The first test series was conducted by the

Hull Section. (Drawing by Michael Wünschmann, 1982)

Inboard Profile, Flight Deck & Hangar Decks 1922. (Drawings by Michael Wünschmann, 1982)

Key:
1. Boiler Rooms
2. Engine Room
3. auxiliary boiler
4. capstan
5. 14cm LA guns
6. fwd aircraft lift (10.35m x 7.86m)
7. drive motors for lifts
8. after aircraft lift (13.71m x 6.34m)
9. aircraft cranes
10. 8cm HA guns (retractable)
11. flight deck (168.25m x 22.6m)
12. island superstructure
13. fwd hangar (fighters)
14. after hangar (bombers)
15. hatches for retractable 8cm HA guns
16. boat deck (port side)
17. accommodation ladders
18. hinged funnel uptakes
19. quarterdeck
20. gyro-stabiliser
21. aviation workshops(?)

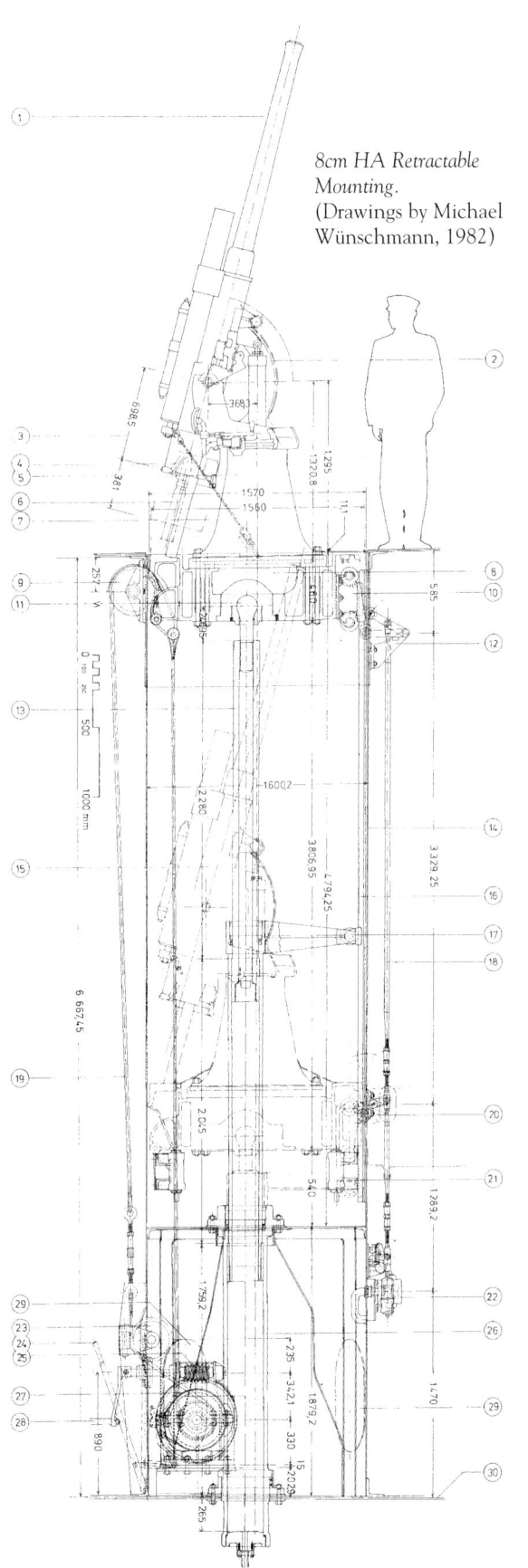

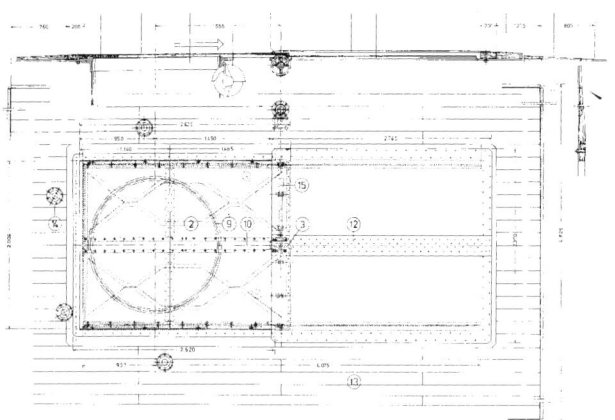

8cm HA Retractable Mounting.
(Drawings by Michael Wünschmann, 1982)

British pilot William L. Jordan and consisted of three landings on each of 22, 24 and 26 February. Jordan was a former pilot in the RAF and was employed as test pilot in the Mitsubishi Engine Works at Nagoya. He flew a Mitsubishi Type 10 fighter (also designed by H. Smith's team), landing on *Hôshô* with the ship steaming into the wind at 10kts in Tôkyô Bay; windspeed over the flight deck varied between 20kts and 35kts. The only mishap occurred when he made the first landing on 24 February, when a hook on one of the wheel shafts broke, causing the plane to tip up and damage its propeller. On every occasion the plane stopped more than 30m before the end of the landing area.

Jordan's landings were observed by many Japanese pilots, some of whom had practised landings on a wooden platform constructed by Mitsubishi to simulate the flight-deck; flush with the ground, the platform was capable of being trained in azimuth to point into the wind. Other pilots had trained on similar platforms built by the IJN at Oppama beach.

The second test series began with two landings made by Lt-Cdr Brackley (ex-RAF pilot and former member of the British Aviation Mission but now under contract to the IJN) using a Vickers 'Viking' amphibian on 13 March. It continued on 14, 16, and 17 March with three landings on each of the three days conducted by Lt Kira Shun'ichi (*Hôshô*'s aviation officer, who had conducted the first test from the 19m platform mounted on 'B' gun turret of the battleship *Yamashiro* on 29 March 1922). The first landing on 16 March was a complete failure: Kira's Type 10 fighter skidded overboard. The pilot was rescued and the following two landings on this day with a reserve aircraft were successful.

The primary aim of both series of trials was to test the suitability of the flight deck and aircraft for deck landings. However, in Kira's case the authorities also wanted to know if Japanese pilots trained by the British Aviation Mission in the Special Aviation Course (September 1921 to November 1922) could successfully conduct carrier landings. Jordan was of the opinion that Japanese pilots had particular difficulty in learning to land without driving the aircraft hard into the deck; several planes sustained serious damage in the aforementioned practice landings.

After some minor modifications to the after part of the flight deck from 2 May to 7 June the third test series began on 20 June and was conducted exclusively by Japanese

HÔSHÔ: THE FIRST AIRCRAFT CARRIER OF THE IMPERIAL JAPANESE NAVY

The aircraft carrier Hôshô, approx. 1928, as modified without island superstructure and tripod mast. (CPL)

pilots such as Kira, Ensign Kamei Yoshio (*Hôshô's* aviation instructor who had made the first take-off from the carrier on 23 February 1923, one day after Jordan's first landings), Ensign Baba Atsumaro and other participants of the Special Aviation Course. The most important result was a list of proposed modifications ranging from enlargement of the searchlight platform to improved seals for the aircraft lifts to stop the ingress of rain into the hangars. As for the aviation equipment the pilots considered the tall bridge structure with its tripod mast a hindrance to vision on a carrier of *Hôshô's* size and requested that it be removed. They also asked for the removal of the collapsible crane, a reduction in the angle of inclination of the flight deck (judged to be dangerous), and the fixing of the funnels in the horizontal position; the latter were to be equipped with a cooling system for the hot exhaust gases to reduce turbulence at the stern. The pilots were unhappy with the small hangar areas and requested that aircraft be permanently assigned to *Hôshô*.

Conversion from Island to Flush Deck Carrier

Hôshô was converted in Yokosuka N.Y. (assisted again by workers dispatched from Asano Co.) from 6 June to 20 August 1924 after tests in the wind tunnel of the Navy Technical Research Institute. The bridge, together with the tripod mast and aircraft crane were removed. The bridge was relocated on the uppermost deck forward of the fore hangar, and was fitted with projecting wings to provide for conning the ship and the control of flight deck operations. The bridge replaced the captain's official and private rooms, which were moved aft. The forward, inclined part of the flight deck was made horizontal both as a response to the pilots' requests and also so as not to restrict the view from the bridge forward. The tripod mast was replaced by a light hinged pole mast to starboard.

The 8cm HA guns were moved close to the position of the former bridge. With the adoption of the British longitudinal wire system their original position had become very inconvenient and it took 30-60mins before the guns were ready for firing. Since the trials had demonstrated that aircraft needed on average only 60m of the 104m long landing area, relocating the guns resolved this problem. Most interesting with respect to gunnery, however, was the criticism of the HA armament as too weak, together with doubts as to the value of mounting low-angle guns. This indicates that aviation specialists not only had recognised the potential danger naval aviation posed to warships, but were of the view that carriers should not operate alone. No modifications were made to the funnels, but from about 1929 they were no longer used in the upright position and were eventually fixed in the horizontal position in 1935/1936.

A fourth series of trials using the Type 13 torpedo bomber and the Type 10 fighter was authorised on 19 July to test the improvements, especially the new flight deck arrangements, and also to secure the qualification of the new torpedo bomber as a carrier plane. Take-off and landing tests on land were begun in the same month, and from the end of August *Hôshô* was designated 'flush deck carrier' (*hira kanpan gata kokubokan*). *Hôshô* was assigned to

Hôshô in 1930 with aircraft on the flight deck. (Hans Lengerer collection)

17

WARSHIP 2008

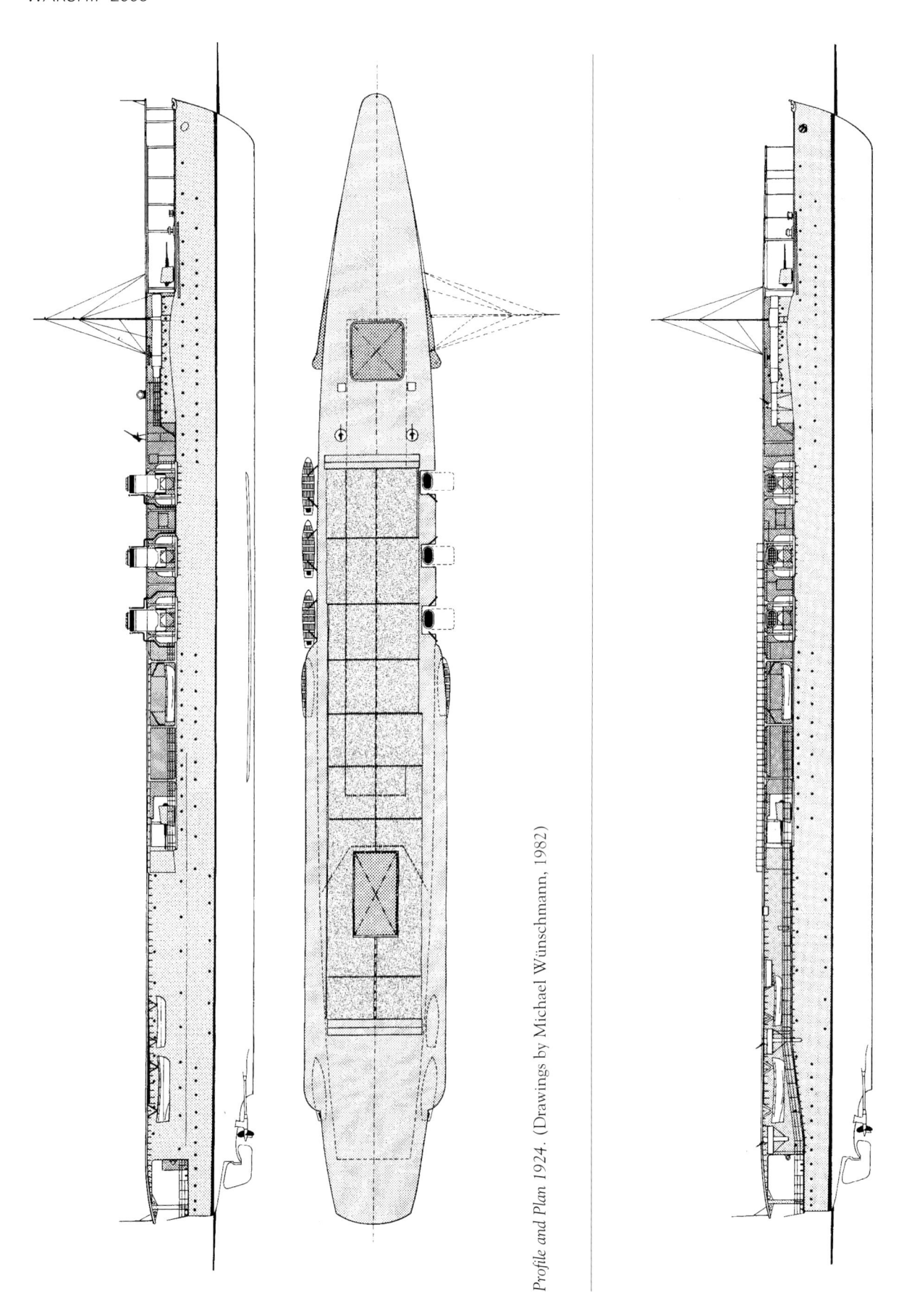

Profile and Plan 1924. (Drawings by Michael Wünschmann, 1982)

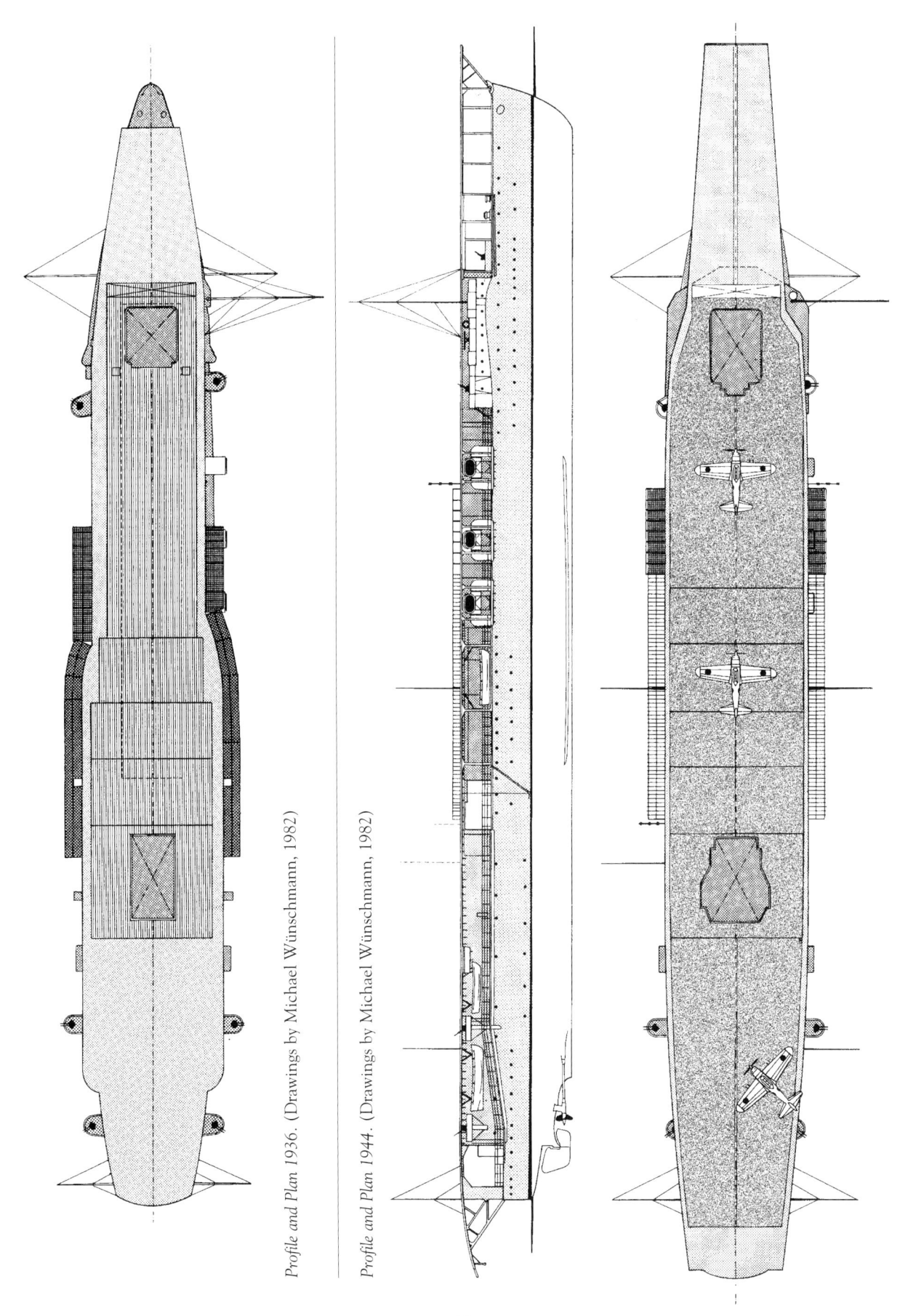

HÔSHÔ: THE FIRST AIRCRAFT CARRIER OF THE IMPERIAL JAPANESE NAVY

Profile and Plan 1936. (Drawings by Michael Wünschmann, 1982)

Profile and Plan 1944. (Drawings by Michael Wünschmann, 1982)

Table 2: Modifications to the Aviation Equipment

Date	Modification	Note
14/11/27-11/1/28	Hangar converted for reserve aircraft; repair of flight deck; fitting of equipment for trials with seaplanes.	From 2/2/28 landing trials with seaplanes.
5/3/28-10/6/28	Fitting of crash barrier and wind shield.	
4/3/29-27/3/29	Equipped with: searchlights for night landings; bomb lifts.	Searchlight tests.
6/11/29-4/2/30	Increase in speed of forward aircraft lift by increase in motor output from 55hp to 100hp.	
15/11/30-7/3/31	Fitting of Kayaba type arrester gear; decking of flight deck renewed.	From 16/2/31 trials with arrestor gear (from June *Akagi* participated) ending with adoption.
12/12/32-27/1/33	Fitting of deck lights on both sides and landing guide lights to starboard.	Tests with guide lights began in autumn of 1932.
15/5/33-9/6/33	Fitting of Kure type arrester gear and increase in speed of after aircraft lift.	Dismounting of Kayaba type uncertain.
13/3/34- ?	Flight deck covering renewed and British longitudinal wire arrester gear removed.	
10/1/35-28/1/35	New fitting of two pairs of Kure type model 4 arrester gear, one pair of Fieux type arrester gear, one landing signal device and one crash barrier.	Landing trials and also quality tests.
1939	Aircraft lifts enlarged (fore: 12.8m x 8.5m; aft 13.7m x 7.0m) Equipped with Type 90 and Type 95 fighters and Type 92 torpedo bombers.	
1940	Equipped with Type 96 fighters and Type 96 torpedo bombers.	

Table 3: Stability after Modification 1936

Item/Condition	2/3 Trial	Full load	Light load	Supplem. light load
Displacement	10,707t	11,443t	8,344t	9,193t
Draught	6.73m	7.27m	5.52m	5.95m
KG	6.59m	6.64m	7.58m	7.19m
GM	0.93m	1.11m	0.08m	0.32m
OG	-0.14	-0.81	2.06m	1.24m
Range	100°	105.5°	66.5°	78°
A/Am	1.47	1.28	2.07	1.83
Ballast	726t	726t	726t	726t + 849t (=1,575t)

Bending moment, maximum stress before and after modification (1936)

(tension and compression expressed in tons per square inch)

Item /Condition	Designed	Completed	Improved
Top tension	9.06	9.02	8.47
Bottom tension	5.81	6.04	5.95
Top compression	4.12	4.27	3.86
Bottom compression	3.70	3.84	3.4

Hôshô in October 1930. Note the destroyers and light cruisers in the background. (Hans Lengerer collection)

An aerial view of Hôshô taken around 1935. (Hans Lengerer collection)

First Fleet from 1 September to 15 November 1924. In addition to her everyday operations with this fleet she conducted a small exercise from 2 to 24 October with six Type 10 fighters and nine Type 13 torpedo planes.

As a result of the fourth trials series and operational experience, several modifications were made to the aviation equipment at Yokosuka N.Y. from 10 March to 2 July 1925. The most noteworthy was the mounting of a crash barrier (*kasso seigen sochi*) abaft the forward lift; this widemeshed but very strong net was used to prevent aircraft landing on from colliding with others preparing for take-off or from falling into the open lift well. The mechanism was operated using hydraulics and the barrier could be raised and lowered within three seconds.

Thus ended the first trial and improvement phase. *Hôshô*'s characteristics had by now reached the stage at which she could be assigned to the fleet as an operational carrier.

Mixed Use for Tests and Operations

Aside from operational tasks such as reconnaissance, bombing and torpedo attacks on ships at anchor or underway, and direct escort ship with anti-submarine and anti-aircraft duties, *Hôshô* was also employed for the development of organisational and tactical directives for the operation of carrier units (on 1 April 1928 she formed the First Carrier Division with *Akagi*). In later years she was used for further tests and trials and finally, after the Battle for Midway, as a training carrier. When first assigned to the fleet one of her primary tasks was to continue gathering data for the aviation equipment of the large carriers *Akagi* and *Kaga* which were then undergoing conversion. The Yokosuka N.Y., the Yokosuka Navy Air Group and *Hôshô* had already received these directives on 7 August 1924, and on 18 March 1926 the second series of take-off and landing trials began.

The improvements and modifications resulting from this second series of trials, together with those relating to the later conversion to training carrier are detailed in Table 2.

Improvement of Stability and Strength

Many ships of the Fourth Fleet were damaged in a typhoon on 26 September 1935. The forward end of *Hôshô*'s flight deck collapsed. The crew cut away the hanging section to port and the ship proceeded slowly back to Yokosuka. This accident, which bore no relation to hull strength, occurred during the period when *Hôshô*'s stability characteristics were being investigated (15 July to 22 November) following the *Tomozuru* incident of 12 March 1934, and found to be insufficient. She was subsequently modified at the Yokosuka N.Y. from 22 November 1935 to 31 March 1936. The principal modifications were:

– the flight deck measured 165.25m; the supporting posts were reinforced and increased in number;
– the arrangement of an internal passageway between the forward and after hangars;
– the removal of (1) the 8cm HA guns, (2) the aircraft crane, (3) the aviation fuel tanks mounted on the upper deck aft, and (4) the hinge mechanism of the funnels, for a saving of 60 tons; the funnels were fixed horizontally with their mouths angled slightly downwards;
– the reinforcement of the front sides of the forward hangar and bridge;
– the partial reinforcement of sheer and bilge strakes and outer plates in the after hangar area above the waterline to improve longitudinal strength.

Stability and maximum stress data following modification are given in Table 3.

Conversion to Training Carrier

Immediately before the outbreak of the Second World War in Europe *Hôshô*'s further use was decided on 12 August 1939 as follows:

> ...Suitable for use as a training carrier in peacetime. As long as Type 95 fighters and Type 96 torpedo bombers continue to be used after the outbreak of a war, *Hôshô* has to escort the main fleet. However, this task shall be executed only during the decisive battle; otherwise she shall be used as a training carrier for landings...

An investigation dated 23 December 1940 revealed that new aircraft types such as the Type 0 ('Zeke'), Type 99 ('Val'), and Type 97 ('Kate') could not be used operationally, and when she was direct escort ship for the main fleet in May/June 1942 *Hôshô* carried six Type 96 torpedo bombers for ASW. *Hôshô* was assigned officially to the Training Fleet in October 1942 (unofficially already in

July), and used for take-off and landing training in the Inland Sea. In order to cater for new aircraft types, particularly the *Tenzan* ('Jill') and *Suisei* ('Judy'), the flight deck was lengthened to 180.80m with a width of 10m (forward), 22.7m (amidships), and 14m (aft) from 27 March to 26 April 1944. At the same time six sets of arrester gear Kure Type 3 Model 10 and Model 11 as well as a Kugishô Model 3 crash barrier were installed. Aircraft lifts and hangars were not modified even though unsuited to the new aircraft types, as *Hôshô* no longer operated her own aircraft. With the flight deck projecting for about 6m over bow and stern, stability was adversely affected, and fears that she might capsize in rough seas meant that operations were strictly restricted to the Inland Sea and favourable weather conditions.

The End

According to Endo Akira (see sources), *Hôshô's* flight deck was damaged by the air raid on Kure naval port on 19 March 1945. Emergency repairs were carried out and on 10 April the captain was ordered to keep her in readiness. However, two days later her status was reduced to '4th reserve ship' and most of the crew was transferred to other units. On 1 June she became 'special guard ship' with most of her crew transferred back. When Kure naval port was air raided again on 24 July 1945 she was slightly damaged, but was repaired within fifteen days.

After the end of the war she was used as a special transport. The fore part of her flight deck was cut off and passenger accommodation was fitted in the hangars. She made nine repatriation cruises and transported about 40,000 soldiers and civilians back to the Japanese homeland up to 15 August 1946; she was then removed from the repatriation list and transferred to the Ministry of Interior on 31 August. She was scrapped by the Kyôwa Shipbuilding Co. Osaka from 2 September until 1 May 1947; the 24-year career of Japan's first and oldest carrier was at an end.

Some corrections to published data:

The date *Hôshô* was laid down is generally stated to be 16 December 1919. However, the basic design as a carrier with a full-length flight deck was completed only during

---

Table 4: CHARACTERISTICS (AS COMPLETED UNLESS OTHERWISE STATED)

Builder and Building Data:
Asano Shipbuilding Co. Tsurumi Shipyard until launch; fitted out Yokosuka N.Y.
Laid down 16 December 1920, launched 13 November 1921, completed and commissioned 27 December 1922.

Displacement:
7,470 tons standard, 9,494 tons normal.

Principal dimensions:
Length (L) 168.25m (oa), 165.05m (wl), 155.45m (pp); Beam (B) 17.98m (wl), Depth (D) 17.14m (keel to flight deck); Draught (d) 6.17m (mean), Freeboard 6.419m (forward), 5.961m (amidships), 3.897m (aft) at 10,797 tons.

Ratios:
L/B 9.47, L/D 9.63, d/L 0.0374, D/d 2.78

Number of watertight compartments:
Hold: 87, second hold deck: 74, wing compartments: 14, total: 175

Flight deck:
Length 168.25m (1936 = 165.25m; 1944 = 180.80m), Width 7.5m forward (1944 = 10.0m), 22.62m amidships (1944 = 22.7m), 10.5m aft (1944 = 14.0m), Area 3,112.6m^2 in 1936, L/B ratio 7.34 (1944 = 7.96).

Hangar:
Two, separated by a transverse passageway and arranged on different decks. Forward hangar: 67.2m x 9.5m and single-deck height for fighters; after hangar: 16.5m x 14m (fwd end) and 29.4m x 12m (after end) and two-decks height for attack aircraft. Total area 1,590.325m^2 (data from 1938).

Aircraft lifts:
Dimensions (L x B): forward lift 10.35m (12.80m) x 7.86m (8.5m); after lift: 13.71m x 6.34m (7.0m); rectangular as completed but irregular form after conversion.

Arrester gear:
British longitudinal wire system + French Fieux transverse wire system, Japanese Type Kayaba, then Kure model 1-3 and finally Kure Type 3 model 10 and model 11.

Crash barrier:
Net in front of the forward lift (1925), Kugishô model 3 (finally).

Aircraft:
1924 Type 10 fighter and Type 13 torpedo bomber; 1928 Type 3 fighter; 1931 Type 90 fighter, Type 89 torpedo bomber (proved unsuited); 1938 Type 95 fighter and Type 92 torpedo bomber; 1940 Type 96 fighter and Type 96 torpedo bomber; no aircraft embarked after Midway, June 1942.

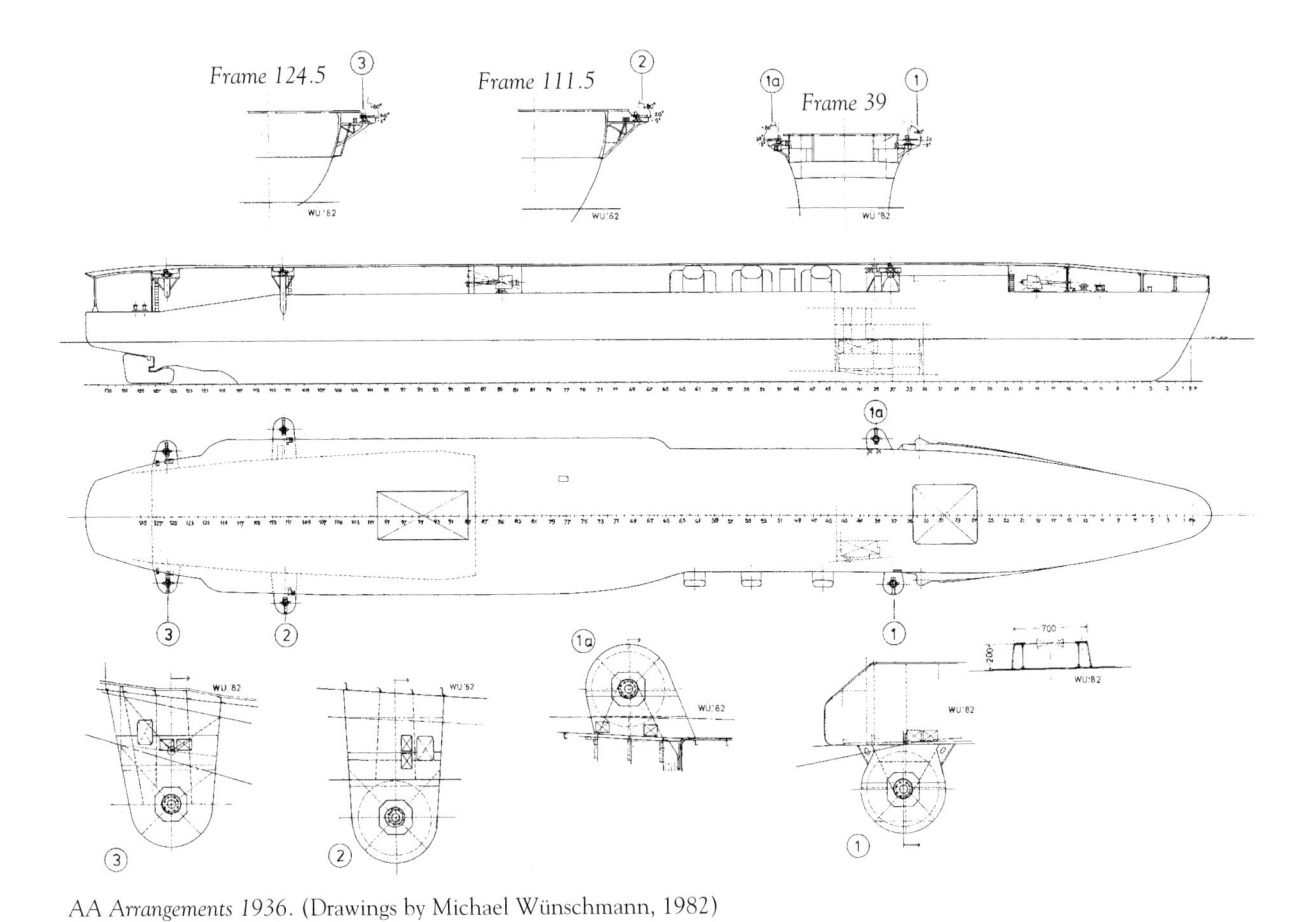

AA Arrangements 1936. (Drawings by Michael Wünschmann, 1982)

Guns:
Four single 50-cal 3rd Year Type 14cm LA guns and two single 40-cal 3rd Year Type 8cm HA guns; two Vickers AAMG in 1932, six twin 13mm Hotchkiss Type 93 AAMG in 1936 (8cm HA removed); about 20 single Type 96 25mm AAMG during Pacific War (14cm removed).

Machinery:
Two sets of Kampon geared turbines each comprising one HP and one LP turbine.
Eight Kampon Ro gô small-tube boilers (four oil-fired, four mixed burners on completion; the latter replaced by oil-fired boilers 28 October 1926 to 31 January 1927); steam pressure/temperature: $18.3 kg/cm^2/138°C$.
Engine Room dimensions: (LxBxH) 14.83m x 12.19m x 6.71m; floor area $178.4m^2$; $173.8shp/m^2$ at 31,000shp.
Boiler Room dimensions: (LxBxH) 28.04m x 12.19m x 6.71m; floor area $337.8m^2$; $91.77shp/m^2$ at 31,000shp.
Two shafts, 250rpm.
Performance: 30,000shp (designed), 31,117shp (trials).
Speed: 25 knots (designed), 26.66 knots (trials), 25.5 knots (1938), 25.2 knots (1944).
Fuel: 2,700 tons fuel oil, 940 tons coal (after refit oil only).
Range: 8,680nm at 12 knots.
Weight (W) 1,227.65 tons; shp/W 25.35 (at 31,117shp)
Funnels: three of hinged type; used in horizontal position only from about 1929 and fixed horizontally in 1936.

Electrical Power:
Four turbo generators of 105kW each, one diesel generator of 105kW; total 525kW

Crew Spaces:

Complement:	53 officers and warrant officers	459 petty officers and men
Area	$1,137.06m^2$	$1,347.51m^2$
Area/man	$20.12m^2$	$3.717m^2$

Water Consumption:
Fresh water 18 litres per man, miscellaneous use 15 litres; total 33 litres per man/day.
Note: This was a high figure for the IJN, exceeded only in the oiler *Kamui* (35.6 litres) and the cruiser *Takao* (34.2 litres).

this month, and the drawings of the machinery spaces were begun on that same day, suggesting that these sources are in error. The reason for the error may be a misprint in the warship list of the annual report of the Navy Ministry for JFY1926 (in previous reports '1920' was given as the year of launch). It is of interest to note that the American naval attaché reported the correct date on 18 November 1921 (Office of Naval Intelligence, Navy Department, Serial No. 840 File No 916-2500). The authoritative *Shôwa Zôsenshi* Vol. 1 gives the launch date as 'December 1920' on p. 472 and '16 December 1920' on p. 781.

In nearly all sources consulted, even Japanese-language sources, the length of the flight deck is given as 158.20m. On the other hand, the flight deck is always drawn over the whole length and length oa is correctly stated to be 168.25m. This mistake may result from an error in the calculation from feet to metres; alternatively it may refer to an earlier design. After the change in April 1919 it had been planned to end the flight deck at the after edge of the after hangar and to mount a large crane on either side (see sketches and drawings); however, this was changed before the ship was laid down and the flight deck was extended to the stern.

Before 1920 the terms *Hikokitaibokan* and *Kôkûtaibokan*, both meaning 'mothership of an air unit' were used alongside *Kôkûbokan* (aircraft mothership or carrier). Of these, *Hikôkitaibokan* was not an official term in the classification list, but the one used before the introduction of *Kôkûtaibokan* by NGS Ordinance No.6 dated 17 May 1916. However, at that time the future carrier was registered as a 'ship for special tasks' (*Kansen ekimo*) and not as a type of warship (*Gunkan*). NGS Ordinance No.1 dated 19 March 1919 (effective 1 April) permitted the use of either *Kôkûtaibokan* or *Kôkûbokan*. In accordance with the recognition of the fighting value of aircraft and their carrier ships Navy Ministry Ordinance No.37 dated 1 April 1920 revised the classification list of naval vessels (*Kantei ruibetsu hôjun*) and the aircraft carrier was shifted to the warship category below the cruiser as *Kôkûbokan*. From this time no other term was used and the aircraft carrier remained in the *gunkan* category until the dissolution of the IJN.

Sources: (Japanese only)

Endo Akira, *Documents on the History of Japanese Warships* (*Nihon gunkan shiko* vol. 2), a privately published series.

Maru Specials: *Japanese Naval Vessels* No.16 *Aircraft carriers Hôshô and Ryûjô*, No.56 *Japanese Aircraft Carrier III*, No.126 *Nihon no kûbô I* (*Hôshô, Akagi, Kaga*) and No.127 *Nihon no kûbô II* (only gyro stabiliser and arrester gear).

Maru Special: *Warship Mechanism* No.3: *Japanese Aircraft Carriers*, 1971.

Nihon Zôsen Gakkai (Ed.), *History of Ship Construction in Shôwa Era* (*Shôwa zôsen-shi*), Hara Shobô, 1977: two vols of which only Vol. 1 used.

Kaigun Suiraishi Kankôkai (Ed.), *History of the Underwater Weapons of the Navy* (*Kaigun suirai-shi*), Shinkôsha, 1979.

Makino Shigeru and Fukui Shizuo (Eds.), *Outline of Warship Construction Techniques* (*Kaigun zôsen gijutsu gaiyô – KZGG*): seven hand-written volumes, 1948-1952 of which Vols. 2 and 7 were used for this article.

These three photos are part of a series that were taken by the US Navy at Kure 12-13 October 1945, while Hôshô was undergoing conversion to a repatriation transport. They show the ship's final appearance, as a training carrier.

Kaigun Henshû Iinkai (Ed.), *The Navy* (*Kaigun*): 15 vols of which Vols.4, 5, 8 and 13 were used.

Bôeichô Bôeikenshûjo Senshibu (Ed.), *A Historical Overview of Japanese Naval Aviation* (*Kaigun kôkû gaishi*), Asagumo Shimbusha 1976: Vol. 96 of the official Senshi Sôsho series.

Fukuda Keiji, *Outline of the Fundamental Design of Warships* (*Gunkan kihon keikaku shiryô*), Kon nichi no wadai shya, Tôkyô 1989.

Fukui Shizuo, 'Reflection on 20 Years of Warship Construction in Japan: Naval Vessels 1926 – 1945' (*Gunkan 20 nenshi no kaiko – Shôwa nenkan okeru kaigun kantei kenzo no gaikyo*) in *Science of Ships* (*Sen no kagaku*) vol. 5 (February to August 1952).

Fukui Shizuo, *Japanese Warships: Development of Ship Construction Technology and Changes in War Vessels Over Time* (*Nihon no gunkan: waga zôkan gijutsu no hattatsu to kantei no hensen*), Shuppan Kyôdôsha, Tôkyô 1956.

Fukui Shizuo, *Pictorial: Fighting Ships of the Imperial Japanese Navy* (*Shashin shû nihon no gunkan – Arishihi no waga kaigun kantei*), Best-sellers Co., Tôkyô 1970.

Fukui Shizuo, *Japanese Naval Vessels Ilustrated, 1869-1945: Vol. 3 Aircraft Carriers, Seaplane Tenders & Torpedo Boat & Submarine Tenders* (*Shashin Nihon kaigun zen kantei shi*), KK Best-sellers Co., Tôkyô 1982.

Fukui Shizuo, *Register of IJN Warships and War Vessels* (*Teikoku kaigun kantei ichiranhyo*): a hand-written 104-page booklet containing warship data using the official name register of the IJN, compiled November 1952 and published privately in September 1971.

Fukui Shizuo, *Illustrated Complete History of the Japanese Warships* (*Shashin nihon kaigun zen kantei shi*), Vol. 1, Best-sellers Co., Tôkyô 1994; also enclosed 'Document Volume' (*Shiryo hen*) compiled by Nakagawa Tsutomu.

Fukui Shizuo, *Survey of Japanese Naval vessels in the Shôwa era, Vol. III: Japanese Naval Vessels which Survived – Their Post-War Activities and Final Disposition* (*Shôwa gunkan haishi III. Shusen to teikoku kantei – Waga kaigun no shûtoku to kantei no kisû*), Shuppan Kyodo Publishers, Tôkyô 1961.

Nagamura Kiyoshi, *A Naval Constructor's Reflection* (*Zôkan kaisô*), Shuppan Kyodo-sha Co., Tôkyô 1957.

Periodicals such as *Ships of the World* (*Sekai no kansen*) and *Sea and Air* (*Umi to Sora*).

HÔSHÔ: THE FIRST AIRCRAFT CARRIER OF THE IMPERIAL JAPANESE NAVY

The lower photo shows the temporary deck built to provide additional accommodation for the role of repatriation transport. (USNHC)

THE ACTION OFF CALABRIA AND THE MYTH OF MORAL ASCENDANCY

British naval historians have long persisted in claiming that the Action off Calabria was instrumental in establishing a psychological advantage over the Italian Regia Marina in the Mediterranean in 1940. **Vincent P. O'Hara** argues that these claims are unsupported by the facts and questions the extent to which they derive from the self-serving proclamations of Cunningham and Churchill

In July, 1940, less than a month after Benito Mussolini declared war, Italy's Regia Marina squared up to Great Britain's Royal Navy in one of the largest sea battles of World War Two: to the British the Action off Calabria, to the Italians the Battle of Punta Stilo. Although no ships were sunk and only a few damaged, English historians consider this battle significant because it established the Royal Navy's 'moral ascendancy' over the Regia Marina. However, just as the two sides cannot agree on the action's name, they interpret its consequences quite differently. A dispassionate examination of the conditions leading to the battle, its conduct and immediate aftermath supports a revised appreciation of Calabria and the entire early course of the Italo-British naval war.

At Calabria each navy sought to take its opponent's measure and gain an early advantage. But each operated under dramatically opposed imperatives which dictated the type of action the admirals could fight. Mussolini, believing the conflict was nearly over, entered the war 'without the logistical doctrine, organisation, or preparations required to fight effectively either a short Mediterranean war or a long one.'[1] Whilst he felt obliged to make a show, hence his army's ineffectual offensive along the French Alpine frontier, he saw no need to risk major warships – expensive assets that represented one of his principal claims to great power status – in a cause already won.

In the summer of 1940 Great Britain's position could hardly have been more different. Just before Italy declared war Winston Churchill, Britain's new prime minister, advised Mussolini that 'whatever may happen on the Continent England will go on to the end, even quite alone, as we have done before …'[2] But understandably Churchill's brave words required action to give them force. 'If there seemed no prospect of a successful decision against Germany herself there was a subsidiary theatre (the Mediterranean) where British forces could be employed to harass the enemy and perhaps inflict serious damage.'[3] To demonstrate British resolve Churchill sanctioned the attack against the French squadron at Mers el-Kébir on 2 July 1940. However, there was a greater prize. The Prime Minister goaded his admirals with reminders of how, shortly before Paris dropped out of the war, French cruisers had bombarded Genoa and escaped unscathed.[4] He believed that a hard blow against Italy – a decisive naval engagement – might even knock Rome out of the ring. Such a victory would also consolidate his own position, which in the early summer of 1940 was none too secure.

This was the background to the Mediterranean naval situation. Great Britain needed victories; Italy did not. The principal objectives of the Regia Marina were the maintenance of maritime communications with North Africa and the Balkans, and to support the military build-up in those theatres.

First Blood

Italy began running regular convoys to Tripoli the day after France's surrender. Because Tobruk lay 500 miles closer to the Egyptian front, within range of British air and naval forces, the Navy transported vital supplies to that port on warships. On 27 June the destroyers *Espero*, *Ostro* and *Zeffiro* (under *Espero*'s Captain Enrico Baroni) departed Taranto on such an operation. This routine mission sparked the Mediterranean war's first surface naval engagement, and provided an interesting preview of both

A Cant Z.501 'Seagull' flying boat. Designed in 1933 this wooden, single-engine high-wing monoplane conducted the bulk of Italy's maritime reconnaissance. In 1941 the Regia Marina deployed 26 squadrons. The Seagull enjoyed good range, but proved slow and vulnerable to even the most outdated British fighters. (USMM)

A pair of British Short Sunderland flying boats. This massive plane first flew in 1937. It had a crew of ten, could stay airborne for 13 hours and proved effective in keeping tabs on the Italian fleet. (USMM)

British and Italian fighting philosophies.

On the morning of 28 June Sunderland flying boat L.5806 operating from Malta spotted Baroni's force 50 miles west of Zakinthos, the southernmost of the Ionian Islands. By coincidence the Mediterranean Fleet had sortied in force for the first time since 11 June to cover convoys sailing to Egypt from the Dardanelles, Greece, and Malta.

The British 7th Cruiser Squadron with *Orion* (flag), *Neptune*, *Sydney*, *Liverpool*, and *Gloucester* under Vice-Admiral John Tovey received L.5806's contact report shortly after noon while southwest of Crete. Leaving two battleships, a carrier, and eight destroyers with the convoy, Tovey led his five cruisers north seeking to engage the enemy.

Liverpool bore 75 miles west southwest of Cape Matapan when she sighted Baroni's ships silhouetted against the late afternoon sun. Three minutes later at 1833 *Liverpool* lofted a salvo toward the enemy destroyers from 22,000 yards. Surprised by the sudden geysers spouting nearby, Baroni immediately turned west southwest and increased speed to 30 knots, the best his old and heavily-laden destroyers could manage in the choppy sea. Just minutes into the action, however, Baroni concluded the enemy would run him down before dark. He made the difficult decision to split his force and ordered *Ostro* and *Zeffiro* to flee at full speed while he zigzagged behind them, laying a thick smoke screen and launching a pair of torpedoes back towards the enemy. In response *Orion*, *Neptune*, and *Sydney* manoeuvred broad on *Espero*'s starboard quarter trying to work around the smoke while *Liverpool* and *Gloucester* pressed forward to close. Twisting and jinking *Espero* fought back against her much larger adversaries and at 1920 landed the first hit of the action, a 120mm (4.7in) shell that exploded on *Liverpool*'s starboard side about three feet above the waterline. Steel splinters pierced the warheads of two torpedoes, which fortunately did not explode. *Liverpool* turned away nonetheless, and *Gloucester* followed. When Tovey saw this *Orion*, *Neptune* and *Sydney* deluged *Espero* with 6in salvos. By 2000, after 90 minutes of non-stop firing, the cruisers finally crippled the elusive destroyer. *Sydney* then closed and applied the *coup de grâce*. *Espero* lost 172 men, but *Ostro* and *Zeffiro* safely made Benghazi.[5]

'Morning showed the muzzles of the (cruiser's) guns stripped of paint, which hung in long reddish-grey streamers almost to the deck.'[6] Tovey's command expended nearly 5,000 6in rounds – 300 tons of ammunition – to sink a 1,500-ton destroyer. Only 800 rounds remained in the entire theatre. This shortage of 6in shells delayed two Malta convoys for nine days.

The Approach to Battle

Italy, meanwhile, notwithstanding the loss of *Espero*, began running regular convoys directly to Benghazi. On the evening of 6 July two light cruisers, four destroyers and six torpedo boats set out for Benghazi escorting a passenger liner and five freighters loaded with 2,200 men, 72 M11/39 medium tanks (the only ones available in all Italy), 237 other vehicles and more than 16,000 tons of fuel and supplies. The Government and *Supermarina*, the Italian naval high command, considered the convoy's arrival critical to the pending invasion of Egypt and the favourable development of the naval war.[7]

Two days previously, *Supermarina* had partially decrypted British orders pertaining to the forthcoming Malta operation. Then, on 7 July, headquarters received notice

HMS Orion, flagship of the 7th Cruiser Squadron. This Leander-class light cruiser reflected British requirements – large numbers of capable cruisers able to protect trade routes. (Author's collection)

Vice-Admiral Inigo Campioni, aged 61 at the time of Punta Stilo, also commanded the Italian Battle Fleet at Cape Teulada. Considered too old and tired by some at naval headquarters, the ministry 'promoted' him to a desk job and he finished the war as governor of the Aegean Dodecanese Islands, where the Germans captured him. Eventually Mussolini had him shot for refusing to renounce the armistice. (USMM)

that British warships had arrived at Malta. This intelligence pointed toward a threat to the vital Benghazi convoy and that day the Regia Marina's Second Battle Force, with six heavy cruisers, four light cruisers and 16 destroyers commanded by Vice-Admiral Riccardo Paladini aboard *Pola* raised anchor. Next, the fleet commander, Vice-Admiral Inigo Campioni, sortied from Taranto in support of Paladini leading the First Battle Force. Campioni had two battleships, six light cruisers and 20 destroyers. The admirals had two missions: to protect the convoy and to intervene in case of a British offensive – if conditions warranted.

The ships spotted at Malta formed just a fraction of the British operation. On 7 July Cunningham cleared Alexandria with three battleships, an aircraft carrier, five light cruisers, and 16 destroyers to meet the Malta convoys. From the other end of the Mediterranean 'Force H', commanded by Vice-Admiral James Somerville and comprising a battlecruiser, two battleships, an aircraft carrier, three light cruisers and 15 destroyers, sailed on 8 July to provide a diversion. Like the Italians, the British committed every large warship available in the Mediterranean to support their operation. Excluding direct escorts the two sides were roughly equal in destroyers, the Regia Marina deployed twice as many cruisers, but in capital ships – the measure of naval power that really mattered according to the wisdom of the day – the British outnumbered their enemy eight to two.

On 8 July an aerial reconnaissance of Alexandria confirmed the departure of the Mediterranean Fleet. Likewise, Italian agents around Gibraltar passed word when 'Force H' raised anchor. Starting at 1000 hours on 8 July Italian aircraft flying out of the Dodecanese and Libya subjected the Mediterranean Fleet to a series of unnerving bombardments. 'They carried out high-level attacks from about 12,000 feet, pressed home in formation in the face of the heavy anti-aircraft fire of the fleet, and for this type of attack their accuracy was very good.'[8] Many bombs fell close, slightly damaging *Warspite* and *Malaya*; *Gloucester* suffered a hit on her bridge, cutting down the captain and 17 other men.

Signals intelligence, later confirmed by aerial and submarine sightings, likewise informed Cunningham that the enemy had an important operation underway.[9] Pondering this news from *Warspite*'s lofty bridge, he saw an opportunity to perhaps provoke the decisive battle that Westminster wanted. And so, Cunningham later wrote: 'it was decided temporarily to abandon the operations in hand, and to move toward Taranto at our best speed to get between the enemy and his base.'[10]

Campioni, loitering off the Libyan coast, monitored the approach of the two enemy prongs. At 1430 on 8 July, correctly surmising that 'Force H' was a diversion, he ordered Paladini to turn north northwest. At 1521 the First Battle Force followed. By 1647, as the convoy arrived safely at Benghazi, both fleets steamed toward Cunningham's position as it had been reported by a shadowing Cant Z506 floatplane.

A confrontation seemed destined for the late afternoon of 8 July, but then the Army-dominated *Comando*

Vice-Admiral Riccardo Paladini, commander of the 2nd Battle Force of the Italian Fleet. He suffered a stroke shortly after Calabria. (USMM)

The Italian heavy cruisers of the 1st and 3rd Divisions at Calabria. (Maurizio Brescia)

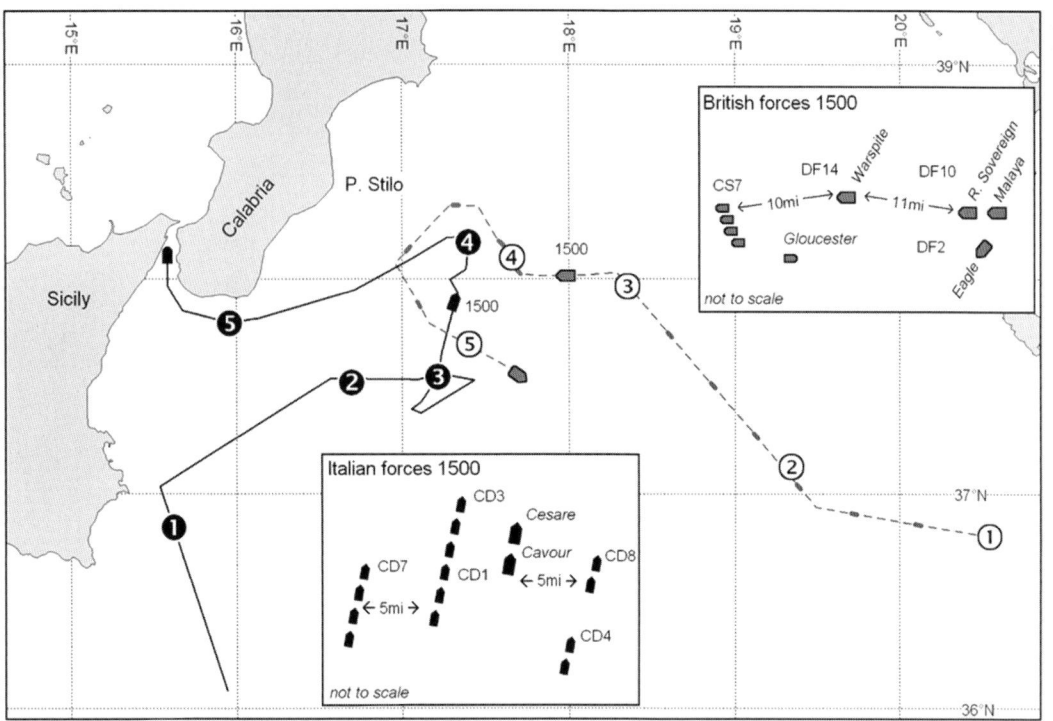

THE ACTION OFF CALABRIA AND THE MYTH OF MORAL ASCENDANCY

Map of fleet movements leading up to the battle. (Vincent P. O'Hara)

The Battle of Calabria/Punta Stilo – General movements 0600 to 2000 hours, 9 July 1940

- ● Campioni's position at time
- ▬▬ General Italian track
- ① Cunningham's position at time
- ▬ ▬ ▬ General British track

Location and time key:
1. 0600 9 July
2. 1000 9 July
3. 1400 9 July
4. 1600 9 July
5. 2000 9 July

CD= cruiser division
DS= destroyer squadron
CS= cruiser squadron
DF= destroyer flotilla

nautical miles
scale: 1:2,895,000

Supremo intervened. Radio intercepts suggested Cunningham planned to be off Calabria (the 'boot' of Italy) by noon on 9 July. Worried that this advance might portend a surface bombardment of Augusta, *Comando Supremo* decided to give the air force, Mussolini's favoured service, a chance to attack the next day and improve the odds prior to the sea battle. However, while Italian Intelligence had intercepted the Mediterranean Fleet's original wireless orders, they remained ignorant of Cunningham's decision – conceived at sea and transmitted by visual signals – to trap Campioni by altering course to the north.

At 0732 hours on the morning of 9 July two Sunderlands from Malta found Campioni's First Battle Force and shadowed him low along the horizon for nearly four hours. Italian planes, meanwhile, fruitlessly crisscrossed the waters south of the British track, deceived by Cunningham's change of course.

Like *Comando Supremo* the British Admiral also wanted to apply airpower to soften up the enemy before engaging. Although a strike launched by *Eagle* at 1145 missed the Italian fleet, a second group of nine Swordfish jumped Paladini's heavy cruisers at 1315 about 45 miles east southeast of Cape Spartivento. For eleven minutes the nimble biplanes braved heavy antiaircraft fire, launching two torpedoes at *Trento*, two at *Bolzano*, and one at *Zara*, but without success. Meanwhile, the sight of carrier-borne

Another view of the Italian heavy cruisers during the battle. (Maurizio Brescia)

planes told Campioni the British were nearby. His cruisers catapulted six Ro.43 float planes and they finally located the British only 80 miles to the northeast. Although the Italian air force had bungled its mission, Campioni reversed course to seek battle.

The Battle

As the Italians manoeuvered, the Mediterranean Fleet steered northwest until 1400 when, satisfied he was between Campioni and Taranto, Cunningham turned

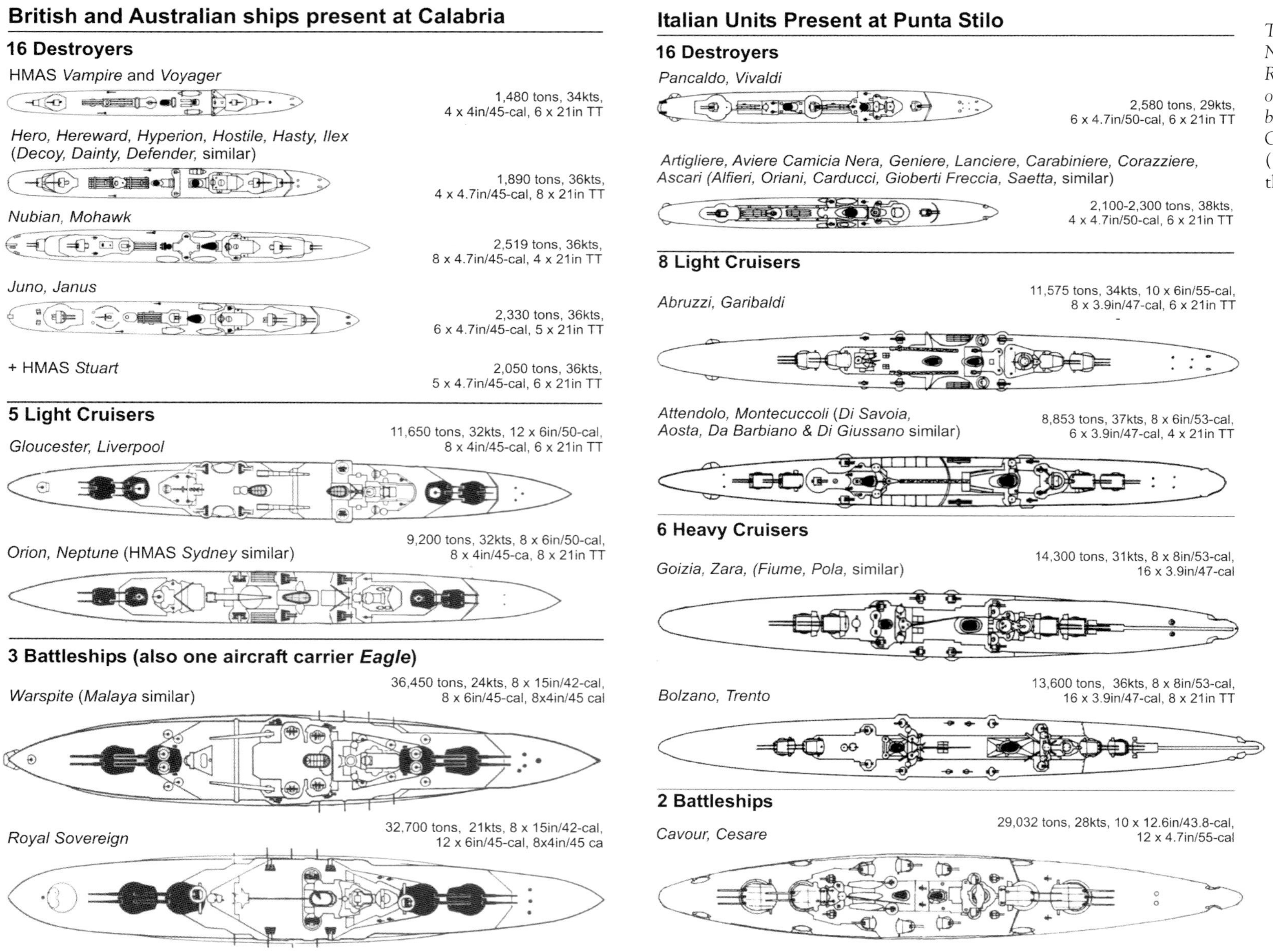

WARSHIP 2008

The Royal Navy and Regia Marina orders of battle at Calabria. (Drawn by the author).

Italian Units Present at Punta Stilo

16 Destroyers
Pancaldo, Vivaldi
2,580 tons, 29kts, 6 x 4.7in/50-cal, 6 x 21in TT

Artigliere, Aviere Camicia Nera, Geniere, Lanciere, Carabiniere, Corazziere, Ascari (Alfieri, Oriani, Carducci, Gioberti Freccia, Saetta, similar)
2,100-2,300 tons, 38kts, 4 x 4.7in/50-cal, 6 x 21in TT

8 Light Cruisers
Abruzzi, Garibaldi
11,575 tons, 34kts, 10 x 6in/55-cal, 8 x 3.9in/47-cal, 6 x 21in TT

Attendolo, Montecuccoli (Di Savoia, Aosta, Da Barbiano & Di Giussano similar)
8,853 tons, 37kts, 8 x 6in/53-cal, 6 x 3.9in/47-cal, 4 x 21in TT

6 Heavy Cruisers
Goizia, Zara, (Fiume, Pola, similar)
14,300 tons, 31kts, 8 x 8in/53-cal, 16 x 3.9in/47-cal

Bolzano, Trento
13,600 tons, 36kts, 8 x 8in/53-cal, 16 x 3.9in/47-cal, 8 x 21in TT

2 Battleships
Cavour, Cesare
29,032 tons, 28kts, 10 x 12.6in/43.8-cal, 12 x 4.7in/55-cal

British and Australian ships present at Calabria

16 Destroyers
HMAS *Vampire and Voyager*
1,480 tons, 34kts, 4 x 4in/45-cal, 6 x 21in TT

Hero, Hereward, Hyperion, Hostile, Hasty, Ilex (Decoy, Dainty, Defender, similar)
1,890 tons, 36kts, 4 x 4.7in/45-cal, 8 x 21in TT

Nubian, Mohawk
2,519 tons, 36kts, 8 x 4.7in/45-cal, 4 x 21in TT

Juno, Janus
2,330 tons, 36kts, 6 x 4.7in/45-cal, 5 x 21in TT

+ HMAS *Stuart*
2,050 tons, 36kts, 5 x 4.7in/45-cal, 6 x 21in TT

5 Light Cruisers
Gloucester, Liverpool
11,650 tons, 32kts, 12 x 6in/50-cal, 8 x 4in/45-cal, 6 x 21in TT

Orion, Neptune (HMAS Sydney similar)
9,200 tons, 32kts, 8 x 6in/50-cal, 8 x 4in/45-ca, 8 x 21in TT

3 Battleships (also one aircraft carrier *Eagle*)
Warspite (Malaya similar)
36,450 tons, 24kts, 8 x 15in/42-cal, 8 x 6in/45-cal, 8x4in/45 cal

Royal Sovereign
32,700 tons, 21kts, 8 x 15in/42-cal, 12 x 6in/45-cal, 8x4in/45 ca

30

THE ACTION OFF CALABRIA AND THE MYTH OF MORAL ASCENDANCY

The Italian destroyera Baleno *(left) and* Fulmine *(right). The destroyers of the 8th Squadron, as well as those of the 15th and 16th Squadrons, missed the battle having been ordered back to Taranto at 0600 hours on 9 July to refuel. Warships never had enough fuel, but this was particularly true of Italy's short ranged destroyers.* Fulmine *had a range of 4,600nm at 12 knots compared to the Royal Navy's 'J' class which could travel 5,500nm at 15 knots. (Maurizio Brescia)*

west to close. At this point Vice-Admiral Tovey's light cruisers of the 7th Squadron, *Orion*, *Neptune*, *Sydney*, *Liverpool* and *Gloucester,* and the Australian destroyer *Stuart* led the fleet by eight miles steaming in a line of bearing at 22 knots. In order to support his vanguard Cunningham divided his battle force and pushed the modernised *Warspite* ahead screened by *Nubian*, *Mohawk*, *Hero*, *Hereward*, and *Decoy*. By 1435 the slower battleships, *Royal Sovereign* and *Malaya*, with *Eagle* and the destroyers *Hyperion*, *Hostile*, *Hasty*, *Ilex*, *Dainty*, *Defender*, *Juno*, *Janus*, *Vampire*, and *Voyager* trailed ten miles behind the flagship. Conditions favoured battle with clear skies, perfect visibility, a fresh breeze north by west and a slight sea. The cruisers carried scarcely 50 percent of their ammunition load and, given the experience with *Espero*, Cunningham apparently anticipated a quick, close range action.[11]

Campioni accomplished the difficult task of bringing his fleet around in good order and steered north northeast at 15 knots, his ships in four columns spaced about five miles apart. From west to east these consisted of the 7th (light cruiser) Division, the 3rd and 1st (heavy cruiser) Divisions, the 5th (battleship) Division and the 8th and 4th (light cruiser) Divisions. Sixteen destroyers screened the various formations. *Supermarina*'s orders were specific: 'Your action today is inspired by the following principles: do not go beyond the range of our aero-naval bases to allow contemporaneous preemptive aerial actions against the enemy. Contact is possible against central armoured groups while they are still separate. Delay gun action to permit disabling of enemy forces by aerial bombardment. At sunset head towards base with larger units. If conditions are favourable, make nocturnal contact with torpedo boats.'[12] Campioni's actions seem, in fact, to have been aggressive in the light of these orders.

At 1447 *Orion* and *Sydney* both spotted smoke on the western horizon and Tovey sent the damaged *Gloucester* to join *Eagle*, which also hauled out of line escorted by the old destroyers *Voyager* and *Vampire*. At 1452 *Neptune* reported two ships southwest by west 28,000 yards away. These were the light cruisers *Abruzzi* and *Garibaldi* of Rear-Admiral Antonio Legnani's 8th Division. Meanwhile Italian lookouts aboard the 4th Division's *da Barbiano* spotted the enemy at 1505. The 8th and 4th Divisions steered north-northeast screened by the destroyers of Captain Lorenzo Daretti's 9th Squadron, *Alfieri*, *Oriani*, *Carducci*, and *Gioberti* and two ships of the 14th Squadron, *Vivaldi* and *Pancaldo*.

The range closed rapidly and more sightings followed as masts emerged above the horizon. At 1508 *Neptune* reported by emergency W/T two enemy battleships 15 miles to the west southwest. Tovey immediately swung north and then northeast. *Abruzzi* and *Garibaldi*, racing at 30 knots, came to the east northeast and gave chase. At 1512, however, Cunningham ordered his cruisers to engage. The 7th came about again, and the action commenced at 1520 when the Italian light cruisers sent salvos arcing toward the British from 23,600 yards. *Neptune* and *Liverpool* replied two minutes later from 22,000 yards, followed by *Sydney* against the 4th Division from 23,000 yards. *Neptune*'s captain R.C. O'Connor reported: '*Neptune* was straddled almost at once … Frequent small alterations of course were made to throw off the enemy cruiser's straddles.' As the pugnacious *Alfieri* closed to 17,000 yards he further noted: '… the gunfire of modern 4.7" gun destroyers can be most threatening to cruisers, when the enemy remains unfired at.'[13]

At 1519 *Alfieri*'s captain Daretti reported: 'Behind the cruiser's smoke I could make out the shapes of other large units that I was not able to specify.'[14] Four minutes later

A tight salvo of British shells falling short of an Italian cruiser. (Maurizio Brescia)

31

Campioni swung his battleships and heavy cruisers to the east northeast to support the light cruisers. The 7th Division (Rear-Admiral Luigi Sansonetti with *Eugenio di Savoia*, *Duca D'Aosta*, *Attendolo*, and *Montecuccoli*) approached the action from the southeast.

At 1524 a shell fired by *Garibaldi* peppered *Neptune's* catapult and seaplane with splinters. British salvos fell tightly bunched, but – as with *Espero* – Tovey's cruisers could not find the range. Throughout this period, *Warspite* had been advancing, her speed now a more cautious 17 knots, and at 1525 great gouts of smoke erupted from her guns as she sent shells streaking toward Legnani's ships.

At 1526 *Barbiano* and *Giussano* of the 4th Division came into range but when giant geysers erupted nearby, the Italian division admirals saw they were clearly out-gunned and they turned away spewing smoke. *Warspite*, meanwhile, in her rush to engage blasted one of her own floatplanes. The British flagship jettisoned the burning aircraft and continued to fire, discharging ten salvos at the enemy cruisers in four and a half minutes – an impressive rate of fire for her 15in guns. Then, rather than pursue, *Warspite* came hard about in a 360-degree turn, although she fired a further six salvos at the enemy cruisers between 1534 and 1536.

Admiral Cunningham was famous for his impatience. 'He would pace one side of the Admiral's bridge, always on the side nearest the enemy; the speed of advance of the battleship was never fast enough for him … This mood was known colloquially among the staff as the "caged tiger act."'[15] However, notwithstanding his reputation, Cunningham knew there were enemy battleships out there. He signalled Tovey: 'Do not get too far ahead of me. I am dropping back on [battle force]. Air striking force will not be ready till 1530.'[16] At 1531 Tovey's cruisers likewise turned away. *Neptune* had expended 136 6in shells during the opening phase.[17]

Three minutes later Legnani spotted Campioni's battleships approaching and he turned west, followed by the 4th Division, clearing the line of fire by cutting between the two Italian dreadnoughts. Campioni later praised his conduct: 'He duplicated exactly what we had executed during our frequent peace time tactical exercises, did not expose himself to 381mm gunfire after he was certain our large ships were heading towards the enemy, and succeeded in withdrawing his ships quickly and brilliantly from the line of fire.'[18]

Trento's 203mm (8in) main battery unleashing a salvo to starboard. (USMM)

The shooting died away from 1536 to 1548 as the Italians advanced and the British regrouped. Cunningham even radioed Tovey: 'Sorry for the delay, but we must call upon reinforcements.'[19] At 1540 Campioni's battleships turned north northeast, steaming at 25 knots, their top gunnery speed. Paladini's heavy cruisers, *Bolzano*, *Trento*, *Fiume*, *Gorizia*, *Zara*, and *Pola* had reached a point 7,500 yards ahead of *Cesare*. Paladini's flagship trailed because the column had executed a simultaneous turn to reach its vanguard position as soon as possible. Sansonetti's cruisers fell in behind *Cavour*. By 1550 when her lookouts located the enemy battleships, *Warspite* had returned to a north-northwest heading steaming at 15 knots while Tovey's light cruisers steered west-northwest, still 13,000 yards ahead of Cunningham. *Malaya* had closed to within 3,000 yards of the flagship, but the *Royal Sovereign* lagged 10,000 yards astern. The British destroyers concentrated by flotillas on *Warspite's* starboard bow.

At 1552 *Cesare's* 320mm (12.6in) guns erupted with yellow smoke and flame sending 1,157-pound shells toward *Warspite* at a range of nearly 29,000 yards. *Cavour*

9 July 1553 hours: Cesare has just opened fire on Warspite. The initial range is 28,900 yards. Her guns are trained abeam, in contrast to Cavour which fired more astern. (USMM)

Cavour's after turret opening fire over her starboard quarter at Malaya. (USMM)

THE ACTION OFF CALABRIA AND THE MYTH OF MORAL ASCENDANCY

THE TACTICAL ACTION 1520-1630

Battleships ● ―――
Cruisers ◆ ―·―·
Destroyers ▲ ········

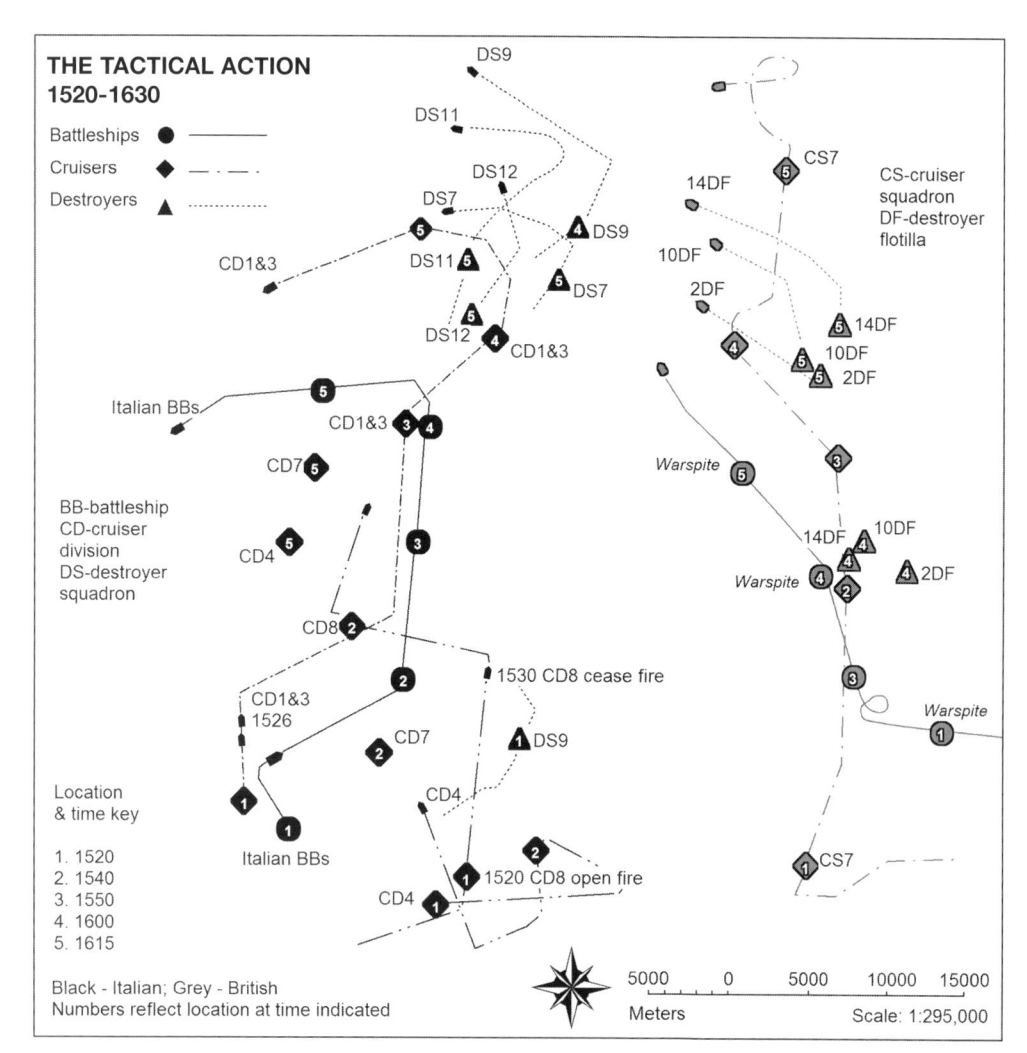

BB-battleship
CD-cruiser division
DS-destroyer squadron

CS-cruiser squadron
DF-destroyer flotilla

Location & time key
1. 1520
2. 1540
3. 1550
4. 1600
5. 1615

Black - Italian; Grey - British
Numbers reflect location at time indicated

Scale: 1:295,000

Map of the tactical action. (Drawn by the author)

Duca d'Aosta of the 7th Division laying smoke. The Italian cruisers turned away shortly after 1525 when they came under Warspite's fire. (Maurizio Brescia)

Dispersed salvos falling around the Italian battleships. The splashes seem small, but their height can be judged by comparing them to their 600ft long targets. (USMM)

Warspite *with enemy salvos falling astern.* (Maurizio Brescia)

Zara straddled. (USMM)

fired next, targeting Malaya by Campioni's express order (which obliged her to switch her main directors at the last minute) on the principle that every opponent should be engaged. Concentrating the 20 big guns of both ships against Warspite would have complicated fire control, but still presented Campioni's best opportunity to take advantage of Cunningham's failure to concentrate, and defeat him in detail. Warspite replied at 1553 firing 1,938-pound shells at a range estimated as 26,000 yards. Malaya also fired, but her broadsides splashed well short. Royal Sovereign strained her engines, but remained far out of range.

The battleship encounter raged for seven minutes. The Italians fired deliberately, observing the fall of each salvo and making corrections as required. Some Italian 'overs' landed amid the British destroyers, and splinters rattled aboard Hereward and Decoy while heavy rounds straddled Nubian twice. Her report noted: '… the second time two shells fell within 10 yards over. One shell grazed the starboard strut of the foremast abreast the steaming light.'[20]

While the heavyweights slugged it out, Paladini steered to close. At 1555 Trento, on her own initiative, lofted three salvos at Warspite from her maximum range of 28,000 yards, targeting the most important enemy unit even if her 8in projectiles could not penetrate the battleship's armoured deck. At 1558 the others, following Paladini's by-the-book orders, engaged the British light cruisers from ranges hovering around 22,000 yards. Tovey's ships, on course 310 degrees, returned Paladini's fire. Warspite's gunners, meanwhile, shot as quickly as they could load. An Italian account noted that: 'the enemy salvos had small dispersion and were progressively centered.'[21]

The decisive moment of the battle arrived when two events occurred near-simultaneously. Warspite's Captain D.B. Fisher noted that from 1556 enemy salvos straddled Warspite and that at 1600 a broadside bracketed the British flagship.[22] A 200 foot geyser from the nearest shell drenched the battleship's deck.[23] Concerned that Cesare had found the range Warspite promptly turned 20 degrees to port and increased speed to 17 knots. Because her Mark VII Dumaresq fire control tables could not stay on target during course changes greater than 10 degrees, the guns temporarily fell silent as the ship steadied on her new course.

The transmitting station of Cesare. (Rivista Marittima)

A sequence of Cesare *under fire. The top photo shows a near miss – on for deflection, but short for range. The second photo records the shell striking the battleship. The explosion is smaller than the splash and thus does not appear as dramatic. This sequence demonstrates why observers so often exaggerated the damage their guns inflicted.* (USMM)

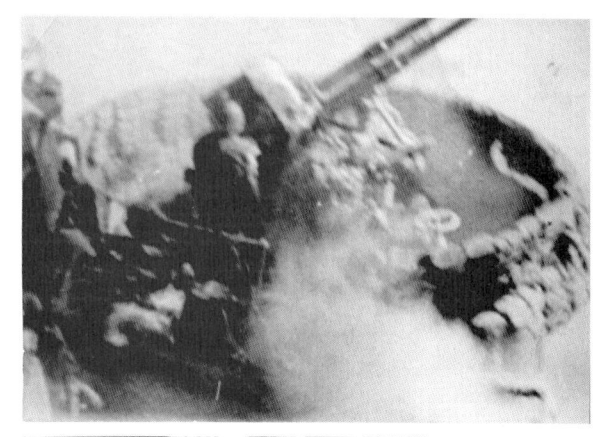

Blast damage aboard Cesare. Warspite's *15in projectile detonated prematurely on the thin plating of the after funnel and tore a 20ft hole in the deck.* (Maurizio Brescia)

Italian lookouts on *Freccia* and *Cesare* both observed *Warspite* heeling and at 1600 *Barbiano*'s Ro.43 floatplane, circling overhead, radioed that the leading enemy battleship had swung out of line.[24] All observed what appeared to be a small fire, and the Italians falsely concluded they had scored a hit.

At the precise moment Italian observers were reporting *Warspite*'s course change a 15in shell from the British flagship's last salvo completed its 33 second flight and, in one of the longest-range gunnery hits in the history of naval combat, struck *Cesare*'s after funnel. The shell detonated prematurely on the funnel's thin inner plate and tore a hole nearly 20ft across. The nose pierced a 37mm magazine and a petty-officer's mess before an armoured bulkhead finally stopped it. Fires erupted and ventilators pushed asphyxiating smoke into the boiler rooms. Boilers 4, 5, 6, and 7 fell off line and *Cesare*'s speed dropped to 18 knots within three minutes. Campioni assumed the worst and, declining to face three more powerful enemy dreadnoughts with only one effective battleship, he ordered his battle line to turn away.

This order came at an opportune moment for the British. Tovey's captains were worried about their ammunition supply.[25] Paladini's heavy cruisers were pulling ahead of Tovey. *Malaya* and *Royal Sovereign* were still strung out. If Campioni had continued on course he would, with his superior speed, have crossed the British T.

Cavour followed *Cesare* around. Both ships fired their after turrets at a more rapid rate until 1608, when Campioni reported, 'the target became hidden by the curtain of smoke extending across our vision laid by our light forces to cover our withdrawal.'[26] During 15 minutes of action *Cesare* expended 74 rounds while *Cavour* contributed 41. *Warspite*'s big guns shot their last round at 1603. In eleven minutes she discharged 17 salvos.

At 1606 Campioni ordered Paladini to retreat as well and the destroyers to cover. Nonetheless, the heavy cruisers continued in action as long as they had targets, *Zara* on *Warspite* and the others against the light cruisers. Tovey's ships fought back. *Neptune* reported: '[we] straddled the target and "rapid groups" was ordered. Eleven broadsides were fired in rapid in 2½ minutes. Only one small line correction was needed …'[27] At 1605 one of *Neptune*'s shells penetrated *Bolzano*'s hull aft and exploded. The wing rudders jammed to port, swinging the ship into an involuntary 180-degree turn while 300 tons of water flooded in. Then, two more shells impacted. The first detonated in the torpedo room killing two men and discharging four torpedoes. The second exploded three feet from the end of B turret's starboard gun, spraying one barrel with metal shards. Nonetheless, *Bolzano* continued to fire, even with her damaged weapon. She freed

Italian heavy cruisers under attack by the Italian air force. From top left to bottom right: Pola, Fiume *and the 1st Division.* (USMM)

the rudders within 90 seconds and came back around, steaming at 36 knots to reclaim her position at the head of the column.

As *Bolzano* dealt with this problem Cunningham's 'ace in the hole' appeared overhead. At 1610 nine Swordfish launched by *Eagle* 25 minutes previously attacked *Bolzano* and *Trento* in three waves. *Bolzano* manoeuvred wildly to avoid the streaking torpedo wakes. The *Eagle's* flyers counted one hit while Italian gunners claimed they downed several attackers, but these reports were all wishful thinking. As the smoke thickened and targets disappeared, Paladini's heavy cruisers stopped firing beginning with *Fiume* at 1605 and ending with *Bolzano* at 1620.

The Destroyer Attacks

When Campioni ordered his destroyers to attack, their screening duties had scattered them throughout the battle zone. Daretti's 9th Squadron, steaming about a mile north northeast of *Bolzano*, charged the British line first at 1607 and launched five torpedoes from ranges of up to 13,500 yards. Based on peacetime exercises, Italian torpedo doctrine called for reserving at least a third of available weapons in the expectation that multiple attack opportunities would arise during an action. This doctrine contrasted sharply with Royal Navy practice of expending all torpedoes against the enemy when opportunity arose. Daretti then ordered his ships to produce white chemical smoke. As he swung away a near miss sprayed *Alfieri* with splinters inflicting light damage.

Next the 7th Squadron's *Freccia* and *Saetta* emerged from behind the battle line's disengaged side. They sallied northeast trailing smoke and closed to 8,500 yards of the British cruisers. At 1618 this pair turned, fired ten torpedoes, and ducked into the thick haze deposited by Daretti's ships. *Saetta's* captain spotted a tall column of water spout up beside *Sydney* and incorrectly claimed a hit.

Meanwhile, the British destroyers formed up in columns of flotillas off *Warspite's* starboard side in order, from northeast to southwest, the 14th (*Nubian, Mohawk, Juno,* and *Janus*), the 2nd (*Hyperion, Hero, Hereward, Hostile, Hasty,* and *Ilex*) and the 10th (*Stuart, Dainty, Defender,* and *Decoy*). At 1614 Cunningham ordered them to counterattack. At 1616 the 10th Flotilla turned together to course 270 degrees and *Stuart* opened fire against the 9th Squadron two minutes later with her A and B mounts from 12,600 yards. Within five minutes, however, the 10th Flotilla had turned away to course 330 degrees and Commander H.M.L. Waller reported: 'By 1630 enemy destroyers were dodging in and out of the smoke, and were being spasmodically engaged by our flotillas for a few salvos at a time until about 1640, when the enemy was enveloped in the smoke screen, and fire was finally ceased.'[28]

The 11th Squadron with *Artigliere, Camicia Nera, Aviere,* and *Geniere* executed the third Italian destroyer attack. At 1606 they left their position to port of the 1st Division and turned to starboard, cutting between *Gorizia* and *Fiume*. A forest of shell splashes surrounded *Artigliere*, the lead ship, as the squadron advanced northeast, trailing dark smoke. She launched at 13,800 yards and her squadron mates followed at 1620 at ranges down to 11,000 yards. Together they put ten torpedoes in the water before retiring unharmed.

The 12th Squadron with *Lanciere, Carabiniere, Corazziere,* and *Ascari* followed the 11th Squadron. Smothered in smoke, they had difficulty spotting targets as they charged from under the stern of the heavy cruiser column. At 1622 *Corazziere* fired three torpedoes at *Malaya*, and *Ascari* aimed one toward a cruiser. Then the squadron emerged into the clear whereupon the entire British fleet, it seemed, deluged them with gunfire. They fled back to the shelter of the smoke as *Nubian* dodged two Italian torpedoes.

There were many British reports of enemy torpedoes and some were clearly imaginary – for example, the six tracks observed passing through the 14th Flotilla at 1610

An SM.79 trimotor bomber of the 233rd Squadron of the 59th Wing (Stormo). These rugged, reliable multi-role medium bombers could carry 2,750lb of ordnance and did quite a bit of damage in the face of heavy opposition. However, their high altitude attacks were generally ineffective. (USMM)

– but other accounts indicate that the Italian attacks were not as futile as generally depicted. For example, *Decoy*'s captain reported: 'At 1700 two torpedo tracks were observed, one passing under the ship and one astern, and one torpedo surfaced on the starboard side about 50 yards away.'[29] Another torpedo 'narrowly missed' *Mohawk*.[30]

The old and large 'Navigatori' class ships *Vivaldi* and *Pancaldo* of the 14th Squadron attempted to attack, but with a top speed of just 28 knots they could not obtain a favourable position.

Throughout the period between 1620 and 1645 the British destroyer flotillas maintained a general heading of west by northwest, keeping their distance from the billowing curtains of smoke and engaging only as enemy ships emerged into view. *Nubian*, for example, fired from 1629 to 1633 and again from 1635 to 1640 against single destroyers bearing west northwest at ranges greater than 12,000 yards. *Hasty*'s remark, 'Enemy destroyers observed making smoke and disappearing behind smoke screen making spotting most difficult', was common.[31] She flung a few salvos at ranges greater than 10,000 yards. *Stuart* expended only 55 shells throughout the entire action and none of the Royal Navy destroyers launched torpedoes.

At 1645, just as the first Italian Air Force bombers Campioni requested several hours earlier finally appeared overhead, the 12th Squadron delivered the day's final attack. It zigzagged southeast between the battle lines seeking an opening. Then *Warspite*'s 6in guns began rumbling at *Lanciere*. She emptied three tubes and cleared the area. By this time dense curtains of smoke separated the fleets.

British aircraft reported *Cesare* and *Cavour* heading southeast, but, during the confused melee, Tovey continued steaming north. His ship's guns had fallen silent by 1633 after moderate expenditures of ammunition, at least compared to the *Espero* action (*Sydney* fired 411 rounds and *Neptune* 512, for example). Moreover, the 7th Squadron was an early target of the Italian air attacks and this absorbed their attention. Fearing to penetrate the smoke (citing a potential 'submarine ambush' as the reason) Cunningham pushed the 14th Flotilla ahead to scout. They worked clear after 1700 and beheld an empty sea.

After reorganizing, the British battleships briefly advanced looking for the cruiser which *Eagle*'s airmen had reported torpedoing. At 1735, when this proved a wild goose chase, Cunningham turned back for Malta. Over the next several hours 76 Italian bombers rained ordnance on the British from high altitude (while 50 bombed their own ships). Whilst the British fleet escaped significant damage (it was reported: 'No ships were hit during any of the attacks though a few splinters from near misses fell on board one or two ships without causing damage.') the attacks were still sufficiently impressive that the action report estimated 'at least 500 aircraft must have taken part.'[32] *Eagle* attracted the most attention and many near misses caused machinery problems which, patched up but not repaired, ultimately caused her to miss the Taranto operation in November 1940.

The Aftermath

Understanding the Battle of Calabria's true impact is critical to appreciating the subsequent course of the Mediterranean war. *Comando Supremo* ordered Campioni to delay action so that Air Force attacks could weaken the enemy. However, when this plan unravelled, the Italian admiral did not hesitate to engage, demonstrating more fighting spirit than the Army-controlled high command. Indeed, considering the balance of forces against him – the three British battleships could fling 93,000 pounds of steel a minute compared to the Italian total of 46,000 pounds – and his government's policy of risk avoidance, Campioni had no business engaging Cunningham at all. Nonetheless, Campioni judged the opportunity worth a gamble and he proceeded to out-manoeuvre Cunningham and position the Mediterranean Fleet for a defeat in detail. Then a hit at extreme range tipped the already unfavourable odds too far against him and Campioni ordered a withdrawal. Even in this manoeuvre, the Italians adeptly kept the British at bay and, if all the British reports of torpedoes narrowly missing or even pass-

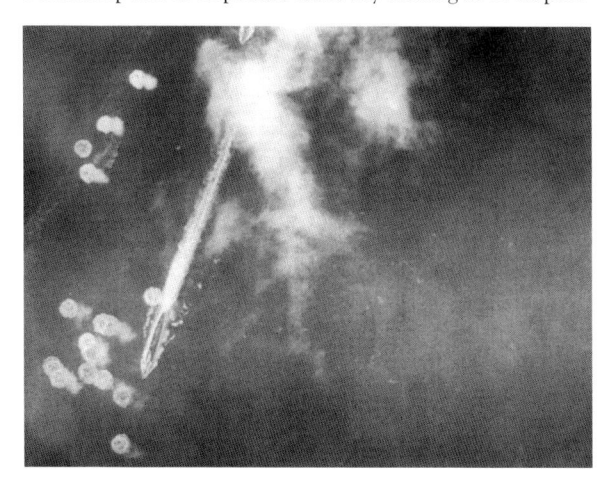

A strike against a British warship after the battle. Seventy-six bombers attacked the Mediterranean Fleet for several hours. They failed to land a single bomb on target, although near misses did result in some damage from underwater concussions and splinters. (USMM)

ing under their warships are correct, the Royal Navy was fortunate not to suffer losses during this part of the battle. Both convoys, the main reason the fleets put to sea in the first place, arrived without loss.

In his official report to the Admiralty (dated January 1941), Admiral Cunningham stated: '[The action] established, I think, a certain degree of moral ascendancy…'[33] These exact words are echoed in most English accounts of the battle: 'The battle off Calabria … confirmed (the British fleet's) moral superiority.'[34]; 'The action was … the first step in the establishment of moral ascendancy over the Italians at sea.'[35]; 'The action off Calabria probably helped to establish the ascendancy over the Italian surface forces …'[36]; 'Cunningham had established the Royal Navy's moral ascendancy over the Italian Fleet …'[37]; and so on. The politically astute Cunningham wrote this report in the afterglow of his unquestioned victory at Taranto. Immediately after Calabria, however, he requested more modern battleships, heavy and anti-air cruisers and a modern aircraft carrier, all of which and more the Admiralty sent, despite the need to secure the home island against invasion.

Far from surrendering any kind of moral ascendancy, Calabria heartened the Regia Marina; Campioni felt he had frustrated the Royal Navy's first offensive thrust, despite unequal odds, and that he had emerged with a draw. This has long been the assessment of most Italian historians.[38]

The Italian Navy repeatedly challenged the British fleet in the months to come. On 31 August 1940 the Italian fleet of four battleships, thirteen cruisers and thirty-nine destroyers 'in magnificent condition as to effectiveness, readiness for action, and fighting spirit' sortied against the Mediterranean Fleet, which had sailed to cover a Malta convoy.[39] *Supermarina* pinpointed the Mediterranean Fleet's location at 1100. Admiral Campioni steamed southeast at 20 knots expecting a battle that afternoon.

The failure of the Italian Air Force to secure hits did not stop it from claiming a great victory, demonstrated with visual aids during a 15 July conference. Mussolini believed that 50 percent of British naval potential in the Mediterranean was annihilated. Ciano wrote on 13 July that 'Perhaps this is somewhat exaggerated,' and that: 'The real controversy in the matter of naval conflicts is not between us and the British, but between our aviation and our navy.' (Rivista Marittima)

Meanwhile, at 1126 Admiral Cunningham received a sighting report of seven enemy cruisers and seven destroyers and he promptly steered to close. However, when an hour later other aircraft clarified that the enemy force also included battleships he abruptly changed his mind. 'In view of the enemy preponderance and the impossibility of coming up with them (they were about 116 miles away) the C-in-C decided not to attack, and course was altered to cover the convoy.'[40]

On 7 September the Italian fleet again sortied when 'Force H' weighed anchor, not knowing Somerville had turned towards the Atlantic. Throughout the month the Italian Navy successfully ran small convoys to North Africa, reinforcing the army for its planned Egyptian offensive. In the middle of September Cunningham bombarded enemy positions in Egypt at the cost of seeing the newly-arrived heavy cruiser *Kent* torpedoed by an Italian bomber. In the beginning and middle of October the British successfully reinforced Malta. Italian battleships, handicapped by ineffective Air Force reconnaissance, sortied on the first occasion, and heavy cruisers on the second, but always too late. The two navies finally tangled during this second Malta convoy, the first of six surface engagements fought during an intensive six week period. Italian actions during this season were hardly consistent with those of a fleet cowering in port afraid to fight a morally ascendant foe.

The war's opening months frustrated both navies because both governments hoped for a short campaign. Mussolini and *Comando Supremo* saw no reason to accept undue risks, holding the view that events elsewhere would probably decide the war before the end of the year. Churchill, meanwhile, hoped a sharp blow might so stagger Mussolini's government that Italy would opt out of the war. London designed the Mediterranean Fleet as the hammer and the Action at Calabria as the moment. The blow failed, however, and as summer passed into autumn it became increasingly clear there would be no quick decisions. Italian bombers and submarines, despite Mussolini's expectations, would not cheaply sweep the British fleet from the seas; meanwhile, despite Churchill's dreams, no modern Trafalgar would bless British arms.

The sea battles fought in the war's opening months had profound consequences, but not those commonly attributed to them. Britain's failure to destroy, much less intimidate Italy's fleet, and Italy's ability to build and maintain armies in the Balkans and Libya, and its closure of the direct Mediterranean route, obliged Great Britain to create an army in Egypt the hard way, by circumnavigating Africa, a journey of 12,000 nautical miles. The length of this journey quadrupled the shipping needed to maintain Britain's position in the Middle East. These requirements, not German U-Boats, accounted for the collapse of imports to Great Britain in the summer of 1940, which dropped 25 percent from 3.94 million tons in August to 2.97 million tons in September.[41] Moreover, during the remainder of the conflict imports never again approached August 1940 levels. The naval war against Italy, meanwhile, continued for three years and three months. When Italy and the Allies finally signed an armistice in September 1943 the Regia Marina remained, bloodied but still effective, veterans of 34 surface actions against the British involving destroyer-sized warships or larger. The vaunted 'moral ascendancy' gained by the Royal Navy at Calabria was simply a wartime myth.

Footnotes:

1. MacGregor Knox, *Hitler's Italian Allies* (London: Cambridge University Press, 2000), p.97.
2. Winston S. Churchill, *The Second World War Volume II: Their Finest Hour* (Boston: Houghton Mifflin, 1949), p.107.
3. Michael Howard, *The Mediterranean Strategy in the Second World War* (London: Greenhill, 1993), p.9.
4. See S.W. Roskill, *Churchill and the Admirals* (New York: William Morrow, 1978), p.178. The bombardment was a short and inconsequential affair against Vado and Genoa.
5. See Christopher Page, ed. *The Royal Navy and the Mediterranean Volume I: September 1939-October 1940* (London: Frank Cass, 2002) pp.22-23. The track chart omits the movements of *Liverpool*. The Admiralty staff history stated: 'This action afforded an early example of the Italians' lack of experience in sea-warfare.' It concluded the Italians should have shadowed and attacked with torpedoes after dark. In fact, Baroni had an exaggerated respect for long range cruiser fire and he had a good chance of escaping if all three ships had run.
6. Hermon G. Gill, *Royal Australian Navy 1939-1942* (Adelaide: Griffin Press, 1957), p.116.
7. 'Mussolini considers the march on Alexandria as practically completed.' Galeazzo Ciano, *The Ciano Diaries 1939-1943* (Safety Harbor, FL: Simon Publications, 2001), p.272.
8. Andrew Cunningham, *A Sailor's Odyssey* (London: Hutchinson & Co., 1951), pp.258-259.
9. F. H. Hinsley, *British Intelligence in the Second World War* (Cambridge: Cambridge University Press, 1993), pp.61-62.
10. Cunningham, *op.cit.* p. 259.
11. '... the right range for any ship of the Mediterranean Fleet, from a battleship to a submarine, to engage an enemy ship with gunfire is POINT BLANK (nowadays 2,000 yards or less) AT WHICH POINT EVEN A GUNNERY OFFICER CANNOT MISS.' Cunningham's verbal instructions for a report, as recounted by the fleet gunnery officer, Barnard, are quoted in S. W. Pack, *The Battle of Matapan* (New York: MacMillan, 1961), p.36.
12. Giuseppe Fioravanzo, *La Marina Italiana Nella Seconda Guerra Mondial, Volume IV, Le Azioni Navali in Mediterrananeo dal 10 Giugno 1940 al 31 Marzo 1941* (Rome: Ufficio Storico Della Marina Militare, 1976), p.122.
13. ADM 199/1048 (TNA): *Naval Actions in the Mediterranean. Neptune* Letter No. 3513 of 14th July 1940, paragraph 8.
14. Fioravanzo, *op.cit.* p.122.
15. Pack, *op.cit.* p.39.
16. ADM 199/1048: Enclosure No 16 to Mediterranean Letter No. 0112/00212/16. Record of Signals Received by the Commander-in-Chief, p.4.
17. ADM 199/1048: *Neptune* Letter, paragraph 12.
18. Francesco Mattesini, *La Battaglia di Punta Stilo* (Rome: Ufficio Storico, 2001), p.71.
19. ADM 199/1048: Signals, p.6.
20. ADM 199/1048: 14th Destroyer Flotilla. Narrative of Action with Enemy Forces on 9th July 1940, p.2.
21. Fioravanzo, *op.cit.* p.124.
22. ADM 199/1048: Action off Calabria, 9th July 1940 from Commanding Officer H.M.S. *Warspite*, p.1.
23. Enrico Cernuschi, *I Sette Minuti di Punta Stilo*. (Rome: *Rivista Marittima* Supplement, February 1998), p.100.
24. Mattesini, *Punta Stilo*, p.207.
25. ADM 199/1048: *Neptune* Letter No. 3513 of 14th July 1940, paragraph 21. 'I was anxious to conserve ammunition.'
26. Peter C. Smith, *Action Imminent* (London: William Kimber, 1980), p.77.
27. ADM 199/1047: *Neptune* Letter, paragraph 17.
28. ADM 199/1047: Action off Calabria, 9th July 1940 from Captain (D) 10th Destroyer Flotilla, HMAS *Stuart*, p.2.
29. ADM 199/1047: HMS *Decoy* Report on Action off Calabria on 9th July, p.2.
30. ADM 199/1048: Action off Calabria, 9th July 1940 from Captain (D) 14th Destroyer Flotilla, p.2.
31. ADM 199/1048: HMS *Hasty* Narrative of Action off Calabria 9th July 1940, p.1.
32. ADM 234/324: 'Battle Summary 8, Mediterranean Operations Operation M.A.5, 7th to 15th July, 1940, Action off Calabria 9th July 1940, p.54 and Operation M.A.5. Bombing Summary, p.2.
33. *London Gazette*, 'Report of an Action with the Italian Fleet off Calabria, 9th July 1940.' (*Supplement*. 27 April, 1948), 26472.
34. David Stevens, ed. *The Royal Australian Navy in World War II* (St. Leonards, Australia: Allen & Unwin, 1996), p.69.
35. P.K. Kemp, *Key to Victory: The Triumph of British Sea Power in WWII* (Boston: Little, Brown, 1957), p.93.
36. S.W. Roskill, *The War at Sea 1939-1945, Volume I: The Defensive* (London: HMSO, 1954), p.299.
37. Julian Thompson, *The War at Sea: The Royal Navy in the Second World War* (Osceola: Motorbooks International, 1996), p.58.
38. 'An objective analysis of the engagement must reach the conclusion that the results were about equal.' Marc'Antonio Bragadin. *The Italian Navy in World War II* (Annapolis: Naval Institute Press, 1957), p.29.
39. Operation 'Hats'. These were some of the ships Cunningham requested after his failure to force a decision at Calabria. See James J Sadkovich. *The Italian Navy in World War II* (Westport, CT: Greenwood Press, 1994), pp.81-84. The quote is from Jack Greene & Alessandro Massignani, *The Naval War in the Mediterranean 1940-1943* (London: Chatham Publishing, 1998), p.93.
40. Admiralty Staff, Historical Section, *Preliminary Narrative for the War at Sea, Volume 1, January-December 1940*, p.198.
41. Kevin Smith, *Conflict Over Convoys: Anglo-American Logistics Diplomacy in the Second World War* (Cambridge: Cambridge University Press, 2002), p.28.

DIMINISHING RETURNS:
Small Battleship Designs, 1919-1953

As the size of battleships increased, navies were subjected to political and economic pressure to design smaller capital ships. In this article **Stephen McLaughlin** describes a number of designs for battleships of reduced size, none of which ever got beyond the drawing board.

From the beginning of the ironclad era the increasing size and cost of warships were constant concerns of both admirals and politicians. One after another, smaller navies that had once been able to maintain respectable squadrons of sea-going ships-of-line found themselves reduced to a small number of coast defence monitors. Even great powers watched in alarm as their battle squadrons shrank in numbers and their naval estimates rose. For example, the 101-gun *Duncan* of 1857 cost £132,697, while the ironclad *Warrior*, laid down only two years later, was at £377,292 almost three times as expensive. Costs continued to rise throughout the remainder of the nineteenth century; by 1891 the price of the latest battleships of the *Royal Sovereign* class was about £914,000 each. Small wonder, then, that second-class battleships were a frequent topic of discussion, and several such ships were built, including the Royal Navy's *Centurion*, *Barfleur* and *Renown*.

Ships of this type were often intended for foreign stations where they would presumably have to face only second-class opponents. But there were some naval theoreticians, like Alfred Thayer Mahan, who considered smaller battleships as the equivalents of the ubiquitous 74-gun ships of the sailing era. It was certainly an attractive analogy, as these figures show:

	Bellona, 74 guns	*Victory*, 100 guns	Ratio: *Bellona*/*Victory*
Tons burthern:	1,615	2,142	75.35%
Crew:	650 men	850 men	76.5%
Broadside:	781lbs	1,032lbs	75.7%
Cost:	£36,917.5	£63,176	69.2%

Notes: Crew is based on the establishment figures. Cost for *Bellona* represents hull, masts and yards, for *Victory* the cost up until her launch. Note that 'tons burthern' was a measure of calculated capacity, not of actual displacement.

Thus a 74-gun ship was almost exactly three-quarters of a 100-gun ship in all important respects, except one: cost. Because bigger ships required rare and disproportionately expensive timbers, a 74-gun ship was actually a better bargain, in terms of fighting power for the cost, than a 100-gun ship.

But when the strength and economics of wooden construction ceased to be limiting factors, the smaller battleship lost much of its viability. The well known square-cube law meant that, as size increased, hull weight (determined to a large extent by the surface area of the hull, hence the square of the dimensions) increased far more slowly than the carrying capacity (dependent upon volume, hence governed by the cube of the dimensions). Although other factors, especially length and depth, influence hull weight, the square-cube law generally gives bigger ships the edge, and as the proportion of weight devoted to the hull decreases, the weight available for 'payload' – weapons, armour and machinery – increases.

The comparatively high speeds of modern warships presented another major difficulty for smaller ships. At the slow speeds of sailing ships, frictional resistance dominates, but as speed increases, wave-making resistance becomes more and more important, with the result that small battleships must have machinery almost as powerful – and almost as heavy and costly – as that of the bigger ships if they are to match them in speed. The effects of this crucial factor can be seen in the fact that several of the small battleship designs included in this article were deliberately intended to be slower than big ships.

A more subtle point comes into play when considering armament. A sailing warship carried numerous relatively small guns, so the armament could be easily sub-divided to match the size of the ship. Thus a 74-gunned ship carried the same kinds of guns as a 100, but carried fewer of them. A modern battleship, on the other hand, was armed with only a few big guns in complex and heavy mountings. These could not be so neatly subdivided – you can't have half or one-quarter of a 16in gun. Each big gun mounting thus represent a sizable 'quantum' of weight, limiting possible reductions; this issue was further complicated by the fact that the number of guns could only be reduced so far before long-range shooting would become ineffective; fire control depended on salvos of several shells to spot the fall of shot in relation to the target and, once the target had been straddled, salvos had to be dense enough to ensure hits. The interplay of these factors can be seen in the designs included here; the two designs with what might be termed 'full' batteries (eight and twelve guns) both feature a small calibre (12in), while those with larger calibre guns (14-16in) had to make do with fewer barrels. The most common battery was six guns (six designs), but one had only four and another five.

Finally, there are some features with a more-or-less fixed size or weight, no matter what the displacement of the ship. For example, the depth of the torpedo protection system, and the thickness of its bulkheads, cannot be reduced in proportion to the displacement if an adequate level of protection is to be maintained. Similarly, the secondary and anti-aircraft batteries had to have some minimum number of barrels to be effective no matter what the size of the ship.

To put it in a nutshell, small battleships quickly ran up against the law of diminishing returns: as size shrank, a greater percentage of a ship's displacement had to be devoted to 'overheads' such as hull weight, torpedo protection, secondary battery and so forth, leaving less for the 'payload' – main battery, armour and propulsion. These technical disadvantages meant that small battleships could not match the fighting power of bigger ships on a ton-for-ton basis. The economics were also weighted against the small ships: ten 35,000-ton battleships could be built more cheaply than thirteen 26,500-ton ships or twenty 17,500-ton ships. In aggregate, the smaller ships will require more horsepower to achieve the same speed as the bigger ships, and they will burn more fuel in doing so; they will require more armour, and – perhaps most critically – they will require more men. Thus the economic justification cited for smaller ships turns out to be a chimera.

In addition to the technical and economic disadvantages, there were sound tactical and strategic considerations militating against the small battleship. On the tactical level, a battle-line composed of a smaller number of big ships will be quicker to maneuvre and change formation than one composed of a larger number of smaller ships; this was one of the advantages cited for *Dreadnought* at the time of her construction. Strategically, big ships can carry more fuel and provisions, making it possible for them to operate at greater distances from their bases. Another strategic rationale given for smaller battleships – the ability to build more ships, allowing more flexibility in the size and composition of individual fleets and squadrons – evaporates when the necessity of concentrating against a single powerful enemy arises, as was the case for both the Royal and Imperial German Navies in the decade before the First World War.

In sum, big ships possess compelling advantages over small ones; but this did not prevent navies and individual designers from trying their hands at designing small battleships.

Small Battleships in an Age of Giants

HMS *Dreadnought* ushered in a period of unprecedented growth in battleship size in the years before the Great War, as the major navies – and even some minor ones – sought to outclass their rivals by building bigger, faster and more powerfully armed battleships. Several of the lesser powers, caught up in the dreadnought craze but lacking the financial means to build big ships, explored the possibilities of smaller battleship designs. Both Greece and The Netherlands considered such ships, but both eventually opted for fully-fledged capital ships. Only Spain managed to build small dreadnoughts – the *España* class. A comparison of the weights of these British-designed ships with their contemporary, HMS *Neptune*, shows some of the sacrifices made in the smaller ships:

The battleship Jaime I *of the* España *class, laid down between 1909 and 1912. Although she carried 80% of the main armament of the contemporary British* Neptune *on 80% of the displacement, sacrifices had to be made in speed and protection. The photo dates from around 1931. (US Naval Historical Center NH 87928)*

	España 1909	*Neptune* 1909	*España/Neptune*
Hull & Fittings:	5,920 tons	6,750 tons	87.7%
Armour & Protection:	3,664 tons	5,706 tons	64.2%
Armament:	2,890 tons	3,569 tons	81.0%
Machinery:	1,390 tons	2,131 tons	65.2%
Equipment:	690 tons	600 tons	115.0%
Coal:	800 tons	900 tons	88.9%
Margin:	186 tons	100 tons	186.0%
Total:	**15,450 tons**	**19,906 tons**	**77.6%**

In terms of armament, the *España* may be accounted a success; on a displacement of less than 80% that of the bigger ship, she managed to carry 80% of the main battery (eight 12in guns compared to *Neptune's* ten) and a more powerful secondary battery (twenty 4in to *Neptune's* twelve). But with a greater percentage of her total displacement devoted to the 'overhead' of her hull and fittings, she had to pay for her relatively powerful armament by trimming in other areas – specifically, in protection and machinery weights. *Neptune's* belt was a full two inches thicker, and she was a knot and a half faster.

The Great War showed that battleships required increased protection against underwater weapons and plunging fire; in other words, future battleships would have to grow larger and more expensive. In Britain, Japan and the United States, a new generation of 'monster' battleships, all of them exceeding 40,000 tons, was on the drawing boards. The Washington Treaty of 1922 put a sudden halt to the trend toward bigger battleships, but by an odd paradox its quantitative and qualitative limits also tended to discourage any impulse toward the small battleship. There seems to have been a general feeling in naval circles that unconventional types of ship might prove disastrous; if the experiment failed to live up to expectation, there would be no way to replace it, so the overall strength of the fleet would be reduced. Moreover, the total displacement limits set by the Washington Treaty meant that any small battleships had to fit exactly within some multiple of 35,000 tons. Thus in the late 1920s Italy considered building three 23,000-ton ships instead of two 35,000-tonners, while France investigated the design of *croiseurs de combat* of 17,500 tons, so that two could be built on the same displacement as a single 35,000-ton battleship. The required features, however, could not always be squeezed into these artificial tonnage quanta; when the German 'pocket battleships' appeared, the French Navy decided that the lightly-protected *croiseur de combat* was inadequate. In the early 1930s its interest shifted to a better protected type of 23,333 tons, but what eventually emerged were the 26,500-ton *Dunkerque* and *Strasbourg*. This left only 17,000 tons for a third capital ship – too small even for an unsatisfactory *croiseur de combat*.

That the laws of physics still favoured the bigger ship can be seen most clearly if we compare the weights of two very similar designs: HMS *Nelson*, the first 35,000-ton battleship, and Vickers' Design 892 for a 26,500-ton battleship, prepared by Sir George Thurston for an article published in the 1926 edition of *Brassey's Naval and Shipping Annual*. Design 892 was in almost every respect a small *Nelson*, making the comparison a very close one:

	Design 892	*Nelson* (Legend)	Design 892/*Nelson*
Hull & Fittings:	11,000 tons	14,250 tons	77.2%
Armour & Protection:	7,000 tons	10,250 tons	68.8%
Armament:	4,850 tons	6,900 tons	70.3%
Equipment:	800 tons	1,050 tons	76.2%
Machinery:	2,730 tons	2,550 tons	107.1%
Margin:	120 tons	–	–
Standard Displ.:	26,500 tons	35,000 tons	75.7%

Thus for three-quarters of the displacement of *Nelson*, Design 892 managed to carry main and secondary batteries that were only two-thirds as powerful as those of the bigger ship – six instead of nine 16in and eight instead of twelve 6in; the proportion of weight devoted to protection is also smaller. One unusual feature is that the smaller ship had more powerful machinery, making her somewhat faster (26kts vs. 23kts); perhaps Sir George found that he had more than enough armament weight for six

An artist's impression of Sir George Thurston's Design 892, in effect a small-scale Nelson. *On a displacement of 26,500 tons the ship was to carry six 16in guns in two triple turrets forward and eight 6in guns in twin turrets abeam the tower structure. She would have been faster than* Nelson *but less well protected. Design 892 was arguably the best-balanced small battleship proposal of the interwar period. (Brassey's Naval and Shipping Annual 1926)*

guns, but not enough for seven, so he applied the excess armament weight to the machinery, giving his ship a turn of speed that might prove very useful if she ran into a more powerful enemy.

In Britain in the late 1920s and early 1930s the whole issue of battleship size became inextricably linked to the small warship proposals of Admiral Sir Herbert Richmond; however, his arguments did not concern the battleship *per se*, but were directed to the question of the minimum size of warships in general. In his writings Richmond tried to establish a theoretical basis for the role, and consequently the size of warships. He concluded that the fundamental role of navies was to protect or attack maritime trade, so they needed ships that were powerful enough to cope with any merchant ship or auxiliary cruiser. This requirement led him to argue that the basic type of warship should displace about 7,500 tons and carry an armament of 6in guns. He believed that larger ships were unnecessary, and that the nations of the world could realise great economic benefits by banning them.

Richmond's arguments did not inspire anyone to give up the battleship, but there was nevertheless much interest at the Admiralty in reducing the size and cost of battleships. At the Geneva Arms Limitation Conference in 1927 the British delegation proposed that, instead of the Washington Treaty standards of 35,000 tons and 16in guns, future battleships should be limited to 28,500 tons and 13.5in guns. At the same time, the Director of Naval Construction's department prepared several sketch designs to explore the characteristics of such ships. The U.S. Navy's leadership, however, was opposed to smaller battleships, primarily because its strategy was dominated by the potential need to fight a trans-Pacific war against Japan. But another sticking point was the question of what would be done with the existing large battleships if a new, lower treaty tonnage limit was adopted. There could be little doubt regarding the fate of a 25,000-ton ship armed with 12in guns in a fight with a *Nagato* or a *Nelson*. On the other hand, if a 12in-gunned ship were protected against 16in guns, its displacement would be increased to 31,000 tons, much of that weight increase being due heavy armour – always an expensive item. Thus the supposed advantages of a reduced treaty limit would be lost. The alternatives were to scrap the existing big battleships, or rearm them with 12in guns. The latter idea summons up some interesting, if bizarre images.

Taken all in all, the USN saw no advantage in reducing the treaty limits any further, so when the British again proposed a limit of 25,000 tons with 12in guns, or 22,000 tons with 11in guns at the London Conference in 1931, the Americans resisted, although the Japanese expressed a willingness to accept limits of 25,000 tons and 14in guns. The end result was an *impasse*, so the existing tonnage and gun-calibre limitations were retained, but the Washington Conference building holiday was extended to 1936.

The French battleship *Dunkerque* has already been mentioned; she was in fact an impressive achievement, but a weight comparison with full-sized battleship *Richelieu*, designed along similar lines, once again demonstrates that smaller size meant making sacrifices:

	Dunkerque	*Richelieu*	*Dunkerque/Richelieu*
Hull	7,011t	8,276t	84.7%
Hull fittings	2,767t	4,706t	58.8%
Armament	4,858t	6,130t	79.2%
Protection	11,040t	16,045t	68.8%
Machinery	2,214t	2,865t	77.3%
Consumables (50%)	1,907t	2,905t	65.6%
Total	**29,797 tonnes**	**40,927 tonnes**	**72.8%**

Note: The figure for consumables for *Dunkerque* has been adjusted to match the percentage for *Richelieu*.

Both designs relied on the concentration of the main battery in two quadruple turrets to achieve a combination of powerful armament, good protection and high speed. Nevertheless, the proportion of displacement devoted to hull weight is larger in the smaller ship, necessitating sacrifices elsewhere; since armament and machinery weights in the smaller ship are proportionally larger, it is the protection and consumables (i.e. range) that suffer most.

The *Dunkerque* had been built in reply to the pocket battleships and so, in the inevitable logic of arms races, Germany, once freed of the Versailles restrictions by the Anglo-German Naval Agreement of 1935, replied to the French ships with *Scharnhorst* and *Gneisenau*, supposed small battleships of 26,000 tons, but with an actual standard displacement of well over 32,000 tons – making them close to full-blown treaty battleships. A number of ships similar in size to *Dunkerque* were subsequently projected or built by various nations (the Dutch battlecruisers for the East Indies, the Japanese B-64/65 design, the Soviet *Kronstadt* class and the American *Alaskas*), but these were all essentially scaled-up cruisers, not battleships, and all of them featured very high speeds and relatively light protection.

By the second half of the 1930s the treaty system was tottering toward collapse, and interest in small battleships virtually disappeared. Although the Second London Naval Conference of 1936 agreed to limit main batteries to 14in guns, there was no interest in further reductions in displacement, and the invoking of the 'escalator clause' the following year, which restored the 16in gun calibre and boosted the permissible battleship size to 45,000 tons, spelled the final end to attempts at limiting battleship size through treaties. Britain, however, still hoped to set an example by voluntarily limiting her new *Lion* class battleships to 40,000 tons.

The Second World War brought home to almost all observers the fact that the days when naval power was measured by the big-gun warship had ended. Even the giant *Musashi* and *Yamato* were sunk by aircraft long before they got within gun range of their intended targets, and new weapons like radio-controlled bombs demonstrated their effectiveness all too clearly by crippling HMS *Warspite* and destroying the Italian battleship *Roma*. Armour against glider-bombs or the guided missiles that were already in prospect, together with protection against the under-bottom explosions of influence mines and torpedoes, would have boosted battleship size to fantastic levels. For the few who believed that battleship building should be resumed, it was obvious that sacrifices would have to be made to keep ships down to feasible dimensions. The Royal Navy's staff considered requirements for new battleships in 1945, including ones for smaller ships – 'small' now meaning 35,000 tons or so – with reduced main batteries and protection. These ideas were soon abandoned. Only in the USSR, where Stalin's antiquated ideas on naval strategy prevailed over the more realistic views of his admirals, was serious attention given to the resumption of big-gun capital ship construction. The trend of the Soviet design work may be gauged from the fact that 70,000-ton ships were dubbed 'medium' designs – ships that would fulfil all the Red Navy's specified requirements would have exceeded 100,000 tons. It was in response to the increasing size and cost of future battleship construction that the Soviet designers came up with what was probably the final serious proposal for small battleships, but the entire scheme came to an end with the death of Stalin in March 1953.

The Designs

What follows is a selection of small battleship designs from the inter-war period, with a couple of post-Second World War proposals included as curiosities. With one possible exception, all of these designs were the products of professional naval architects and so may be considered more or less technically feasible, even if suspect in other regards.

1. Scheme A-2, United States, 1919

By 1918 the U.S. Navy was preparing to lay down the *South Dakota* class, 43,200-ton monsters armed with twelve 16in guns. But the size of these ships worried Rear Admiral David W. Taylor, Chief Constructor of the U.S. Navy, and in March 1919 he asked the Preliminary Design branch of the Bureau of Construction and Repair to prepare a series of small battleship designs. These were to be armed with two twin 16in turrets each, with speeds varying from 20 to 29kts. Taylor hoped that the resulting ships would be in the neighbourhood of 13,000 tons, so he was very disappointed when even the slowest variant (shown in the drawing) weighed in at 21,000 tons; the 29-knot variant was no less than 37,000 tons, a striking illustration of just how expensive high speed could be. Among the factors driving up the displacement was the use of a complete five-bulkhead side-protection system and the need for increased deck protection to resist plunging fire at long ranges.

Using triple 16in turrets, which had been developed for the *South Dakota* class, rather than twins for the main battery would have allowed a more powerful design with a modest increase in displacement. But Taylor was apparently sufficiently disappointed with the results of the twin-turret series to abandon all further work on small battleships.

2. Soliani's 'Semi-Submerged Battle Monitors', 1920

Whereas Taylor sought to trim displacement by reducing the number of main battery guns, Nabor Soliani, Chief Constructor of Italy's Ansaldo shipbuilding firm, took a far more radical approach. In a paper presented to the Italian Society of Naval Architects and Marine Engineers in December 1920, Soliani suggested that his country's defensive needs could be met by an unusual type of battleship that he dubbed the 'semi-submersible battle monitor'. Soliani's ships would take on water ballast before going into action until all that remained above water would be the guns and conning tower. This would allow the elimination of heavy side armour, saving greatly on displacement and cost. With a speed of about 18kts the ships would be relatively slow – and even slower when in battle trim with increased draught – but Soliani did not see this as a major drawback for defensive ships. His calculations indicated that stability would be satisfactory, although the reserve of buoyancy would be very low.

Those commenting on Soliani's proposal criticised the relatively low speed of the design, and pointed out that the virtual absence of freeboard would put severe limits on the ship's ability to fight her guns in any sort of a seaway. The small reserve of buoyancy was also seen as an Achilles' heel, making the ship liable to loss after even

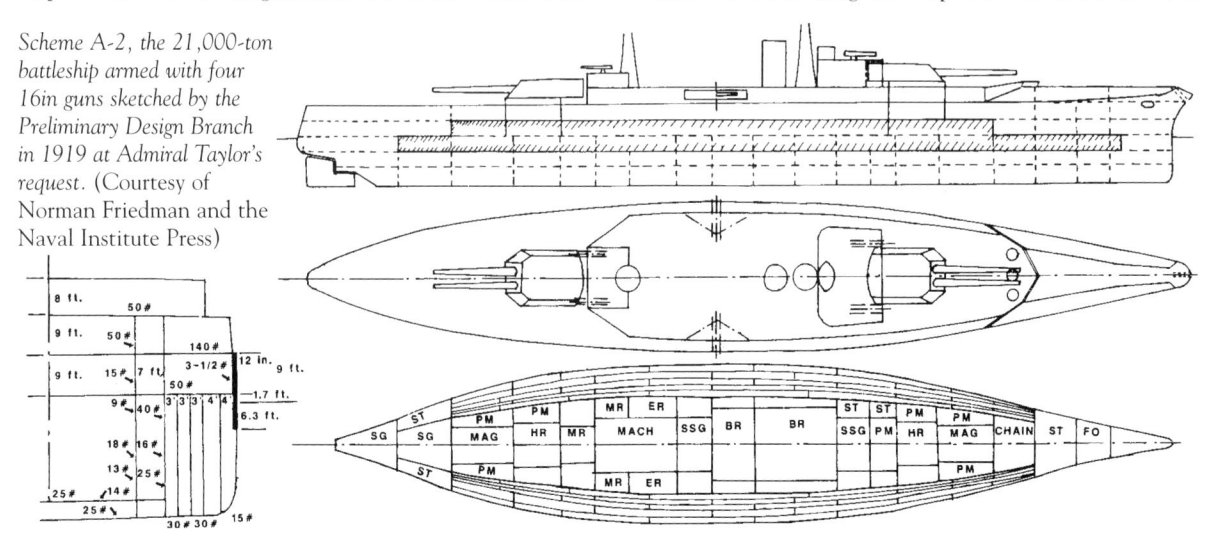

Scheme A-2, the 21,000-ton battleship armed with four 16in guns sketched by the Preliminary Design Branch in 1919 at Admiral Taylor's request. (Courtesy of Norman Friedman and the Naval Institute Press)

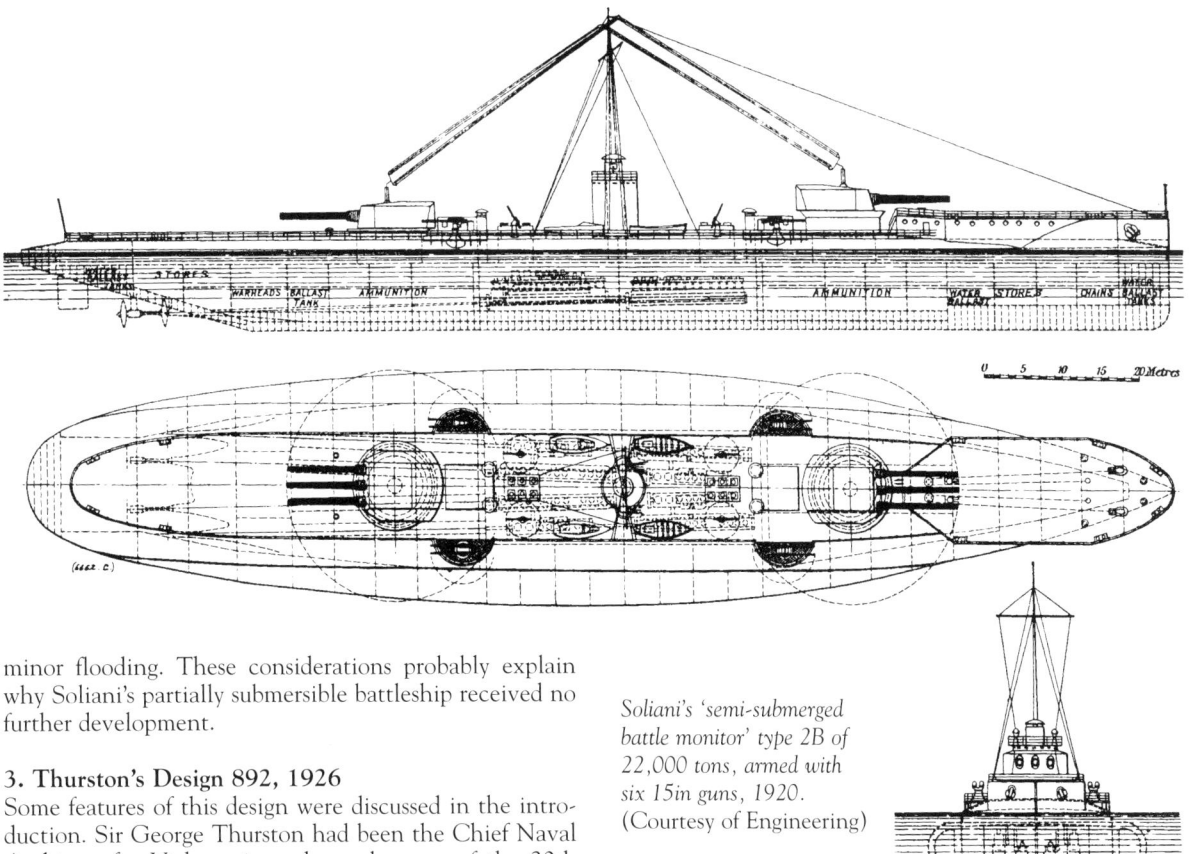

DIMINISHING RETURNS: SMALL BATTLESHIP DESIGNS, 1919-1953

minor flooding. These considerations probably explain why Soliani's partially submersible battleship received no further development.

3. Thurston's Design 892, 1926

Some features of this design were discussed in the introduction. Sir George Thurston had been the Chief Naval Architect for Vickers since the early years of the 20th century, and had proven himself to be both a competent warship designer and a clever salesman, often working closely with the infamous Basil Zaharoff. Before the Great War his company had eagerly sought contracts with the ambitious navies of South America, Turkey, Spain and China, while even major powers like Japan and Russia did not hesitate to call on Vickers for warship designs. But

Soliani's 'semi-submerged battle monitor' type 2B of 22,000 tons, armed with six 15in guns, 1920. (Courtesy of Engineering)

after the war business was slow, and Vickers was in financial difficulties. Sir George hoped to re-ignite the naval passions of the South American republics by offering innovative designs, and to this end he published an article in the 1926 edition of *Brassey's Naval and Shipping*

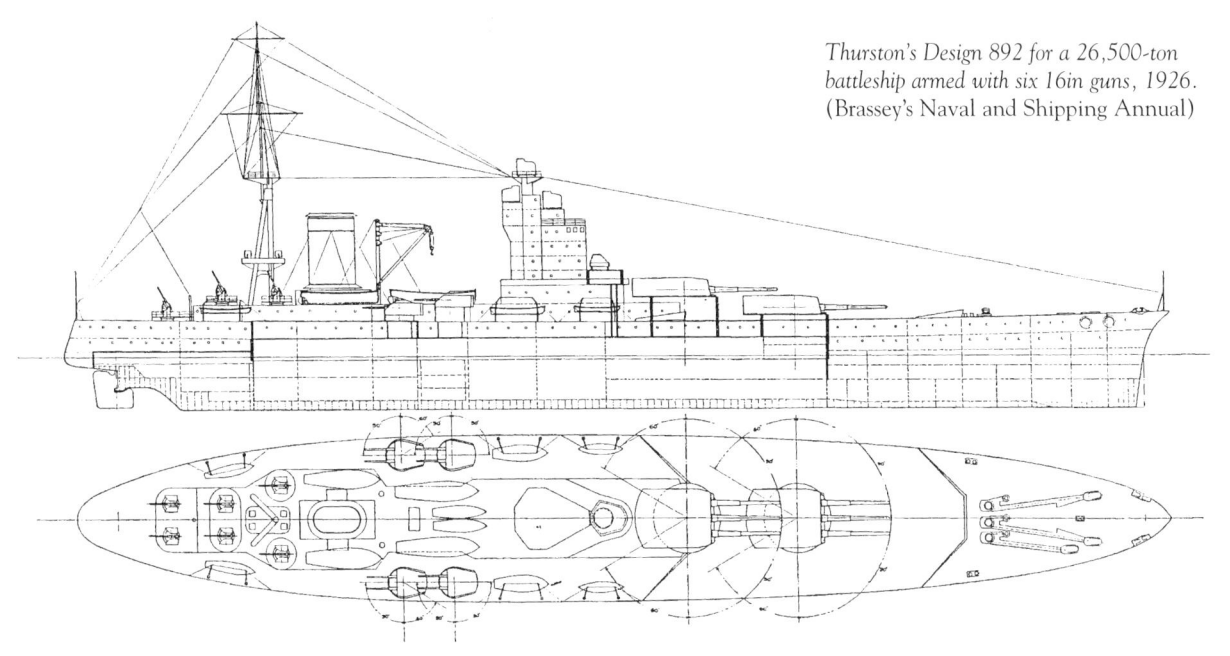

Thurston's Design 892 for a 26,500-ton battleship armed with six 16in guns, 1926. (Brassey's Naval and Shipping Annual)

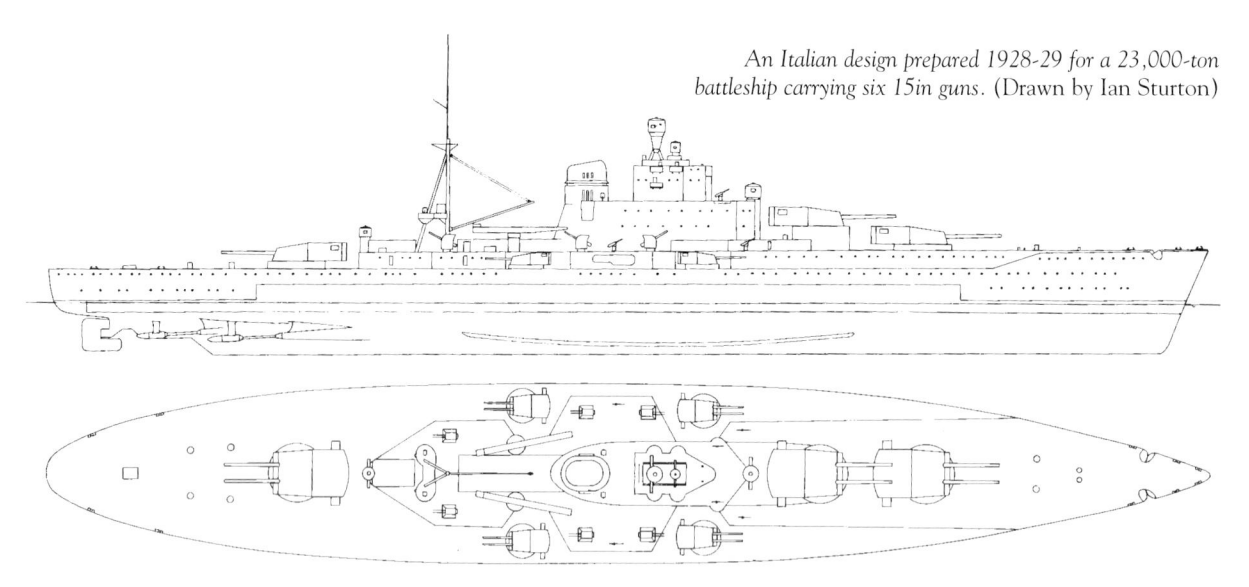

An Italian design prepared 1928-29 for a 23,000-ton battleship carrying six 15in guns. (Drawn by Ian Sturton)

Annual in which he proposed several unusual types of battleship, the implication being that Vickers would be only too happy to build any of these ships for a client. One of these was a 26,500-ton ship armed with six 16in guns in two triple turrets forward, to all intents and purposes a scaled-down *Nelson*. It is perhaps the most feasible and attractive small battleship scheme of the era, foreshadowing in many ways the French *Dunkerque*. Sir George was able to provide his ship with protection almost equal to that of *Nelson*, as well as a speed of 26 knots, fast enough to allow the ship to choose her range when fighting most of the world's battleships, or to escape from more powerful enemies.

Unfortunately for Vickers, none of the South American nations was inclined to resume the pre-war dreadnought-building craze, so Sir George's ideas remained unrealised.

4. 23,000-ton Design, Italy, 1928/29

The Washington Treaty allowed Italy to lay down a new 35,000-ton battleship in 1927 and a second in 1929, and in 1928-1929 the *Stato Maggiore della Marina* (Naval General Staff) began investigating how best to use the permitted tonnage. The Stato Maggiore believed that three new battleships would have to be built, to ensure that at least two ships were available at all times. Given the available tonnage, this meant three small battleships of about 23,000 tons.

This size ruled out a battery of 16in guns, but six 15in guns would be possible, arranged in twin turrets rather than triples so that, if one turret were put out of action, two turrets with four guns would remain. Full-fledged secondary and heavy AA batteries were included, and a high speed of 28 to 29kts was specified, in part to allow the ships to escape from superior enemy forces. The scale and extent of the armour protection is uncertain, although the maximum armour thickness is quoted as a respectable 330mm.

The fly in the ointment was that France might reply to Italy's 23,000-ton ships with battleships of 35,000 tons, so some preliminary design work was also done on larger ships armed with six 16in guns. However, in the end battleship construction was postponed; when it was finally resumed in 1934, the chosen type of ship was the large *Littorio* class.

5. Design 12B, Great Britain, 1929

During the Geneva Arms Limitation Conference in 1927, Britain suggested a modification of the Washington Treaty's qualitative limits – instead of 35,000 tons and 16in guns, the new limits would be 28,500 tons and 13.5in guns. At the same time the Admiralty had sketch designs drawn up for ships of this size, although for some reason these were armed with 14in, not 13.5in, guns. The British proposals at the Geneva Conference were not supported by the other powers, but this did not end official interest in reducing the size of battleships. In 1928/1929 a series of designs developed by the Director of Naval Construction's department included ships with 14in, 12in and even 10in guns.

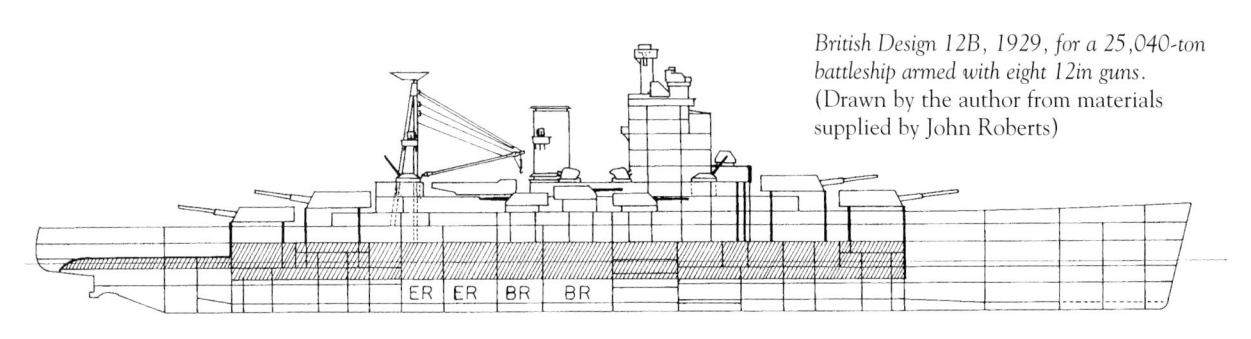

British Design 12B, 1929, for a 25,040-ton battleship armed with eight 12in guns. (Drawn by the author from materials supplied by John Roberts)

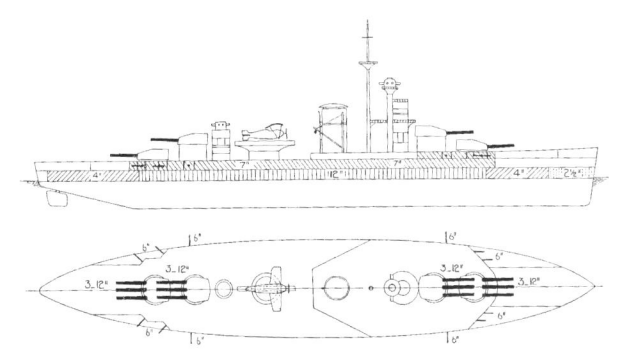

Thurston's 'battleship of the future', 1933; she was to displace 25,000 tons and carry twelve 12in guns. (Brassey's Naval and Shipping Annual)

One of these designs is illustrated here; it follows British practices of the day, with a tower mast almost identical to that of *Nelson*, and the main battery distributed in the preferred four twin turrets. Note that there is a full suite of twelve 6in guns – illustrating the fact that, even on a reduced displacement, some things could not be reduced. Perhaps the most interesting feature of the design is the use of between-deck 4.7in AA mountings.

6. Thurston's Battleship of the Future, 1933
Having designed an attractive mini-*Nelson* for *Brassey's Naval and Shipping Annual* in 1926, Sir George Thurston returned to the theme of small battleships in the 1933 edition of the same yearbook and presented what may well be the ugliest of all the inter-war proposals. This time Sir George was not aiming to sell ships to Latin American powers – he had retired from Vickers in 1929 – but to forecast the likely future shape of battleships for even the major powers. His method of analysis was peculiar to say the least: he compared the British *Nelson*, Japanese *Nagato*, American *Colorado*, French *Bretagne*, Italian *Duilio* and the German pocket battleship *Deutschland* as if their varying sizes, armaments, speeds and protection represented deliberate choices in battleship design, rather than reflecting the differing eras of their construction and the artificial limitations placed upon their designers. The result of this hodgepodge approach to design was the conclusion that future battleships would be armed with high-velocity 12in guns, that they would be smaller than ships like *Nelson*, yet they would nevertheless require protection – especially horizontal and underwater – more or less on a par with the bigger ships. He completely failed to grasp the purpose of 'all-or-nothing' protection, and argued that citadel armour was necessary to protect the ship's personnel.

Even a close reading of Sir George's article fails to reveal by what logic he reached his conclusions; but whatever it was, he managed to design what was essentially a pre-war dreadnought, albeit with fairly heavy horizontal protection. It is not surprising to find that, whereas Thurston's 1926 proposals had generated some interest in the naval press (if not, alas, among prospective customers), his 1933 article seems to have been almost completely ignored.

7. Acworth's 'Battleship of To-morrow,' 1934
Captain Bernard Acworth, D.S.O., RN (Retired), achieved a certain notoriety in the 1930s because of his controversial writings on naval topics. Acworth considered the potential of aircraft to be highly overrated, argued that navies didn't need large staff organisations, believed that 'scientific' (a word he always put within quotation marks) devices like hydrophones were 'fraudulent,' and that radio was of doubtful utility, given Britain's

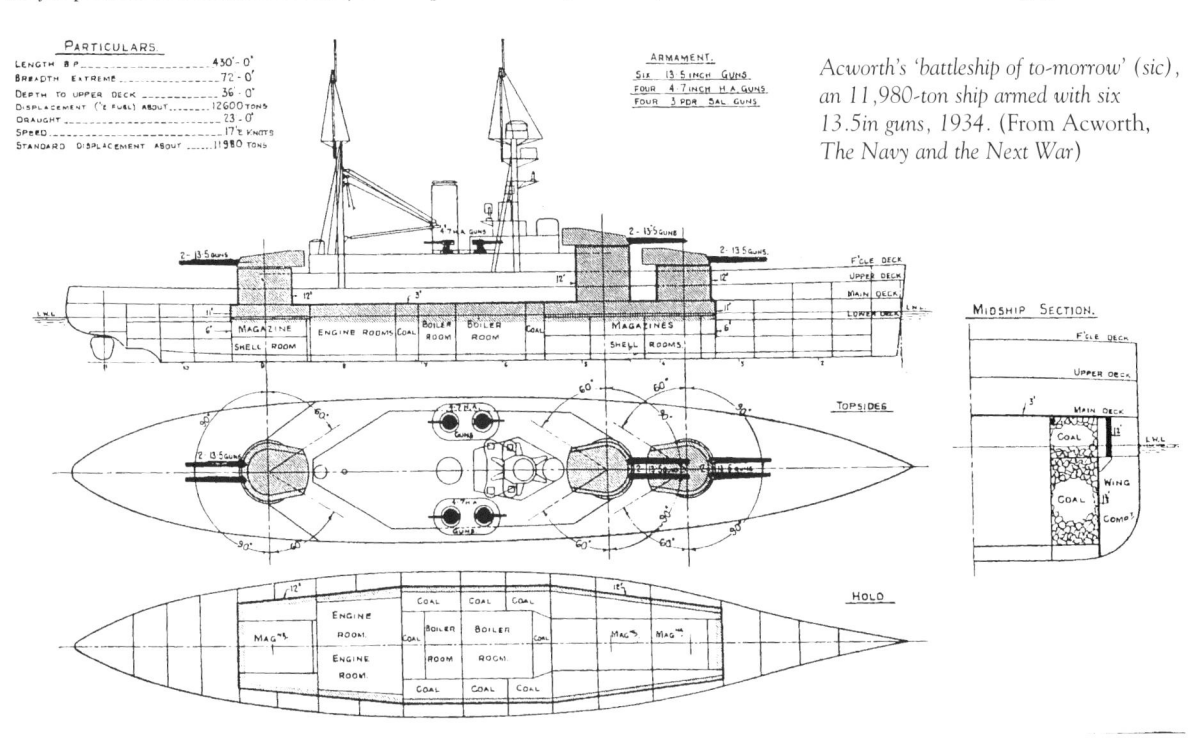

Acworth's 'battleship of to-morrow' (sic), an 11,980-ton ship armed with six 13.5in guns, 1934. (From Acworth, The Navy and the Next War)

extensive network of cable communications. In light of the events and developments of the Second World War, this can only be regarded as a pretty dismal track record for a self-appointed prognosticator.

Acworth also believed that battleships could be much reduced in size, and that they should be coal-fired. Working with an unnamed naval constructor, Acworth produced a design for a 12,600-ton ship with an armament of six 13.5in guns and a 12in belt; deck protection was weak because Acworth believed that fighting at long ranges was foolish. He never explained how a squadron of his slow (17.5-kt) ships were supposed to get close enough to, say, a *Colorado* or a *Nagato* – both of which were considerably faster – to overwhelm them with short-range fire.

Despite professional naval opinion, which generally recognised Acworth for the crank that he was, his notions met with some sympathy in political circles. This led Sir Stanley Goodall, the DNC, to complain in his diary that ministers were taken in by Acworth's arguments, and his 1937 paper for the Institution of Naval Architects, on 'Uncontrolled Weapons and Warships of Limited Displacement,' may have been aimed at least in part at Acworth's ideas. Goodall returned to the subject the next year when Acworth presented a paper on 'Alternative Firing of British Men-of-War' to that same institution, severely criticising Acworth's battleship. He noted, among other things, that its stability would be 'entirely inadequate'. Acworth countered that the initial stability of the ship would be as good as that of a First World War-era battleships; this missed Goodall's point, which was that the internal belt armour would leave the ship's outer hull vulnerable along the waterline even to small-calibre shells; the loss of waterplane caused by such damage would have been fatal to the small ship.

Goodall's reaction, while certainly justified, was perhaps a bit harsh, and suggests that he found Acworth and his political supporters particularly annoying. Fortunately for the Royal Navy, Acworth's ideas, including his small coal-fired battleship, had no influence on naval construction or policy, despite the political interest they garnered.

8. The 'Small Displacement Capital Ship', 1942

With the resumption of battleship construction in the latter half of the 1930s, whatever official interest there had been in small battleships disappeared. However, in the early 1940s Walter E. Strope and Stanley J. Dwyer, students at the Webb Institute of Naval Architecture in Glen Cove, New York, decided to explore the practicality of small battleships as a joint senior thesis. They felt that their project would help 'to clarify the controversy over the problem of size' in battleships. Moreover, if a small battleship proved to be viable, it might allow useful capital ships to be built at shipyards too small for full-sized battleships; they also felt that such ships might be suitable for Latin American navies and so would be 'helpful in promoting hemisphere defense'.

Strope and Dwyer deliberately avoided any consideration of tactical or strategic issues, concentrating solely on the technical possibilities. They fixed the standard displacement of their design at 15,000 tons, since this would make it relatively easy to compare the qualities of the resultant design with ships in the 30,000-ton range such as USS *Colorado*, as well as the brand new 45,000-ton *Iowa* class; in other words, two small battleships should equal a *Colorado*, three of them should match an *Iowa*. Their guiding philosophy was that 'any feature which does not contribute to the strength of the ship in the battle-line' could be sacrificed to achieve the target displacement – specifically, speed and secondary armament.

The authors went into considerable detail, even performing detailed calculations of damaged trim and stability; their work approached the level of a preliminary design in the USN, and in fact Strope joined the Preliminary Design Branch of the Bureau of Ships after his graduation. The extent of their work probably owed a good deal to the head of the Webb Institute, Rear Admiral George H. Rock, USN (Retired), a former Chief Constructor of U.S. Navy; Rock often discussed the design with the two students during its development, and presumably provided a great deal of advice and guidance.

The resulting design was certainly interesting, but the

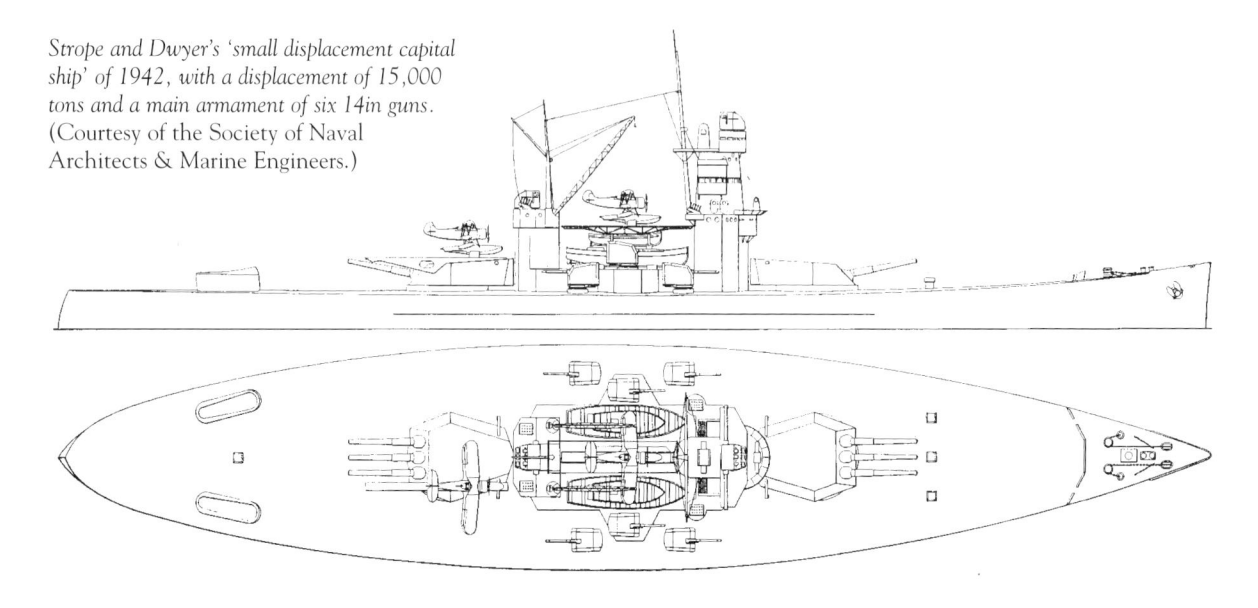

Strope and Dwyer's 'small displacement capital ship' of 1942, with a displacement of 15,000 tons and a main armament of six 14in guns. (Courtesy of the Society of Naval Architects & Marine Engineers.)

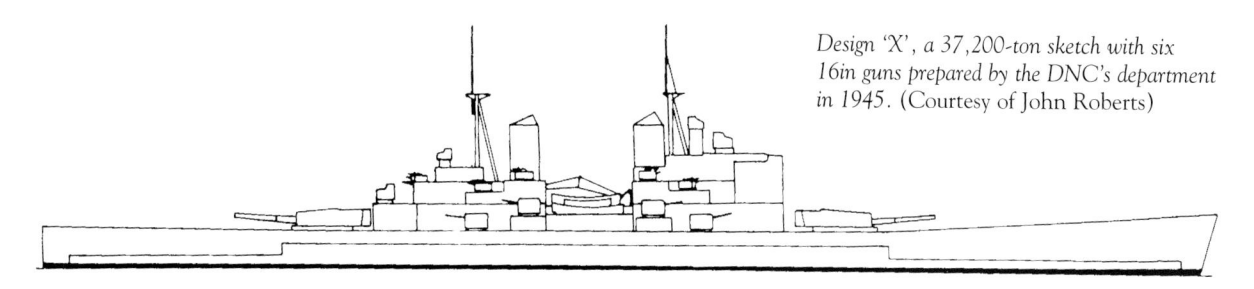

DIMINISHING RETURNS: SMALL BATTLESHIP DESIGNS, 1919-1953

Design 'X', a 37,200-ton sketch with six 16in guns prepared by the DNC's department in 1945. (Courtesy of John Roberts)

naval constructors and naval officers who commented on it pointed out a number of critical shortcomings. Chief among these was the low speed – virtually every professional who discussed the paper noted that recent war experience emphasised the tactical and strategic value of speed, especially in joint formations with aircraft carriers. Another defect was the strange funnel arrangement, which featured long horizontal ducts that ran below decks to the quarterdeck, where two low funnels were placed. The authors felt that this system avoided the drawbacks of smoke near the command and fire-control positions, but the horizontal ducts would have formed a dangerous path for flooding between compartments in the event of damage. In fact, the ship's ability to resist damage was generally considered suspect; in the interests of saving weight, the citadel was compressed to less than half the ship's length, which created long 'soft' ends. Moreover, there was no way to avoid a centreline bulkhead in the large machinery compartments, creating the danger of off-centre flooding. All in all, the naval officers and constructors saw no future for the small battleship, and some went so far as to suggest that the aircraft carrier was becoming the principal type of warship.

9. 'Design X', Great Britain, 1945

After the suspension of work on the *Lion* class battleships in May 1940, the Royal Navy's staff returned from time to time to the question of future battleship construction, updating the requirements as war experience dictated. By February 1945 the DNC, Sir Charles Lillicrap, was estimating that a ship meeting all the latest requirements would displace 67,000 to 70,000 tons; subsequent refining brought this down to 59,100 tons standard, but this was still considered excessive. Soon after this Lillicrap had a design prepared that reduced the ship's size by limiting the main battery to two triple 16in turrets and the belt armour to 9in. The resulting sketch, designated 'X', was for a ship of 35,000 tons, with a heavy AA battery. Unfortunately, the sketch does not appear to have survived, but John Roberts has provided an estimate of its appearance based on the known characteristics and general British practices of the time.

The small battleship was severely criticised by the staff, which felt that its armament was inferior to that of existing foreign battleships. As a result, in April 1945 a Committee on the Size of Battleships was established, and some further work was done, generally heading toward a ship of about 45,000 tons. However, interest in new battleships petered out after the war due to a combination of Britain's harsh economic conditions and the increasing menace of new airborne and underwater weapons.

10. Small Battleship Design, Soviet Union, 1952-1953

The last known small battleship designs – and perhaps the last battleship designs seriously considered by any power – were drawn up by the Soviet Ministry of Shipbuilding in 1950-1953. After the end of the Second World War, Stalin still hoped to build a powerful fleet of big-gun capital ships; this desire came close to reality in the *Stalingrad* class (Project 82) battlecruisers, laid down in 1951-1952. Stalin also hoped to build a new class of battleships in the near future, but the design of these ships proceeded at a leisurely pace; by 1950 it was still only at the preliminary design stage. This called for a ship of 73,000 tons armed with nine 16in guns and featuring very heavy protection.

By this time, however, the naval architects at the Shipbuilding Ministry were beginning to express doubts as to the utility of such large battleships, proposing instead the construction of 'small' battleships in the 35,000-ton range. The basic argument ran along the following lines: by

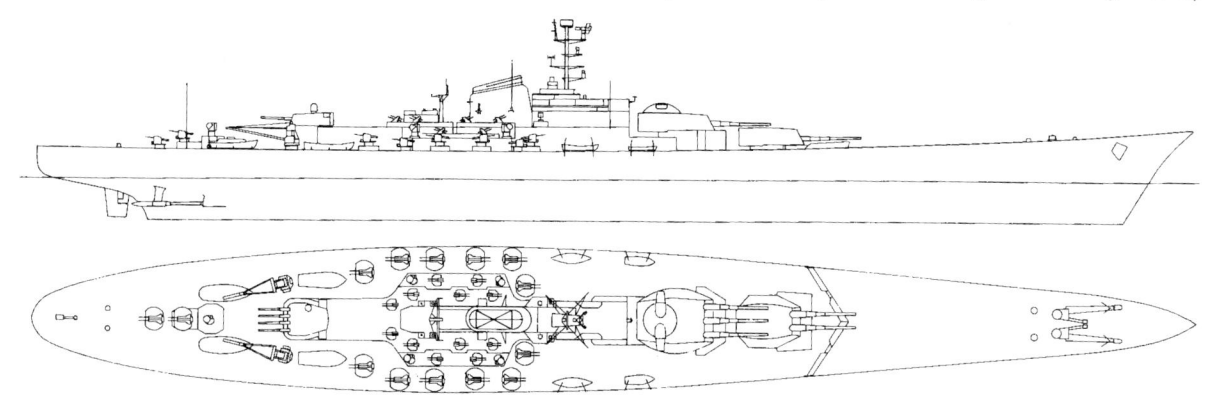

Soviet Design II+III+3, a 39,250-ton 'small' battleship design carrying five 16in guns, prepared circa 1951. (Drawn by Ian Sturton)

Small Battleship Design Characteristics 1919-1953

	No. 1 Taylor's Scheme A-2	No. 2 Soliani's Semi-submersible Battle Monitors Type 2B	No. 3 Thurston's Design 892	No. 4 Small Battleship	No. 5 Design 12B
Date:	1919	1920	1926	1928/1929	1929
Country of Origin:	United States	Italy	Great Britain	Italy	Great Britain
Displacement					
Standard				23,000	25,040
Normal	21,000	22,000	27,500		
Full Load		25,000		27,000	
Length					
pp			600ft		610ft
waterline	510ft			184.5m	
overall	523ft	150m		190.0m	
Beam	80ft	29m	92ft	26m	96ft
Draft	25ft	10m	29ft	8m	27ft
Armament	4 x 16in (2x2) 12 x 6in (6x2) 2 x 3in AA	6 x 381mm (3x2) 8 x 120mm (4x2) 4 x 102mm AA	6 x 16in (2 x 3) 8 x 6in (4 x 2) 6 x 4.7in AA	6 x 381mm (3 x 2) 8 x 152mm (4 x 2) 12 x 100mm (6 x 2)	8 x 12in (4x2) 12 x 6in (6x2) 8 x 4.7in (4x2) 4 pom-poms (4x8)
Aircraft Equipment	N/A	N/A	N/A	2 catapults	1 catapult
Machinery	Turbo-electric?	Diesels	Turbines	Turbines?	Turbines
Shafts		4	4	4	2?
Power		24,000bhp	66,000shp	?	37,000shp
Speed		18kts	26kts	28-29kts	23kts
Protection					
Belt	12in	150mm	14in magazines 13in machinery	330mm?	10in magazines 8in machinery
Deck	3.5in	150mm	6.25in magazines 3.75in machinery	?	6in magazines 4in machinery

making full use of modern fire-control and radio gear, two or three relatively small, fast battleships, each armed with a limited number of main battery guns, could concentrate their fire to achieve superiority over a single larger opponent. Moreover, a single small battleship could also fulfil the duties of a *Stalingrad* class battlecruiser, making for a simpler and more flexible fleet structure. The size of the individual ships could be kept down by limiting their underwater protection, since the distribution of the guns in several separate hulls increased the overall survivability of the armament – one ship might be damaged or sunk by underwater attack, but the other ships and their guns would remain ready for action. Since their high speed would allow the small battleships to choose their range and relative position, the armour protection could be heavily skewed toward fighting on forward bearings, allowing a reduction in side armour. There would be no heavy AA battery, since this task would be assigned to escort ships.

Based on these theories, the naval constructors of the Shipbuilding Ministry drew up a spectrum of designs. The design that seemed to be the favourite was designated II+III-3, armed with five 16in guns in a twin and triple turret forward, tipping the scales at 39,250 tons standard, making its classification as a 'small' battleship somewhat dubious. In addition to her main battery, she carried a single quad 180mm turret aft; during the approach to battle, these guns were to fire high-explosive shells intended to wreck the enemy's radar and fire-control installations. The likelihood of hitting with such guns at ranges on the order of 30,000m or more is a moot point.

The Soviet Navy's leadership never accepted the small battleship concept proposed by the Shipbuilding Ministry, and the argument over what type of battleship to build continued until Stalin's death in March 1953. At that point all design and construction work on big-gun capital ships was cancelled, bringing to an end the long and not always distinguished history of the small battleship.

Acknowledgements:

I would like to express my gratitude to John Roberts, who generously provided information on both the Royal Navy's 1929 design and the 1945 Battleship 'X' scheme. I would also like to thank Ian Sturton for graciously agreeing to draw two of the ships. As usual, Jan Torbet provided invaluable editorial assistance.

Sources:

Acworth, Bernard: *The Navy and the Next War: A Vindication of Sea Power*, Eyre & Spottiswoode (London: 1934).
Brown, David K. Brown: 'Sir Stanley V Goodall, KCB, OBE, RCNC', *Warship 1997-1998*, pp.52-63.

No. 6	No. 7	No. 8	No. 9	No. 10
Thurston's Battleship of the Future	Acworth's 'Battleship of To-morrow'	Small Displacement Capital Ship	Battleship 'X'	Design II+III-3
1933	1934	1942	1945	1952-1953
Great Britain	Great Britain	United States	Great Britain	Soviet Union
25,000	11,980	15,000	37,200	39,250
	12,600	16,900		
			44,500 (deep)	42,300
560ft	430ft		680ft	
		470ft	720ft	260m
				31m
92ft	72ft	84ft	106ft	9m
29ft 6in	23ft	27ft	?	
12 x 12in (4x3)	6 x 13.5in (3x2)	6 x 14in (2x3)	6 x 16in (2x3)	5 x 406mm (1x2, 1x3)
12 x 6in (12x1)	4 x 4.7in HA	6 x 5in (6x1)	12 x 4.5in (6x2)	4 x 180mm (1x4)
8 x 4.7in AA	4 x 3pdr saluting	4 multiple 40mm	54 x 40mm (9x6)	24 x 57mm (12x2)
2 x 21in TT				48 x 25mm (12x4)
1 catapult		2 catapults		
Turbines	?	Turbines		Turbines
?	2	2		3
30,000shp	?	20,000shp	125,000shp	210,000shp
22kts	17.5kts	21kts	29kts	32.7kts
12in	12in	14in	9in	250mm max
				(500mm for bkhd)
5in	3in	4in	6in	185mm total

Dumas, Robert: *Les cuirassés Dunkerque et Strasbourg*, Marines editions (Nantes: 2001), p.21.

Dumas, Robert: *Le cuirassé Richelieu 1935-1968*, Marines editions (Nantes: 2001), p.10.

Friedman, Norman: *U.S. Battleships: An Illustrated Design History*, Naval Institute Press (Annapolis 1985), pp.167-169, 224-228.

Giorgerini, Giorgio and Augusto Nani: *Le navi di linea italiane 1861-1969*, Third edition, Ufficio storico della Marina Militare (Rome 1973), pp.31, 33.

Higham, Robin: *The Military Intellectuals in Britain: 1918-1939*, Greenwood Press (Westport, CT, 1981), pp.51-66.

Hunt, Barry D: 'Smaller Navies and Disarmament: Sir Herbert Richmond's Small Ship Theories and the Development of British Naval Policy in the 1920s.' In: *Dreadnought to Polaris: Maritime Strategy Since Mahan* (edited by A.M.J. Hyatt; Toronto: The Copp Clark Publishing Company, 1973), pp.47-63.

'The Italian Society of Naval Architects and Marine Engineers', *Engineering*, 14 January 1921, pp.40-41.

Jordan, John: 'The Origins of *Dunkerque* and *Strasbourg*', *Warship 1999-2000*, Conway Maritime Press (London, 1999), pp.99-114.

Lavery, Brian: *The 74-gun Ship Bellona* (Anatomy of the Ship series), Naval Institute Press (Annapolis, 1985).

McKay, John: *The 100-gun Ship Victory* (Anatomy of the Ship series), Naval Institute Press (Annapolis, 1987).

McLaughlin, Stephen: *Russian and Soviet Battleships*, Naval Institute Press (Annapolis, 2003), pp.428-431.

Raven, Alan and John Roberts: *British Battleships of World War Two: The Development and Technical History of the Royal Navy's Battleships and Battlecruisers from 1911 to 1946*, Naval Institute Press (Annapolis, 1976), pp.146-156.

Roberts, John: 'Penultimate Battleships', Part 2, *Warship Vol. V* (1981), pp.266-274.

Soliani, Nabor: 'The Future of Warships', *Engineering*, 7 January 1921, pp.25-27.

Strope, Walmer Elton and Stanley J. Dwyer: 'Reinvestigation of the Practicality of the Small Displacement Capital Ship', *Transactions of the Society of Naval Architects and Marine Engineers*, Vol. 50 (1942), pp.268-305.

Thurston, George: 'Battleship or Aircraft Carrier?', *Brassey's Naval and Shipping Annual 1926*, pp.79-93.

Thurston, George: 'A Problem of the Navy', *Brassey's Naval and Shipping Annual 1933*, pp.81-95.

Thurston Notebooks, National Maritime Museum, Greenwich.

IMPERIAL JAPANESE MINELAYERS *ITSUKUSHIMA, OKINOSHIMA,* AND *TSUGARU*

Hans Lengerer continues his study of the Imperial Japanese Navy of the interwar period with a detailed look at the three purpose-built cruiser minelayers.

The production of mines was begun in Japan by Satsuma Daimyate in 1857, and three of these controlled mines were laid in Kagoshima Bay when the capital and its coast defence batteries were attacked by a British fleet commanded by Vice-Ad. Augustus Kuper in 1863.

After the formation of the Imperial Japanese Navy the first import of controlled mines was in June 1878, when the British-built armoured frigate *Fusô* (I) entered Yokohama with two British-made mines aboard. Akabane Production Branch Factory started the production of controlled mines in 1882 and four years later the independent type mine was introduced when the British-built protected cruiser *Naniwa* arrived in Japan and brought electric-type automatic mines. From that time the construction of specialised ships for laying mines became necessary, and until the end of Meiji era (1912) more than thirty boats displacing from 50 tons to 320 tons were built either from wood or steel.

During the Russo-Japanese War (1904-05) the contact mine with automatic mooring anchor and inertia firing unit was widely used, and exerted its effect by sinking capital ships, cruisers and smaller vessels of both adversaries. The IJN used not only the aforementioned vessels but also destroyers, torpedo-boats, shipborne torpedo-boats and mobilised civilian vessels classified as auxiliary minelayers. However, the lessons of the war indicated clearly that minelaying from these vessels was a difficult, time-consuming and often also dangerous task. The Naval General Staff (NGS) therefore proposed the conversion of the old cruisers *Naniwa* and her sister *Takachiho* to large type minelayers (*Ko-shu kirai fustetsukan*) on 25 October 1909 (see *Warship* 2004). After the loss of both ships in 1912 and 1914 respectively, the 2nd class cruiser *Tsugaru* (ex-Russian *Pallada*) was converted. In 1917 the mercantile-type first purpose-built cruiser minelayer *Katsuriki Maru* was completed, and the 1st class cruiser *Aso* (ex-Russian *Bayan*) was converted.

On 1 April 1920 warship classification was revised and the minelayers *Tsugaru, Aso* and *Katsuriki* were enrolled in the 'warship' (*gunkan*) category. *Tsugaru* was removed two years later and because it was foreseen that *Aso* would follow soon (she was in fact stricken only on 1 April 1931). Another veteran of the Russo-Japanese War, the British-built 1st class cruiser *Tokiwa*, was converted in 1922-23.

At the time of the so-called Eight-Eight Fleet (planning was halted by the conclusion of the Washington Naval Arms Limitation Treaty in 1922) 5,500-ton type light cruisers and destroyers of the *Minekaze* class were fitted for laying the No.1 mine (a tethered mine for tactical use), and at that time total minelaying capacity was fairly large. The construction of a cruiser minelayer of 5,000 tons was also included in the Eight-Eight Fleet Completion Programme of 1920. However, this programme had to be revised completely, and it was not until the New Supplementary Programme of 1923 that a minelaying cruiser, *Itsukushima*, and a fast netlayer (*Kyusetsumokan*) were authorised; the latter type, the first of which would be named *Shirataka*, would also have a minelaying capability.

In the Supplementary Programme of 1927 two 5,000-ton cruiser minelayers were requested as replacements for *Aso* and *Tokiwa*, together with twelve 1,200-ton light minelayers and one 5,000-ton fast netlayer, but only one 1,200-ton minelayer was authorised; this was *Yaeyama*, completed in 1932. Finally, as the result of a special provision in the London Treaty of 1930, the construction of two offensive-type cruiser minelayers was authorised in the First and Third Replenishment Programmes of 1931 and 1937 respectively. These ships would be named

Okinoshima and Tsugaru (II), and will be described in detail together with the smaller type Itsukushima.

However, before turning to these three ships it will be helpful to provide a brief overview of the cruiser minelayers operated by the IJN. These may be divided into the following categories:

– a large type capable of sailing to advanced bases and enemy coasts for contested minelaying;
– a medium ocean-going type with limited offensive minelaying capabilities;
– a small type to protect approaches, coastal areas and ports.

The 'fleet type' units were:

– four converted cruisers, of which three were classified officially as cruiser minelayers while the first, *Takachiho*, was sunk before the introduction of this category;
– one mercantile-type small cruiser minelayer, *Katsuriki*;
– one small type cruiser minelayer, *Yaeyama*;
– one medium type cruiser minelayer with some offensive minelaying capabilities, *Itsuksushima*;
– two large cruiser minelayers with full offensive minelaying capabilities, *Okinoshima* and *Tsugaru* (II);
– four small combined minelayers / fast netlayers: *Shirataka, Hatsutaka, Aotaka, Wakatake*;
– three converted wartime standard freighters of which one, *Minoo*, was included in the warship category while the other two, *Eijo Maru* and *Koryu Maru*, were classified as auxiliary minelayers.

The Medium Cruiser Minelayer Itsukushima

Itsukushima was the first ship designed and built as a cruiser minelayer after the introduction of this ship type into the classification list. She had some characteristic features and differed very much from the earlier *Katsuriki* and the contemporary combined netlayer/minelayer *Shirataka*. Her distinctive features were concerned not only with mine stowage but also her general configuration, superstructures, machinery, and guns.

The NGS requirement was for:

– stowage of an unprecedented number of mines;
– long range;
– sufficient gun power for defence against the attacks of ocean-going destroyers.

These features clearly indicated a vessel capable of sailing to advanced bases and enemy coasts to engage in offensive minelaying.

The Navy Technical Department (NTD) had no experience in the design of a cruiser minelayer of this type, so the Fundamental Design Section was heavily influenced by the Royal Navy's minelaying cruiser *Adventure*, which was being fitted out at that time. The calculations at the preliminary stage suggested a displacement of at least 3,000 tons. Following these studies a large offensive-type cruiser minelayer was requested and the funding for one ship authorised in 1923 as part of the New Fleet Replenishment Programme. However, owing to i) the postwar recession, which affected shipbuilding, shipping and other associated industries, ii) the massive damage resulting from the Kantô Great Earthquake, requiring immense sums for reconstruction, and iii) the mood of disarmament in the wake of the First World War and the Washington Treaty, the budget of the IJN was much reduced; some construction was postponed and some designs underwent major revisions. *Itsukushima* belonged to the latter category. The standard displacement was reduced by one third; however, it was found that the original staff requirements could still be meet by a reduction in speed and, to a lesser extent, in gun armament. This meant that some of the light cruiser characteristics disappeared, although *Adventure* was still the model for features like the flush deck and the internal mine hangar.

Itsukushima was laid down by the Uraga Dock Co. on 2 February 1928. She was launched on 22 May 1929 and completed on 26 December after a building period of nearly two years.

Hull and Superstructure

The general arrangement was determined primarily by the use of the main deck as a mine hangar. In order to obtain sufficient space *Itsukushima* had a flush deck – seldom used by Japanese designers. The main deck was continuous through the whole length of the ship. Directly beneath and forward of the bridge structure were located part of the officers' accommodation and staterooms, and from the after end of the superstructure to the stern there was a

An oblique port side view of Itsukushima with her 14cm guns trained to port. When this photo was taken in 1937 Itsukushima was the largest of the Japanese minelayers, and was also considered the most important one. The main recognition features were (1) a flush deck, (2) a short funnel just abaft amidships, and (3) a tall, rounded tower bridge set atop the long forward deckhouse. The main armament was heavy for a 2,000-ton ship: three 14cm low-angle guns and two 8cm (actual calibre 7.62cm) HA guns. The photo was published in Recognition Journal 12 Aug 1944, p. 12. (Hans Lengerer Collection)

large mine hangar for 500 No.5 mines. In the forward part of the mine hangar four sets of rails were fitted, but over most of its length there were six. The mines were stowed on the rails and moved by electric drive (*Dendo fusetsu sôchi* – most probably an endless chain system) until discharged via the six mine doors at the stern. This arrangement contributed much to the lowering of the centre of gravity (CG), and hence improved stability (GM). Its success led to it being repeated in the large cruiser minelayers built during the 1930s.

The adoption of six sets of rails – a feature unique to *Itsukushima* – was to enable a mine barrage off an enemy base or port to be laid in a short time. The arrangement of the six mine doors required a specially-configured stern, in which the sides were cut away to accommodate the doors for the outer sets of rails, while the four central doors were mounted flush with the rectangular transom. There was a control station for the mines on the centre-line between the inner pairs of doors at main deck level, and a second station above it on the upper deck. In order to obtain the required stiffness the upper deck was supported by deep girders, stanchions 100mm in diameter and also a centre-line bulkhead with a few arch openings to allow passage between the port and starboard mine bays.

The internal mine hangar was the most characteristic feature of *Itsukushima*. Mines, rails, and mine personnel were not exposed to weather conditions as was the case with upper-deck installations, and the working space was fully enclosed; safety and reliability were thereby significantly improved.

Abaft the bridge and forward of the funnel there were three mine elevators to port and three to starboard to transport the mines from the upper deck to the main deck. The elevators were connected to transverse transport rails each with two turntables, and these rails in turn were linked to the mine recovery rail. The latter was located to starboard on the upper deck, and ran from the bow to the after transverse rail. From just abaft the bridge, ie the position of the forward transverse mine rail, a mine rail to port extended to the funnel. There was also a davit at the bow to take on board mines used for training, etc. Smaller davits were arranged at the stern to handle depth charges and mine-sweeping gear, etc.

The large mine hangar effectively displaced part of the accommodation, traditionally located within the hull, to a broad shelter deck about 20m in length directly beneath the bridge structure. This housed the official and private rooms of the captain and first officer, and the private rooms of the division heads (mine, gunnery, navigation etc.). This arrangement was a departure from traditional practice.

The bridge structure was similar to that of the destroyers of the 'Special Type' (*Fubuki* class), and was erected on the shelter deck with the rear end almost flush with its after wall. This meant that the officers' living spaces were concentrated around the bridge. Behind the compass bridge there was a light tripod mast, complete with topmast, crow's nest and two yards. Abaft the shelter deck there was a large deckhouse that housed the galleys for officers, petty officers and ratings; the roof was used as the boat deck. Fore and aft of the low funnel there were two small deckhouses: the forward one housed the after W/T room, while the after one housed the bathroom and heads for the crew. Two 75cm searchlights were located in tubs *en echelon* atop the after W/T room. Between the two after 14cm gun mountings there was a deckhouse for munitions handling, topped by a short pole mainmast.

The quarterdeck from the after 14cm gun mounting to the stern was reserved for depth charges and tethered anti-sweep devices (*Bosogu*). The latter essentially comprised an anchor (weight 599kg), a blimp-shaped buoy with large wings, and a single serrated strong 'V' cutter to cut minesweeping and towing ropes to prevent the sweeping of mines by the enemy. Two pairs of rails were fitted on both sides of the quarterdeck of which the inner ones, which led to the inboard edges of the stern cutaways, were used for laying the anti-sweep devices.

On the lower deck, which was not continuous, the living spaces of the crew were arranged forward and also aft of the machinery spaces. At the after end of this deck were the depth charge magazine, store rooms for the various 'divisions', and motor rooms for the mine elevators and rails, steering compartment and tiller flat. The hold deck beneath it housed the generators, the auxiliary boiler room, the shell rooms and powder magazines, food storage and other store rooms; however, most of this area was occupied by trim, ballast and heavy oil tanks.

There were 78 watertight compartments of which nine were above the main deck. The bow had the typical Japanese warship form, namely double curvature with the forefoot largely cut away to be able to overrun a No.1 tethered mine should this become unavoidable.

Machinery

Another new departure for the designers was the adoption of diesel engines. Aside from the small tanker *Tsurugizaki* (1,970 tons, built at Kure N.Y. in 1918) *Itsukushima* was the first Japanese surface warship to be propelled by diesels. Diesel propulsion was adopted in part out of a desire for particularly compact machinery spaces in order to accommodate the voluminous mine hangar (see Table 1 for a comparison with the later *Okinoshima*, which had steam turbine propulsion), and also to obtain a large operational radius due to the comparatively low fuel consumption. As stated before, this meant that *Itsukushima* comfortably met range requirements, but at the expense of a tactical speed significantly lower than that originally envisaged.

At the time of building no suitable engine was available in Japan. Therefore the Ra Type No.1 diesel (built under licence from the Rauschenbach Co. of Switzerland but actually designed by MAN of Germany) was chosen because this four-cycle, single-action, six-cylinder (diameter 450mm, stroke 420mm) engine had been fitted in IJN's first minelaying submarine *I 21* (later *I 121*) with good results. In order to save money, the diesels of the former German minelaying submarine *U-125* (IJN designation: *O1*), after land trials had proven their reliability, were connected to the outer shafts while the engine for the centre shaft was newly manufactured by Niigata Iron Works.

The original engine developed 1,200bhp at 450rpm, but for reasons not known by the author its rating was reduced to 1,000bhp at 400rpm. Therefore, even with her unusual three-shaft system total output was only 3,000bhp, thereby limiting maximum speed to a barely acceptable 17knots. In later cruiser minelayers diesel propulsion was abandoned, probably because of the lack of a suitable lightweight, high-performance and reliable operating diesel. However diesels were again adopted for the light minelayers of the *Sarushima* type completed in 1934.

Directly behind the propeller on the centre shaft a German Oertz-type rudder with a surface area of 4.12m^2 was fitted experimentally instead of the usual balanced type. *Itsukushima* was the IJN's first warship with this rudder and the results, shown in Table 2, were very satisfactory.

Electricity was generated by two 175kW and one 45kW piston (reciprocating) generators to make a total of 395kW.

Armament

The mine hangar was designed to accommodate either 500 No.5 mines or 300 No.3 mines. Some particulars of these types are listed in Table 8.

The main guns were intended to engage small warships up to the destroyer type while executing offensive minelaying, and *Itsukushima* had gun power spproaching that of a light cruiser, with three 3rd Year Type 14cm/50-cal LA guns on the centreline. No.1 gun was mounted forward of the bridge on the shelter deck, with No. 2 and No.3 guns at upper deck level fore and aft of the mainmast. For defence against air attacks there were 3rd Year Type 8cm/40-cal HA guns on either side of the after end of the bridge; the guns were mounted on semicircular platforms extending out from the shelter deck supported by strong pillars.

The rangefinders were: one 3.5m type atop of the compass bridge to provide ranging for the main guns; and two 2m HA type for the 8cm guns. One of the latter was mounted forward of the 3.5m type, the other on a pedestal at the after end of the roof of the large deckhouse for the ship's boats. According to Fukuda, *op. cit.* p. 18, she also had one 1.5m RF.

An unusual feature of the armament was a long-range depth charge thrower purchased from the British Vickers Co. *Itsukushima* was the only IJN ship to be experimentally equipped with this thrower, which was located abaft the third 14cm gun on the centreline. It could be trained and laid like a gun and the throwing distance (maximum 1,512m) was adjusted by the elevation angle of the barrel. It was fitted with reloading gear, the depth charges being loaded from a stowage rack. The DCT fired a special type of depth charge, but there were also 18 standard depth charges (most probably Type 88) that were launched by means of rails fitted on the quarterdeck, the second pair of

Table 1:
A COMPARISON OF THE MACHINERY OF ITSUKUSHIMA AND OKINOSHIMA

	Itsukushima	*Okinoshima*
Type of propulsion	diesel	steam turbine
Power rating	4,211bhp	9,000shp
Engine/Motor Room		
length	13.6m	12.2m
width	13.0m	10.2m
height	4.6m	6.2m
area	157m^2	134.64m^2
No. of boilers	none	4 (mixed firing)
Boiler Room		
length	n/a	13.2m
width	n/a	11.6m
height	n/a	6.2m
area	n/a	167.04m^2
Total area mach. spaces	157m^2	301.68m^2
Power/space ratio	26.8bhp/m^2	29.8shp/m^2
Weight of Machinery		
Power rating	4,365.8bhp	9,000shp
Weight	225.6 tonnes	411 tonnes
Power/weight ratio	19.35bhp/tonne	21.89shp/tonne

Source: Fukuda, *op. cit.* p.149, p.152

Table 2: TURNING CAPABILITIES BEFORE AND AFTER STABILITY IMPROVEMENT

Standard speed

Rudder angle	Time for 180° turn	DA (m)	DT (m)	Maximum list
15° Starboard	3m06s (2m35s)	478 (392)	677 (560)	3° (5.5°)
20° Port	2m51s (2m49s)	446 (416)	635 (610)	3.5° (4.3°)
35° Port	2m16s (2m14s)	344 (312)	496 (460)	3.5° (5.0°)

8/10 Full speed

15° Starboard	2m10s (2m14s)	391 (412)	520 (570)	4.5° (7.0°)
20° Port	2m07s (2m10s)	380 (386)	493 (547)	5.5° (6.5°)
35° Starboard	1m44s (1m43s)	297 (324)	381 (300)	6.0° (7.9°)

Results of 4 August 1933 and (14 May 1935) respectively, the latter after the modification. The displacement was 1,957 (2,539) tonnes, draught 2.79m (3.17m) fwd, 3.35m (3.98m) aft, and trim 0.56m (0.81m). Am/A(n) was 49.9 (58.1).

Source: KZGG, Vol. 4, *op. cit.* p. 794

In Fukuda, *op. cit.* p.124 the following data are given:

Displacement 1,997 tonnes, speed 16.25 knots, relation between Am (lateral middle line area) and An (rudder area) 49.86 and relation between DT (transfer) and L (keel angle) 3.34.

A port view of Itsukushima *taken on 27 May 1930 (Navy Memorial Day – Battle of Tsushima) at Tôkyô. Note the visitors and photographers aboard. Note also the typical bow shape of the Japanese naval vessels and the distinctive configuration of the stern. The 8cm HA gun abeam the tower bridge appears to be at maximum elevation.* (Hans Lengerer collection)

Bow view of Itsukushima *also taken on 27 May 1930. The forecastle and deckhouse are packed with visitors to the ship.* (Hans Lengerer collection)

rails being used for the anti-sweep device described above. A similar DCT of modified design was projected for the anti-aircraft destroyers of the *Akizuki* class but never entered service; *Itsukushima* therefore remained the only ship fitted with this weapon.

Between the larger deckhouse and the small one with the searchlight platforms on its roof four paravanes were mounted on the upper deck. The two 75cm searchlights were of the standard type, and the 30cm signal searchlight also belonged to this type.

Later Modifications

Despite the reduction in topweight realised by locating the mine hangar on the main deck, *Itsukushima*'s stability proved to be inadequate, with excessive GM and OG values when completed. In addition, CG was high and the ship rolled badly. After the capsizing of the torpedo-boat *Tomozuru* in March 1934 her stability was investigated and she was taken in hand at Uraga Dock the following year for modification.

In order to reduce GM, waterline beam was decreased by one metre. The outer plates were removed and the shape of the frames modified; the outer plates were bent to conform to the new shape and then re-riveted. Below the waterline bulges were fitted with fixed ballast in the lower compartment. Fixed ballast was also fitted in the hull bottom, the total weight being 135 tonnes. In addition, 160 tonnes of sea water ballast was drawn in when the ship was in light load condition to attain so-called 'supplemented light load' condition. These measures were aimed at lowering the centre of gravity (CG), and were supplemented by shortening the funnel and mainmast and removing some unnecessary fittings to reduce topweight.

Modifications were also made to the armament:

Stern view of Itsukushima also taken on 27 May 1930. Note the six mine doors at the stern (the starboard door is obscured by the central projection of the stern). The small superstructure on the centre line above the stern is the minelaying control station. (Hans Lengerer collection)

- The two 3rd Year Type 8cm/40 HA guns were replaced by Type 93 13mm twin MG (this also helped to reduce topweight).
- The Vickers depth charge thrower was replaced by a Type 93 DCT (a copy of the US Navy's 'Y-gun'). This may have been because the long range of the Vickers model could not be matched by the available submarine detection apparatus.
- The electric depth meter was replaced by a Type L sound depth meter (*Onkyorokushingi*).
- A Type 93 Sonar was fitted.

Itsukushima was the first cruiser minelayer fitted with Sonar and one of the first ships of the IJN to have this device.

After conversion GM and OG values were within acceptable ranges; there was also a marked improvement in stability and rolling characteristics (see Table 3).

Further Modifications
To the author's great regret practically nothing is known about changes and modifications executed between 1935 and *Itsukushima*'s loss on 7 October 1944 to a torpedo

Table 3: STABILITY CHARACTERISTICS OF ITSUKUSHIMA

	Light load condition	Supplemented light load
Displacement:	2,000.9t	2,117.6t
GM:	0.488m	1.070m
OG:	–	1.490m
Stability range:	84.8°	96°

Notes:
GM = metacentric height; the vertical distance between the centre of gravity (G) and the metacentre (M).
OG = height of centre of gravity (G) above waterline (O).

Source: KZGG, Vol. 4, op. cit., p. 792

Roll Period:

	Itsukushima	Itsukushima	Okinoshima
Displacement:	2242t	2540t	4642t
GM:	0.965m	0.947m	1.602m
P:	10.02 secs	10.4 secs	10 secs
K:	4.9m	4.96m	6.3m
Beam (wl):	12.75m	12.75m	15.74m
K/Bwl:	0.385	0.39	0.4

Notes:
P = period of roll.
K = radius of gyration of the ship about a longitudinal axis through G.

fired from the Dutch submarine *Zwaardvisch*. It is reported that the 13mm MG were replaced by a Type 96 25mm triple MG, and she was fitted with radar (Type 13?) in 1944. However, even this cannot be confirmed.

The Large Cruiser Minelayer Okinoshima

Okinoshima was the IJN's first purpose-built large cruiser minelayer, representing the 'offensive' type. She had the large mine capacity, long range and heavy armament necessary for contested minelaying in remote seas and advanced bases in southern waters. Her capabilities approached those of the minelaying cruiser except for speed, which was restricted by treaty regulations.

This type had long been requested by the Naval General Staff but had not been realised due to budget restrictions after Washington and the priority accorded to other categories of warship. The London Treaty of 1930 extended qualitative and quantitative limitations to the so-called 'auxiliary vessels' such as cruisers, destroyers and submarines, categories on which the IJN had focused during the 'battleship holiday'. However, despite new qualitative restrictions on vessels outside these categories, Japan did secure permission for the construction of two new cruiser minelayers of less than 5,000 tons standard and with a maximum speed of 20 knots as replacements for the elderly converted armoured cruisers *Aso* and *Tokiwa*.

Okinoshima was included in the First Replenishment Programme authorised by the Diet in 1931 (for more data on this programme see the author's article on the *Hatsuharu* class in *Warship* 2007). She replaced the ex-Russian *Aso* removed from the list on 1 April 1931.

The NGS requirements were as follows:

Displacement (st.):	5,000 tons
Speed:	20 knots
LAG:	four 15.5cm guns
HAG:	at least four AA guns
Mines:	500 minimum
Range:	5,000nm at 14 knots

The basic design was completed the following year. The standard displacement was reduced to 4,800 tons to save expense, and the 15.5cm/60-cal main guns newly designed for the cruisers of the *Mogami* class were replaced by the older model 3rd Year Type 14cm/50-cal gun, which was readily available. All of the other NGS requirements were fully met.

Before the ship was laid down the *Tomozuru* Incident led to a review of the design, which was for a shallow-drafted ship with high freeboard and large superstructures and an unfavourable wind sail area – all indicators for stability problems. Based on these findings the design was revised. Standard displacement was further reduced from 4,800 tons to 4,470 tons, and length(oa) from 138.5m to 124.5m. Boilers were changed from mixed firing to oil burning and the four single 14cm guns became two twin mountings.

Six months after the *Tomozuru* Incident *Okinoshima*'s keel was laid at Harima Shipyard on 27 September 1934, and she was launched on 15 November 1935, about a month and a half after the Fourth Fleet Incident. As in the case of the small cruiser minelayer *Yaeyama*, electric welding had been employed extensively for the hull structure, and similar defects quickly became apparent. As the hull grew on the building slip the welded frames and plates were exposed to considerable strain and significant deformations were observed. In the course of the investigation following the Fourth Fleet Incident the hull structure was re-inspected, but fortunately the scantlings had been designed with large margins and the stress was within acceptable limits, so small-scale remedial work sufficed to resolve the problem.

Okinoshima was completed on 30 September 1936 with the principal particulars as shown in Table 5. Among the changes should be noted the reduction in length by 14m and of the standard displacement by 400 tons to 4,000 tons, the increase in range, and the improvements in stability.

Hull and Superstructures

Okinoshima had a flush deck like *Itsukushima* with moderate sheer at the bow and a squared-off transom stern, albeit without the side cut-aways of the latter. She had a large bridge structure forward topped by the fire control director and rangefinder for the main guns and a light tripod mast at its after end. As in the other IJN cruiser minelayers the bridge was located atop a shelter deck within which were housed the official and private rooms of the officers. This was again necessary because the upper mine hangar was placed on the main deck, while the

A port-side view of the minelayer Okinoshima. (Hans Lengerer collection)

Table 4: Weight Distribution in the Trial Condition

	Itsukushima		Okinoshima	
	Tonnes	Percentage	Tonnes	Percentage
Hull:	877.5t	43.7%	1,786.6t	38.3%
Machinery:	220.6t	11.0%	398.3t	8.5%
Fittings:	47.3t	7.3%	242.2t	5.2%
Permanent equipment:	46.8t	2.3%	140.2t	3.0%
Consumable equipment:	94.9t	4.7%	199.3t	4.3%
Guns:	105.9t	5.3%	136.3t	2.9%
U/W weapons (incl. mines):	318.0t	15.8%	666.4t	14.3%
Electrics:	73.3t	3.6%	110.0t	2.4%
Aviation:	–	–	27.7t	0.6%
Navigation:	2.5t	0.1%	?	?
Heavy oil fuel (own use):	96.7t	4.8%	561.1t	12.0%
Coal:	1.3t	0.1%	16.3t	0.4%
Light oil:	10.0t	0.5%	6.4t	0.3%
Reserve feed water:	6.7t	0.3%	26.2t	0.6%
Heavy oil (for supply):	–	–	395.6t	7.7%
Miscellaneous:	9.4t	0.5%	15.5t	0.3%
Total	2,010.4t	100%	4,661.1t	100%

Hull Strength

With regard to the stress which became so important in the calculation of the hull strength after the Fourth Fleet Accident the following data, taken from Fukuda, *op. cit.* p.126, may suffice

	Itsukushima	Okinoshima
Top tension:	6.01	6.04
Bottom compression:	5.05	4.48
Top compression:	2.14	2.00
Bottom tension:	2.76	1.94

Note: Unit is tons per square inch. While the IJN changed to the metric system during the early 1920s strength calculations continued to be made using the British units – a slightly bizarre anomaly.

Displacement and Dimensions

	Itsukushima	Okinoshima
Full load condition:	2,093.5t	5,063.3t
Trial condition:	2,010.4t	4,661.1t
Normal condition:	1,799.6t	3,759.4t
Light load condition:	1,550.8t	2,897.8t
Length (pp):	100.00m	113.59m
Beam (max.):	12.80m	16.20m
Depth of hull:	7.64m	9.70m
Frame spacings:	0.80m	1.10m

Source: 'Weight and Centre of Gravity Data for Miscellaneous Warships' by Constructor LT Tôyama, Engineer Imai, Assistant engineers Takahashi and Ogino (all belonging to the 'Preliminary Design Group' of the NTD); second correction added in October 1941, p. 55. P.56 gives a breakdown of hull weight but is too detailed for inclusion, while p.57 details the displacement conditions recorded above.

The legend of weight of *Okinoshima* as first designed (5,000 tonnes) may be found in Fukuda, *op. cit.* p. 49 (this also gives data for *Itsukushima*); centre of gravity data is on p. 64 and speed, horsepower, and displacement data of *Okinoshima* on p. 117. Lack of space prevents the publication of these and further data.

Complement vs. Area & Volume of Living Spaces in *Itsukushima*

No. of officers and warrant officers:	21
Area of living space: officers and warrant officers:	191.215m^2
Area of living space per man: officers and warrant officers:	**8.908m^2**
Volume of living space: officers and warrant officers:	395.880m^2
Volume of living space per man: officers and warrant officers:	**18.451m^2**
No. of petty officers and ratings:	206
Area of living space: petty officers and ratings:	457.310m^2
Area of living space per man: petty officers and ratings:	**2.219m^2**
Volume of living space: petty officers and ratings:	931.050m^2
Volume of living space per man: petty officers and ratings:	**4.5196m^2**

Source: Fukuda Keiji, *Outline of the Fundamental Design of Warships* (*Gunkan kihon keikaku shiryô*), p. 176

Table 5: CHARACTERISTICS OF OKINOSHIMA AS DESIGNED AND COMPLETED

	Original design	Revised design	As completed
Standard displacement:	4,800 tons	4,470 tons	4,000 tons
Trial displacement:	5,400 tonnes	5,000 tonnes	4,661 tonnes
Length (wl):	135.00m	119.29m	118.19m
Length (oa):	138.40m	124.50m	124.50m
Beam (wl):	16.20m	15.74m	15.64m
Beam (max):	16.50m	16.20m	16.20m
Depth:	10.10m	9.70m	9.70m
Draught (mean):	4.40m	5.49m	5.15m
Engine power:	9,000shp	9,000shp	9,000shp
Boilers:	4 mixed firing	4 oil burning	4 oil burning
Engines:	2 geared turbines	2 geared turbines	2 geared turbines
Speed:	20kts	20kts	20.48kts
Fuel:	750t coal	–	–
	350t heavy oil	850t (+200t supply)	561t (+360t supply)
Range:	5,000nm @14kts	5,000nm @14kts	5,000nm* @14kts
LAG:	4 – 14cm (4 x I)	4 – 14cm (2 x II)	4 – 14cm (2 x II)
HAG:	2 – 8cm (2 x I)	2 – 8cm (2 x I)	2 – 8cm (2 x I)
Mines (No.6 Mod.2);	500	500	500
DC:	36	18	22
Searchlights:	3 x 90cm	3 x 90cm	3 x 90cm
Catapults:	1	1	1
Seaplane:	1	1	1
Stability data			
GM:	0.740m	1.350m	1.399m
OG:	1.600m	0.210m	0.487m
Stability range:	87.5°	96.3°	102°
DS/W:	1.187	0.943	?
A/Aw:	2.236	1.430	1.702

* 9,500nm with 850t f.o.

Okinoshima could be employed as an escort. In this view she has a Kawanishi E7K 'Alf' long-range reconnaissance aircraft on her catapult. (Hans Lengerer collection)

An aerial view of Okinoshima. (Hans Lengerer collection)

lower mine stowage was arranged on the lower and hold decks forward of the boiler rooms, requiring some living spaces to be relocated to the superstructure.

The minelaying arrangements differed from *Itsukushima* in that there were only two sets of internal mine rails at main deck level, with a further two sets on the upper deck. Mines were laid from the (inboard) stern doors at main deck level, or from the outer corners of the transom stern. The arrangement of the mines on four levels – the two lower levels being for stowage only – required an extensive system of mine elevators, rails and turntables, and it took a considerable time to lay all 500 No.6 mines Model 2 via the four sets of rails.

Abaft the shelter deck there was a deckhouse with the direction finder platform at its forward edge, searchlight platforms behind to port and starboard and a single funnel at its after end, the latter on the centreline like the direction finder. At the forward and after edges and at both sides of this deckhouse the transfer stations for embarking the mines were mounted, with the loading hatches directly beneath to transport the mines to the hangar and stowage rooms.

Between the funnel and the after deckhouse there was a catapult for a floatplane; the catapult was on a high pedestal to keep it clear of the boat deck. Besides the four motor-boats and cutters stowed here there were two whalers on davits on both sides of the hull abeam the light tripod foremast.

The after deckhouse was built around a heavy tripod mainmast equipped with a large derrick on its forward side to handle the aircraft and the boats; abaft the mast a third searchlight platform was located at the after end of the roof of the deckhouse.

Machinery

Okinoshima was fitted with two sets of Kampon (*Kaigun kansei honbu* = Navy Technical Department) high pressure (HP) and low pressure (LP) turbines connected to the propeller shafts via reduction gearing. The steam for the operation of the turbines was supplied by four Kampon type Ro Go (B) oil-fired boilers fitted with air preheaters. As originally projected the boilers were to have had mixed firing; however, the dimensions of the boilers remained unchanged, the modification being limited to a change in the burner system. Therefore the boilers had surplus power compared to the designed output of the turbines, which produced 9,000shp for 20 knots, the maximum speed permitted by the treaty restrictions.

Saturated steam with a pressure of 20kg/cm^2 was used. The heating area amounted to 276.6m^2; the air preheaters 53.4m^2. The volume of the combustion chamber was 9.14m^2 and the planned combustion 4.0kg/m^2/h. Each boiler was fitted with six oil burners each capable of burning 250kg of heavy oil per hour.

The total weight of the machinery was 408 tonnes including feedwater and oil, and 367 tonnes in the 'empty' condition. Propeller diameter was 2.7m, pitch 2.45m – a major increase from the diesel-driven *Itsukushima*, whose propellers had a diameter of 1.6m with 1.71m pitch.

As designed *Okinoshima* had bunkerage for 850 tonnes of heavy oil with an additional 200 tonnes for supply to other ships, but following trials it was found that this amount was sufficient for an endurance of 9,500nm at 14 knots. This range was considered excessive, and fuel capacity was reduced to 561 tonnes normal plus 360 tonnes supply.

Electricity was generated by two 100kW turbo generators and two 80kW diesel generators for a total of 360kW.

Armament

The four main guns were the same 14cm model as adopted for *Itsukushima*, but *Okinoshima* had twin mountings fitted with open shields which were disposed on the centreline on the forecastle, forward of the shelter deck, and on the quarterdeck abaft the tripod mainmast. The high performance 3rd Year Type 15.5cm/60-cal guns which formed the main artillery of *Mogami* class cruisers in their light cruiser configuration could not be mounted due to insufficient weapon production capacity.

Atop the bridge structure there was a Type 91 fire con-

Table 6: HULL COEFFICIENTS AND RATIOS

	Itsukushima	Okinoshima
Block coefficient (Cb)	0.475	0.473 (0.548)
Prismatic coefficient (Cp)	0.551	0.543 (0.565)
Midship area coefficient (Cm)	0.862	0.872 (0.970)
Waterline coefficient (Cwl)	0.663	0.672 (0.668)
Length-to-beam-ratio (L/B)	8.16	7.582 (8.335)
Draught-to-length-ratio (d/L)	0.031	0.047 (0.0326)
Beam-to-draught-ratio (B/d)	3.96	2.568 (3.68)
Length-to-depth-ratio (L/d)	13.7	12.3 (13.4)

trol director with the 4.5m-base rangefinder on a platform behind. In addition, rangefinders of 1.5m base length were located on either side of the bridge at 01 deck level. Behind the light tripod foremast 8cm HA guns of the same type as mounted on *Itsukushima* were mounted on either side of the shelter deck, and for close-range AA fire Type 93 13mm twin MG were mounted at the same deck level on either side of the bridge structure. Two Type 92 90cm searchlights were mounted on platforms to port and starboard forward of the funnel and a third was located on a platform abaft the mainmast. It is probable that the control station for laying mines from the upper deck was located in the support for the after searchlight platform.

Okinoshima was the first cruiser minelayer to be equipped with a floatplane. The Kure No.2 Model 3 catapult was located between the funnel and the tripod mainmast, and a single Type 94 three-seat reconnaissance seaplane was carried.

A Type 94 depth charge thrower together with its stowage rack was mounted near the stern. *Okinoshima* carried 22 depth charges which were stowed below.

First War Loss of a CM
Okinoshima was employed during the China Incident for the transport of troops, landing forces and supply materials utilising her large mine hangar and stowage. After the opening of the Pacific War she participated in the Rabaul and Tulagi landing operations. She was sunk in Queen Carola Bay on the west coast of Buka Island (Solomons) on 12 May 1942 after heavy damage by a torpedo fired from US submarine *S 42* in the St. George Channel (05°06 S/153°48 E – about 15 miles southwest of Cape St. George) on the previous day and unsuccessful attempts by the transport *Kinryu Maru* and the destroyer *Mochizuki* to save her. She became the first war loss among the IJN's cruiser minelayers and was removed from the register of Imperial warships on 25 May.

Table 6 gives the hull coefficients and ratios in order to provide a comparison between the medium and large type of cruiser minelayer. The data in parentheses for *Okinoshima* are those of the initial design and reveal considerable modifications during the design process.

The Large Cruiser Minelayer Tsugaru

As stated before, in the wake of the London Treaty of 1930 the Japanese NGS had requested two large offensive type cruiser minelayers, but only the *Okinoshima* was initially authorised. The review of her design after the *Tomozuru* Incident highlighted several defects, particularly the high OG and lack of stability, leading to modifications to the design. During the preparation of the Third Naval Replenishment Programme the NGS held a conference on the *Okinoshima* type cruiser minelayer, and the ship designed as an improved type was *Tsugaru*. Her design number H-10 suggests that there were other sketch designs, as that for *Okinoshima* had been H-6.

The principal differences between these two large cruiser minelayers were their dimensions, construction methods, armament and supplies. The major changes were as follows:

– In order to improve stability the dimensions were slightly modified, as was the general layout. These changes were also directed at increasing the mine capacity.
– Riveting was used instead of electric welding for the structural members of the hull to improve hull strength. This was a technical regression prompted by the Fourth Fleet Accident and Hiraga Yuzuru's dogmatic view about the application of electric welding (see *Hatsuharu* in *Warship 2007*).
– In order to improve the speed of minelaying the number of rails on the main deck was doubled and four minelaying doors were fitted at the stern.
– The main armament was revised to two Type 89 12.7cm/40-cal HA guns in twin mountings in place of the older Type 3 14cm/50-cal LA gun. When *Tsugaru* was designed, air attacks were assessed as being more dangerous than attacks by small naval vessels (against which the 12.7cm had an acceptable capability), so

Table 7: GENERAL CHARACTERISTICS OF OKINOSHIMA & TSUGARU

	Okinoshima	Tsugaru
Trial displacement	4,661 tonnes	4,400 tonnes
Length (wl)	118.19m	121.00m
Beam (wl)	15.74m	15.58m
Draught (mean)	5.15m	4.92m
Armament	4 – 14cm LAG (2 x II)	–
	2 – 8cm HAG (2 x I)	4 – 12.7cm HAG (2 x II)
	4 – 13mm AAMG (2 x II)	4 – 25mm AAMG (2 x II)
Mines	500 x No.6 Model 2	600 x Type 93 Model 1
Searchlights	3 x Type 92 90cm	3 x Type 92 90cm

A rare view of the cruiser minelayer Tsugaru. *She had 12.7cm twin DP guns fore and aft in place of the 14cm guns of the* Okinoshima. (Hans Lengerer collection)

reinforcement of AA capabilities was considered a priority. For fire control the latest Type 94 director was mounted atop the bridge structure.
- Some changes were made to the supply materials, and special tanks for aviation fuel were fitted.

Table 6 gives a comparison between the general characteristics of *Okinoshima* and *Tsugaru*.

The funding for the construction of *Tsugaru* was authorised as part of the Third Fleet Replenishment Programme in 1937. She was laid down at Yokosuka N.Y. on 5 July 1939, launched exactly eleven months later on 5 June 1940, and was completed on 22 October 1941, less than two months before the outbreak of the Pacific War.

Hull and Superstructure

Tsugaru resembled *Okinoshima* very closely. The main differences were:

– mounting of a Type 94 HA fire director (combined with 4.5m stereo HA rangefinder) atop the bridge structure;
– change in the configuration of the tripod foremast (the mainmast was less extensively modified);
– relocation of the direction finding station abaft the funnel (in *Okinoshima* it was forward of the funnel);
– relocation of the after searchlight platform from the roof of the after deckhouse to the mainmast starfish;
– modification of the shape of the stern close to the waterline
– mounting of the spare floats for the seaplane on either side of the shelter deck at the after end of the bridge structure.

The arrangement of the mine hangar, mine storage compartments and minelaying rails on the upper and main decks was similar to *Okinoshima*. The mine stowage compartments were located on the lower deck and the hold deck forward of the machinery spaces with four to six sets of rails on the lower and hold decks and six to eight on the main deck. A mine elevator was placed at the after end on the centreline and connected to each line using a turntable. The mine hangar on the main deck was separated into three separate compartments by the boiler uptakes and ventilation trunking. There were four to six sets of mine rails at the foward end, while above the boiler rooms the mines were stowed on two sets of rails on either side of the funnel uptakes and ventilation ducts. In the after part of the mine hangar there were eight sets of mine rails throughout the broadest section of the hull, reducing to six and finally to four sets of rails as the hull narrowed aft (see plans, p.65) . Mines were laid from these four lines via the four minelaying doors at the stern.

One of the key features of *Tsugaru* was provision for carrying not only heavy oil for supply but also aviation fuel, lubricants and bombs. Capacity was 102 tonnes of heavy oil, 125 tonnes of aviation fuel, several tonnes of aviation lubricants and a few No.6 and No.25 type bombs. The aviation fuel was stowed in three fully welded tanks located abaft the engine rooms and fitted as in the IJN's aircraft carriers (ie not connected to any structural member of the hull and enclosed by a void space).

Machinery

Tsugaru was propelled by the same main engines and boilers as fitted in *Okinoshima*, and she was designed to have the same speed and range. However, owing to the trial results of her half-sister, whose range was estimated as 9,500 nautical miles at 14 knots, the heavy oil bunkerage (own use) was decreased from 850 tonnes to 580 tonnes. Even with this marked reduction *Tsugaru* had a great deal in reserve, as her own trials suggested a figure of 6,383nm at 14 knots, far in excess of the required 5,000nm.

In accordance with current practice the electrical sup-

WARSHIP 2008

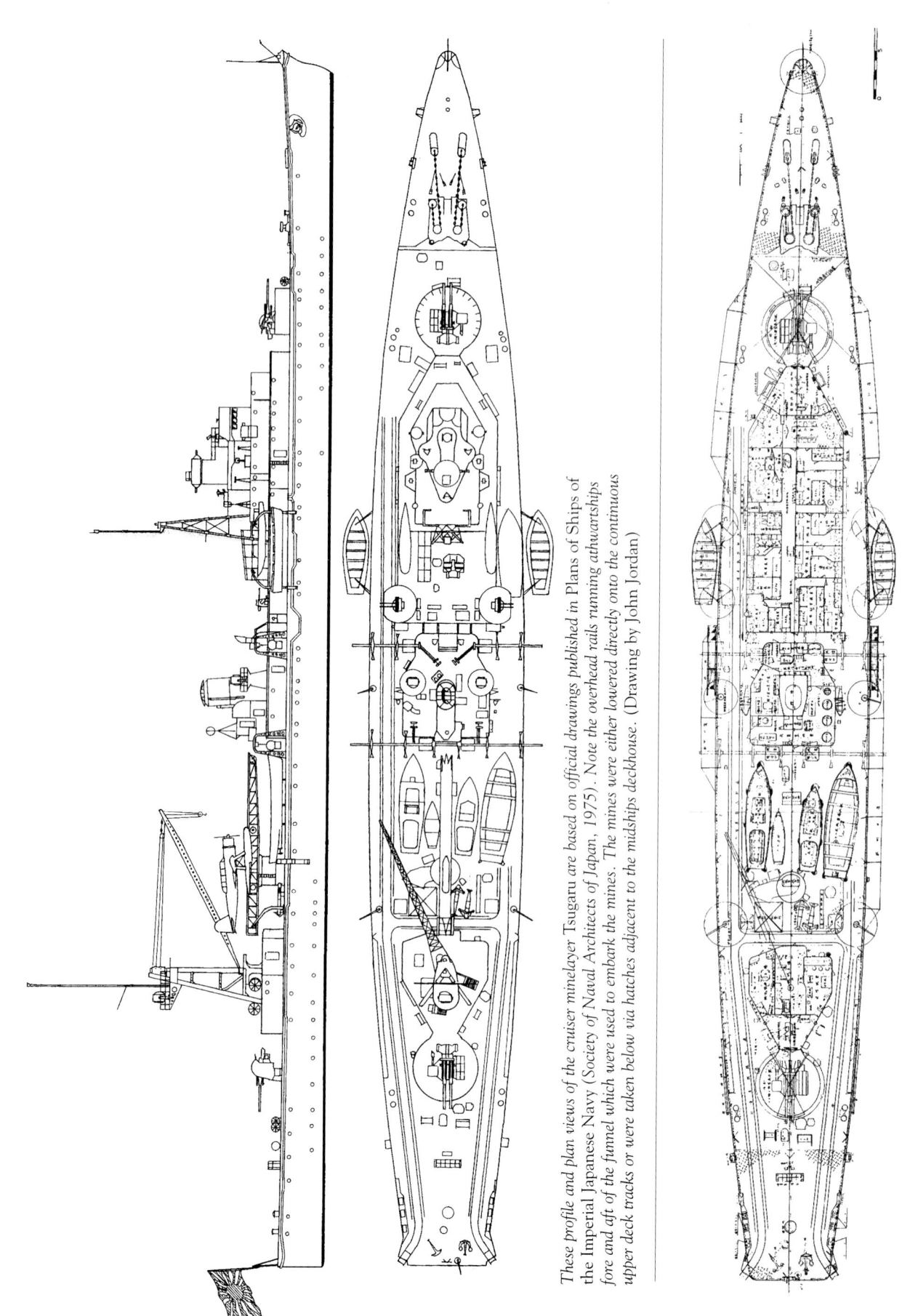

These profile and plan views of the cruiser minelayer Tsugaru are based on official drawings published in Plans of Ships of the Imperial Japanese Navy (Society of Naval Architects of Japan, 1975). Note the overhead rails running athwartships fore and aft of the funnel which were used to embark the mines. The mines were either lowered directly onto the continuous upper deck tracks or were taken below via hatches adjacent to the midships deckhouse. (Drawing by John Jordan)

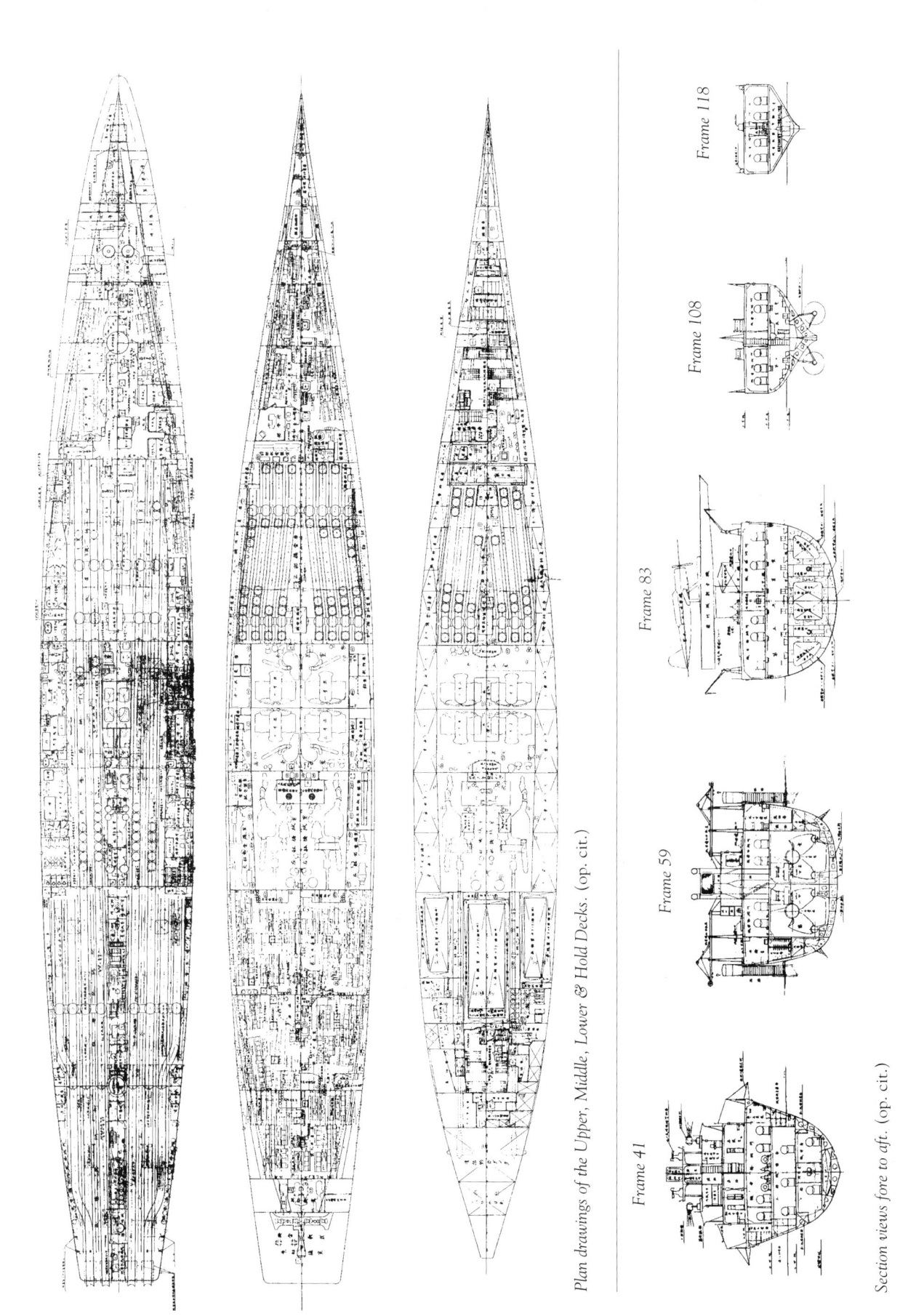

IMPERIAL JAPANESE MINELAYERS ITSUKUSHIMA, OKINOSHIMA, *AND* TSUGARU

Plan drawings of the Upper, Middle, Lower & Hold Decks. (op. cit.)

Frame 118

Frame 108

Frame 83

Frame 59

Frame 41

Section views fore to aft. (op. cit.)

Table 8: MINE DATA

The principal particulars of the mines carried by these three cruiser minelayers are listed below.

The No.5 mine Modification 1 was an improved type of No.5 mine. It was developed after the detonation of three mines aboard of the cruiser minelayer *Tokiwa* in August 1928 – an incident in which 35 men were killed. The method of priming was revised from bottom type to chemical reaction type.

The No.6 mine was a modification of mines imported from the British Vickers Co.

The Type 93 mine, formally adopted in September 1934, was an improved Type 89 mine. It was the standard mine of the IJN, was mass produced before the outbreak of the Pacific War and laid in defensive mine fields. A total of 55,646 mines of this type were manufactured; Models 1, 2, 3, and 4 differed only in minor details, mainly relating to improvements and an increase in the number of horns to ensure detonation against submarines.

	No.5 mine Mod.1	No.6 mine Mod.1	No.6 mine Mod.2	Type 93 mine
Characteristics	Safety device changed to increase safety owing to *Tokiwa* mine detonation accident	Tethered mine with horns, very heavy charge	Improved No.6 Mod.1	Tethered mine
Year adopted	1934	1925	1933	1934
Cable (diam. x length)	9mm x 100m	10mm x 300m	10mm x 205m	12mm x 150m
Mine casing (diam. x height)	830 x 853mm	1,050 x 1,150mm	1,050 x 1,021mm	860 x 860mm
With base (height x width)	1,474 x 830mm	1,776 x 1,050mm	1,782 x 1,050mm	1,513 x 1,020mm
Charge	83kg Shimose hexagonal	215kg Shimose hexagonal	200kg Shimose cast	100kg Type 88 or Type 97
Total weight of armed mine	520kg	1,156kg	1,080kg	710kg

Source: *Kaigun suirai-shi*, pp. 295-296, 299 (with omissions)

ply was changed from 230V DC to 440V AC. She was fitted with two 180kW turbo and 110kW diesel generators, making a total of 580kW. This was a major advance on *Okinoshima*, which had only a 360kW generating capacity, less even than the 395kW of the much smaller *Itsuksushima*. The author can find no explanation for this anomaly.

Armament

The mine hangar and mine stowage compartments were designed to accomodate 600 Type 93 Model 1 mines. The weight of this type was 710kg, so the total weight of mines carried amounted to 426 tonnes; the No.6 mine Model 2 carried by *Okinoshima* weighed 1,080kg, for a total weight of 540 tonnes. This was effectively a reduction of 114 tonnes, but stowage space had to be slightly increased owing to the larger number of mines carried.

As for the gun armament the designers took into account recent advances in aviation and changed both the main guns and the light AA weapons to the most recent types, the danger from the air being a more realistic proposition than a gunnery battle with an enemy surface vessel. In order to ensure that the fire of the two Type 89 12.7cm/40-cal twin HA guns was as effective as possible the fire control system adopted was of the most advanced type.

The searchlights were of the same type as fitted in *Okinoshima*, namely the Type 92 90cm, which had far better characteristics than the older 75cm type of *Itsukushima*.

ASW equipment comprised a Type 93 hydrophone and Sonar, a Type 94 DCT ('Y-gun') plus stowage rack, 18 depth charges and the usual mine rails on either side of the stern.

Wartime Modifications and Fate

During the war the catapult and the seaplane were removed and the close-in AA weapons increased by a 25mm triple mounting and a 25mm twin mounting. However, the information given in Japanese secondary sources cannot be regarded as reliable, as most ships carried more than officially recorded, and it has also been stated that a 13mm twin mounting was also installed. Type 21 radar (air search) was fitted to improve AA defence by early detection and warning of incoming aircraft.

Tsugaru was hit and damaged on four occasions: twice by submarine torpedo attacks and twice by aircraft. She was finally sunk off the northern tip of Halmahera Island (02°10 N / 128°05 E) by a torpedo fired from the US submarine *Darter* (SS 227), which attacked a convoy escorted by her on 29 June 1944.

THE ODYSSEY OF VON SPEE AND THE EAST ASIATIC SQUADRON, 1914

Philippe Caresse looks at the origins and formation of the German East Asiatic Squadron and traces its passage across the Pacific Ocean following the outbreak of war in 1914 to its final defeat and extermination at the Falklands

At the beginning of the 1870s German warships had been involved in the purchase of land from local princes in the Pacific Ocean. In the islands of Samoa the Anglo-American communities viewed the introduction of Prussian traders into the region with concern. It was only in 1879 that a Captain Zembsch was nominated Consul General in Apia. After reestablishing order in the islands, a legitimate government was recognised and displayed open sympathies with the few German nationals. Within a short time Samoa would become the first German colony. Before achieving this Bismarck would be compelled to protect himself from Russia by signing the Triple Alliance. Moreover, Germany was under no illusion that the fleet was as yet powerful enough to protect its sea lines of communication with far-off stations such as Samoa. Despite this, influential traders began to make incursions into these territories, and there was no doubt that they should be accorded assistance and protection. After a brief hesitation Bismarck laid the keystone of a unified German Empire.

The warships which at that time were deployed overseas were old frigates equipped with broadside cannon of little military value, but with the new policy of colonial expansion it would be necessary to provide warships worthy of the name. On 23 November 1897 Kaiser Wilhelm II authorised the creation of a squadron of cruisers in the Far East. By the end of the nineteenth century this squadron comprised the cruisers *Kaiser* (flag), *Deutschland* and *Kaiserin Augusta*. During the Boxer Rebellion more modern cruisers such the *Hertha* and the *Hansa* were despatched to join *Kaiserin Augusta*. On 20 June 1900 the German Ambassador von Ketteler was assassinated in Peking, resulting in the mobilisation of a major part of the fleet in this corner of the globe: no fewer than fifteen warships, including the four battleships of the *Brandenburg* class. The expeditionary force, consisting of 19,602 men under the command of Weltfeldmarschall von Walders, quickly restored order, and a peace treaty was signed with China on 7 September. This served to reinforce the lesson that a fleet in the Far East was indispensable.

That same year the first true armoured cruiser of the Imperial German Navy, the *Fürst Bismarck*, moored at Tsingtao. This base, which had been purchased from China, was the most modern in this part of the world. It could support and maintain numerous warships, and the town itself provided plenty of distractions for men on leave and comfortable accommodation for the ships' officers. The cruiser squadron now had its own dockyard. Tirpitz himself commanded this formation; his successors were Rear-Admiral von Diederichs, Vice-Admiral Geissler, Rear-Admiral Krosigt and, from January 1913, Vice-Admiral Graf von Spee. The latter would become the legendary commander of the East Asiatic Squadron,

Vice-Admiral Graf von Spee, commander of the East Asiatic Squadron. (Billdienst)

WARSHIP 2008

The launch of the armoured cruiser SMS Gneisenau *14 June 1906 at the Weser Shipyard, Bremen. (Private Collection)*

and would fly his flag in the armoured cruiser *Scharnhorst*, which would be accompanied at the heart of the squadron by her sister *Gneisenau*.

Characteristics

Construction data and the general characteristics of *Scharnhorst* and *Gneisenau* are given in Table 1.

The hull was divided into fifteen watertight compartments. The double bottom extended for some 50% of the length of the ship. Freeboard was 7.1m forward and 4.8m aft. The depth of the keel was 12.65m. The limit for capsizing was 41° at full load displacement; the GM was 1.18m at the same displacement. The ship submerged by one centimetre for each additional 23.69 tonnes.

The eighteen Schultz-Thornycroft boilers were in five boiler rooms. The central propeller was 4.7m in diameter and the propellers on the wing shafts 5m in *Scharnhorst*; the figures for *Gneisenau* were 4.6m and 4.8m respectively. There was only a single rudder. On trials *Scharnhorst* achieved 23.5 knots with 28,783ihp, *Gneisenau* 23.6 knots

Gneisenau *fitting out in a floating dock. (Private Collection)*

with 30,396ihp. The 110V electricity supply was provided by four 260kW turbo-generators.

Armament

The main artillery comprised eight 21cm SK C/04 L/40 guns. Four of these were in twin turrets fore and aft and the remaining four in casemates amidships. The 21cm SK L/40 could fire 108kg armour piercing (AP) shells to a range of 16,300kg with a muzzle velocity of 890m/s (780m/s?). Elevation was −5° to +30°, and the firing cycle was three rounds per minute. The magazines held 700 rounds.

The secondary armament comprised six 15cm SK C/97 L/40 guns in casemates, protected by 150mm armour. Each of these guns could fire a 45.3kg shell to a range of 13,700m with a muzzle velocity of 800m/s. The firing cycle was 7rpm, and the magazines held 1020 rounds (170 per gun).

To repel torpedo-boats *Scharnhorst* and *Gneisenau* were armed with eighteen 8.8cm SK C/97 L/35 guns. These

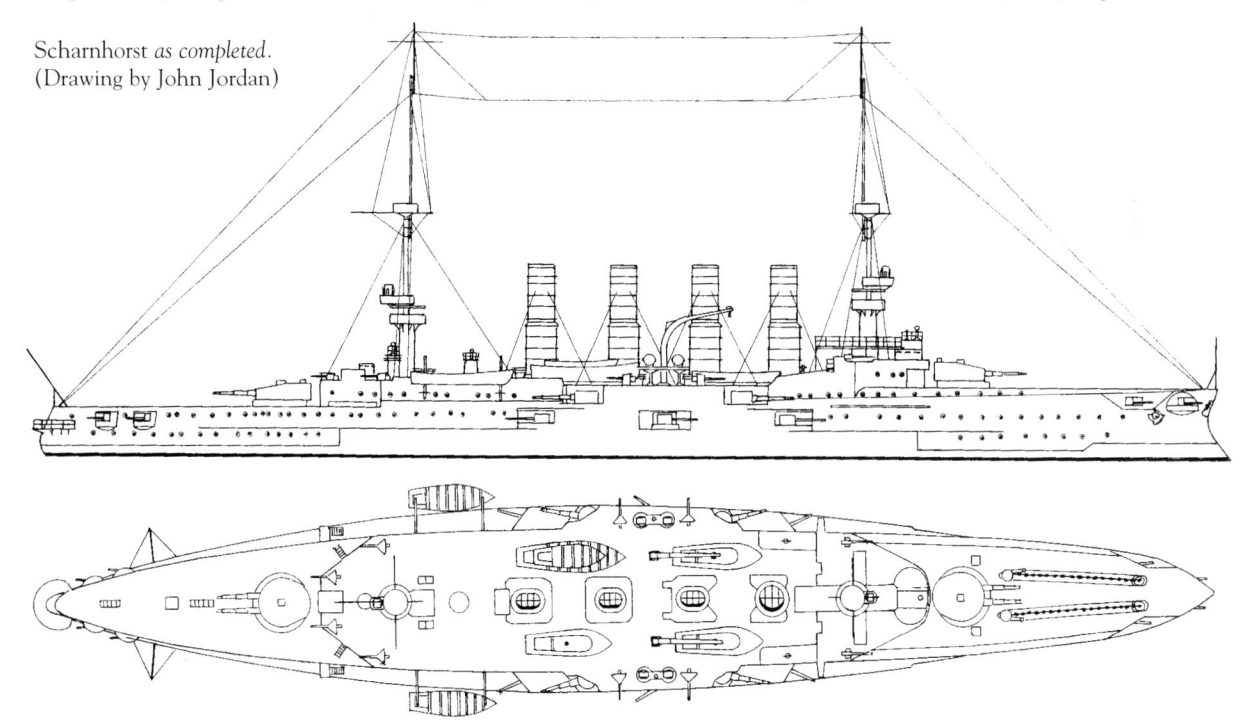

Scharnhorst as completed.
(Drawing by John Jordan)

Table 1: SCHARNHORST & GNEISENAU

Construction data

Name	Builder	Laid down	Launched	In service	Cost
Scharnhorst	Blohm & Voss	Jan 1905	22.03.06	04.10.07	20,319 DM
Gneisenau	Weser	Dec 1904	14.06.06	06.03.08	19,243 DM

Note: *Scharnhorst* was cruiser 'D', laid down on slipway no.175 at Hamburg; *Gneisenau* was cruiser 'C', laid down on slipway no.144 at Bremen.

General Characteristics

Displacement:	11,800 tonnes normal
	13,200 tonnes full load
Length:	143.75m wl, 144.6m oa
Beam:	21.6m
Draught (max):	7.96m (normal), 8.37m (full load)
Machinery:	18 Schulz-Thonycroft boilers; three triple expansion engines on three shafts; 26,000ihp = 22.5kts (designed)
Endurance:	coal 800 tonnes (normal), 2000 tonnes (full load); 5120nm at 12kts, 4800nm at 14 kts.
Armament:	eight 21cm SK C/04 L/40 (2 x II, 4 x I), six 15cm SK C/97 L/40 (6 x I), eighteen 8.8cm SK C/97 L/35; four 45cm torpedo tubes (underwater).
Protection:	
hull:	150-80mm belt; 50mm deck
turrets:	170mm faces; 150mm sides; 30mm roofs and rear
conning tower:	200mm forward section with 30mm roof; 500mm after section with 20mm roof

The Scharnhorst *in her overseas livery. The hull is painted light beige ('wet canvas') and the superstructures and funnels in yellow.* (Billdienst)

fired a 7kg shell to a range of 9100m. The firing cycle was 10rpm and there were 2700 shells in the magazines. Eight of the mountings were in casemates at the bow and the stern, the remaining guns being mounted in the superstructures: two in the bridge structure, four amidships and four atop the after superstructure.

The four 45cm torpedo tubes were beneath the waterline: one in the bow, one in the stern and one on either beam directly below the bridge. There were eleven reserve torpedoes.

Equipment

The complement of boats comprised two 16m motor launches, two 16m long boats, a 10m pinnace, two 9m cutters, three 6m gigs and a smaller rowing boat. These boats were stowed on either side of the funnels and on davits outboard of the mainmast.

The two bow anchors were of the Hall type. A spare anchor of the same type was stowed abeam the forward 21cm turret to port, and the stream anchor was stowed

Postcard of the armoured cruiser Scharnhorst *and her distinctive heraldic badge.* (Private Collection)

THE ODYSSEY OF VON SPEE AND THE EAST ASIATIC SQUADRON, 1914

Scharnhorst on gunnery exercises. This ship would repeatedly win the firing competition sponsored by the Kaiser. (Billdienst)

beneath the overhang of the sternwalk aft.

There were six 110cm searchlight projectors, initially disposed as follows: one on each of the mast platforms and four on the platforms located between the second and third funnels. These arrangements proved unsatisfactory and the platforms between the funnels were removed. Their four projectors were relocated as follows: two abaft the bridge, a second projector on the mainmast platform and the fourth on the upper platform of the foremast.

The complement comprised 35 officers and 726 petty officers and men. When the ship was serving as a divisional flagship there was an additional staff of three officers and 25 men, and if serving as a squadron flagship an admiral's staff of 14 officers and 62 men would have to be accommodated.

Von Spee Goes to War

At the beginning of the year 1909 it was decided to send home from Tsingtao the armoured cruiser *Fürst Bismarck*, and to replace her with a comparable but more modern unit. The primary mission of the ships was to demonstrate German naval power in the Far East, so the ship would need to be fast, elegant and powerful. The *Scharnhorst* was

Captain Felix Schultz, commander of the Scharnhorst. (Private Collection)

Captain Maerker, commander of the Gneisenau. (Private Collection)

The two sons of the admiral, Otto Ferdinand and Heinrich Franz von Spee, serving aboard the light cruiser Nürnberg and the Gneisenau respectively. (Private Collection)

The Scharnhorst *at her moorings off Nauru.* (Billdienst)

chosen. Her crew, frequent winners of the Kaiser Cup, the Imperial Navy's premier gunnery competition, were experienced and dedicated to their ship.

Scharnhorst left Kiel 1st April 1909 and completed the long voyage without any particular problem. As flagship of the squadron she would cruise the Pacific, making port visits which could not fail to impress the men embarked in her.

Von Spee would join her in January 1913. Maximilian Johannes Maria Hubertus Reichsgraf von Spee was born in Copenhagen 22 June 1861. He joined the Imperial Navy as an officer cadet 23 April 1878 and achieved rapid promotion. On 27 January 1905 he was appointed Captain (*Kapitän zur See*), on 27 January 1910 he was promoted to Rear-Admiral (*Konteradmiral*) and became Vice-Admiral (*Vizeadmiral*) 15 November 1913. For von Spee service in the Imperial Navy represented the ultimate goal in life, and he ensured that his sons followed him into the profession. Ensigns Otto Ferdinand and Heinrich Franz von Spee were appointed to the light cruiser *Nürnberg* and to the armoured cruiser *Gneisenau* respectively.

It had been envisaged for some time that the East Asiatic Squadron would be reinforced by a second cruiser,

Scharnhorst *and* Nürnberg *alongside at Tsing-Tao in 1910.* (Billdienst)

and the name *Blücher* had been mentioned. However, for reasons of homogeneity it was *Scharnhorst*'s sister *Gneisenau* which joined her from 10 November 1910. Moreover, besides the two armoured cruisers, the force now included three light cruisers: the 3700-tonne *Emden*, the 3500-ton *Nürnberg*, and the 3300-tonne *Leipzig*. The average speed of these ships was 23/24 knots and they were armed with ten 10.5cm guns.

For coast defence there were the sea-going gunboats *Jaguar*, *Tiger*, *Iltis* and *Luchs*, the smaller gunboats *Tsingtau*, *Vaterland and Otter*, and the torpedo-boat S90. These were of limited military value, but possessed a handful of guns capable of causing serious damage to a landing force. Von Spee also had a fleet replenishment vessel, the *Titania*.

In the summer of 1914 we find the armoured cruisers on a cruise in the South Seas with port visits planned for the Marianas and Samoa, returning at the end of September via Fiji. The crews had been renewed on 2 June with the arrival of the steamer *Patricia*, bringing 1600 men including Captain Maerker, due to relieve Captain Brüninghaus aboard the *Gneisenau* – *Scharnhorst* was commanded by Captain Felix Schultz at this time.

On 12 June the British armoured cruiser *Minotaur* made a courtesy visit to Tsingtao. After various festivies, which included official receptions and football matches, *Minotaur* left on the 16 June. On 20 June, following a spell in dock, *Gneisenau* had sailed followed by her sister-ship. On 22 June Maerker was at Nagasaki to take on 400 tonnes of coal. He left the port the same evening and after four days sailing crossed the Tropic of Cancer. On 28 June the ship stopped at Pagan in the Marianas, sailing again that same evening. On the following day, while the ship was being hammered by severe storms, information arrived on the bridge that the Archduke Ferdinand had been assassinated in Sarajevo. Von Spee, who himself had just arrived in the Marianas, suspected that in the event of war he would not be left to his own devices, and set about reassembling his forces. On 30 June *Gneisenau* put into Saipan and then the island of Rota, where the officers engaged in stag hunting. On 7 July *Scharnhorst* and *Gneisenau* joined up at the Truk archipelago. The *Titania* and the collier *Fukoku Maru* would be the next to arrive.

That summer only the cruiser *Emden* (Cdr. von Müller) remained at Tsingtao. The *Nürnberg* (Capt. von Schönberg) was on the west coast of Mexico and the *Leipzig* (Capt. Haun) had left the Bay of Kiao-Chu on 7 July to relieve her. Another warship would also become involved in the future operations of the squadron: the *Dresden*, sister of the *Emden*, which was in the Caribbean at Port-au-Prince in company with the light cruiser *Karlsruhe*. At Haiti these two cruisers exchanged their respective commanding officers. *Dresden* would recover her former CO, Cdr. Lüdecke, who because of his experience had been given the job of working up the recently-completed *Karlsruhe*. As for Cdr. Köhler, who had commanded the *Dresden* during her campaign in Mexico, he would now take commend of a turbine-powered ship.[1] From 28 July both ships were ordered to join the squadron flagship in the Marianas.

At Truk the crew was busy coaling ship before being put ashore to visit the atoll. In order to gain access to the well-sheltered anchorage without striking a reef, divers were clearing one of the channels with explosives. On 9 July von Spee received a cable outlining the possibility of hostilities with the countries of the Entente: Great Britain, France and Russia. On 15 July the squadron raised anchor and made for Ponape. During the voyage there were gunnery exercises before arrival on 17 July. The anchorage was safe; however, the ships had to keep some of their boilers lit and *Scharnhorst* had to move her berth several times.

On 27 July the von Spee received a new message from Germany:

> Diplomatic relations between Austria-Hungary and Serbia broken off. Russia favouring Serbia. Political tensions between Double and Triple Entente possible.

> Samoan cruise will probably be discontinued. Await developments in Yap area.

On the day of 29 July, von Spee conducted an inspection aboard the *Gneisenau* and ordered her officers to disembark all non-essential items and inflammable materials. Personal effects, all the souvenirs amassed by the crew during their port visits, the wooden tables, the carpets, etc., were landed and stowed on Langar Island. On 2 August the order to mobilise against France and Russia was broadcast by radio, then on 6 August Britain's declaration of war became official.

With hostilities imminent the East Asiatic Squadron exchanged its livery of light beige ('wet canvas') hull and yellow superstructures for the medium grey now standard in the Imperial Navy.

Crossing the Pacific

The *Nürnberg* rejoined von Spee on 6 August and immediately began coaling. Departure was scheduled for that same evening and, at 1600, *Titania* was the first to slip her moorings. An hour later it was the turn of the two armoured cruisers and finally, after having filled her bunkers, the light cruiser set sail towards the north. On 11 August von Spee was at Pagan joined, on the following day, by the *Emden* and the armed merchant cruiser *Prinz Eitel Friedrich*.

The German General Staff was under no illusions: a treaty of alliance existed between Britain and Japan, and there was no doubt that Tsingtao would have to be abandoned. The East Asiatic Squadron could therefore no longer count on its dockyard for repair and maintenance, and the resupply of provisions and coal would now become that much more difficult. Meanwhile the numerous cargo vessels at anchor would ensure that the precious foodstuffs so important to the squadron were distrinuted. On 12 August the *Scharnhorst* was informed via Yap that

Scharnhorst moored in Manila Bay in 1914. (Private Collection)

WARSHIP 2008

Coaling on the Scharnhorst *– an arduous and unpleasant task. With a bunker capacity of 2000 tonnes* Scharnhorst *burnt 100 tonnes a day at cruise speed, 500 tonnes a day at higher speeds.* (Private Collection)

the Japanese Fleet had departed for the southern seas. It would be folly to wait around in these waters; decisive action was required.

On the morning of 13 August von Spee invited aboard the various COs of his squadron in order to outline to them the situation. There was no dissent from the admiral's decisions save from von Müller, who wished to use his cruiser for commerce raiding in the Indian Ocean. After reflection, von Spee gave his consent and allocated a collier to him to provide for his needs.

At 1800 the supply ships headed east. There were, in two columns, the *Yorck, Prinz Waldemar, Holsatia, Mark, Longmore, Gouverneur Jaschke, Staatssekretär Krätke* and *Markomannia*. In their holds they carried 19,000 tonnes of coal, 4,000 tonnes of drinking water, plus sufficient provisions for the 12,000 miles which separated them from South America. Two miles souh of them were the *Scharnhorst, Gneisenau, Nürnberg, Emden, Titania* and *Prinz Eitel Friedrich*.

At 1400 on 14 August von Spee gave freedom of action to the *Emden*, which departed with the *Markomannia*. Von Müller transmitted to the *Scharnhorst*: 'I thank your Excellency for the confidence placed in me. I wish the Cruiser Squadron a happy crossing and success.'[2]

Despite the spartan conditions on the messdecks, which had not been designed to operate in the suffocating, humid Pacific weather, morale was excellent. Quarter succeeded quarter, broken up by exercises which left no opportunity for homesickness. On 19 August the *Nürnberg* led the fleet into Eniwetok lagoon. In this shel-

Stokers aboard the flagship. (Bilddienst)

74

tered anchorage coaling commenced at dawn the following day. To encourage the crews the ships' bands played stirring music. Beneath the tropical sun coaling was an unpleasant and exhausting task. After having emptied their holds the *Gouverneur Jaschke* and *Staatssekretär Krätke* were ordered to remain at the anchorage until 24 August, then to proceed to Jaluit.[3]

During the night, a strong gust of wind parted the ropes of the boats moored under *Gneisenau*'s stern, and the boats disappeared into the shadows. A man fell into the water while trying to secure them; fortunately he was picked up by one of *Nürnberg*'s boats. In the early hours of the morning all the boats were recovered intact except for a dinghy loaded with soap which capsized and sank. At the time little attention was paid to this loss, but it was to be keenly felt later.

At 0600 on 22 August the squadron sailed. In order to gather information, which was almost totally lacking, von Spee ordered Schönberg to make for Honolulu and to transmit his intentions to Berlin in order to prepare for his arrival off the coast of Chile. When she arrived at Pearl Harbor the *Nürnberg* had trouble coaling, and her CO had to make personal respresentations with the American Rear-Admiral Moore in order to obtain the 700 tonnes required to fill his bunkers. He then busied himself transmitting von Spee's instructions to the Naval General Staff in Berlin. These were that 5000 tonnes of coal, together with sufficient provisions to feed 1000 men for three months, should be despatched from San Francisco to Juan Fernandez. A similar supply should subsequently be directed to Valparaíso. At Oahu the light cruiser embarked fresh fruit and vegetables, as well as some reservists and volunteers, before departing hastily with the news that the Japanese battlecruiser *Kongo* was operating in these waters.

In Micronesia the *Scharnhorst* and her group skirted the eastern side of the Marshalls while conducting firing practices. The *Titania* towed targets and each ship of the squadron took turns to loose off a few rounds. In the course of a manoeuvre the *Gneisenau* struck the bow of the towing ship. The cruiser had part of her side plating carried away and the *Titania* lost her anchor. The damage to both ships was minor, and repairs were undertaken in transit. On 27 August the fleet anchored at Majuro, an atoll in the Ratak island group. The *Prinz Waldemar* and *Longmore* were emptied of their cargoes and were granted freedom of action when the warships departed. During this halt the auxiliary cruiser *Cormoran* (which was none other than the *Riasan* captured by the *Emden*), as well as the cargo ships *O.D.J Ahlers* and *Göttingen* joined up with the fleet. On 30 August von Spee resumed his passage towards the east and detached, in order to hunt for maritime traffic off the west coast of Australia, the *Kormoran*, *Prinz Eitel Friedrich* and *Mark*.

On Sunday 6 September the *Nürnberg* again took her place in the squadron. Her presence was of short duration as, having transmitted the most important information and distributed provisions to the other ships of the squadron, she was ordered to proceed to Fanning Island where, aided by the *Titania*, she was to cut the cable linking Australia to Vancouver. The *Scharnhorst*, the *Gneisenau* and their supply ships dropped anchor at

The engine room on the Scharnhorst. (Billdienst)

Christmas Island on 7 September. The *Nürnberg* and her companion rejoined them the following day. While at the anchorage von Spee and his staff had time to analyse the press cuttings which Schönberg had sent them. From them they deduced that Samoa, the former German colony, had fallen into the hands of New Zealanders backed by a powerful squadron which included the battlecruiser *Australia*. Von Spee determined to attack the port of Apia even if the formidable *Australia* was still present. He estimated that a few well-placed torpedoes would be sufficient to put the latter out of action, while the lesser ships would be sunk by gunfire! This would have been a risky course of action given the characteristics of the enemy battlecruiser, and appeared not to take into full account the dangers to which he would be exposing his ships.[4]

On 9 September *Scharnhorst* and *Gneisenau* set course for the Samoa islands. Early on the 14 September the two cruisers separated and stood towards the shore so that their silhouette would be unrecognisable. Unfortunately for them the port was deserted except for an ancient wreck rotting away deep in the anchorage and an American three-master. As there were many German nationals ashore and the ships had a finite stock of munitions it was decided that there was little point in shelling

The French gunboat Zélée, commanded by lieutenant de vaisseau Destremau. (DR)

the town. Although the radio station did not fail to transmit a warning of their presence these transmissions were jammed by von Spee's radio operators.

The ships then continued on towards Apolima Strait, where a ship's boat was sighted. The latter was occupied by two men who approached the *Scharnhorst* to inform her that the *Australia* and the French *Montcalm* had been in these waters as late as 31 August. They further stated that troops had been landed to take control of the archipelago. Frustrated, the two armoured cruisers set course first to the north-west, in order to confuse any lookouts ashore, then to the east towards the island of Suvorov where they were to coal from the *Ahlers*. When they arrived there the swell was such that coaling was impossible, and they headed for Tahiti. For this eventuality the orders were as follows: destruction of enemy vessels, the dockyard and any coastal batteries, and the landing of a an armed force to seize the coal reserves. Von Spee justified this operation in the following terms:

> The detour via Tahiti can be undertaken at the expense of the excess coal available, given that we shall almost certainly be able to capture coal reserves ashore. It also means that there is a prospect of replenishing our fresh provisions; there is the chance of an encounter with enemy vessels (*Kersaint* or *Montcalm*), and our presence will in any case disrupt enemy traffic (particularly English mail steamers) and as a military operation will raise the morale of the crews.

The Attack on Tahiti

On 21 September a stop was made at Bora Bora in order to fill the bunkers with anthracite. Apparently the French knew nothing of the declaration of war, and it even proved possible to barter with the indigenous inhabitants. By paying cash it was a simple matter to purchase cows, sucking pigs, fruit and vegetables. The leader of the landing party obligingly provided an inventory of the garrison of Papeete: the gunboat *Zélée*, the German cargo ship *Walküre*, a few gendarmes and twenty-five soldiers. It was estimated that such a small force could be easily overcome; the reality was to be far less straightforward.

At 1600 the ships sailed for Tahiti, arriving off the coast the following morning. A series of mishaps then dogged the execution of the German plans. In the first instance a navigational error displaced the squadron 14 miles to the west, where its presence was spotted by the islanders of Moorea. Secondly, the captain of the *Zélée*, LV Maxime Destremau, had no intention of giving way without a fight. He had been appointed *commandant d'armes* on 4 August by Admiral Huguet and, fully aware of the weakness of his ship, had disembarked his guns, which were subsequently relocated ashore. To defend the approaches there were now two 100mm and four 65mm guns. In order to intervene against possible landing sites, six 37mm guns were installed on motor vehicles. For a brief moment Destremau would have to call the Governor, Monsieur Fawtier, to order when the latter proposed surrendering the town to the enemy. He bluntly informed him that he had received no such order from himself, and promptly left ready to fight.

At 0630 the German squadron was in sight, the 6000-tonne supply of coal was set on fire, and EV Barbier was blowing up the buoys for the access channel, which it was planned to block by scuttling a ship.

On the heights the first shots from the 65mm guns rang out. On the *Scharnhorst* flags were hoisted, and the 21cm

German postcard showing the destruction of the Zélée *at Papeete 22 September 1914. (Private Collection)*

and 15cm guns began to fire on the forts. The latter took care not to reply so as not to reveal their positions. Soon, inside the harbour, the *Zélée* and the *Walküre* alongside her were taken under fire. At 0820 von Spee realised that the coal supply had been fired, but he continued shooting at the gunboat. The *Zélée* shook under the impact of the shells, her funnel collapsed, and some of the 'overs' set a copra warehouse on fire. Enseigne Barbier, who had remained on board, determined to scuttle his ship in the channel. He ordered the sea-cocks to be opened and abandoned ship, leaving the *Zélée* capsizing to port as her boilers exploded.

At 0920 the *Scharnhorst* ceased fire, having received the signal that 26 German hostages had been taken ashore; moreover, it was no longer possible to seize the anthracite ashore. Forty-six 21cm shells and 35 15cm shells had been expended without result, von Spee had revealed the position of his squadron, and at 1015 he gave the order to head for the Marquesas Islands at 10 knots. Destremau and his men had saved Tahiti; the gunboat and the *Walküre* had been lost, but honour had been preserved.[5]

Von Spee Makes for South America

The *Scharnhorst* and *Gneisenau* left the archipelago of Touamotous to starboard as they headed for Contrôleur Bay where *Nürnberg* was awaiting them. On 26 September, at Nuku Hiva, all crews were in their working overalls for the inevitable coaling. Maerker replenished from the *Ahlers* and the *Holsatia*, Schultz from the *Göttingen* and the *Titania*. After three days of this gruelling work the men were permitted to go ashore. On 30 September the *Gneisenau* made for Hiva Oa to requisition stores from the Hamburg-based Kayser Company, while the *Scharnhorst* did the same at the Scharf warehouse at Port-Anne-Marie. After three months at sea soap, meat and fresh vegetables were well received on the mess-decks. On the afternoon of 2 October the flagship, together with the *Nürnberg*, sailed in company with the *Yorck* and *Göttingen*. The O.J.D *Ahlers et Holsatia* remained at anchor, due to make their way to Hawaii. The following day the *Gneisenau* rejoined the formation which was now headed for Easter Island. The *Titania*, which could no longer keep up, made her way independently towards the same destination.

During the crossing the ships' doctors had to deal with an outbrak of dysentery. Then, during the night of 4/5 October, radio contact was made with the *Dresden* which was 2500 miles from the squadron. Contact was also made with the *Leipzig*, which would rejoin shortly. On 12 October von Spee found Lüdecke in the anchorage of Cook Bay on Easter Island. The latter was accompanied by the *Baden* with 6000 tonnes of coal, and also had news for von Spee: the armoured cruisers *Good Hope* and *Monmouth*, the light cruiser *Glasgow* and the auxiliary cruiser *Otranto* had left Punta Arenas in Chile on 28 September heading west. Also the Japanese armoured cruiser *Idzumo* was reported to be on the west coast of Mexico.

Whatever the rumours the first priority was reprovisioning. The first night in this anchorage was interrupted when

The Gneisenau *in heavy seas. This photo is often captioned as showing the cruiser rounding Cape Horn, but the awning on the after deck suggests that the image was taken earlier, when this part of the world was still at peace.* (DR)

a false alarm led to the order to raise steam. All were agreed that it was preferable to fight at sea than at anchor. When in the morning the alarm proved to be false order was reestablished and the men were able to go ashore to top up the cold storage rooms. While some hunted or engaged in transactions, the remainder of the crews topped up the fuel bunkers with the 'black diamonds' which were indispensable for the insatiable boilers. On 14 October it was the turn of the *Leipzig* to enter port accompanied by three colliers. The cruiser also brought warm clothing as the temperature would soon be dropping. The holds of the *Yorck*, *Karnak* and *Anubis* were emptied. *Yorck* then left with the *Titania* for Más a Fuera, and the other two ships made for Chile. Von Spee's fleet had never been so large, but the anchorages were not secure and the ships had to be moved on several occasions. The swell was such the the *Nürnberg* saw one of her propeller blades twisted in a minor collision with the *Baden*. It was necessary to induce a list of 15° to port in order to proceed with repairs. In a further setback two men aboard the *Gneisenau* died of dysentery.

Finally, on 19 October, all anchors were weighed and the ships formed up in a single line with Más a Fuera, one of the islands of the Juan Fernández group, as their new destination. Only the *Nürnberg* was delayed as she needed to complete work on her damaged propeller. During the voyage there were numerous gunnery practices. Von Spee was by now convinced that he was inevitably going to come up against an adversary absolutely determined to halt his progress. On 24 October the *Leipzig* left for Más a Tierra Island where she should have found the colliers, but her search was in vain. On 26 October the squadron anchored in the shelter of a huge cliff on the northwest side of Más a Fuera. Blocks of lava prevented any disembarkation. Putting aside the constant noise of the steam winches filling the empty bunkers with coal, the sailors were able to abandon themselves to a distraction about which they became more and more enthusiastic: fishing, as these waters were teaming with fish. Once she had emptied her holds the *Göttingen* departed – she would subsequently be interned – and an old friend, the *Prinz Eitel Friedrich*, came to take her place in the anchorage. Twenty hours later the German squadron left this inhospitable place and continued its progress to the east. During the night, radio messages from the *Good Hope* and *Monmouth* were picked up; their clarity suggested that these ships were close by. On 30 October the *Prinz Eitel Friedrich* and the *Göttingen* headed for Valparaíso.

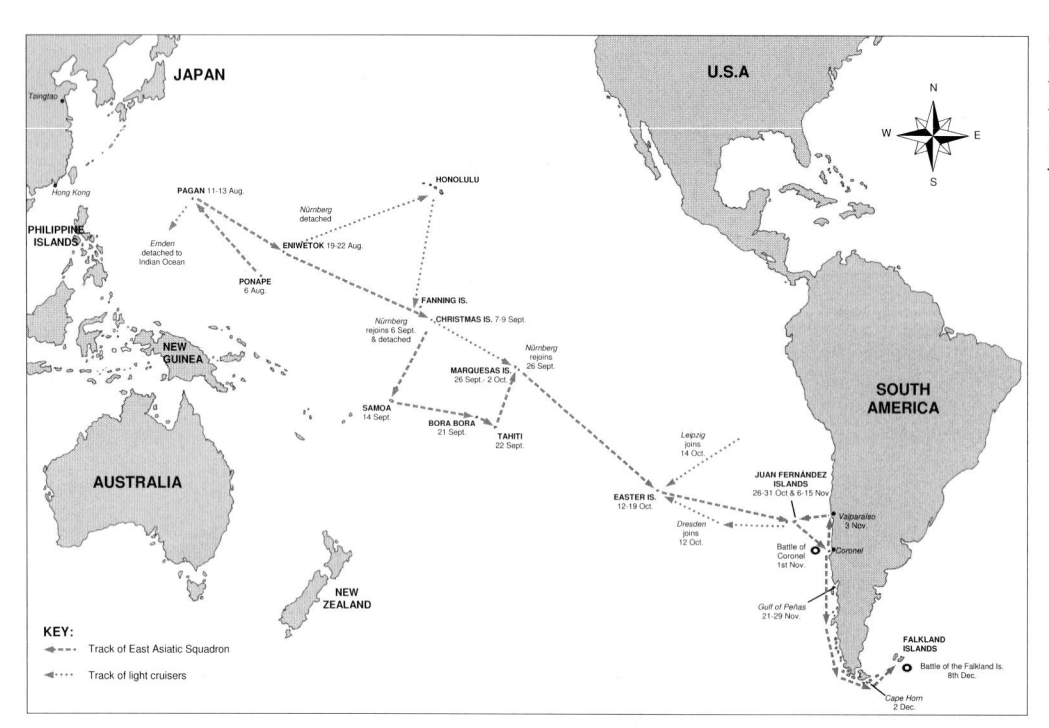

Track of the East Asiatic Squadron, August-December 1914. (Map by John Jordan)

Admiral Cradock to the Sacrifice

On 31 October at 1630 von Spee set his course to the south and received, that same night, a message of great consequence transmitted by the *Göttingen*: 'English cruiser at anchor in Coronel roads, 31 October at 7pm'. Leaving his transports behind von Spee ordered speed to be raised to 14 knots in the hope of intercepting the English ship. On 1st November the formation was running parallel to the coast, headed for Santa Maria Island. The light cruisers were stationed on either flank in order to stop and examine merchant ships. The *Leipzig* had in fact just stopped a sailing vessel while at 1500 the crews were preparing for action stations. The wind was strengthening from the south but at 1545 speed had been built up to 18 knots. The small cruisers were from this point virtually out of sight, but despite this Action Stations was sounded at 1620 and there was little doubt aboard the *Scahrnhorst* that the days of the British cruiser were numbered.

The enemy vessel had now been located but as the distance closed it became clear that there was not just a single pillar of smoke on the horizon but three! The distance was about 15 miles and there was a Sea State 6. Immediately the orders went for the *Nürnberg* and the *Dresden*, now 25 miles astern, for the *Gneisenau*, which was on a scouting mission towards the Bay of Arauco, and for the *Leipzig* to take station on the flagship. The long-awaited moment had arrived, and in their repsective conning towers the British and German admirals, both of whom were personally acquainted, were about to lead their men to death or glory.

In order to counter von Spee's squadron, which the British Admiralty was now convinced to be headed for South America, London had allocated to Admiral Cradock a somewhat ill-matched force. His instructions were clear:

There is a strong possibility of *Scharnhorst* and *Gneisenau* arriving in the Magellan Straits or on west coast of South America. Germans have begun to carry on trade there. Leave a sufficient force to deal with *Dresden* and *Karlsruhe*. Concentrate a squadron strong enough to meet *Scharnhorst* and *Gneisenau*, making Falkland Islands your coaling base. *Canopus* is en route to Abrolhos; *Defence* is joining you from the Mediterranean. Until *Defence* joins keep at least *Canopus* and one 'County' class cruiser with your flagship. As soon as you have superior force, search Magellan Straits, being ready to return and cover Plate, or search north as far as Valparaíso. Break up German trade and destroy German cruisers.

The *Defence* would never join Cradock, and the latter was never informed of the Admiralty's intentions regarding this ship. In view of the course von Spee had taken following his attack on Apia, to the northwest, the Admiralty was convinced that he was returning to the China Sea, and that it was no longer necessary to allocate to the admiral in command of the West Indies station a large number of powerful warships. Cradock nevertheless decided to cross the Magellan Straits and to make for Punta Arenas, where he arrived 28 September. The *Dresden* had reported his presence in these waters and some of the German supply ships had been seen at Valparaíso and Coronel. Cradock's presence on the western coast of South America was therefore fully justified. His squadron currently comprised the armoured cruisers *Good Hope* (flagship, Capt. Franklin) and *Monmouth* (Capt. Brandt), the light cruiser *Glasgow* (Capt. Luce) and the auxiliary cruiser *Otranto* (Capt. Davidson). The elderly battleship *Canopus*, now obsolete but armed with four 12in and twelve 6in guns, could also join his squadron.

Following the visit to Punta Arenas Cradock had divided his forces. Three of these ships were to patrol off

Valparaíso while the *Good Hope* returned to the Falklands to coal. In the meantime the radio station in the Fiji islands had intercepted a message from the *Scharnhorst* stating that she was headed for Easter Island. There were, moreover, three light cruisers escorting her. On 8 October Cradock asked the Admiralty the anticipated date of arrival of the *Defence* because he was anxious to assemble his ships. The British finally realised that von Spee could disrupt traffic on either side of Cape Horn. It was therefore also necessary to watch over the South Atlantic, and Admiral Stoddart received the order to base himself at Montevideo (Uruguay) with the armoured cruisers *Carnavon* and *Cornwall*, the light cruiser *Bristol*, and the auxiliary cruisers *Macedonia* and *Orama*. There was still no question of reinforcing Cradock's squadron, and the armoured cruiser *Kent*, which was due to join him, was diverted to the Canaries. The ancient *Canopus* was not expected at Port Stanley before 15 October, and when she arrived the *Good Hope* weighed anchor straight away to join *Monmouth*. In any case the battleship could make no more than 12 knots, and Cradock rightly questioned whether it was not wise to dispense with her services in order to retain his freedom of manoeuvre.

Sir Christopher George Francis Maurice Cradock was born on 2 July 1862 at Harforth in Yorkshire. He joined the Navy in 1875 and took part in the campaigns in Egypt 1884 and the Sudan 1891. He was promoted rear-admiral in 1910. Three years later he was charged with the protection of the north american coasts from the St Laurent to Brazil. Before leaving the Falklands, the admiral gave the Governor of the island a letter to be forwarded to his family n the event of his death. This may have been an indicator of Cradock's view as to the probable outcome of the battle which he would surely have to fight. Once underway he transmitted a message to the Admiralty urging the despatch of the *Defence*, but as the *Karlsruhe* had once again revealed her presence, the armoured cruiser remained under Stoddart's orders. On 30 October the *Glasgow* was at Coronel and signalled that the German ships were off the coast of Chile. The *Good Hope* and *Monmouth* therefore left Vallenar Roads on the day that *Canopus* arrived at Port Stanley. The latter had machinery problems, and Cradock gave her captain 24 hours to effect repairs. In the meantime he ordered *Glasgow* and *Otranto* to rendez-vous with him 50 miles to the west of Coronel.

On 1st November the *Glasgow* was the first to make out smoke to starboard, at 1515. The *Otranto* confirmed the sighting five minutes later. The *Good Hope* waited for the line to be formed before increasing to full speed. Battle ensigns were hoisted. The flagship was followed by *Monmouth*, *Glasgow* and *Otranto*.

The Battle of Coronel

At 1735 the *Scharnhorst* was headed south southwest, and von Spee took advantage of the delay to notify the distribution of fire to his squadron. The flagship was to fire on the *Good Hope*, *Gneisenau* the *Monmouth*, *Leipzig* and *Dresden* the other two British cruisers. The *Nürnberg*, which was still some distance away, would probably not be able to close up in time to participate in the battle.

At 1734 Cradock assumed a course of 40° towards his adversary, transmitting to *Canopus* (Capt. Grant) more than 250 miles away: 'I am engaged in attacking the enemy'. His fleet was silhouetted against the setting sun, whereas von Spee's force remained enshrouded in the increasing gloom. This unwise tactical disposition would place his force at a disadvantage, particularly as his crews were largely composed of reservists whose training left much to be desired. Cradock, however, was not a man to run away.

At 1834 the distance was a mere 10,400m and it was at that moment that *Scharnhorst* opened fire, closely followed

Table 2: THE BATTLE OF CORONEL

Cradock's Squadron

	Good Hope	Monmouth	Glasgow	Otranto
Displacement:	14,100 tons	9800 tons	4800 tons	12,000 tons
Speed:	23 knots	23 knots	25 knots	15 knots
Complement:	900	678	480	350
Armament:	2 x 9.2in* (2 x I)	14 x 6in	2 x 6in (2 x I)	8 x 4.7in* (8 x I)
	16 x 6in* (16 x I)	(2 x II, 10 x I)	10 x 4in* (10 x I)	
Protection:	Belt: 6in	Belt: 4in		None
	Deck: 2-3in	Deck: 2in	Deck: ?-2in	

Von Spee's Squadron

	Scharnhorst/Gneisenau	Dresden/Nürnberg/Leipzig
Displacement:	11,800 tonnes	3300-3700 tonnes
Speed:	22.5 knots	23-24 knots
Complement:	760-840	320-360
Armament:	8 x 21cm (2 x II, 4 x I)	10 x 10.5cm (10 x I)
	6 x 15cm (16 x I)	
Protection:	Belt: 150mm	
	Deck: 50mm	Deck: 20-30mm

* Metric equivalents: 9.2in = 23.4cm; 6in = 15.2cm; 4.7in = 12cm; 4in = 10.2cm

by the other German cruisers. In the early stages of the battle only the 21cm guns rang out as the 15cm guns, which were closer to the waterline, were handicapped by the heavy seas, which disrupted their aim. After two ranging shots Schultz scored a hit on the *Good Hope*, between the conning tower and the forward 9.2in turret, provoking a fire. Her sister *Gneisenau* was hitting her own opponent hard. She scored a major hit on her bow which put the twin forward turret out of action. At 9200m the secondary guns of British squadron entered the action but found it difficult to establish a rythm. *Glasgow* was unwilling to be left out of the action and engaged *Leipzig*. Despite her efforts, the heavy seas made it difficult for her to get the range. For the *Otranto* the situation would rapidly become dramatic. With her high sides, the former liner was an easy target. *Dresden* had already scored a hit on her promenade deck and her captain wisely decided to leave the line.

In order to close the range, Cradock changed course to the southwest, but his flagship was already badly battered. There were at least twenty fires raging as a consequence of around thirty shell hits. At 1853, fearing a torpedo attack von Spee opened the range. On the *Good Hope* a huge column of flame was seen to rise abaft the fourth funnel and the ship was ravaged by fire from end to end. In the midst of the confusion *Monmouth* manage to secure a 6in shell hit on the after turret of the *Gneisenau*, but the shell failed to pierce the armour. *Geneisenau* was also struck on her armoured belt by a 9.2in shell from *Good Hope* which had little effect. Despite these minor successes the English cruiser was suffering terribly. The roof of her after turret had been blown away and dense smoke was emerging from it. The foremast had been shot away and the spotting top had fallen onto the suprstructure, with the result that at 1850 the *Monmouth* left the line and attempted to shelter closer to the coast. Lacking a target *Gneisenau* shifted her fire onto the opposing flagship, which was by now in a desperate condition.

At 1923 a violent explosion between the second and third funnels shook the *Good Hope*. Debris was thrown more than 60 metres. In a final death charge the ship headed directly for the *Scharnhorst*, perhaps intending to ram; no one will ever know. Enveloped by the gathering darkness and a dense cloud of smoke the cruiser sank beneath the waves between 2000 and 2030. There were no survivors; Admiral Cradock, his flag staff, numerous midshipmen not yet 18, and 900 men went down with the ship. The *Good Hope* sank in the approximate position 36°59S, 73°55W. Admiral von Spee ordered his squadron to cease fire at 1926, and ordered his light cruisers to seek out the remaining enemy ships to attack them with torpedoes.

In the twilight the *Glasgow*, which had been struck by five shells, ceased fire and the Germans lost her from sight. She passed the *Monmouth*, which failed to answer her signals. Captain Luce decided not to risk his ship to no purpose and, with the three cheers of the armoured cruiser ringing out, vanished into the shadows.

The *Leipzig* left at 18 knots heading northwest. The *Nürnberg*, which had not arrived in time for the battle, sighted a cruiser at 2005 but could not gain on her. On the other hand, another vessel was approaching which appeared to be in a poor state. Not knowing the identity of the ship, Captain Schönberg approached cautiously until only a short distance away, then illuminated the ship with one of his searchlight projectors. The wreck of a warship appeared in the beam, its ensigns still flying. At 2050 the *Nürnberg* fired off a number of 10.5cm shells and a torpedo which missed its target. The *Monmouth* failed to react, but did not lower her colours. At a range of 600m the shells began to rain down again and the brave cruiser finally turned over on her starboard side. At 2058 she disappeared beneath the waves.

The Germans did not stay long in these waters; nobody knew for certain the location of the *Glasgow*, and the heavy seas made it impossible to lower boats. *Monmouth* had disappeared together with her entire complement of 678 officers and men. The *Nürnberg* turned to the south southwest and rejoined the *Scharnhorst* at 2130. Von Spee set his course north northeast. The following day he addressed to the squadron the following message:

> With God's help we have achieved a great victory, for which I express to the crews my gratitude and my congratulations.

The *Scharnhorst* had suffered only light damage caused by two shells which failed to explode. The *Gneisenau* had minor damage from a shell which struck the bridge, another on the after 21cm barbette, one on the armoured belt and a fourth on the roof of one of the starboard casemates. Temporary repairs were quickly effected. In terms of casualties among the crews only two men were wounded. Moreover the light cruisers were completely undamaged. The only downside to the action was that the squadron had expended almost 50% of its munitions, and it would prove impossible to replenish.

There are two small memorials commemorating the battle of 1st November 1914. The first is located in Stanley Cathedral on the Falkland Islands and the second in the Plaza des 21 de Mayo in the town of Coronel itself.

The Last Stop at Valparaíso

Following the defeat at Coronel a British agent at Valparaíso sent a message to London stating that the *Monmouth* had been sunk, and that the *Good Hope* had blown up and had almost certainly foundered. In the meantime, on 1st November, the British consul at Valparaíso signalled to the First Sea Lord that von Spee's squadron had reached the Chilean coast. On 3 November the consul signalled to Cradock:

> *Defence* has been ordered to join your flag urgently. *Glasgow* is to make contact with the enemy. You should remain in contact with *Glasgow* while concentrating the remainder of your squadron, including the *Canopus*. It is important that you make your junction with *Defence* as soon as possible in order to make contact with the enemy.

This message, intended for an admiral who had ceaselessly requested reinforcement, was long overdue. It was not received because at the time of its transmission *Good*

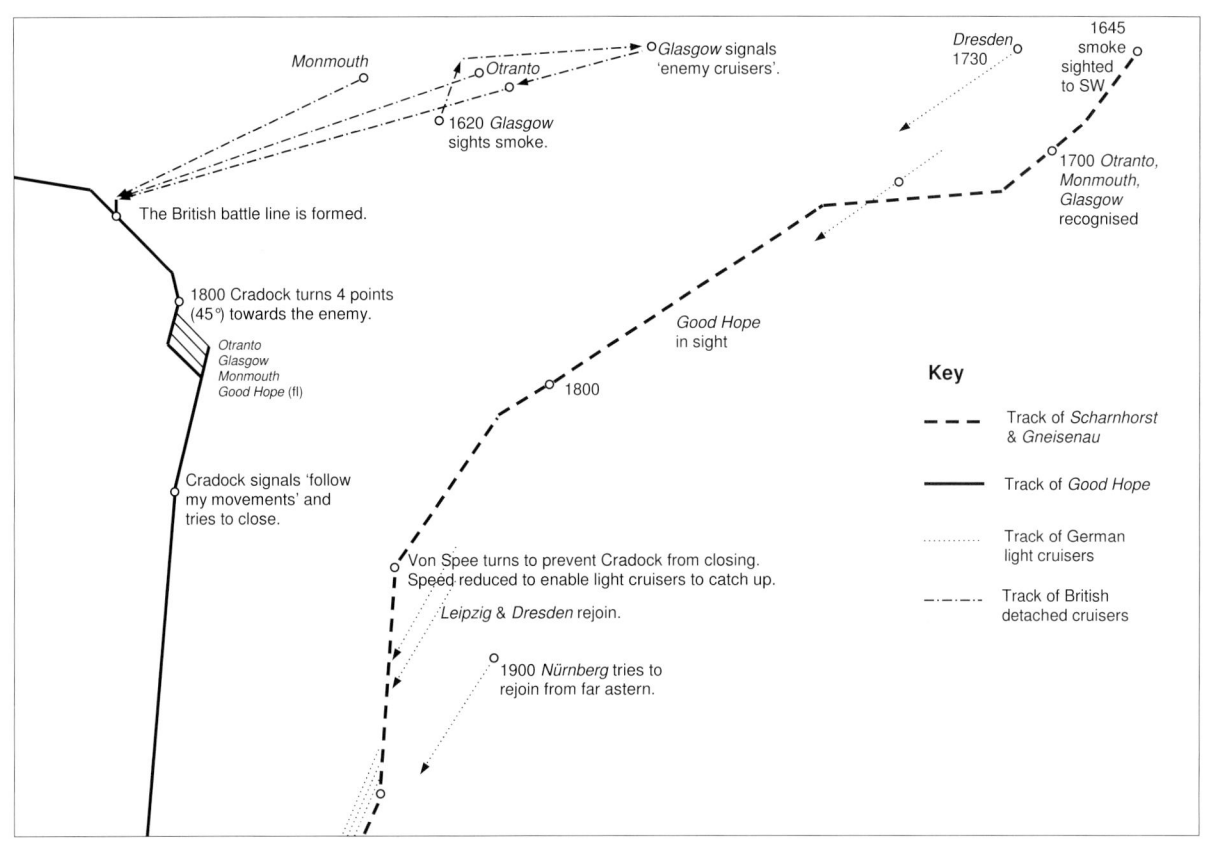

THE ODYSSEY OF VON SPEE AND THE EAST ASIATIC SQUADRON, 1914

The Battle of Coronel, 1 November 1914. Above: the approach; right: the engagement. (Maps by John Jordan)

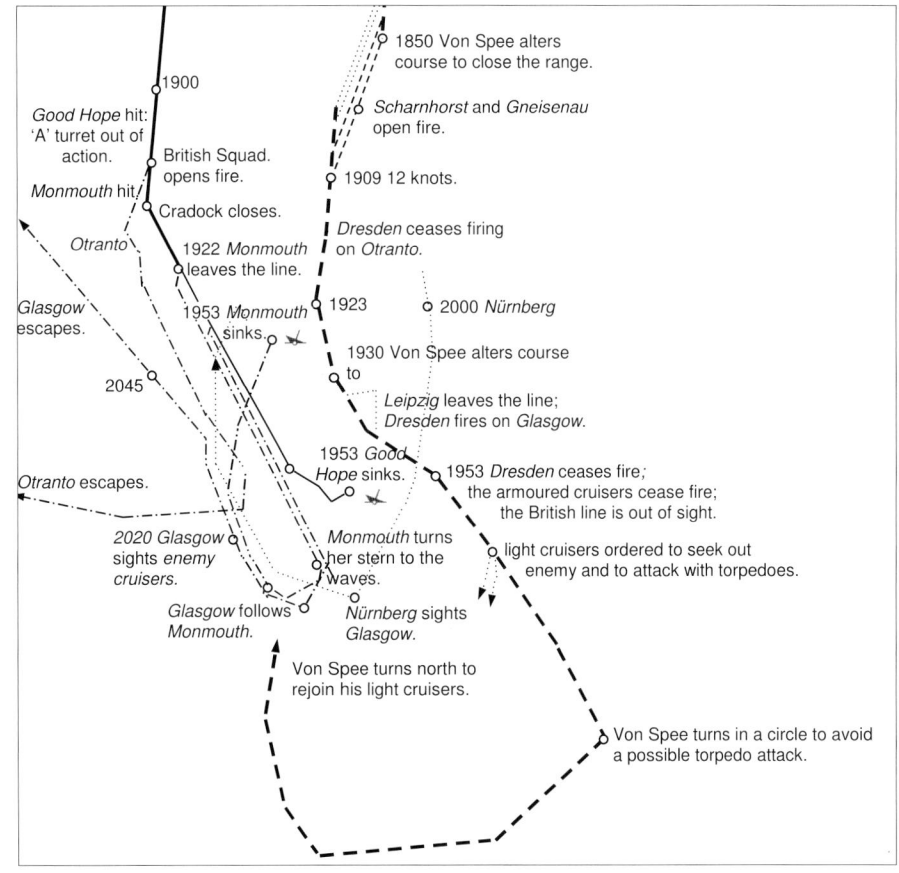

Hope had already been on the bottom of the ocean for nearly 48 hours!

News of the defeat struck the British Admiralty like a bomb. It was the first reverse of this magnitude for more than a century. News had arrived from the *Glasgow*, which had passed through the Magellan Strait on 4 November, and from the *Otranto* which had successfully rounded Cape Horn. Henceforth all the naval forces off South America would be concentrated on Admiral Stoddart at Montevideo. Mercantile traffic was stopped and there was a request for the *Canopus* to be beached in the harbour mouth at Port Stanley to serve as a 'floating battery'.

In the higher echelons of the Admiralty, the First Lord Winston Churchill demanded the despatch of the battle-cruiser *Invincible* to the South Atlantic. On 4 November, shortly after the announcement of the *débâcle* at Coronel, the new First Sea Lord, 'Jackie' Fisher, ordered the C-in-C Grand Fleet, Admiral Jellicoe, to prepare for imminent departure not one but two battlecruisers: *Inflexible* was to join *Invincible*; moreover a third battlecruiser, *Princess Royal*, was to be deployed to the North Atlantic. Vice-Admiral Sturdee was charged with the annihilation of von Spee's squadron.[6]

Before setting sail for the South Atlantic the two battlecruisers were to be docked, and Devonport dockyard stated that work on them would take until 13 November. Fisher was having none of this and insisted that they should be ready to leave on 11 November, failing which civilian workers would have to be embarked to complete the work. On that date the battlecruisers left for Saint Vincent at a speed of 18 knots. On 26 November Sturdee was at Abrolhos Rocks, 400 miles to the north of Rio de Janeiro. He then had to gather together his force, which besides the two battlecruisers was to comprise the light cruiser *Bristol*, the armoured cruisers *Carnarvon*, *Cornwall* and *Kent*, and, inevitably, the *Glasgow*.

On the afternoon of 2 November von Spee announced that he intended to call in at Valparaíso. The following day, at 1100, the *Scharnhorst*, *Gneisenau* and *Nürnberg* entered the harbour. Since international law did not permit a stopover by more than three ships at once in a neutral port, the *Leipzig* and *Dresden* waited 150 miles offshore to the west.

A rapturous welcome awaited the victorious admiral and his men, there being many German expatriates in this maritime town of Chile. It was the first port visit worthy of the name since Nagasaki, and the sailors were impatient to let their hair down ashore. Numerous journalists came aboard to gather details of the battle which had just taken place. The consul himself was received aboard the flagship, and von Spee entrusted to him his war log. In the evening the admiral was invited to a German club ashore, and insisted that the reception should be as low-key as possible. In the meantime he exchanged lengthy telegrams with Berlin and was informed of the latest developments in Europe. While his ships were being resupplied with provisions and coal, the admiral attended the reception as agreed, and when an admirer presented him with a bouquet of flowers he remarked that he would do better to keep them for his funeral!

Was von Spee conscious at this point that his days were numbered? If so he did not allow his pessimism to be communicated to his men, for on the morning of 3 November he was busy holding a reception for reservists who had come to enrol in the the fleet. One hundred and twenty-seven had the honour of being accepted into the 'glorious

Gneisenau during her visit to Valparaíso. (Billdienst)

Scharnhorst replenishes at Valparaíso. (Billdienst)

The light cruiser SMS Leipzig at Valparaíso. (Billdienst)

Admiral von Spee goes ashore at Valparaíso. We see him here in the company of the German Consul and his Chief of Staff. (Private Collection)

China Squadron'. At 1100 the armoured cruisers and the light cruiser weighed anchor and set course for Más a Fuera where they arrived on 6 November. There they found the *Leipzig* which was in the process of coaling from the four-masted French barque *Valentine*. Fitted out at Dunkerque and carrying 3500 tonnes of Welsh coal, the latter had been captured at night and towed to the German anchorage. That evening the *Baden* brought in the Norwegian sailing ship *Helicon* which was quickly moored alongside the *Gneisenau*. On 8 November the *Dresden* arrived with the American steamer *Sacramento*, which was carrying 7000 tonnes of coal and 1000 tonnes of fresh provisions. Soon the last two of the cruisers could put into Valparaíso to give leave to their crews. The *Prinz Eitel Friedrich* was also present at Más a Fuera and was ordered to sink the *Valentine*, on which a fire had broken out, and the *Titania*, which in view of her extreme age was now only a liability. This sad task was carried out on 14 November three miles from the coast.

It was at about this time that von Spee learned that Tsingtao had fallen to the Japanese and that the *Emden* had been sunk. On Sunday 15 November at 1600 all of the ships left for the Bay of Saint Quentin except for the *Prinz Eitel Friedrich*, which was to become a solitary commerce raider. The voyage had barely commenced when the *Scharnhorst* stopped briefly to bury at sea a sailor who had accidentally met his death during coaling.

On 18 November the *Dresden* and *Leipzig* joined the formation, having sunk a former auxiliary vessel of Cradock, the cargo ship *North Wales*. They brought a message from the German High Command ordering a slowing of the war on commerce and suggesting a return to Germany via the Denmark Strait, where a collier would be waiting. Von Spee was asked to reply giving his intentions and the munitions situation. He replied:

> I envisage a breakthrough of the cruiser squadron to Germany. The current situation with regard to munitions is as follows: each of the large cruisers has 445 21cm and 1100 15cm shells; the smaller cruisers 1860 rounds.

A rumour was circulating that a battlecruiser, almost certainly the *Von der Tann*, was to be deployed to the Atlantic to create a diversion. This was subsequently to prove unfounded.

However, von Spee still had some way to go. At dawn on 21 November the squadron penetrated into the Gulf of Peñas in thick fog. The weather was cold and the steam heating system was activated, but the location was impressive with mountains covered with forests and an immense glacier. Insensitive to the panorama the boilers continued to claim their ration of coal and everyone had to buckle down to the demanding task of coaling. Saint Quentin was the assembly point for the supply ships. Present were the *Seydlitz* (8008 BRT) from Australia, the *Ramses* (7127 BRT), the *Memphis* (7074 BRT) and the *Luxor* (7109 BRT). The cruisers had arrived with the *Baden*, *Santa Isabel* and *Amasis*, making for an impressive concentration of German ships in this small bay. Three supply ships were emptied of their cargo and von Spee set off once again with the *Baden*, *Santa Isabel* and *Seydlitz*, loaded with 17,000 tonnes of anthracite. In order to relieve the monotony of the voyage, it was announced that the Kaiser had awarded 300 Iron Crosses 2nd Class, and an Iron Cross 1st Class for the commander-in-chief. With their bunkers fully topped up and sacks of coal stowed in every available corner, the cruisers of the East Asiatic Squadron prepared to round Cape Horn. The weather conditions in this mythical place lived up to tradition, to the extent that the supplementary bags of coal had to be heaved over the side to reduce topweight. On 2 December the famous Cape was glimpsed through the rain, and an iceberg 600 metres wide passed close to the ships. Suddenly the *Genisenau* sighted a sailing ship to port and the *Leipzig* was ordered to investigate. It turned out to be the Canadian *Drummuir* carrying 2750 tonnes of Welsh coal. In order to proceed with a further replenishment von Spee ordered the squadron to head for Picton Island, where the squadron anchored at dawn on 3 December. The *Drummuir* had been taken in tow and now transferred her cargo to the *Baden* and *Santa Isabel* while the *Seydlitz* supplied the cruisers. The task completed the men went ashore to hunt, and even von Spee was seen walking with the captain of the *Gneisenau* on the desert shore.

On 6 December the Canadian vessel was towed out by the *Baden* and sunk by the *Leipzig*. The *Seydlitz* was given the job of picking up the crew. A final briefing was given by the admiral to his commanders before the ships again made out to sea. He informed them that he intended to attack Port Stanley and to capture the Governor of the Falkland Islands. The *Gneisenau* and the *Nürnberg* were to carry out this mission at 0800 on 8 December. Certain commanders, including apparently the captain of the *Gneisenau*, voiced concerns, arguing that there would

On 2 December 1914, the East Asiatic Squadron rounds Cape Horn. (Süddeutscher Verlag)

undoubtedly be powerful warships in this key British base and that they would reveal their positions to little purpose. Despite these arguments von Spee was set on his course of action.

The Germans weighed anchor on the afternoon of 6 December. They passed by Tierra del Fuego at 10 knots with the *Leipzig* one mile ahead of the squadron. During this time the landing parties were preparing their equipment between decks. The *Gneisenau* was to anchor off Port Stanley and lower boats for the assault on the town while the *Nürnberg* provided fire support. At 0200 on 8 December the Falkland coasts were in sight, the weather conditions were unusually favourable, and only a light northeasterly breeze was ruffling the surface of the waves. At 0500 Maerker received the signal from the admiral to commence execution of the plan and, in company with the *Nürnberg*, he set off to the north at a speed of 14 knots. From the outset a miscalculation had resulted in an hour's delay to the original timetable, and the *Canopus* had plenty of time to spot the enemy ships and to identify them. At 0750 the battleship transmitted: 'Two unidentified vessels approaching from the south'.

The British squadron charged with intercepting von Spee's ships had arrived at Port Stanley at 1030 the previous day. All ships had been placed on a two-hour alert and coaling had begun immediately. Only the *Cornwall* was permitted to keep one of her boilers fired up. On 8 December the *Carnarvon* and *Bristol* had finished coaling and from 0720 it was the turn of the *Inflexible* to come alongside the colliers. At 0750 Sturdee was informed that a four-funnelled ship accompanied by another with two funnels was on a southerly heading. He immediately ordered the *Invincible* and *Inflexible* to disengage from the cargo ships and all ships to raise steam. At 0845 the *Kent* was in the harbour approaches where the auxiliary cruiser *Macedonia*, which had earlier been on patrol, was waiting for her. These two ships were joined an hour later by the two battlecruisers accompanied by the *Carnarvon* and the *Glasgow*. Sturdee had time to have breakfast before going to sea and preparing to avenge the honour of the Royal Navy. By nightfall of that fateful day von Spee and all but one of his senior officers would be dead and the elite East Asiatic Squadron would have ceased to exist; only the light cruiser *Dresden* would escape Sturdee's ships.

Notes:

1. On 4 November 1914 the *Karlsruhe* was destroyed by the accidental explosion of one of her magazines in the position: 11°07'N & 55°25'W. The survivors were rescued by two naval auxliaries and repatriated to Germany aboard the *Rio Negro*. The cruiser had sunk 17 steamers during the first months of the war.
2. The *Emden* undertook a memorable commerce-raiding cruise in the Indian Ocean. She was sunk on 9 November 1914 at the Cocos Islands by the Australian cruiser *Sydney*.
3. These two steamers were interned at Honolulu in September 1914.
4. The *Australia* displaced 18,750 tons, was armed with eight 12in guns and had a top speed of 25 knots. She would have been a formidable opponent for two armoured cruisers, however well-trained their crews.
5. One would expect to see the exploits of Destremau duly recognised; nothing could be farther from the truth. Governor Fawtier submitted a falsified report in which he accused Destremau of insubordination. Ordered to return to France aboard the *Montcalm*, Destremau was placed under arrest for two months. He would die of diptheria at Saint Anne's Hospital 7 March 1915. His reputation would be restored only on 19 December of the same year with the publication of the Official Report.
6. Sturdee would be promoted Admiral in 1917 and Admiral of the Fleet in 1921; he died 7 May 1925.

ITALIAN FAST COASTAL FORCES: DEVELOPMENT, DOCTRINE AND CAMPAIGNS, 1914-1986

Part One: from the Beginning to 1934

The narrow waters of the Adriatic were favourable to both the torpedo and the mine, and the Italian Regia Marina was quick to exploit the potential of the fast torpedo boat in these waters. This article by **Erminio Bagnasco, Enrico Cernuschi** and **Vincent P. O'Hara** traces the development of the Italian MAS boat from its conception to the interwar period.

Until the mid 19th century one of the constants of naval warfare was that nothing could challenge a battleship at sea except another battleship. A series of technological innovations, beginning with the introduction of the explosive shell in 1824, followed by the use of the steam engine and then iron armour, changed the nature of the main battle force, but not the general principle, true since the galleys of ancient times, that on the high seas small warships could not challenge the giants.

During the Victorian age, as technology altered the appearance of the battleship, it also fostered the evolution of whole new classes of cheap, insidious naval weapons which gave David, for the first time, the opportunity to defy Goliath with the help of daring, stealth and – last but not least – luck. All navies tried to exploit the possibilities presented by this development, but no navy did it better than Italy's Regia Marina. This article chronicles the development, doctrine and operational history of Italy's innovative and successful family of giant killers, its fast coastal forces.

The story begins with the history of the torpedo. The first torpedoes were floating packets of explosives – what today would be called a drifting mine. They suffered the disadvantage of being completely passive and the spear torpedo boat, a miniature man of war that carried this explosive charge on the tip of a long (but rarely long enough) pole projecting from the boat's bow, was developed in the late 1850s to give the torpedo mobility. This primitive torpedo boat, along with the even less effective towed torpedo, was used by both sides during the American Civil War and by other navies up until the 1880s, but the limitations of such craft were obvious.

In 1860, fearing an Italian blockade and raids against the Austrian coastline, a Habsburg navy captain, Johann Luppis, conceived the idea of the *Kustenbrander* ('Coastal Fire Ship'), a small, unmanned vessel with glass sails guided by wires from shore. Within a year, this weapon evolved into a semi-submersible boat packed with explosives and propelled by a clockwork engine, designed to ram blockading warships. After some unsuccessful trials Luppis approached Robert Whitehead (a British engineer living in Austria) for assistance in 1864. Although mechanical issues killed the concept, it gave Whitehead the idea for his locomotive torpedo which, by 1867, had developed into the recognisable ancestor of today's underwater weapon.

Whitehead's invention first armed battleships and cruisers, but it was not long before the concept of the spar torpedo boat and the locomotive torpedo merged in the British torpedo-boat *Lightning*. Completed in 1877, *Lightning* was a 32.5-ton steam launch, 87ft long with a top speed of 19 knots. The fast torpedo boat (a contemporary ironclad could reach at best 15 knots), armed with a powerful fire and forget weapon represented a revolution

The prototype MAS 1 as a minelayer. (Erminio Bagnasco)

in naval warfare, at least in theory, and the world's navies were quick to sieze upon and improve the concept. In fact *Lightning* marked the genesis of new warship classes the displacement of which, in the quest for speed and better sea-keeping characteristics, soon grew to more than 200 tons. By 1892 the *Lightning*'s progeny had evolved into the flexible and revolutionary 30-knot warship of 250 plus tons known, originally, as the torpedo-boat destroyer and then simply as the destroyer.[1]

The original vision of a host of small, stealthy torpedo boats was not completely lost in this process, however. Naval thinkers speculated that the torpedo would be most effective at night when delivered by a swarm of unseen small craft from short range, which would then run like the wind from their much larger and more powerful targets.

The problems blocking the realisation of this vision were machinery and seaworthiness. The steam technology of the day (in spite of improvements and the introduction of the turbine) soon dictated a compromise between seaworthiness and speed which imposed a displacement average of about 100 tons and a top speed, at best, of 27 knots during the golden years of the torpedo boat age.

As a matter of fact a very small torpedo-armed unit was available: steam launches with a displacement ranging between 8 and 15 tons and armed with torpedoes were used by almost every navy from 1882 until the beginning of the First World War. They were silent, but at no more than 15 knots, too slow. They also suffered from an extremely limited range and, worst of all, lacked the seaworthiness to operate independently. These limitations forced these small steam picket boats to depend upon a mother ship, usually a cruiser or a battleship. They required good weather and, being too slow to run down a ship underway, their target needed to be a sitting duck – a combination of conditions rarely encountered in wartime. Nevertheless, these boats performed well in a few specific situations, particularly harbour penetration actions. A good example was the Italian raid on Beirut harbour on 24 February 1912. In a daring and lucky attack carried out (against all the rules) in full daylight, two torpedoes launched by the Italian cruiser *Garibaldi*'s picket boat sank the Turkish armoured gunboat *Avnillah* (2,362t). Meanwhile the cruiser *Ferruccio*'s launch torpedoed a barge. Another famous action occurred on the night of 16 April 1915 when two British boats from the battleships *Triumph* and *Majestic* torpedoed the stranded Royal Navy submarine *E 15* during the Gallipoli campaign to keep it out of Turkish hands.

These exploits – exceptions that proved the rule – confirmed that the classic torpedo boat doctrine of fast, small and expendable was impracticable because the delivery systems had grown to 100-200 tons per ship, thus becoming too big and expensive and, above all, too few. This led from the beginning of the 20th Century to the practical abandonment of the small torpedo boat by most major navies, except, due to the particular nature of these seas, those operating in the Adriatic and Baltic.

The Advent of the Petrol Engine

The construction of the first practical internal combustion engine by the German Nikolaus Otto in 1876, followed by Rudolph Diesel's diesel engine in 1892, sparked a revolution in naval propulsion. The on-going development of Otto's engine led to compact power plants with greater relative output. Internal combustion thus seemed to promise (despite its volatile fuel) the ability to merge the stealth, economy and punch of the old steam launch with the speed and sea-keeping qualities of the bigger torpedo boat. Prototypes (ranging in displacement from 4.5 to 8 tons) proposed between 1903 and 1906 by French, American, Italian and British enterprises, however, all failed to realise the promise of the new powerplant. Other attempts to shoe-horn internal combustion engines into iron hulls, like an 8-tonne FIAT prototype launched in 1906, or the ten

A steam torpedo launch of the 'Garibaldi' cruiser division taken at La Spezia early 20th Century. (Erminio Bagnasco)

32-ton boats armed with a single 18in torpedo built in the United States and delivered to Russia in 1905, proved operationally useless. The hard truth was that their engines lacked the power needed. All this changed in 1914.

During the summer of 1914 the Regia Marina's recently appointed Chief of Staff, Adm. Paolo Thaon di Revel (who conceived and ordered the 1912 Beirut picket boat action), refused to let the offensive possibilities presented by swarms of small, fast MTBs be ignored. He had the vision of using a wooden motor boat as an MTB rather than the much larger and heavier classic torpedo boat hull. He got this idea from observing the motor boats made by the Venetian yard SVAN (*Società Veneziana Automobili Navali* – Venice Motor Boat Company, founded in 1909) that plied the lagoon, serving the city's many deluxe hotels. From the economic point of view his idea allowed the Regia Marina to acquire ten MTBs, each armed with two 450mm (17.7in) torpedoes and crewed by eight men,

MAS 7 in Brindisi roads, 1916. This is one of the early 'SVAN 12t' boats equipped with a torpedo-rack launching system. In the background are the armoured cruisers Pisa *(left) and* San Giorgio *(right). (Erminio Bagnasco)*

A 1916 view of a MAS of the 'SVAN 3-22' series, armed in the gunboat configuration, taken in Grado. (Aureliano Molinari)

for the same price as a single 120-tonne boat of the Italian 'PN' class armed with two torpedoes, manned by a crew of 23 and having only slightly better seakeeping qualities.

Thaon di Revel's idea proved more difficult to implement than expected, however. The first SVAN project was too small, while a further design seemed incapable of obtaining the promised top speed of 30 knots. A visit to the United States by a Regia Marina party in the autumn of 1914 to find a better MTB alternative proved vain. Staff then rejected a proposal made in November 1914 by Maccia Marchini, a yard on the Lake of Como, for an 8-tonne hard-chine, 15-metre (50ft) boat designed to achieve 30 knots, judging it too small and insufficiently seaworthy. In March 1915 the SVAN program finally commenced with the order for a pair of 13-tonne hard-chine hull, 16-metre (53ft) prototypes armed with two heavy stern torpedo tubes and named *MAS 1* and *MAS 2*.[2] Completed that same year, these boats suffered from serious trim problems and their two 200hp Isotta-Fraschini L.56 engines proved less powerful than planned; with torpedoes aboard maximum speed was only 20 knots, ten less than anticipated.

It is interesting to consider that as Italy struggled to develop a small and expendable MTB the Royal Navy was likewise travelling down a parallel but inverse path. The British envisaged their MTB, developed in 1916 as the 40ft, 5-ton, step-hulled CMB boat, as a weapon that could offer the same modest advantages of the old steam picket boats with a better post-launch survival speed. The British did not foresee it engaged in night patrol work, which was to be the Italian MAS's primary task. It is one of history's many ironies that while the British soon abandoned the CMB's harbour attack mission and that same boat evolved into a true 11-ton MTB, able to achieve 36 knots – albeit in the calmest of waters – the Italian boats gained renown by forcing enemy harbours, although they never neglected their primary task conducting thousands of fatiguing, uneventful patrols along the enemy's sea routes.

Evolution of the 'Mosquito Fleet'

On 16 July 1915, even before the first trials of the new wooden MTBs, Thaon di Revel ordered a batch of MAS boats (*MAS 3* to *22*) similar to the prototypes, the first of which entered service on 28 March 1916. This class was then followed by an almost continuous stream of orders for progressively enhanced 12-tonne boats of similar design.[3]

The earliest and most important improvement was the replacement of the stern torpedo tubes which, combined with their faulty engines, soon reduced *MAS 1* and *2* to the role of miniature minelayers. The follow-up boats used the light Vickers side racks scavenged from the retired steam picket torpedo boats, which solved stability problems caused by the weight of the torpedoes.[4] Another improvement was the use of convertible weapon systems which allowed the boats to be quickly reconfigured as MTBs, MGBs (with one 47/40mm gun and two 6.5mm Colt machine guns) or, later, as minelayers. Armoured cockpits appeared in 1918 for some boats operating along the Army front lines. With the proliferation of Austrian

MAS 15 armed with torpedoes, taken in Venice. (Erminio Bagnasco)

MAS 68, an ELCO ASW boat built in the United States, at Castellamare di Stabia July 1917. (Erminio Bagnasco)

boom defences the Italians fitted net cutters to the noses of their torpedoes for use during harbour penetration actions. The adoption of radios, on the other hand, was not possible until mid-1918 because the wireless sets available were too cumbersome. Instead, these were fitted into the larger ELCO MAS boats used as ASW pickets.

MAS and ASW

From the late autumn of 1916 the increasing menace of German submarines in the Mediterranean sea lanes and the lack of specialised sub-chasers forced the Regia Marina to employ about 100 MAS boats in an ASW role arming them with 47/40 guns, machine guns, depth charges and a towed torpedo.[5] Lacking any underwater search device (hydrophones were introduced on Italian MAS in 1918), using expensive petrol as fuel and being restricted to coastal routes, these boats were far from ideal for such work. The anti-submarine MAS were joined, from May 1917, by the much more suitable 24.4m 44-tonne ELCO motor launches, of which U.S. yards built 66 and Italian yards nine to a slightly modified design before the end of the war and a further 39 later. Although the Italian Navy classified them as MAS because they had petrol engines like their smaller Adriatic cousins, these bigger and slower boats lacked torpedoes, were used only for ASW duties and are thus only mentioned in the present study.

The ASW coastal forces deployed by Italy totalled about 300 units by 1917-1918, supported by more than a hundred flying boats and seven airships, not to mention a system of defended anchorages and booms along the coastal routes. It may have seemed quite a rag-bag according to modern concepts of warfare, but the MAS boats proved effective nonetheless. In 1918 one German submarine commander lamented that: 'The greatest danger came from aircraft by day and fast motor-boats by night'.[6]

The Refinement of Doctrine

According to Thaon di Revel's original concept of a mass 'mosquito fleet', the 1915 plan was to commission 100 MAS boats every year with the ultimate goal being a force of 300 torpedo-armed craft available at any given time. Wood and a skilled labour force, distributed among ten yards, were not a problem, but a lack of steel crippled domestic engine production and imports could not help as, until the end of the war, it was impossible to find abroad a petrol engine both affordable and powerful enough to allow the boats to exceed 24 knots.[7] The grand total of 12-tonne attack and SVAN-derived boats ordered during the war thus totalled only 212 units, of which 161 commissioned before the Armistice.

The general MAS program was sub-divided as follows (see table for breakdown and characteristics):

A Group: attack boats of the SVAN 12-tonne type and derivatives;
B Group: MAS *da crociera* ('cruise' MAS) of the SVAN 19-tonne type with semi-hard chine hull and devoted to ASW duties only;
C Group: ELCO ASW types;
D Group: *veloci* and *velocissimi* ('fast' and 'very fast') experimental types.

In the event this shortfall in the numbers envisaged by Thaon di Revel proved tolerable because doctrine evolved as the experiences of war demonstrated the importance of quality. In this case quality was in the form of superior personnel rather than improved engines or weapon systems. The Regia Marina discovered that only well trained crews and hand-picked officers, gifted both with seamanship and initiative, could effectively man the torpedo-armed MAS boats. The attack flotillas active from the Adriatic Sea bases of Brindisi and Venice totalled, as a consequence, no more than twenty (later thirty) boats at a time.

Thus doctrine came to consider the boats as elite but expendable weapons to be used against high value targets in carefully crafted operations. This concept formed the foundation of Italy's successful employment of MAS boats during both World Wars. The opposite doctrine, that of cheap attack craft to be squandered in mass attacks, as adopted by the German Navy in 1944 and 1945, proved more deadly to their courageous operators than to the Allied invasion fleets.

The MAS Boats at War

The first success accomplished by Italy's 'mosquito fleet' occurred on 22 May 1916 off Trieste when MAS 19 captured the *Leni*, a large armed Austro-Hungarian motorboat. Two nights later the same MAS chased an enemy tug off Trieste and forced it ashore. During the night of 6 June, 100-tonne torpedo boats towed MAS 5 and 7, led by Lt. Pagano di Melito, across the Adriatic, a common practice to increase the range of the MAS boats. The MAS sneaked up on the Austrian steamer *Lokrum* (924 GWT) anchored in Durazzo roads and MAS 5 dispatched her with two torpedoes fired from 200 yards in the first successful MTB torpedo attack worldwide.

Lieutenant di Melito's two boats then penetrated the Albanian harbour of San Giovanni di Medua on 16 June 1916, but found no targets. Ten days later they were back off Durazzo where they sank, with one torpedo, the freighter *Sarajevo* (1,111 GWT). MAS boats forced Durazzo Roads again on the nights of 4 July, 24 July, 2 August and 3 November 1916 without further successes, although their daring raids provided good grist for the propaganda mill.

On the night of 1-2 November 1916 the mosquito fleet undertook a new penetration mission in the Fasana Channel near the main Austro-Hungariann naval base at Pola Harbour where the torpedo boat 9 *PN*, commanded

Replacing a Sterling 200hp petrol engine on MAS 25, a 'SVAN/Ansaldo' boat. (Erminio Bagnasco)

by Lt. Cdr. Domenico Cavagnari, the Regia Marina's future Chief of Staff, used lead weights to lower the boom protecting that anchorage. MAS 20 slipped through and, after almost two hours searching, torpedoed the old centre battery ship *Mars* (7,430t) believing she was a cruiser. The torpedoes failed to explode,[8] but the close call forced the Austro-Hungarian Navy to allocate more resources to harbour defence while the Regia Marina's morale was boosted by the safe recovery of the MAS by 9 *PN*, which lingered by the boom far longer than originally planned to grant the tiny motor boat and her crew a chance of survival.

After a further uneventful Durazzo trip on 25 August 1917 MAS boats tried to force Trieste on 28 August but on this occasion the Austrians were vigilant and the mission had to be cancelled.

The following month MAS boats had encounters on the night of 23-24 September, when MAS 16 fought a brief gun action with the Austrian torpedo boat 95 *F* (244t), which believed she was facing a similarly sized torpedo boat, and on 16 November when Lt. Cdr. Costanzo Ciano (appointed in July 1917 commander of the 1st MAS Flotilla of Venice) led, off Cortellazzo in the upper

An MAS of the 'Orlando 1' type ('91-102' series) running her sea trials, early 1917. (Cantiere Orlando, Leghorn)

Adriatic, a daylight charge with MAS *13* and *15* against the pre-dreadnoughts Wien and Budapest which, with an escort of ten sea-going torpedo boats, were bombarding Italian shore positions. The attack had no result, although an Italian 152mm (6in) battery hit the enemy battleships during the action.

Meanwhile, the Regia Marina was evaluating its wartime experiences and planning MAS operations more scientifically. It ingeniously introduced two 5hp electric motors aboard some boats which allowed them to creep along silently at 3.6 knots for up to ten miles. This innovation, together with an hydraulic shear on the bow (the two modifications added an additional tonne to the already overweight MTBs) allowed MAS *9* and *13*, under the command of Lt. Luigi Rizzo, to force Trieste Harbour on 10 December 1917. The boats used their shears to snip the protective hawsers, a process that required two hours. In a trip of 20 minutes they silently threaded through the harbour to their targets and inspected them at their leisure to ensure the absence of torpedo nets. MAS *9* proceeded to hit Wien with two torpedoes amidships causing the old battleship to rapidly capsize, while MAS *13*'s weapons ran past their target, Budapest, and exploded on the beach. The boats escaped at full speed and met their escorts, PN *9* and *11*, ten miles offshore.

It is relevant to note that in September 1917 an electric motor-equipped boat carrying Adm. Thaon di Revel himself scouted Trieste. The admiral wanted to verify the feasibility of the mission before ordering his men to force the harbour. Thaon di Revel's sponsorship of 'his' MAS MTBs and the strong 'band of brothers' spirit of their men soon became legendary, with the help of the press, which was glad to glorify their exploits. In the same way the characteristics of the MAS came to be exaggerated as a result of their reputation; they were credited with a speed of 30 knots even though they achieved at best 24 knots without torpedoes, which was much slower than the Austro-Hungarian sea-going torpedo boats of the 74 T, 82 F and 98 M classes.

On 10 February 1918 MAS *94*, *95* and *96* penetrated the fishing harbour of Buccari. Again they missed the merchant vessels they attacked, but newspaper articles about the raid written by the famous poet Dannunzio (a volunteer aboard MAS *96*) allowed the Italians to reap a propaganda coup.

Much more importantly from a historical point of view was the 13 May 1918 action, when Lt. Cdr. Pagano di Melito led MAS *99* and *100* against an Austro-Hungarian convoy off Durazzo, sinking the steamer Bregenz (3,905 GWT). This was the first torpedo success for the Italian MTBs on the open seas. Two days later the same boats tried to force Antivari harbour in Montenegro, but enemy gun batteries repelled the attack. A similar mission against Trieste failed that same night.

The Sinking of the Battleship Szent István

In the early morning of 10 June 1918 off the Dalmatian island of Premuda MAS *15* and *21*, under the command of Lt. Cdr. Rizzo – the same officer who had sunk Wien –

Mid-Adriatic, morning of 10 June 1918 off Premuda Island: the Austro-Hungarian battleship Szent István *sinking after being hit by torpedoes launched by* MAS 15. *(Ufficio Storico Marina Militare)*

encountered the dreadnoughts Szent István and Tegetthoff escorted by one destroyer and six sea-going torpedo boats. The Austrian battle fleet was attempting its first general action since 24 May 1915, but the endeavour ended in disaster when the Italian MTBs made a daring daylight attack. The Austrian lookouts did not sight the enemy until a torpedo slammed into the Szent István, causing the new battleship to founder two and half hours later.[9] Rizzo escaped without damage as the torpedo boat *76 T*, which pursued MAS *15*, took avoiding action after Rizzo released two depth charges in *76 T*'s path. The Habsburg ship claimed she had been unable to match the enemy's speed. As one historian noted: 'It was probably the high point of the war for the Italian navy'.[10]

The MAS boats' fame was by now widespread and the British asked for a section to mount a sneak attack against the battlecruiser Goeben inside the Dardanelles straits. The Regia Marina, which had already planned in 1917 to send a MAS flotilla to Palestinian waters to operate with the small Italian expeditionary force active there, dispatched two boats to the Aegean Sea that autumn, but the Allies signed an armistice with Turkey before the action could materialise.

MAS boats made two further penetrations of Durazzo on 8 September and 2 October 1918. A torpedo struck the enemy torpedo boat *87 F* during the second action, but the warhead did not detonate.[11] A major assault planned against Pola spearheaded by the old battleship Re Umberto, modified to ram the enemy booms and open passage to twelve MAS which would then attack the Habsburg battle fleet, was called off on 4 November 1918 due to the Austrian armistice, which was signed just before the assault ship's modifications had been completed.

As a matter of fact the MAS exploits, along with the Regia Marina's submarines, flying boats and the actions of the solitary attack craft, dominated public attention then and later, overshadowing the 24 surface engagements fought by Italian cruisers, destroyers and torpedo boats against similar Austro-Hungarian warships in the Adriatic during the 1915-1918 war. Yet, these boats were also in the public eye because they were so active and proved

A MAS 'SVAN 12t' squadron (from the left: MAS 54, 55, 56 and 57) leaving Imperia-Porto Maurizio harbour on an ASW patrol, Summer 1917. (Erminio Bagnasco)

extremely flexible weapons. MAS boats served more than 650,000 hours at sea, operating not only in the classic offensive patrol and escort roles, but also as scouts, minelayers, landing boats for commando parties and informers, in support of flying boats and small attack craft and even as fire support vessels along the coasts, the Venice lagoon, and on inland waterways. A flotilla was even active from May 1917 on Lake Garda performing

MAS 116, *a 'SVAN 19t' first batch ('115-139' series) boat in Venice awaiting sea trials, March 1918. (Erminio Bagnasco)*

many *coups de main* against the Austrian held shore.[12]

The legend of the MAS – orchestrated by the effective Italian propaganda machine of the age – arose from their victories, more spectacular and with greater public appeal than any others achieved by the Regia Marina, and their officers became the 'stars' of the navy. This phenomenon was accelerated by the skills and personality of the man who rose to command the *Ispettorato dei MAS* (which provided both training and planning for all MAS flotillas), Of these the most prominent was Captain Costanzo Ciano, father of the more famous Galeazzo Ciano, Mussolini's son-in-law and Italy's future foreign minister.[13] Ciano was an efficient self-made man, a courageous and ambitious leader and an adroit propagandist. His personality and skills soon enabled him to expand his original MAS command to include all Italian coastal ASW forces, justifying this extra fief by the ASW forces' common use of petrol engines. Most of the Regia Marina staff rightly considered this initiative a step in creating Ciano's personal 'Petrol Navy' and a springboard to his becoming chief of the whole service at a later date.

Whatever his purpose Ciano's Super Coastal Force Command was disbanded shortly after the war ended and, on 19 May 1919, Ciano resigned from the Navy even before his supporter Thaon di Revel resigned his own post on 24 November 1919. The troubled history of this Super Command, however, would have serious consequences in 1940, as we will appreciate in the second part of this study.

View from the Other Side of the Hill

For its own part the Austro-Hungarian Navy was frustrated by the initiative of Italy's MAS boats and never appreciated their faults – mainly slow speed and limited

MAS 222, an 'Orlando' second batch boat, in the 1920s. The 'Orlando' MAS, being capable of 26 knots, were slightly faster then the original 'SVAN 12t' boats. (Guido Alfano)

range. The Austrians, in fact, attributed to them imagined characteristics and even as late as the 1930s they related in official histories and memoirs that they had been unable to chase down MAS boats which were, in fact, nearly ten knots slower than the pursuer. The Habsburg navy even concluded that the MAS were armoured, as they consistently escaped in the face of intense counterfire. Overall, the Austrians proved unable to develop an adequate response to the problems presented by Italy's mosquito fleet.[14]

After pursuing a 32-knot torpedo hovercraft (the *Versuchsgleitboot*) in 1915, which proved noisy and completely unseaworthy, the Austrian answer to the MAS menace was to design and order, in December 1916, nine 26-tonne *Panzerboote* ('armoured boats', *Mb 107-115*). In a case of too little too late the first three were launched but not commissioned before the end of the war. These MTBs,

The two Isotta Fraschini L.700 engines of a '397-400' MAS. Behind them the auxiliary engine IF L.250. The sea trials of these 30t boats proved disappointing as with 1900hp they achieved no more than 28 knots. (Andrea Tani)

WARSHIP 2008

MAS 430 *cockpit: in front of the helm is the gas-engine command and the compass; above are the torpedo aiming sights.* (Guido Alfano)

MAS 426 *entering La Spezia harbour in the early 1930s. The 'SVAN 14t' boats of the '423-426' series were able, at last, to achieve a top speed of 40 knots thanks to the introduction of the new Isotta Fraschini 500hp engines which gave a 107hp/tonne power to displacement ratio.* (Erminio Bagnasco)

armed with one 66/45 gun, two machine guns and two 45cm (17.7in) bow-mounted torpedoes, had a planned speed of 24 knots, but the weight of a 40mm armour belt rendered such speeds impossible from their three 200bhp engines, as postwar trials made by the Italians with *Mb 107* confirmed. This induced the Regia Marina to deliver the boat to the Customs Service, which soon paid her off.

After ordering in Germany seven 7-tonne motor boats of the LM type (which were never delivered) the last choice of the Austro-Hungarian Navy to face Italy's coastal forces was a tiny 6.5-tonne MTB, *Gleitboot No. II*, designed to reach 33 knots and armed with a single 35cm (13.8in) torpedo. As with the *Panzerboote*, the prototype of this fast attack craft was not commissioned before the end of the war. She sailed under the Italian tricolour in November 1918, but was soon discarded being considered of little value and without any chance of further development.

The 1920s and the Search for Velocissimo

After the end of the war the Regia Marina disbanded its fast coastal force and distributed the boats among the coastal department commands on the various Italian seas. From the 1920s to the mid-1930s the total availability of the MAS force was about 30 boats, all of the attack type, as the entire ASW organisation had been dissolved as being unnecessary in time of peace.

This force was a mixed bunch of veterans (originally designed for a service life of just four years) and prototypes which reduced, of course, the general level of efficiency. This situation was not unique to Italy as other major navies (except the Soviets) did not maintain fast coastal forces during these years. In spite of a brisk business exporting MAS boats, designs and engines to the USSR, China, Romania, Sweden and Finland, the development of Italian coastal forces doctrine also languished during these years. The reasons were both psychological and technical.

Being deeply persuaded, at least since mid-1916 and the ensuing Jutland controversy, to be a young service of increasing intellectual, scientific and technical ability,

MAS 431 *in foreground at Spezia, mid-1930s. With her hydroplane one-step hull she was the test boat for the following '500' series MAS boats which adopted a higher performance hydroplane two step hull.* (Guido Alfano)

MAS 428 *during her trials in 1926. These SVAN motor gunboats were too slow and not really suited to their anticipated missions.* (Erminio Bagnasco)

growing stronger in the face of the declining British and French navies, the Regia Marina's rising stars snubbed their service's traditions of individual initiative and innovation and instead embraced Mahan's classic doctrine of Sea Power as measured by the battleship and its big guns. In such an environment the MAS service, still subdivided into the many local commands, was not a paying destination for any ambitious officer interested in future high command.

Nonetheless, Italy continued to develop the MTB concept and to improve its designs. Some ideas, like that of a radio controlled MAS, proved to be a dead end. High speed and increased seaworthiness were the two most sought-after improvements. The Adriatic Sea's extremely variable weather conditions did not permit adoption of the British solution: stepped hulls which allowed good speed on the power plants then available. Thus the development of Italy's postwar boats witnessed a series of hard-chine hulls aiming towards a craft that could achieve 40 knots. As the ideal 100hp/tonne power/displacement ratio was as yet unobtainable – at their best the engines of the 1920s gave only 75hp/tonne – the experiments (see the attached table) were long and disappointing. At last in 1927 the Navy's designers adopted in the latest prototype three of the new Isotta Fraschini Asso 500s, a 12-cylinder engine developing 500hp at 1,850rpm, instead of the prior solution of two FIAT 750hp engines.

With a displacement of 13.7 tonnes the new prototype

MAS 432, a 'Velocissimo SVAN 14t' boat, at top speed. (Guido Alfano)

A detail of the after part of MAS 432 with the new torpedo launching racks. (Erminio Bagnasco)

MAS 423, a SVAN boat of the hard chine type, exceeded the long dreamed goal by reaching 43 knots during her maiden trials in 1928, by far the highest speed obtained by an Italian MTB up to that point. Five similar boats (MAS 432-436) quickly followed, with an additional unit, MAS 437, being an experimental two-shaft Diesel prototype. In the meanwhile, however, a dark horse had entered the contest.

The new boat was a very different 16-tonne prototype called MAS 431; it was originally put forward in 1929 as a private venture by the Baglietto yard at Varazze (near Genoa) and was finally delivered in 1932. With two FIAT M900 750hp engines, 431 was, at 42 knots, faster than the SVAN products 432-436 even if her power/displacement ratio was 17hp lower. She obtained her high speed by sacrificing the normal keel and chine, hitherto a feature on all Italian MAS, for a hydroplaning one-step hull. While this adaptation gave the boat high speed and good handling, qualities believed necessary to assure safe withdrawal from an ambush zone or after an attack, it limited her ability to operate in any kind of open waters. Although two similar MAS were built for China the following year 431 remained, until the 1935 Ethiopian crisis, a lone prototype.

In parallel to these traditional designs the Regia Marina had tried since 1918 to develop a bigger fast MTB called an *autocannoniera* ('motor gun boat'). The prototypes (MAS 427-429), of about 32 tonnes, had a displacement hull and were intended for torpedo, gunnery and minelaying duties on the high seas but they proved unable, in spite of SVAN's hopes, to reach the planned speed of 30

Italian MAS boats 1914-1934

Type	Boats	Yard	Year Ordered	Year Delivered	Displacement (t)	Dimensions (m)
Group A						
SVAN 12t	1-2	SVAN	1915	1916	13	16x2.6
SVAN 12t	3-22	SVAN	1915	1916-17	11.9/12.4	16x2.6
SVAN 12t	53-62	SVAN	1916	1917	11.3/12.4	16x3
SVAN 12t	140-202	Various	1917	1918-19	12/12.9	16x2.6
SVAN 12t	319-323	SVAN	1917	1919	14.2	16x3
SVAN 12t	325-326	Picchiotti	1917	1918	13/13.6	16x3
SVAN/Ansaldo	23-52	Ansaldo	1915	1916-17	11.5	16x3
Orlando 1	91-102	Orlando	1917	1917-18	11.5/12.4	16.1x2.8
Orlando 2	218-232	Orlando	1917	1918-19	12/12.9	16.5x3
Baglietto	203-217	Baglietto	1917	1917-18	13/13.9	16x2.6
SVAN Pecoraro	324	SVAN	1917	–	12/12.8	16x3.25
Group B						
SVAN 19t 1	115-139	SVAN	1917	1918	19	18x3.2
SVAN 19t 2	233-252	Ducrot	1917	1918-19	19.4	18x3.6
Baglietto 1914	318	Baglietto	1917	1917	19.9	17.5x3.9
GROUP C						
Elco USA	63-90, 103-114, 253-302	ELCO USA	1916	1917-19	43.8	24.4x3.7
Elco Italy	303-317, 327-376	Various Italian	1917	1918-22	44.6	24.4x3.7
Group D						
Veloce Baglietto	397-400	Baglietto	1917	1920-24	30	21.2x4.2
Veloce SVAN	401-410	SVAN	1917	1923-24	28.5	22x4
Velocissimo SVAN	411-422	SVAN	1918	1919-23	22.5	18x3.6
Post War						
SVAN 14t	423-426	SVAN	1923	1928-30	13.8	16x3.25
SVAN 14t	430	SVAN	1923	1930	13.7	16x3.25
Auto cannoniera	427-429	SVAN	1923	1925-27	31.85	24x4
Baglietto 1931	431	Baglietto	1929	1932	15.9	16x3.95
Velocissimo SVAN 14t	432-436	SVAN	1929	1930-34	14.5	16x3.25
Velocissimo SVAN 19t	437	SVAN	1929	1934	19	17x3.6
Baglietto 1934	438-441	Baglietto	1933	1934-35	36.8	22.5x4.3

Displacement in tonnes, speed in knots, range in nautical miles.
Boats with two displacements show value for gun configuration followed by torpedo configuration.

knots. From 1928 the Albanian Customs Service successfully employed four similar boats, displacing 46 tonnes and with a length of 24.4 metres, rated for 17 knots and armed with machine guns; however, three further *autocannoniere* of 32 tonnes, ordered from SVAN by Turkey in 1928 and delivered in 1931, were unable to reach their designed speed of 32 knots. The penalty the Venetian enterprise had to pay as a consequence bankrupted the yard and ended its contributions to Italy's mosquito fleet.

After this incident and not discounting the ASW school's 1933 order for four 16-knot MAS (*438-441*) armed with machine guns and depth charges, inspired by the wartime ELCO boats and intended to use up the remaining stock of old American-built Standard engines, the evolution of Italy's fast MTB fleet stopped from 1931 until 1935, when the whole Mediterranean situation changed, suddenly and dramatically, in a crescendo which finally culminated in the Second World War.

Footnotes:

[1] For an account of torpedo boat development in the Royal Navy see David K Brown, 'Steam Torpedo Boats of the Royal Navy', *Warship* 2005.

[2] The original meaning of MAS is much debated as the documents of the time used, at first, both *Motobarca Armata Silurante* ('Torpedo Armed Motor Barge') and *Motobarca Armata SVAN* ('SVAN Armed Motor Barge'). In November 1915 the description officially became *Motobarca Anti Sommergibili* (MA/SB). However, *Motoscafo Anti Sommergibili* came into general use as *Motoscafo* (motor boat) was a more

Hull Type	Motors No x Type/Shafts	HP	Max Speed	Range (nm) at Speed	Gun	Torpedo	ASW
HC	2 IF L56/2	450	23	160/23	1x47mm, 1MG	removed	none
HC	2 IF L56/2	450	24	190/16	1x47mm, 2MG	2x356 or 450mm	1TT, 4-6DC
HC	2 Sterling/2 or 2 FIAT A12/2	400 480	22-25	200/20	1x47mm, 2MG	2x450mm	1TT, 4-6DC
HC	2 Sterling/2 or 2 FIAT A12/2	400 480	24-25	200/22	1x57mm, 1MG	2x450mm	1TT, 4-6DC
HC	2 Sterling/2 or 2 FIAT A12/2	400 480	26	180/26	3MG	2x450mm	1TT, 4-6DC
HC	2 Sterling/2 or 2 Fiat A12/22	400 480	23	175/22	1x57mm, 1MG	2x450mm	1TT, 4-6DC
HC	2 Sterling/2	400	22	200/22	1x47mm, 1MG	none	1TT, 4-6DC
HC	2 IF L250/2	500	26	170/24	1x47mm, 2MG	2x450mm	1TT, 2-4DC
HC	2 IF L250/2	500	26	170/24	1x57mm, 2MG	2x450mm	1TT, 2-4DC
HC	2 FIAT L56/2	480	24	200/24	1x47 or 57mm, 1MG	2x450mm	1TT, 10DC
HC	2 Sterling/2	400	>23	200/22	1x57mm, 1MG	2x450mm	1TT, 4DC
N	2 IF L250/2	500	22	300/18	1x76mm, 1MG	none	2TT, 20 DC
N	3 IF L250/2	500	21	300/18	1x76mm, 1MG	none	2TT, 20 DC
HC	4 IF L250/2	500	20	200/18	1x57mm, 1MG	none	2TT, 20 DC
N	2 Standard/2	460	17	600/17	1x76mm, 1MG	none	2TT, 10 DC
N	2 Standard/2	460	17	900/16	1x76mm, 1MG	none	2TT, 12 DC
HC	2 IF L700 +1 IF L250/3	1600+300	28	110/28	1x76mm, 1MG	4x450mm, then 2	1TT, 4DC
HC	2 IF L700 +1 IF L250/3	1600+300	27	120/27	1x76mm, 1MG	2x450mm	1TT, 4DC
HC	2 IF L700/2	1600	25	100/25	3MG	2x450mm	1TT, 4DC
HC	3 IF Asso 500/3	1500	40	127/36	2xMG	2x450mm	1TT, 6DC
HC	2xFIAT M900/2	1500	41	148/16	2xMG	2x450mm	1TT, 6DC
N	3 IF L350/3	1200	26	318/26	1x76, 2MG	2x450mm	1TT, 10DC
OS	2xFIAT M900/2	1500	41	100/40	2xMG	2x450mm	1TT, 5DC
HC	3 IF L350/3	1500	40	124/36	2xMG	2x450mm	1TT, 4DC
HC	2xFIAT V 1616/2 Diesel	1500	40	100/40	2xMG	2x450mm	1TT, 4DC
N	2xStandard/2	460	17.5	164/16	1MG	none	1TT, 5DC

Abbreviations: IF – Isotta Fraschini, MG – 6.5mm machine gun, TT – towed torpedo, DC – depth charge, HC – hard chine, N – normal, OS – one step.

3. appropriate and elegant word than Motobarca. It was only in the mid-1930s that the word 'Motoscafo' become official at last, even if the ASW role was secondary. The famous Italian poet Dannunzio – himself, at age 55, a MAS volunteer – penned in the meanwhile the MAS motto: *Memento Audere Semper*, Latin for 'Always Remember to Dare'.
3. A lone exception was the Orlando 12-tonne type, inspired by the classic SVAN MAS, but which was only 1.5 knots faster, thus not justifying the change from the standard model.
4. This solution may seem intuitive, but the German Navy maintained a sole, heavy torpedo tube for her LM class MTBs while Britain adopted a stern slide system which required a peculiar launch sequence.
5. The Austro-Hungarian submarine force consisted of coastal boats that were unable to attack the main Italian shipping route in the Western Mediterranean. During the war 27 Austro-Hungarian submarines sank 196,103 GWT of Allied and neutral shipping while 57 German submarines active in the Mediterranean sank 3,487,171 tons between 1915 and 1918. During the war Italy also pressed into ASW coastal service about 200 ex-civilian yachts, trawlers, tugs, fishing vessels, small steamers and motor boats.
6. Paul G. Halpern, *The Naval War in the Mediterranean 1914-1918* (London: Allen & Unwin, 1987), p.455.
7. The British CMBs adopted the stepped planing hull as their original engines could not develop more than 250bhp (the Royal Navy later adopted an Italian FIAT petrol engine of 275bhp on some CMBs). The Germans, using petrol engines originally developed for their airships, could not generate more than 210hp for the single motor in their LM-type MTBs ordered in 1917.
8. Defective detonators and poorly trained maintenance personnel were the biggest torpedo problems the Regia Marina faced during the Great War. Between 1915 and 1918 at least eleven Italian torpedoes impacted but failed to detonate, sparing eight Austro-Hungarian warships (a dreadnought, a destroyer, a torpedo boat, a sloop, three submarines and a harbour guard ship) and one freighter. The 1919 seizure of the Whitehead enterprise at Fiume, with its research department and well trained personnel, helped the Italian Navy quickly remedy its torpedo defects.
9. The low level of training of the main Austro-Hungarian battle force and the final collapse of that navy's morale, as demonstrated by the many mutinies that erupted in the last two years of the war, was a consequence of the situation in the upper Adriatic where the Regia Marina's initiative and ongoing guerrilla war confined the Habsburg battleships to harbour. The *Szent István* spent 94.4 percent of the war at anchor. Not counting her final mission and a lone sortie to Pago Island, she sailed only 54 times on a voyage of 45 minutes, keeping within a defended boom net barrage, to practice gunnery in the Fasana channel. On the other hand, Rizzo's role in sinking two large enemy warships demonstrated how the ingredients of skill and daring were vital to the successes enjoyed by Italy's fast coastal forces.
10. Paul G. Halpern, *The Battle of the Otranto Straits* (Bloomington, IN: Indiana University Press, 2004), p.143.
11. It was only a deferred payment. The torpedo boat 87 F become the Yugoslavian T5 and was seized by the Regia Marina in 1941, serving under Italian colours with the same name. She was then transferred, in December, 1943 to the Royal Navy which handed her back to the small Yugoslavian fleet.
12. The Italian small attack craft of the First World War, from the climbing boats of the *Grillo* class, one of which tried on the night of 13 May 1918 to force Pola, to the semi-submersible '*Mignatta*', which sank on Halloween night 1918 the Austro-Hungarian dreadnought *Viribus Unitis*, were conceived and manned by the Venice MAS command under the direct supervision of Thaon di Revel who, even when again appointed chief of staff on 9 February 1917, had saved for himself his former Upper Adriatic Command which he had held since 12 October 1915.
13. Before that day Costanzo Ciano had penetrated the Austrian harbour of Parenzo on 12 June 1916 with the destroyer *Zeffiro* and the torpedo boats 40 PN and 46 OS, shelling the local flying boat station and seizing some PoWs.
14. Twelve MAS were lost during the war, mostly by accidents caused by their dangerous petrol engines. Only MAS 16 fell to enemy shore fire in the River Piave on 14 December 1917. Before the Austrians could survey the wreck, however, the Italians were able to float and recover the hull. The Austro-Hungarian desire to study those unpredictable boats induced them to land, on the night of 5 April 1918, a party near Ancona to seize a MAS. This attempt failed and all the raiding sailors were captured.

Sources:

Andriola, Fabio. *Luigi Rizzo*. Rome: ed. Ufficio Storico della Marina Militare, 2000.

Bagnasco, Erminio. *I MAS e le motosiluranti italiane*. Volume I: *MAS e mezzi d'assalto italiani* and Volume II *Unità veloci costiere italiane*: Rome: Ufficio Storico Marina Militare, 1967; second edition 1969; third edition 1996-1998.

—. *Le motosiluranti della seconda guerra mondiale*. Parma: Alberelli, 1977.

—. 'Lo sviluppo e l'impiego dei MAS nella prima guerra mondiale', *Rivista Marittima*, June 1965.

Bagnasco, Erminio and Enrico Cernuschi, 'Antisom' part one, *STORIA militare*, June 2001.

Bagnasco, Erminio and Achille Rastelli, *Navi e marinai italiani nella Grande Guerra*. Parma: Alberelli, 1997.

Chiggiato, Artù. 'Le pirobarche di cento anni fa', *Rivista Marittima*, marzo 1980.

—. 'Il cantiere 'S.V.A.N.' di Venezia, ricordi di un cantiere scomparso', *Rivista Marittima*, April, 1979.

Ferrante, Ezio. *Il Grande Ammiraglio Paolo Thaon di Revel*. 'Rivista Marittima' Supplement. August/September 1989.

Fraccaroli, Aldo. *Italian Warships of World War One*. London: Ian Allan, 1970.

—. 'Osarono sempre', *Storia Illustrata*. August, 1974.

Halpern, Paul G. *The Battle of the Otranto Straits: Controlling the Gateway to the Adriatic in WWI*. Bloomington, IN: Indiana University Press, 2004.

—. *A Naval History of World War I*. Annapolis: Naval Institute Press, 1994.

—. *The Naval War in the Mediterranean*. London: Allen & Unwin, 1987.

Rastelli, Achille and Alessandro Massignani, ed. *La guerra navale 1914-1918*. Valdagno: Gino Rossato, 2002.

Santini, Aldo. *Costanzo Ciano*. Milan: Camunia, 1993.

Sokol, Hans. *La guerra marittima dell'Austria-Ungheria*. Rome: Istituto Poligrafico dello Stato, 1931-1934.

THE SOVIET PROJECT 7/7U DESTROYERS

The destroyers of the Project 7 and Project 7U classes were the workhorses of the Soviet Navy during the Second World War. However, the design was seriously flawed, being adapted from Italian destroyers intended to serve in a less demanding environment. **Vladimir Yakubov** and **Richard Worth** tell their story.

The Russians went into the First World War with shipyards busily engaged on a promising set of projects. They came out of the First World War, and the subsequent domestic mess, with their economy in distress, their heavy industry in shambles, and their building programmes in disarray. Yet a remnant of the promising classes survived.

The *Novik* class raised the bar for destroyers around the world: robust ships, fast and heavily armed. The programme began with the name ship commissioned in 1913 and plans for 65 half-sisters to follow, but after cancellations and war casualties and wrecks, only seventeen units survived to give service in the Soviet era. Respectable ships by 1913 standards, they seemed less so after their first decade, and their limited numbers meant sketchy coverage in the Baltic and Black Seas, to say nothing of the Arctic and Far East. With this obvious need for a new destroyer programme, the specifics of design and timetable remained at the discretion of the leadership, a group devoted to strong-armed optimism.

Throughout the interwar years, the disparity between the planners' ideals and actual industrial capacity resulted in a succession of grand expectations and stifling reality. The first destroyer project fitted this model. Allowing themselves no baby-steps, the Soviets fixed their eyes on France's powerful *contre-torpilleurs* and opted for a similarly ambitious design, the *Leningrad*-class flotilla leaders. Compounding the challenge, the design bureaucracy underwent a thorough reshuffling at precisely this time. The flotilla leader began at the Scientific-Technical Committee before transferring to V. A. Nikitin at the newly formed Central Shipbuilding Design Bureau. Nikitin had first-hand experience with destroyers, having overseen the refurbishment of *Yakov Sverdlov* (ex-*Novik*) in 1927. At that time, it was noticed that *Novik*'s original draught markings had been painted 200mm too high on the hull, perhaps in a deliberate attempt to conceal overweight. Nikitin would eventually have his own adventure with destroyer overweight, too severe for paint to disguise.

Working with P. O. Trakhtenberg, Nikitin proved unable to redeem the *Leningrad* project from mismanagement and industrial overreach. The name ship was launched in 1933, a year before turbine production became established and three years before the 130mm/50 gun was accepted into service. Delayed also by the need to replace defective components, the ships averaged about five years' construction time. Nevertheless, the *Leningrads* succeeded in topping their 40-knot specification, which put them roughly 10 knots above the speed of the *Noviks* they were nominally intended to lead.

The Italian Connection

Ruminations on a new type to follow the *Leningrad* leaders coalesced by 1931 into a pair of 40-knot designs of 1300-1400 tonnes which differed mostly in their machinery arrangements. The following year, with *Leningrad* construction underway, designers could focus on this *Novik* replacement, a design more homogeneous with *Leningrad* in speed and in weaponry and, as things turned out, with a similarly tortuous gestation. The effort began with a commonsensical attempt to get assistance from the experienced professionals in Italy. In March 1932, Nikitin and other Soviet specialists under K. I. Dushenov, a key proponent of the *jeune école*, ventured to Italy where they had the opportunity to see various *jeune école* ships including destroyers: *Dardo* of the *Freccia* class and *Baleno* of the *Folgore* class. The visit proved fruitful. Among the successes was an Italian agreement to provide drawings of the *Folgore*. Adapted to meet Soviet specifications, the new design began to take shape under Nikitin's watchful gaze. (Nikitin had many responsibilities, including sorting out the problems with the *Leningrads*, and Trakhtenberg performed much of the work.) Italian assistance continued in the form of tank tests using wooden models (which, the Italians noted, were less likely to deform than the Soviets' paraffin wax models). The end product would be a unique Soviet variation on the original, but much attention would come to focus on two very Italian features.

In planning the hull structure, Soviet designers adopted a combination of framing plans like that used by the Italians, with longitudinal framing amidships and transverse framing at the ends. This gained the benefits of both structural systems but necessitated great diligence in designing the transitional zones fore and aft. In using a Mediterranean ship as a model, the Soviets accepted the challenge of adapting it for harsher environments.

Leningrad had her machinery arranged in the unit system of alternating boiler and engine compartments, which enhanced the ship's survivability by reducing the chance of a single hit disabling both engines or all the boilers. *Folgore* had the more conventional arrangement with the boiler rooms ahead of the two engine rooms. The earliest studies for Project 7 considered both these machinery options, and the Soviets eventually chose the Italian example as being less technically demanding with

Table 1: Gnevnyi class (Project 7)

Ship	Builder	Assembled	Laid down	Re-Laid	Launched	Completed	Planned completion
Gnevnyi	#190 Zhdanov Yard (L)	–	8 Dec 35	–	13 Jul 36	23 Dec 38	1937
Groznyi	#190 Zhdanov Yard, (L)	–	21 Dec 35	–	31 Jul 36	9 Dec 38	1937
Gromkiy	#190 Zhdanov Yard, (L)	–	29 Apr 36	–	6 Dec 37	31 Dec 38	1937
Gordyi	#190 Zhdanov Yard (L)	–	25 Jun 36	–	10 Jun 37	23 Dec 38	1937
Gremyashchiy	#190 Zhdanov Yard (L)	–	23 Jul 36	–	12 Aug 37	28 Aug 38	1937
Steregushchiy	#190 Zhdanov Yard (L)	–	12 Aug 36	–	18 Jan 38	30 Oct 39	1937
Grozyashchiy	#190 Zhdanov Yard (L)	#189 Ordzhonikidze Yard (L)	18 Jun 36	–	5 Jan 37	17 Sep 39	1937
Stremitel'nyi	#189 Ordzhonikidze Yard (L)	–	22 Aug 36	–	4 Feb 37	18 Nov 38	1937
Sokrushitel'nyi	#189 Ordzhonikidze Yard (L)	–	29 Oct 36	–	23 Aug 37	13 Aug 39	1937
Smetlivyi	#189 Ordzhonikidze Yard (L)	–	17 Sep 36	–	16 Jul 37	6 Nov 38	1938
Lovkii	#189 Ordzhonikidze Yard (L)	–	17 Sep 36	–	–	–	1938
Legkii	#189 Ordzhonikidze Yard (L)	–	16 Oct 36	–	–	–	1938
Bodryi	#198 Marti Factory (N)	–	31 Dec 35	–	1 Aug 36	6 Nov 38	1937
Bystryi	#198 Marti Factory (N)	–	17 Apr 36	–	5 Nov 36	7 Mar 39	1937
Boykiy	#198 Marti Factory (N)	–	17 Apr 36	–	29 Oct 36	9 Mar 39	1937
Besposhchadnyi	#198 Marti Factory (N)	–	15 May 36	–	5 Dec 36	2 Oct 39	1937
Bezuprechnyi	#200 61 Kommunar (N)	–	23 Aug 36	–	25 Jun 37	2 Oct 39	1937
Bditel'nyi	#200 61 Kommunar (N)	–	23 Aug 36	–	29 Jun 37	22 Oct 39	1937
Burnyi	#200 61 Kommunar (N)	–	17 Aug 36	–	–	–	1938
Boevoy	#200 61 Kommunar (N)	–	17 Aug 36	–	–	–	1938
Pronzitel'nyi	#200 61 Kommunar (N)	–	15 Oct 36	–	–	–	1938
Porazhayuschiy	#200 61 Kommunar (N)	–	25 Dec 36	–	–	–	1938
Rezvyi	#198 Marti Factory (N)	#202 Voroshilov Factory (V)	5 Nov 35	23 Aug 36	24 Sep 37	24 Jan 40	1937
Reshitelnyi (i)	#198 Marti Factory (N)	#199 Amurski Shipyard (K)	5 Nov 35	20 Sep 36	18 Oct 37	–	1937
Rastoropnyi	#198 Marti Factory (N)	#199 Amurski Shipyard (K)	27 Feb 36	5 Nov 36	25 Jun 38	5 Jan 40	1937
Razyashchiy	#198 Marti Factory (N)	#202 Voroshilov Factory (V)	27 Feb 36	15 Nov 36	24 Mar 38	20 Dec 40	1937
R'yanyi	#198 Marti Factory (N)	#202 Voroshilov Factory (V)	31 Dec 35	18 Sep 36	31 May 37	11 Aug 39	1937
Rezkiy	#198 Marti Factory (N)	#202 Voroshilov Factory (V)	5 May 36	20 Aug 38	29 Apr 40	16 Aug 42	1937
Retivyi	#198 Marti Factory (N)	#199 Amurski Shipyard (K)	23 Aug 36	29 Jul 37	27 Sep 39	10 Oct 41	1938
Reshitelnyi (ii) (ex-*Pospeshnyi*)	#198 Marti Factory (N)	#199 Amurski Shipyard (K)	23 Aug 36	23 Aug 37	30 Apr 40	5 Sep 41	1938
Revnostnyi (ex-*Provornyi*)	#198 Marti Factory (N)	#199 Amurski Shipyard (K)	23 Aug 36	17 Sep 37	22 May 41	14 Dec 41	1938
Raz'yaryonnyi (ex-*Peredovoy*, ex-*Razvitoy*)	#198 Marti Factory (N)	#199 Amurski Shipyard (K)	15 Sep 36	17 Sep 37	22 May 41	14 Dec 41	1938
Rekordnyi (ex-*Prytkiy*)	#198 Marti Factory (N)	#202 Voroshilov Factory (V)	25 Sep 36	July 1937	6 Apr 39	9 Jan 41	1938
Redkiy (ex-*Pylkiy*)	#198 Marti Factory (N)	#199 Amurski Shipyard (K)	28 Sep 36	17 Nov 38	28 Sep 41	29 Nov 42	1938
Razumnyi (ex-*Prochnyi*)	#200 61 Kommunar (N)	#202 Voroshilov Factory (V)	7 Jul 36	16 Aug 37	30 Jun 39	7 Nov 41	1938

Key:
(L) Leningrad   (N) Nikolayev   (V) Vladivostok   (K) Komsomol'sk-an-Amur

the additional advantage of lower weight.

Other features were pure Soviet. While *Folgore* had a concentrated armament of two twin 120mm mountings totaling 40 tonnes, Project 7 had four 130mm singles adding up to 51 tonnes, not to mention a pair of 76mm anti-aircraft guns. The stern design, a squared form which was also a feature of the *Leningrads*, facilitated minelaying. Technical plans were finalised on 21 December 1934.

Characteristics (GNEVNYI AS COMPLETED, 1938)

Displacement:	1425/1612 tonnes standard (designed/completed), 1955/2039 tonnes full (designed/completed)
Dimensions:	112.8m oa x 10.2m x 4.8m
Machinery:	three boilers, 2-shaft Kharkov GTZA-24 geared turbines, 50,500shp = 38.33 knots (39.37 knots reached at trials)
Bunkerage:	126 tonnes normal, 252 tonnes full, 518.8 tonnes maximum, range 2640nm at 19.83 knots
Armament:	four 130mm/50 B-13 guns with 150 rounds per gun (including 5 ready rounds per gun), 175 overload
	two 76mm/55 34-K dual-purpose guns with 300 rounds per gun (including 84 ready rounds per gun), 350 overload
	two 45mm/46 21-K anti-aircraft guns with 500 rounds per gun (including 180 ready rounds per gun), 660 overload
	two 12.7mm DShK or DK machine guns
	six 533mm 53-38 torpedoes in two triple 39-Yu mounts (plus six reloads)
	60 Model KB-3 mines or 65 Model 1926 mines or 95 Model 1912 mines
	two depth charge racks with ten BB-1 and fifteen BM-1 depth charges
Complement:	197 peacetime, 236 wartime

Table 2: STOROZHEVOI CLASS (PROJECT 7U)

Ship	Builder	Laid down	Re-laid	Launched	Completed
Storozhevoi	#190 Zhdanov Yard (L)	26 Aug 36	Jan 38	2 Oct 38	6 Oct 40
Sil'nyi	#190 Zhdanov Yard (L)	26 Oct 36	Jan 38	1 Nov 38	31 Oct 40
Surovyi (ex-*Letuchiy*)	#189 Ordzhonikidze Yard (L)	27 Oct 36	1 Feb 39	5 Aug 39	31 May 41
Serdityi (ex-*Likhoy*)	#189 Ordzhonikidze Yard (L)	27 Oct 36	15 Oct 38	21 Apr 39	15 Oct 40
Smelyi	#190 Zhdanov Yard (L)	26 Oct 36	Mar 38	30 Apr 39	31 May 41
Stoikiy	#190 Zhdanov Yard (L)	26 Aug 36	Mar 38	26 Dec 38	18 Oct 40
Slavnyi	#189 Ordzhonikidze Yard (L)	31 Aug 36	31 Jan 39	19 Sep 39	31 May 41
Strashnyi	#190 Zhdanov Yard (L)	26 Aug 36	Mar 38	8 Apr 39	22 Jun 41
Skoryi	#190 Zhdanov Yard (L)	29 Nov 36	23 Oct 38	24 Jul 39	1 Aug 41
Statnyi	#190 Zhdanov Yard (L)	26 Dec 36	29 Dec 38	24 Nov 39	18 Jul 41
Svirepyi	#190 Zhdanov Yard (L)	29 Nov 36	30 Dec 38	28 Aug 39	18 Jul 41
Strogiy	#190 Zhdanov Yard (L)	26 Oct 36	26 Oct 38	31 Dec 39	22 Sep 42
Stroynyi	#190 Zhdanov Yard (L)	26 Dec 36	29 Dec 38	29 Apr 40	22 Sep 42
Smyshlennyi (ex-*Poleznyi*)	#200 61 Kommunar (N)	15 Oct 36	27 Jun 38	26 Aug 39	10 Nov 40
Soobrazitel'nyi (ex-*Prozorlivyi*)	#200 61 Kommunar (N)	15 Oct 36	3 Mar 39	26 Aug 39	7 Jun 41
Sposobnyi (ex-*Podvizhyi*)	#200 61 Kommunar (N)	7 Jul 36	7 Mar 39	30 Sep 39	24 Jun 41
Svobodnyi (ex-*Besshumnyi*)	#200 61 Kommunar (N)	23 Aug 36	1938	25 Feb 39	2 Jan 42
Sovershennyi (ex-*Besstrashyi*)	#200 61 Kommunar (N)	17 Sep 36	1938	25 Feb 39	30 Sep 41

Characteristics (STOROZHEVOI AS COMPLETED, 1941)

Displacement:	1686/1727 tonnes standard (designed/completed), 2246/2279 tonnes full (designed/completed)
Dimensions:	112.5m oa x 10.2m x 3.98m
Machinery:	four watertube boilers, Kharkov GTZA-24 geared turbines, 54,000shp = 40.28 knots
Bunkerage:	207 tonnes normal, 337 tonnes full, 510 tonnes maximum, 2700nm at 19 knots
Armament:	four 130mm/50 B-13 guns with 150 rounds per gun (including 5 ready rounds per gun), 190 overload
	two 76mm/55 34-K dual-purpose guns with 300 rounds per gun (including 58 ready rounds per gun), 340 overload
	three 45mm/46 21-K anti-aircraft guns with 500 rounds per gun (including 180 ready rounds per gun), 660 overload
	four 12.7mm DShK or DK machine guns
	six 533mm 53-38 torpedoes in two triple 1-N mounts
	58 KB mines or 62 Model 1926 mines or 96 Model 1912 mines
	two depth charge racks with ten BB-1 and twenty BM-1 depth charges
Complement:	207 peacetime, 271 wartime

Silhouettes offer a clear distinction between the single-funnel Project 7 (left) and the two-funnel Project 7U. (Boris Lemachko Collection lemachko@mtu-net.ru)

Construction of the Project 7, also known as the *Gnevnyi* class, began under the 1933-1938 Naval Shipbuilding Programme with plans eventually totaling fifty-three units scheduled for completion in 1937-38. At that time, the *Novik*s would redeploy to the Northern Fleet while the *Gnevnyi*s took over in the more 'active' sectors: 21 in the Baltic, 10 in the Black Sea, and 22 in the Pacific. Construction began at two Baltic shipyards and two Black Sea yards. It appears that all these units began construction, though not all would reach completion:

Zhdanov, Leningrad:	17 units
Ordzhonikidze, Leningrad:	8 units
61 Kommunar, Nikolayev:	12 units
Marti, Nikolayev:	16 units

Twelve Marti units were transported in sections by rail to Far East yards for assembly. When a storm drove one of these ships, *Reshitelnyi*, onto the rocks before commissioning, *Razumnyi* was sent as a substitute.

Project Problems

Anyone familiar with the difficulties experienced in the *Leningrad* project, which comprised just six ships, should have anticipated the problems with Project 7. Weight calculations fell well short of reality. Turbine production imposed delays, and none of the scheduled 1937 completions materialised. While the project struggled forward in the face of the limitations of Soviet industry, Stalin himself stepped in to make matters worse.

On 13 May 1937, the Spanish Civil War was less than a year old when a British destroyer patrolling off Almería, HMS *Hunter*, triggered an underwater explosive that left her dead in the water. Days later and thousands of miles away, this event worked its way into the conversation at a Council of Labour and Defence meeting presided over by Stalin, and it dredged up the old question of machinery dispersal. One official remarked that large ships warranted such protection while humbler ships like destroyers were expendable. Stalin was shocked, shocked to find such personal insensitivity in the Soviet leadership.

So it came to pass that Stalin's delicate soul finally settled the technical debate on propulsion layout. This raised doubts about the Project 7 hulls, none of which had reached completion at that point. Their prospects looked poor through August – most probably, all but a few units would be swept up in rampant scrapping – but with the help of a new proposal, Project 7 survived in fairly good shape. The units farthest along would continue to completion. Only six nascent hulls were broken up and cancelled, and the remaining eighteen would be re-laid to a new design with machinery in the unit arrangement. This was Project 7U (U = *Uluchshennyi*, improved).

The episode created more casualties than just six scrapped hulls. Project 7 earned the dreaded 'wrecking' label, a buzzword for obstruction to Soviet progress. Nikitin, who claimed to have supported unit machinery from the start, emerged from it all with body and career intact. However, Trakhtenberg came to an unhappy end around this time; details remain unclear.

The imposing task of squeezing the unit system into a hull with minimal alterations fell into the hands of O. F. Yakob, who hammered out a successful solution quickly enough for construction to resume the following January. All eighteen *Storozhevoi*s reached completion, even those still building at the start of Operation Barbarossa.

Did the switch justify the effort? Certainly not. In wartime, *Slavnyi* became the sole example of a ship whose unit machinery layout saved her from power loss after battle damage, while the design detour effectively 'sank' six Project 7 hulls outright and delayed the completion of eighteen subsequent units. (The extent of delay is difficult to assess, given the pre-existing turbine shortage.) After costing uncounted man-hours in shipyards and design offices, Project 7U increased the pricetag: 21-28 million rubles per Project 7 unit, but 33 million for the improved version. The claim of improvement is itself spurious; Project 7U was a design of generally lesser capability. Yakob's finest efforts could not provide machinery dispersal without sacrifices in other areas. Crew accommodations shrank, operational radius declined, and weight calculations veered into unreality.

Gnevnyi herself had turned out more than 10% overweight, and though it was understood that *Storozhevoi* would incur further weight gain in her conversion, designers anticipated a 60-tonne increase rather than the hundreds of tonnes it eventually became. Much of the excess took the form of topweight, so the expected reduction in stability – an 11% cut in metacentric height – became 30%. Given that the Project 7 design had deliberately sacrificed *Novik* standards of stability even before its overweight became clear, the Project 7U mistakes had alarming ramifications.

A formal investigation began in summer 1940 with intensive recalculation of weights and minutely scrutinised inclining experiments. World events eventually truncated the process, but designers understood enough to calculate solid ballasting for the ships, with 89 to 126 tonnes being fitted. Operations would always require a close eye on fuel oil bunkerage, more so as war service added weight to the already overloaded ships.

And still this was not the end of the problems for the Project 7/7U destroyers. Service during the Winter War had revealed deficiencies in the hull structure, and the 1940 weight investigation had looked also into this issue. This led to some units receiving reinforcement to their bows, a partial solution that overlooked half the problem.

In May 1942, *Gromkiy* ran into a Force 8 storm while returning from a bombardment mission in the Arctic. Heavy seas snapped her bow, almost removing it, and only strenuous effort by captain and crew brought her safely home. *Sokrushitel'nyi* had less luck: the following November, Arctic seas tore off her stern; crippled, she sank. It is no surprise that the Northern Fleet commander stated outright his preference for *Noviks* over modern ships.

The misgivings of those who hesitated to model a Soviet ship on a Mediterranean design had unhappy vindication. The issue was not hull strength in general, a matter the Soviets understood; for example, in adapting Italian cruiser design, they reduced the gap between transverse frames by 34%. However, the inherent discontinuity in areas where longitudinal and transverse framing came together necessitated extreme care in detail design. The record of battle damage shows that the Project 7/7U ships did not simply crumple when roughly handled; out of twenty instances of underwater damage, eleven ships survived. *Besposhchadnyi*'s experience is instructive: operating near Odessa on 22 September 1941, she underwent attack by 22 Stukas dropping dozens of bombs. A near miss deformed her plating and caused leakage between the after gun mountings – precisely the point at which *Sokrushitel'nyi* broke apart. Two bombs hit the bow, one exploding on board and the other passing through to explode in the water nearby. The bow split, not quite separating, and a severe trim had water lapping at the foremost gun mount. Yet *Besposhchadnyi*'s hull held together, and she withdrew under her own power.

Weaponry

All the modern Soviet destroyers in the Second World War carried the 130mm/50 gun, a weapon that attempted to emulate the performance of the old 130mm/55 gun using a shorter barrel – an ambitious goal. The ensuing technical problems delayed introduction of the gun until 1936, mere months before *Leningrad*'s completion. Problems with the gun, which included rapid barrel erosion, prompted a frenzy of remedial measures and several variant fixes. In the end the gun served well enough, though with some logistical and operational complications due to the variants. Table 3 gives data for the 130mm/50 and a comparison with the longer gun.

The new main battery represented the most important

Table 3: 130mm GUN PERFORMANCE

Gun	Ammunition	Shell weight (kg)	Velocity (m/s)	Range (m)
130mm/55	Semi-AP Model 1928	33.5	861	18,656 (20°)
Firing cycle: 7.5-12 sec.	HE Model 1928 OF-054	33.4	861	22,314
Elevation limits: -8° to +30°	Shrapnel	29.2	890	16,827
Loading angle: any	Diving	33.15	237.7	3110
	Distance Grenade[1]	33.4	861	22,314
	Illumination C-072	34.3	675	10,608 (22°)
130mm/50 B-13	Semi-AP Model 1928 PB-46	33.4	870	25,731
(with small grooving)	HE Model 1928 OF-46	33.4	870	25,731
Firing cycle: 6-10 sec.	Distance 3S-46	33.4	870	22,314
Elevation limits: -5° to +45°	Diving	33.15	237.7	3200
Loading angle: any	Illumination SP-46	34.5	675	10,608
(with ANIMI liner)	Semi-AP Model 1928 PB-46	33.4	870	25,515
(with NII-13 liner)	Semi-AP Model 1928 PB-46	33.4	870	25,597
	HE Model 1928 OF-46	33.4	870	25,597
	Distance 3S-46	33.4	870	22,314
	Diving	33.15	238	3110
	Illumination SP-46		675	
	Anti-radar RP-42/46		750	

[1] An anti-aircraft shell set to detonate at a certain distance.

Table 4: Radar fits of the Project 7/7U destroyers at the end of the war

Ship	Air-detection radar	Fire-control radar
Gromkiy	Gyuys-1	–
Gremyashchiy	Type 286M	–
Bodryi	Type 286	Type 284
Rezvyi	Type 291	–
Rastoropnyi	Type 291	–
Razyashchiy	Type 291	–
Rezkiy	Type 291	–
Retivyi	Type 291	–
Reshitelnyi	Type 291	–
Raz'yaryonnyi	SF-1	–
Rekordnyi	Type 291	–
Redkiy	Type 291	–
Razumnyi	SL	–
Boykiy	Type 286	–
Groznyi	SF-1	–
R'yanyi	Gyuys-1	–
Vitse-Admiral Drozd	Type 291	Type 284
Slavnyi	Type 291	–
Strashnyi	Type 291	–
Sil'nyi	Type 291	Type 284
Strogiy	Gyuys-1	–
Soobrazitel'nyi	Type 291	–

advance on the *Novik* design. The 130mm gun nearly doubled *Novik*'s 17.5kg shell weight and added almost 10km of range, greatly improving performance in the primary wartime duty of Soviet naval artillery, bombardment of German troops. The Mina-7 fire-control system, advanced by destroyer standards, derived from Italy's Galileo system. It included a TsAS-2 computer, a KDP_2-4 director with two DM-4 4-metre stereoscopic rangefinders, and two 1-N night viewfinders. The computer could manage target speeds of 40 knots to a range of 27,300m, engaging multiple enemies by day or night, and calculating for intermittently visible targets.

At the beginning of the war, the Soviet Union lagged behind other navies in electronics; only one ship carried radar, the cruiser *Molotov*. No other ship acquired radar until the beginning of Lend-Lease. Project 7/7U destroyers started receiving their sets in 1942. By war's end, all remaining units received air-detection radars, mostly British Type 291. Fire-control radar remained a rarity.

As was the case in most navies in the 1930s, the leadership failed to appreciate the aviation threat and the difficulty in shooting down aircraft. No attempt was made to provide dual-purpose mountings for destroyer main batteries, but from the start, Project 7 included an intermediate anti-aircraft calibre rather than relying on the small, fast-firing cannon. Never shy about innovation, the Soviets tried to develop an automatic 37mm gun in the

Table 5: Anti-aircraft Guns

Gun	Ammunition	Shell weight (kg)	Velocity (m/s)	Range (m)
76mm/55 34-K				
Firing cycle: 3-4 seconds	Distance O-361D	11.5	810	8970
Elevation limits: -5° to +85°	HE-Frag O-361K	11.9	801	14,640[1]
	Shrapnel Sh-361	11.5	813	8600[1]
	AP BP-361	11.5	816	4000[2]

[1] With time fuze.
[2] Maximum range for armor penetration.
All shells had a ballistic ceiling of 9300m, cut to 8000m by time fuzing, and 6500m was considered the effective limit.

45mm/46.1 21-K				
Rate of fire: 25-30 rpm	Frag-tracer OT-033	1.065	880	
Elevation limits: -10° to +85°	Frag-tracer OP-73A	1.41	760	9200
	HE O-240	2.14	335	5000

Based on an army anti-tank gun, this was a hand-loaded, single-shot weapon of the sort common in various navies of the late 1930s. For the most part, it was replaced by the 37mm gun by the middle of the war.

37mm/74 70-K				
Rate of fire: 160-180 rpm	Frag-tracer	0.732	880	4000[3]
Elevation limits: -10° to +85°	AP-tracer	0.758	880	4000[3]

[3] Ballistic range was 8400m, but rounds self-destructed at 4000m. Effective ceiling was 4000m.
A major improvement over the 45mm, this was developed from a Bofors 25mm design.

12.7mm/79 DShK				
Rate of fire: 600 rpm cyclic	AP-incendiary B-32	0.134	830	5400
Elevation limits: -34 to +85	AP Model 1930 B-30	0.124	850	5400

The gun gave a realistic 125rpm rate of fire. Effective range was 3500m, or 2500m against aircraft. Early in the war, some units mounted the DK, an early magazine-fed version of the DShK with a cyclic rate of 360 rpm; it went out of production in 1935.

Table 6: Changes in Project 7 Anti-aircraft Batteries

Unit	Year	Anti-aircraft outfit
All ships as built	to summer 1941	two 76mm/55 34-K, two 45mm/46 21-K, two 12.7mm DK (2xI)
All Northern Fleet ships	1942-45	two 76mm/55 34-K, three 37mm/74 70-K, six 12.7mm Colt-Browning (2xII) and DShK (2xI)
Groznyi	1943	two 76mm/55 34-K, four 37mm/74 70-K (six in 1944), six 12.7mm Colt-Browning (2xII) and DK (2xI)
Grozyashchiy	1943	three 76mm/55 34-K, four 37mm/74 70-K (six in 1944), six 12.7mm DK (2xI) and Vickers (1xIV)
Bodryi, Boykiy, Besposhchadnyi	1943-1945	two 76mm/55 34-K, five 37mm/74 70-K, six 12.7mm Colt-Browning (2xII) and DShK (2xI)
Rezvyi	1945	two 76mm/55 34-K, four 37mm/74 70-K, four 12.7mm DShK (4xI)
R'yanyi	1945	two 76mm/55 34-K, four 37mm/74 70-K, three 12.7mm DShK (4xI)
Post-war modernization	1950s	eight 37mm/74 V-11 (4xII)

Table 7: Changes in Project 7U anti-aircraft batteries

Unit	Year	Anti-aircraft outfit
All ships as built	to summer 1941	two 76mm/55 34-K, three 45mm/46 21-K, four 12.7mm DK (4xI)
All Baltic Fleet ships	1944-45	three 76mm/55 34-K, six 37mm/74 70-K, four 12.7mm DShK (4xI)
Sil'nyi	1942	two 76mm/55 34-K, five 37mm/74 70-K, two 20mm Oerlikons, eight 12.7mm Vickers (1xIV) and DK (4xI)
Svirepyi	1943	three 76mm/55 34-K, two 45mm/46 21-K, two 37mm/74 70-K, seven 12.7mm Colt-Browning (2xII) and DShK (3xI)
Soobrazitel'nyi, Sposobnyi	1943	two 76mm/55 34-K, seven 37mm/74 70-K, eight 12.7mm Colt-Browning (2xII) and DK (4xI)
Storozhevoi	1944	three 76mm/55 34-K, two 45mm/46 21-K, four 37mm/74 70-K, four 12.7mm DShK (4xI)
Soobrazitel'nyi	1947	eight 37mm/74 70-K, twelve 12.7mm Colt-Browning (6xII)
Post-war modernization	1950s	eight 37mm/74 V-11 (4xII)

early 1930s, but the project flopped; an order for fifty guns ended with only five completed and none accepted by the navy. Consequently, the Navy went to war depending on a converted 45mm anti-tank gun firing a contact-fuzed shell. Only in 1941 did production of the Swedish-type 37mm 70-K cannon give the fleet an effective weapon, and the mass rearming of the ships went on until the end of the 1942.

Apart from the homegrown weaponry, Lend-Lease provided standard Western arms like the 20mm Oerlikon cannon and 0.50-calibre machine guns (Vickers and Colt-Browning). The destroyers continued to mount machine guns as anti-aircraft weapons to the end of the war.

Anti-aircraft fire control was a problematic area for the Project 7/7U ships. Each mounted a DM-3 3-metre rangefinder – abaft the second torpedo mount in Project 7, forward of the mount in Project 7U – but a fully integrated system never materialised. The Soyuz system for the 76mm battery appeared just before the war, but multiple production problems delayed its deployment so that few units received it: *Svobodnyi*, *Sposobnyi*, *Storozhevoi*, *Strogiy*, perhaps *Skoryi* and *Statnyi*. The system included a computer similar to the main TsAS-2, a Gazon vertical gyroscope, and an SVP-29 stabilised viewfinder. It sufficed against level bombers but was useless against dive-bombers. The smaller-calibre guns always operated under local control.

All the torpedoes (see Table 8) were wet-heater types. The 53-27 went out of production in 1935. The 53-38 and 53-38U, based on an Italian torpedo purchased in 1932, became the predominant wartime models. The 53-39 had only limited production. The Soviets used TNT, perhaps mixed with HND or tetryl to gain a slight boost in destructiveness. The torpedoes had no independent fire control but relied on the ship's main system. All Soviet flotilla craft were fitted with mine rails. The types of mine carried are listed in Table 9.

The depth charges carried are listed in Table 10. These were the standard Soviet wartime types, and both used TNT as their explosive; additional depth charges became available via Lend-Lease. Each ship had two lever racks, each carrying ten BB-1's while twelve BM-1's were stored in a magazine and eight on ready racks. During the war, each ship received two BMB-1 launchers capable of firing a BB-1 up to 110m.

No Soviet ship carried an active sonar at the start of the

Table 8: TORPEDOES

Torpedo	Weight (kg)	Length (m)	Explosive (kg)	Range settings
53.3cm 53-27	1710	7.0	265	3700m at 45 knots
53.3cm 53-38	1615	7.2	300	4000m at 44.5 knots, 8000m at 34.5 knots, 10,000m at 30.5 knots
53.3cm 53-38U	1725	7.4	400	4000m at 44.5 knots, 8000m at 34.5 knots, 10,000m at 30.5 knots
53.3cm 53-39	1780	7.5	317	4000m at 51 knots, 8000m at 39 knots, 10,000m at 34 knots

Table 9: MINES

Mine	Type	Fuze	Maximum depth (m)	Weight (kg)	Explosive (kg)
Model 1912 (M-12)	moored contact	percussion mechanical	130	600	100
Model 1926 (M-26)	moored contact	percussion mechanical	130	960	250
KB-3	moored contact		260	1065	230

Each of these mines had a TNT charge.

Table 10: DEPTH CHARGES

Depth charge	Weight	Explosive	Sinking speed	Damage radius	Depth settings
BB-1	165kg	135kg	2.3-2.5m/s	8-20m	20m-100m
BM-1	41kg	25kg	2.1-2.3m/s	3.5-5m	

war, making do with Mars hydrophones and the Arktur underwater communication system – both entirely inadequate in submarine detection as they could not function at speeds exceeding 3 knots. Lend-Lease Asdic began to make its way on board in early 1942, and by the end of the war all Project 7/7U ships were so equipped.

Propulsion

While the *Leningrad*-class leaders achieved and even surpassed their design speed, their three-shaft system proved complex, heavy, vulnerable, and uneconomical, sending the Project 7 ships in a simpler direction. In an example indicative of the times, the Kharkov-made GTZA-24 turbines were designed to make 27,000shp but officially rated at 24,000shp. The engineers understood the consequences of failing to achieve the design figure, so they lowered it. Their caution was vindicated when the brand-new Gnevnyi maintained only 50,500shp on her two shafts during trials with the maximum attained power being 53,000shp. There were three Yarrow-type boilers, with the after pair making 98.5 tonnes of steam per hour and the forward one making 83 tonnes per hour because of the smaller heating area (1077m^2 instead of 1264m^2) dictated by the narrower beam there. Steam pressure was 26.65kg/cm^2 pressure and maximum temperature 340-360°C.

Project 7U used similar boiler conditions (26.5kg/cm^2 pressure and 340°C) but added another boiler, each of the four making 80 tonnes of steam per hour. This was expected to increase the engine rating to 60,000shp, but once again the crafty designers officially lowered expectations by 3000shp per shaft.

Delays in turbine delivery made it clear that Kharkov couldn't keep up with demand, so orders went out for twelve sets from Vickers and Parsons. The British turbines were rated at only 24,000shp, which cut 2-3 knots from the nominal 39 knots of the Kharkov ships, but they could function from a cold start without preheating. Vickers turbines went into seven Baltic units (plus one set kept in reserve), and three Parsons sets went into Black Sea ships (one set in reserve).

Fuel stowage defied standardisation with a wide range from normal to maximum loads. The double bottom could hold fuel, but stability concerns made it undesirable to pump out those spaces. Even when that was done, the ships lacked range. For extended operations along the Romanian coast, *Besposhchadnyi* had to load her no.7 magazine with an extra 90 tonnes of fuel. The Project 7U redesign worsened matters by simultaneously adding a boiler and reducing bunkerage volume; *Soobrazitel'nyi*

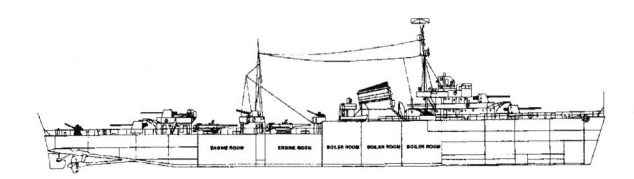

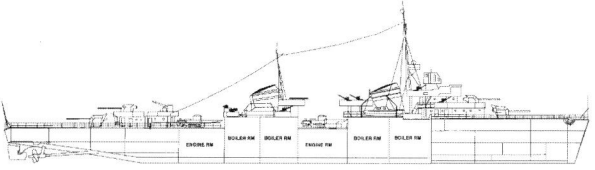

Machinery arrangments in the Project 7 (above) and Project 7U (right). With one additional boiler, the newer ship had a separate funnel for each pair of boiler rooms. (Drawings by Rob Lundgren)

managed just 1380 miles at economical speed in 1943, less than half the original Project 7 design range of 3000 miles. However, in other regards the machinery worked well, and ships maintained high speed for extended periods without complaints of unreliability.

Postwar

Eighteen units from Project 7 and ten from Project 7U survived the war, and most were rewarded with modernisation. They landed their former anti-aircraft weaponry and shipped instead a new set of 37mm/74 cannon, the same gun as in wartime but now fitted in four twin V-11 mounts. Standardised Soviet radar and Asdic replaced the Lend-Lease equipment. Tripod masts and enlarged superstructures altered their silhouettes. Standard displacement swelled yet again, now over 1900 tonnes with speed dipping to 34-35 knots. With the shipbuilding industry's focus on its newest and best ships, these refits received low priority, and the work dragged out for as long as eight years – rather a waste, as the ships served as little as two years between refit and decommissioning. Most units then retired to auxiliary duties lasting into the 1960s. A lucky foursome transferred to the Chinese Navy, which bought them extra decades of life.

Career Highlights

Like their counterparts in other navies, the Soviet destroyers spent much of their wartime service in the nerve-racking drudgery of patrol and escort work. Bombardment duty offered somewhat more gratification, but there were few of the minelaying missions that had figured prominently in prewar planning.

I) Project 7:
Northern Fleet

Gremyashchiy ('Thunderous'): commissioned into Baltic Fleet 30 October 1938; to Northern Fleet September 1939; damaged by near-miss bombs 18 and 22 August 1941; attacked *U-435* 30 March 1942; refit 13 January to 29 April 1942; bombardment missions 9 and 26 October 1944; major refit 19 January 1945-28 December 1949; stricken from combat duty 3 April 1956; designated as test ship OS-5 27 December 1956; used in nuclear tests 1955-

Table 11: SPEED AND RANGE VARIATION IN PROJECT 7 DESTROYERS

Ship	Year	Actual speed (knots)	Actual range (nm at 19 knots)
Gnevnyi	1938	38.38	2720
Stremitel'nyi	1938	38.26	3055
Bodryi	1938	39.05	2190
Bezuprechnyi	1939	38.73	3145
R'yanyi	1939	38.60	2700
Rastoropnyi	1940	37.98	2970
Redkiy	1942	37.35	3040
Gremyashchiy	1942	37.00	1670
Groznyi	1943	36.00	1690
Grozyashchiy	1944	39.40	2800
Boykiy	1944	34.00	1350 (at 16 knots)
Steregushchiy	1948	35.20	2500
Razumnyi	1957	34.80	2300

Table 12: SPEED AND RANGE VARIATION IN PROJECT 7U DESTROYERS

Ship	Year	Actual speed (knots)	Actual range
Storozhevoi	1941	40.28	2700 nm at 19 knots
Strashnyi	1941	39.6	
Svirepyi	1943	38.00	1800 nm at 19 knots
Sposobnyi	1943	36.80	1380 nm at 20 knots
Soobrazitel'nyi	1943	36.80	1380 nm at 19 knots
Storozhevoi	1944	38.90	1800 nm at 17 knots

1957; scuttled in shallow water near Novaya Zemlya (extant), October 1957.

Gromkiy ('Loud'): commissioned into Baltic Fleet 9 December 1938; to Northern Fleet first half of 1939; White Sea flotilla training duty until 29 September 41; bombardment missions, firing 480 130mm rounds, October-December 1941; damaged by heavy seas 24-25 December 1941; rescue of *Gromkiy*, providing 117 tonnes

The Project 7 Gremyashchiy in 1942. (Drawing by Sergei Balakin, via Arseny Malov)

Remains of Gremyashkiy at Novaya Zemlya after serving in nuclear tests. (Boris Lemachko Collection lemachko@mtu-net.ru)

Northern Fleet's Gromkiy *showing details of the superstructure.* (Boris Lemachko Collection lemachko@mtu-net.ru)

of fuel, incurred grounding damage that required two months of repair 6 March 1942; attacked a submarine target but no kill, 27 June 1942; re-boilered August 1942 to March 1943; returned to Baltic 26 June 1948; major refit until 21 August 1956; stricken, redesignated as target ship *TsL-74* 18 April 1958; sold for scrap 15 September 1960.

Groznyi ('Terrible'): commissioned into Baltic Fleet 31 December 1938; to Northern Fleet May 1939; under repair November 1940 to 8 June 1941; laid two minefields (142 mines) September-October 1941; four bombardment missions (1332 rounds) September-October 1941; shelled Varda Island with RN ships 25 November 1941; ran out of fuel in heavy storm, rescued by *Groznyi* and other ships 6 March 1942; six bombardment missions (872 rounds) April-May 1942; almost lost bow in heavy storm 8 May 1942; repairs until 8 October 1942; rescue of *Sokrushitel'nyi* crew, bow cracks once again appeared 21 November 1942; refit, 27 March 1948-31 December 1954; stricken 17 February 1956; reclassified as test ship *OS-3* 27 December 1956; used in nuclear test 7 September 1957; sunk at Novaya Zemlya, 10 October 1957.

Stremitel'nyi ('Impetuous'): commissioned into Baltic Fleet 29 November 1938; to Northern Fleet 9 May 1940; hit by four or five bombs, broke in two at Polyarnyi, 121 dead, 20 July 1941; parts of the hull raised April 1942; stern used to repair *Raz'yaryonny*.

Sokrushitel'nyi ('Destructive'): commissioned into Baltic Fleet 13 August 1939; to Northern Fleet November 1939; refit 18 July 1940-4 July 1941; White Sea flotilla until 29 September 1941; eleven bombardment missions (1297 rounds) October 1941-January 1942; escorted convoy PQ-13 during attack by German destroyers 28 March 1942; repairs summer-autumn 1942; stern broke off in heavy weather, ship sank, 35 dead 20 November 1942.

Baltic Fleet

Gnevnyi ('Angry'): commissioned into Baltic Fleet October 1938; active in the Winter War, shelling Finnish positions; bow lost on mine in Gulf of Riga (20 dead, 23 wounded), scuttling by gunfire attempted but incomplete 23 June 1941; finished off by German aircraft 26 June 1941.

Gordyi ('Proud'): commissioned into Baltic Fleet 23 December 1938; active in the Winter War; rescue of *Gnevnyi* and *Serdityi* crews, summer 1941; Tallinn evacuation, heavily damaged by a mine, towed to Kronshtadt under air attack (267 bombs dropped) 30 August 1941; repairs until November 1941; evacuation of Hango, struck two mines within ten minutes and sank, 88 survivors 14 November 1941.

Smetlivyi ('Sly'): commissioned into Baltic Fleet 6 November 1938; active in the Winter War; minelaying operations in Irben Gulf summer 1941; gunfire support of troops around Tallinn; Tallinn evacuation 28-30 August 1941; artillery support for the defence of Leningrad September-October 1941; evacuation of Hango, loaded with 560 evacuees when mined forward suffering medium damage, able to restore power until striking second mine that detonated the forward magazine and broke off the bow, drifting ship then hit third mine that split remaining hull, sank with only 350 survivors (80 crew and 270 evacuees) 4 November 1941.

Steregushchiy ('Watchful'): commissioned into Baltic Fleet 30 October 1939; took part in the Winter War; escorted damaged cruiser *Maxim Gorkiy* 23 June 1941; attacked German convoy while under heavy air attack 18 July 1941; began repairs September 1941; attacked by a dozen or more Ju-87's while defending Leningrad, hit by three bombs, able to reach shallow water despite machinery room hit, sank partly capsized in 5.5m of water 21 September 1941; some items salvaged; raised and repairs started July 1944; repairs finished, ship back in service 1948; stricken 28 January 1958; scrapped 1959.

Grozyashchiy ('Threatening'): commissioned into Baltic Fleet 17 September 1939; active in the Winter War, captured Finnish steamer *Aiva*; heavy damage to forward hull from explosion during minelaying operation, able to make port by steaming in reverse 20 July 1941; under repair 24 July-2 September 1941; after bombardment mission near Oranienbaum struck a reef and damaged screws, 9 September 1941; struck by three bombs while in dry dock, large fire extinguished by flooding the dock 21-23 September 1941; repairs until summer 1942; assigned for major refit 24 June 1952; refit canceled due to general condition 24 August 1953; scrapped.

Black Sea Fleet
Bodryi ('Sprightly'): commissioned into Black Sea Fleet 1 March 1939; repairs June 1939-April 1940; under repair again August-October 1940; covered the withdrawal of Danube flotilla June 1941; defence of Odessa, delivery of supplies and shelling Germans August-September 1941; evacuation of Odessa October 1941; damaged by German bombers 31 October 1941; bombed again while under repair in Sevastopol 2 November 1941; repairs until mid-December 1941; Tuapse amphibious landing, carried troops 16 December 1941; major re-supply operation to Sevastopol 20 December 1941; repairs February-July 1942; hit by three bombs, stern settled to the bottom 16 July 1941; re-floated but stern broke off in dry dock; under repair until 31 December 1944; major refit 1951-31 December 1953; target ship *TsL-3* 17 February 1956; training station *UTS-8* 13 October 1959; scrapped sometime in the early 1960s.

Boykiy ('Active'): commissioned into Black Sea Fleet 17 May 1939; defence of Odessa, supporting amphibious landing at Grigir'evka August-September 1941; defence of Sevastopol October-December 1941; amphibious landing at Feodossiya, transport and bombardment duties 28-30 December 1941; collided with transport *Serov* near Novorossiysk 13 January 1942; shelled German troops in Crimea February-March 1942; bow heavily damaged during storm, cracks appearing and damage to the forward gun 22 March 1942; six supply runs into Sevastopol, damaged by aircraft, up to July 1942; repairs until autumn 1942; shelled Tuapse 6 October 1942; sortie against German communications with cruiser *Voroshilov* and three other destroyers, *Voroshilov* mined and sent back to port with two destroyers while *Boykiy* and *Besposhchadnyi* continued and attacked a German 'convoy' sinking two 'transports' (postwar research showed that they most likely shelled rocks in the fog) 29 November-2 December 1942; bow once again damaged in heavy seas with numerous cracks appearing, 5-6 February 1943; operations against German communications spring-summer 1943; after loss of three destroyers in October 1943, retained mostly in port until the end of combat in September 1944; major refit 1948-27 December 1951; stricken and redesignated as test ship *OS-18* 17 February 1956; sunk in the shallow water near Tendra spit (extant) 9 February 1962.

Besposhchadnyi ('Ruthless'): commissioned into Black Sea Fleet 2 October 1939; storm damage to bow 9-10 October 1939; defensive minelaying sorties 22-30 June 1941; defence of Odessa, amphibious landing at Grigir'evka August-September 1941; bomb damage, bow nearly severed 22 September 1941; bow removed in Odessa, ship towed backward to Sevastopol 23 September 1941; under repair including bow parts salvaged from sunken *Bystryi*, work completed November 1941; bomb hit plus two near misses, heavy damage to the machinery rooms and a large fire 12 November 1941; put into dry dock 14 November 1941; however, evacuated to Poti 17 November 1941; repairs until September 1942; raids on Romanian and Bulgarian coast November-December 1942; escort, transport, and bombardment duties, winter-spring 1943; attacked by German bombers while returning from the Crimean raid with leader *Kharkov* and destroyer *Sposobnyi*, first *Kharkov* hit and crippled, then *Besposhchadnyi* hit and crippled, and *Sposobnyi* attempted towing operations, but more planes came and hit all three ships, sinking them with only 176 of 903 crewmen surviving (41 from *Besposhchadnyi*) 6 October 1943.

Bystryi ('Fast'): commissioned into Black Sea Fleet 7 March 1939; mined while leaving Sevastopol, sinking partly capsized in shallow water (24 dead, 81 wounded) 1 July 1941; raised in poor condition 13 July 1941; repair reluctantly begun, hull patched; hit by two bombs and sunk September 1941; bow scavenged to repair *Besposhchadnyi* autumn 1941; raised for scrapping 1945.

Bezuprechnyi ('Irreproachable'): commissioned into Black Sea Fleet 2 October 1939; minelaying operations (219 mines) July 1941; defence of Odessa, heavily damaged by numerous near-miss bombs (over 400 splinter holes including 152 below the waterline) August-September 1941; evacuation from Tendra spit October 1941; hit anchor chain of SS *Mestkom* 8 December 1941; bombardment duties January-March 1942; made her last successful supply run into Sevastopol 24 June 1942; bombed while attempting transport run to Sevastopol, sunk with three people surviving out of about 400 26 June 1942.

Bditel'nyi ('Vigilant'): commissioned into Black Sea Fleet 22 October 1939; bow damage from grounding 24 September 1941; repairs until October 1941; evacuated troops to Sevastopol November 1941; bombardment missions February-March 1942; rescued 143 survivors of sunken transport *Svanetiya* (753 dead) 17 April 1942; seven supply runs into Sevastopol February-June 1942; shelled Feodossiya 9 May 1942; one of the last large ships to reach Sevastopol 25 June 1942; helped rescue damaged destroyer *Tashkent* 26 June 1942; bombed at Novorossiysk, torpedoes in forward mount detonated, after magazines detonated, ship sank 2 July 1942; raised in pieces and scrapped 1948-52.

Pacific Fleet

Razumnyi ('Intelligent'): commissioned into Pacific Fleet 7 November 1941; to the Northern Fleet through the northern (Arctic) route 15 July 1942 to 14 October 1942; rescue of *Sokrushitel'nyi* survivors 20-22 November 1942; teamed with leader *Baku* to skirmish with German surface forces 20-21 January 1943; under repair February 1943; hit by a bomb 3 April 1943; repairs until 14 June 1943; shelled Varde Island 26 October 1944; attacked and damaged a German submarine 8 December 1944; major refit 1954-30 June 1957; stricken and redesignated as target ship *TsL-29* 6 February 1960; accommodation ship *PKZ-3* 15 September 1960; earmarked for scrapping 4 July 1962; nevertheless converted to target ship *SM-14* 23 October 1962; sold for scrap 4 May 1963; scrapped in Murmansk 1963-64.

Raz'yaryonny ('Furious'): commissioned into Pacific Fleet 14 December 1941; to Northern Fleet through the northern (Arctic) route 15 July 1942 to 14 October 1942; repairs until 1 January 1943; ran aground, bow damage 8 January 1943; repairs until 25 June 1943; torpedoed by *U-293* (38 killed, 17 wounded), eventually losing stern, but successfully towed back to port 23 January 1945; under repair (using stern from *Stremitel'nyi*) until 1946; stricken 17 February 1956; test ship *OS-4* 27 December 1956; nuclear tests 7 September 1957; scuttled near Novaya Zemlya October 1957.

R'yanyi ('Fervent'): commissioned into Pacific Fleet 11 August 1939; major refit 1946-4 February 1949; target ship *TsL-33* 18 April 1958; sunk in the Sea of Japan during live-fire exercises 8 January 1961.

Rezvyi ('Lively'): commissioned into Pacific Fleet 24 January 1940; sold for scrap 3 April 1958.

Razyashchiy ('Pounding'): commissioned into Pacific Fleet 20 December 1940; major refit 9 October 1948-30 September 1950; target ship *TsL-39* 18 April 1958; sunk during live-fire exercises 9 July 1961.

Rekordnyi ('Record-setting'): commissioned into Pacific Fleet 4 January 1941; major refit 20 October 1949-17 December 1952; transferred to the Chinese Navy as *Anshan* 6 July 1955; modernised as missile destroyer May 1969-February 1970; stricken 1986; extant as museum in Quindao from 24 April 1992.

Rezkiy ('Brusque'): commissioned into Pacific Fleet 16 August 1942; major refit 28 November 1952-15 January 1955; transferred to the Chinese Navy as *Fushun* 6 July 1955; modernised as missile destroyer 1971-1974; stricken and scrapped late 1980s.

Rastoropnyi ('Swift'): commissioned into Pacific Fleet 5 January 1940; major refit 10 June 1949-31 May 1951; stricken 17 February 1956; converted to Project 32a rescue ship *SDK-12* 1956-1958; in reserve 15 December 1960; target ship *TsL-1* 14 September 1963; sold for scrap 27 April 1965.

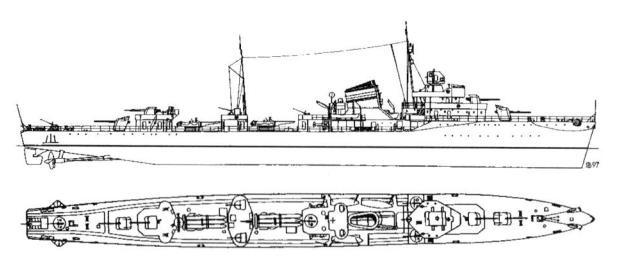

The Project 7 Razumnyi *in 1943.* (Drawings by Sergei Balakin, via Arseny Malov)

Retivyi ('Zealous'): commissioned into Pacific Fleet 10 October 1941; major refit 24 November 1951-11 January 1954; transferred to the Chinese Navy as *Jilin** 14 January 1955; modernised as missile destroyer 1971-1974; stricken September 1991; extant as training station at Dalyan Naval Institute.

Reshitel'nyi ('Resolute'): commissioned into Pacific Fleet 5 September 1941; major refit 3 July 1951-8 October 1953; transferred to the Chinese Navy as *Chang Chun* 14 January 1955; modernised as missile destroyer 1971-1974; stricken August 1990; extant as tourist attraction in Rushan.

Revnostnyi ('Eager'): commissioned into Pacific Fleet 14 December 1941; scheduled for transfer to the Northern Fleet, but damaged in collision with transport *Terney* 18 July 1942; missed departure date during ten days of repairs, remained in the Pacific; major refit 30 November 1951-26 December 1952; stricken and redesignated target *TsL-37* 18 April 1958; training station *UTS-88* 19 January 1959; sold for scrap 28 December 1961.

Redkiy ('Rare'): commissioned into Pacific Fleet 29 November 1942; major refit 15 November 1952 to 4 January 1956; stricken and redesignated target *TsL-38* 18 April 1958; sold for scrap 26 February 1962.

II) Project 7U:
Baltic Fleet

Storozhevoi ('Protective'): commissioned into Baltic Fleet 12 April 1941; minelaying operations with three other destroyers 24 and 26 June 1941; while returning to base struck by S-boat torpedo, forward magazine exploded, forward end obliterated, remainder of ship towed to Tallinn and then to Kronshtadt 27 June 1941; placed in dry dock 7 July 1941; hit by a German shell 24 May 1942; repaired using forward end of unfinished Project 30 destroyer *Organizovannyi* resulting in unique Project 7U/30 ship, launched on 9 October 1942; bombardment missions 25 October 1942-May 1943; reclassified as a training destroyer 17 February 1956; sold for scrap 11 March 1958; scrapped at Liepaya 1958-59.

Stoikiy ('Steadfast'): commissioned into Baltic Fleet 12 April 1941; minelaying operations in Irben Gulf June 1941; narrowly avoided S-boat torpedo 27 June 1941; screw damage from grounding near Moonzund 12 July 1941; repairs until 20 August 1941; shelled Finnish troops near Vyborg (490 rounds fired) 25 and 27 August 1941; defence of Leningrad (576 rounds fired), hit by German 210mm round 21 September-15 October 1941; repairs until November 1941; evacuation of Hango and Gogland Island 1-29 November 1941; Leningrad blockade 1942-1944; renamed *Vitse-Admiral Drozd* (in honor of fleet commander killed in 1943) 13 February 1943; major refit 2 November 1951-7 February 1956; stricken from combat rolls and redesignated target ship *TsL-54* 6 February 1960; sank at anchor near Cape Taran during storm 2 July 1960.

Sil'nyi ('Strong'): commissioned into Baltic Fleet 12 April 1941; minelaying operations in Irben Gulf June 1941; with *Serdityi* intercepted German minelaying force and disrupted its mission, scored no hits, one 105mm hit on *Sil'nyi* 6 July 1941; grounding damage to screws in Moonzund July 1941; repairs until 23 August 1941; shelled Finnish troops near Vyborg (500 rounds fired) 25 August 1941; shelled German troops near Leningrad (500 rounds fired) 15-21 September 1941; bomb hit and several near misses 21 September 1941; repairs until 30 December 1941; hit by 128mm shell 12 December 1941; Leningrad blockade 1942-44; hit by artillery shell April 1942; repairs until 24 April 1942; repair period November 1944-mid 1945; major refit 19 November 1948-10 December 1954; stricken from combat rolls, target ship *TsL-43* 20 February 1959; sold for scrap 21 January 1960; scrapped at Tallinn.

Serdityi ('Enraged'): commissioned into Baltic Fleet 12 April 1941; minelaying operations in Irben Gulf June 1941; with *Sil'nyi* intercepted German minelaying force and disrupted its mission 6 July 1941; with *Steregushchiy* attacked a German convoy, subjected to air attacks (German and Soviet?), splinter damage 18 July 1941; bomb hit on the forward superstructure, ship lost power, near miss damaged fuel tanks, severe fire detonated depth charges, ship sank 19 July 1941; raised in pieces and scrapped 1949-1952.

Slavnyi ('Famous'): commissioned into Baltic Fleet 31 May 1941; minelaying operations June 1941; escorted battleship *Oktyabr'skaya Revolyutsiya* from Tallinn to Kronshtadt 1 July 1941; defence of Tallinn 18 July-28 August 1941; shock damage from two mine explosions 28 August 1941; repairs until 21 September 1941; Hango evacuation, misidentified and sank Soviet MO-112 subchaser by gunfire 1 November 1941; return to Hango interrupted by damaged steering 29 November 1941; steering by engines finally reached Kronshtadt 6 December 1941; Leningrad blockade 1942-44; hit by German shells 25 October 1942 and 1 May 1943; shelled Finnish troops near Vyborg 19 July 1944; major refit 10 July 1947-6 July 1955; stricken and redesignated target *TsL-44* 6 February 1960; floating target *SM-20* 30 June 1961; sold for scrap 4 March 1964; scrapped at Liepaya.

Surovyi ('Severe'): commissioned into Baltic Fleet 31 May 1941; artillery support in Narva area (186 rounds fired) 23 July 1941; two sorties with *Statnyi* against German targets in Gulf of Riga August 1941; sortie with destroyer *Artem* against German convoy in Gulf of Riga 21 August 1941; evacuation of Tallinn, damaged by two nearby mine explosions 28 August 1941; repairs 3-23 September 1941; evacuation of Hango 3 November 1941; en route to Hango, collided with minesweeper *T-217*, bow damaged, a mine then damaged the stern, shafts immobilised, ship scuttled by depth charges 13 November 1941.

Smelyi ('Brave'): commissioned into Baltic Fleet 31 May 1941; defence of Moonzund and Gulf of Riga June-July 1941; mined in Irben Strait, bow nearly broken off with keel bent down and grounded, ship scuttled by MTB 27 July 1941.

Svirepyi (Fierce): commissioned into Baltic Fleet before completing acceptance trials 22 June 1941; escorted battleship *Oktyabr'skaya Revolyutsiya* from Tallinn to Kronshtadt 1 July 1941; amphibious assault on Virtsu Island 18 July 1941; fended off S-boat attack 20 July 1941; defence of Tallinn August 1941; retreat from Tallinn, towed damaged destroyer *Gordyi* 28 August 1941; defence of Leningrad September-November 1941; 203mm shell hit 1 October 1941; three sorties to cover rescue attempt of damaged troopship *Iosif Stalin* 23 November-6 December 1941; Leningrad blockade 1942-43; artillery support around Leningrad January 1944; major refit in the Neptune Shipyard at Rostock GDR 10 July 1947-2 January 1951; sold for scrap 28 January 1958.

Skoryi ('Rapid'): commissioned into Baltic Fleet before completing acceptance trials 18 July 1941; defence of Tallinn August 1941; hit by a 150mm round 26 August 1941; attempting to tow damaged leader *Minsk* during Tallinn retreat, ran onto mine that broke the ship's back, sank within minutes 28 August 1941.

Strashnyi ('Awesome'): commissioned into Baltic Fleet before completing acceptance trials 22 June 1941; air attacks, damage from near misses 13 and 15 July 1941; mined while en route to Tallinn for repairs, bow nearly blown off, ship retained power and successfully steamed astern 16 July 1941; repaired with new bow including parts from sunken *Steregushchiy* 23 September 1941-15

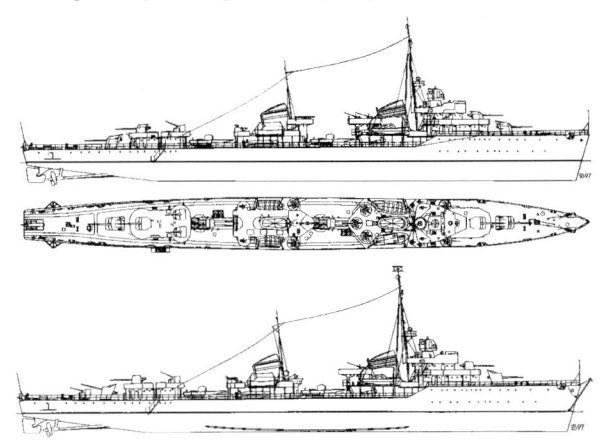

Soobrazitel'nyi *in 1944 and (bottom)* Sil'nyi *in 1945.*
(Drawings by Sergei Balakin, via Arseny Malov)

This composite photo of Strogiy *in 1944 shows two of the realities for ships caught in the Leningrad area: ice and elaborate attempts at camouflage.* (Boris Lemachko Collection lemachko@mtu-net.ru)

April 1942; Leningrad blockade 1942-43; gunfire support (229 rounds fired) early 1944; major refit 10 July 1947-10 January 1953; training station *UTS-83* 18 April 1958; sold for scrap 12 January 1960.

Statnyi ('Stately'): commissioned into Baltic Fleet before completing acceptance trials 9 July 1941; two raids with *Surovyi* in Gulf of Riga August 1941; mined at Tallinn, bow broke off and sank, remaining hull grounded; five days of refloating efforts, air attacks restrict work to nighttime; ship sank in storm 23 August 1941; raised and scrapped 1957.

Strogiy ('Strict'): commissioned into Baltic Fleet while not fully complete 30 August 1941; towed to the Neva River for bombardment duty (118 fire missions) September 1941; completed 15 September 1942; artillery support throughout Leningrad blockade (4669 rounds fired); ran acceptance trials August-October 1945; converted to Project 32 rescue ship 30 November 1953-1958; renamed *SDK-13* 20 March 1956; renamed *SS-18* 27 December 1956; transferred to the Northern Fleet 11 October 1958; converted to target ship *SM-16* 14 September 1963; sold for scrap 26 June 1964; scrapped in Murmansk 1964-65.

Stroynyi ('Slim'): commissioned into Baltic Fleet while not fully complete 30 August 1941; steamed to the upper reaches of the Neva River to provide artillery support September 1941; completed 15 September 1942; artillery support throughout Leningrad blockade; ran acceptance trials August-October 1945; converted to Project 32 rescue ship 30 November 1953-1956; renamed *SDK-10* 20 March 1956; renamed *SS-17* 27 December 1956; converted to target ship *TsL-2* 27 August 1963; sold for scrap 27 August 1965; scrapped in Liepaya 1965-66.

Black Sea Fleet

Soobrazitel'nyi ('Shrewd'): commissioned into Black Sea Fleet 7 June 1941; sortied for strike on Constanza with cruiser-destroyer force, *Moskva* sunk by a mine, *Kharkov* damaged by artillery, imaginary torpedo attack prompts dropping of depth-charges on imaginary submarine contact 25 June 1941; shelled troops around Odessa (364 rounds fired) 29-31 August 1941; towed damaged *Besposhchadnyi* from Odessa to Sevastopol 23-25 September; Kerch-Feodossiya amphibious assault, shelled Germans (385 rounds fired) 25 December 1941-3 January 1942; amphibious assault on Sudak 15 January 1942; bombardment missions in Crimea late January 1942; storm damage to bow 21 February 1942; bow again damaged in storm during supply run to Sevastopol 6-7 March 1942; supply run to Sevastopol, attacked by torpedo planes, eight torpedoes evaded 27-28 May 1942; assisted leader *Tashkent*, removed 1975 evacuees 27 June 1942; repairs July-August 1942; bombardment near Novorossiysk (345 rounds fired) 1-2 September 1942; shelled Yalta with *Boykiy*, two ships fired 300 rounds, chased off an MTB attack 2 October 1942; cruiser-destroyer raid on Romanian coast, fired 196 rounds, escorted mine-damaged cruiser *Voroshilov* back to port 29 November-3 December 1942; covered minesweeper sortie along Romanian coast 12-14 December 1942; raided Romanian coast 26-29 December 1942; bombardment near Novorossiysk, storm damage to bow 31 January-4 February 1943; not in combat operations due to worn condition throughout 1944; patrolled near Yalta during Yalta

The Project 7U Soobrazitel'nyi *in 1943.* (Drawing by Sergei Balakin, via Arseny Malov)

THE SOVIET PROJECT 7/7U DESTROYERS

conference February 1945; major refit 19 December 1945-25 August 1947; converted to Project 32 rescue ship 29 December 1951-1958; renamed *SDK-11* 20 March 1956; renamed *SS-16* 12 February 1957; placed in reserve 27 March 1960; target ship *TsL-3* 14 September 1963; sold for scrap 19 March 1966.

Smyshlenyi ('Clever'): commissioned into Black Sea Fleet 10 November 1940; sortied with cruiser-destroyer force for strike on Constanza but left behind after grounding damage 25 June 1941; defence of Odessa and Sevastopol August-December 1941; bombardment mission 28 November 1941; amphibious assault on Feodossiya December 1941; attempt to land second wave in raid on Evpatoriya prevented by storm, first wave annihilated 5 January 1942; storm damage 21 February 1942; ran into Soviet minefield, crippled by explosion 5 March 1942; able to restore power, escorted homeward at 8 knots, power lost due to lack of fresh boiler water, attempts at towing unsuccessful in stormy seas, ship sunk by progressive flooding, most crewmen killed by exploding depth charges, only two survivors 8 March 1942.

Sposobnyi ('Capable'): commissioned into Black Sea Fleet 24 June 1941; defence of Odessa September 1941; supply runs to Sevastopol September-November 1941; shelled Germans around Sevastopol (621 round fired) December 1941; mined near Novorossiysk during transport run to Feodossiya (106 people dead), bow lost, able to return to

Soobrazitelniy *survived to become a Project 32 NBC rescue ship. Here she is,* renamed SS-16. (Boris Lemachko Collection lemachko@mtu-net.ru)

Novorossiysk steaming astern 8 January 1942; near-missed by bomb while under repair in Novorossiysk, splinters detonated 130mm ready-service rounds and started fire, 41 dead, 45 wounded 10 April 1942; evacuated to Tuapse 22 April 1942; repairs until May 1943; summer-autumn 1943 escort duties; bombed and sunk with *Kharkov* and *Besposhchadnyi* 6 October 1943.

Sovershennyi ('Absolute'): at 90% readiness 22 June 1941; mined during trials, over 1000 tonnes of flooding 30 September 1941; towed back to dry dock 1 October 1941; hit by two bombs in dry dock, extensive fire, further

Few destroyers had a busier wartime career than Soobrazitelniy. *This view shows the characteristic Soviet stern form with two depth charge racks paired closely at the centreline between the mine rails.* (Boris Lemachko Collection lemachko@mtu-net.ru)

bombs caused dry dock to flood, ship's back broke, ship settled at 25° list 12 November 1941; hit by two 150mm artillery rounds 14 November 1941; ship disarmed; dry dock repaired 20 February 1942; work resumed on the ship, hull restoration 20 February 1942-May 1942; hit by another bomb early June 1942; hit by a heavy artillery shell, ship sank 15 June 1942; raised and scrapped 28 October 1945.

Svobodnyi ('Free'): at 83.8% readiness 22 June 1941; evacuated to Sevastopol August 1941; commissioned into Black Sea Fleet 2 January 1942; defence of Sevastopol, bombardment missions January-May 1942; supply run into Sevastopol, struck by eight bombs while unloading, massive fires and explosions, ship sank at 50° list, 67 dead 9-10 June 1941; raised and scrapped 1953.

Conclusion

Gnevnyi's trials, an ongoing revelation of quirks and flaws, merely confirmed that Project 7 exceeded any realistic expectations, a lesson already played out with the *Leningrad* and *Uragan* programmes. The policy of overly ambitious plans resulted in inferior products, waste, and frustration.

The Project 7/7U destroyers were not good ships, inferior in some ways to the *Noviks* they were meant to replace. In combining transverse and longitudinal framing, hull strength suffered, as seen through recurring incidents of damage by heavy seas. Miscalculations left the ships overloaded and wanting for stability. The lack of range imposed strict limits on their operations.

On the positive side of the ledger, these ships provided numbers at a time when few destroyers were available to cover four major theaters. Their reliable power plants provided good speed. The 130mm guns and modern fire control systems represented a major advance compared to the *Noviks*, especially important for the Soviet Union's war which relied so heavily on naval gunnery support. The wartime record shows a busy set of ships whose operations subjected them to repeated hazards and a high attrition rate. As an important step in the Soviet Union's industrial redevelopment, they prepared the way for subsequent classes like the well-rounded *Ognevois*.

Sources:

Balakin, S. A. '*Gremyashchiy*' *i drugie: Ehskadrennye minonostsy proekta 7*, Modelist-Konstruktor, Morskaya Kollektsiya 2/1996.

Balakin, S. A. *Legendarnye semerki: esmintsy stalinskoi serii*, EKSMO, 2007.

Balakin, S. A. '*Soobrazitel'nyi*' *i drugie: Ehskadrennye minonostsy proekta 7U*, Modelist-Konstruktor, Morskaya Kollektsiya 6/1997.

Morin, A. B. *Ehskadrennye Minonostsy tipa Gnevnyi*, Gangut, 1994.

Platonov, A. V. *Ehntsiklopediya Sovetskih Nadvodnyh Korabley 1941-1945*, Poligon, 2002.

Platonov, A. V. *Sovetskie Minonostsy*, Galeya-Print, 2003.

Platonov, A. V.; S. V. Aprelev, D. N. Sinyaev. *Sovetskie Boevye Korabli 1941-1945: IV Vooruzhenie*, Tsitadel', 1997.

Rohwer, Jürgen and Mikhail Monakov. *Stalin's Ocean-Going Fleet: Soviet Naval Strategy and Shipbuilding Programmemes 19351953*, Frank Cass Publishers, 2001.

Shirokorad, A. B. *Ehntsiklopediya Otechestvennoy Artillerii*, Harvest, 2000.

Spasskiy, I. D. *Istoriya Otechestvennogo Sudostreniya: Tom IV*, Sudostroenie, 1996.

Westwood, J. N. *Russian Naval Construction 1905-1945*, Macmillan Press Ltd., 1994.

Even in calm seas, the overloaded Project 7U had no surplus of freeboard. (Boris Lemachko Collection lemachko@mtu-net.ru)

THE CRUISER *DE GRASSE*

Ordered from the Arsenal de Lorient on 18 October 1938 as the first of a new class of light cruisers, *De Grasse* had her construction suspended on 10 June 1940 when she was 28% complete. Launched postwar to clear the slipway, she would await the redesign and funding necessary for work to be resumed. She would eventually be completed as the prototype of a new series of French anti-aircraft cruisers. In this article, using official documentation only recently made available, **John Jordan** and **Bruno Gire** recount the story of the ship's design and construction from conception to completion.

Following the London Treaty of 1930 the French Marine Nationale had authorised six light cruisers of the *La Galissonnière* class: two under the 1931 Estimates and a further four under the 1932 Estimates. Although France had failed to ratify the treaty itself because of fundamental disagreements with the procedures adopted for calculating overall tonnage limits, the French government had felt morally obliged to conform where possible to its spirit, and the new cruisers were designed within the qualitative limits which the British had been attempting to secure ever since the Geneva Conference of 1927: a standard displacement of 7000/8000 tons and an armament of 6in (152mm) guns. The result had been a well-balanced ship with a displacement of 7600 tons (7720 tonnes), an armament of nine 152mm guns in triple turrets, a maximum speed of 31-32 knots, and an armour belt 105mm thick.[1]

The Italians had likewise failed to ratify the London Treaty, primarily because their negotiators entered the conference with a brief to demand parity with the French, and as the latter had failed to agree to quantitative limits the Italian delegation was not in a position to sign up to anything other than the qualitative agreements which made up Part II of the treaty. Since the policy of the Regia Marina of 1930 was to match new French construction ship for ship the six *La Galissonnières* were answered by six new light cruisers of comparable size and power. The first pair of cruisers of the *Montecuccoli* class were essentially an enlargement of the earlier 'Condottieri' types, which emphasised high speed at the expense of hull strength and protection. In the second pair of ships of the *D'Aosta* class standard displacement was increased to 8450 tonnes (see table), allowing a modest increase in protection. However, the new French cruisers had a much more substantial impact on the third pair, the *Abruzzi* class. The latter were of a completely new design which prioritised gunpower and protection over speed, and with a standard displacement of 9592 tonnes and a main armament of ten 152mm guns were more than a match for the 7720-tonne French ships.

The London Treaty of 1936

France not only took part in the new London Conference which took place in 1935, but was happy to sign and ratify the subsequent treaty. Following the withdrawal of the Japanese from the Treaty System and Germany's renunciation of the Treaty of Versailles it was clear that no agreement could be reached on quantitative limits to naval construction, and this effectively removed the obstacles to French signature on a new agreement. Unrestricted building programmes both in Europe and in the Pacific

Table 1: *FRENCH AND ITALIAN CRUISERS OF THE EARLY 1930S*

	La Galissonnière	Montecuccoli	Duca d'Aosta	Abruzzi
Built	6 ships, 1931-37	2 ships, 1931-35	2 ships, 1932-36	2 ships, 1933-37
Displacement	7720t	7524t	8450t	9592t
Speed	31-32kts	37kts	36kts	34kts
Armament	9 x 152mm	8 x 152mm	8 x 152mm	10 x 152mm
	8 x 90mm	6 x 100mm	6 x 100mm	8 x 100mm
	4 x TT	4 x TT	6 x TT	6 x TT
	3 aircraft	2 aircraft	2 aircraft	4 aircraft
Protection (vert)	105mm	60mm	70mm	100mm
(hor)	38mm	30mm	35mm	40mm

would result; however, one of the key clauses of the London Treaty of 1936 was the restriction of cruiser displacement to 8000 tons (8127 tonnes) standard.[2]

When in early 1936 the French Navy sat down to consider the design of the next generation of cruisers it found that not only would it be unable to match the 9500-tonne displacement of the latest Italian ships, but that the new limit permitted an increase in displacement (standard) of only 400 tons (406 tonnes) over the *La Galissonnières*. The Naval General Staff therefore requested that the constructor branch, the STCN, look at how best to use this additional 406 tonnes in order to secure improvements with a focus on i) speed, ii) armament and iii) protection.

In a note dated 25 June 1936[3] the STCN first of all focused on the cost of general improvements which were now considered desirable in the light of trials with *La Galissonnière*, which had been proceeding since the Spring of 1935. These would comprise a wooden quarterdeck from the stern to abeam the hangar, an increase in the size and number of boats (to be matched by a corresponding increase in the capacity of the twin handling cranes), and replacement of the single telescopic catapult, which in the 7600-ton cruisers was located atop turret no.3 and therefore subject to vibration problems, by twin catapults mounted either atop the hangar or on the after deckhouse which might replace it (see below).

Two further modifications would need to be taken into account before considering radical improvements in the performance of the ships. The 152mm triple turrets of the 7600-ton type were capable of a maximum elevation of 45° but could be loaded only at elevations of 15° or below, which reduced the firing cycle considerably at longer ranges. It was therefore proposed that the guns on the new ships should be capable of being loaded up to their maximum angle of elevation of 45°. The new ships would also need an increase in SHP simply to cope with the increase in displacement. The 7600-ton cruisers had an overload power rating of 100,000shp to deliver 35 knots on their 8-hour speed trial, and it was calculated that this figure would need to be increased to a minimum of 105,000shp in the 8000-ton cruisers. The STCN recommended going to 110,000shp, considering this to be the maximum figure possible with a two-shaft installation; four shafts would have an unacceptable cost in machinery weight.

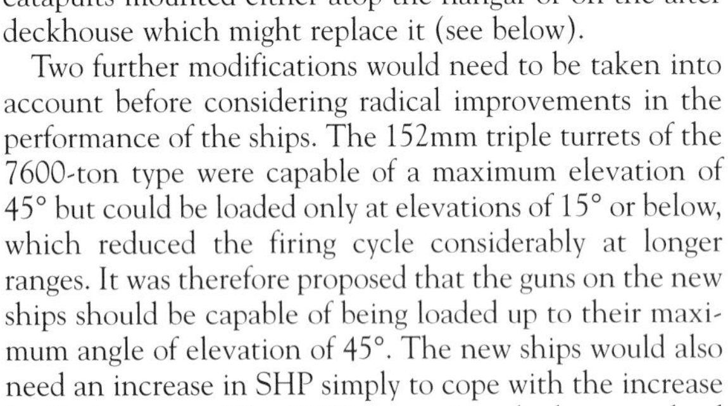

The cruiser Marseillaise *of the 7600-ton type, seen here in July 1939. Note the aviation arrangements of these ships, with a telescoping catapult atop turret no.3 and a large double hangar. The opening for the canvas recovery mat in the transom stern is particularly prominent in this view; the handling crane is stowed flat on the quarterdeck. The aircraft atop the hangar is a Loire 130 reconnaissance aircraft.* (Marius Bar)

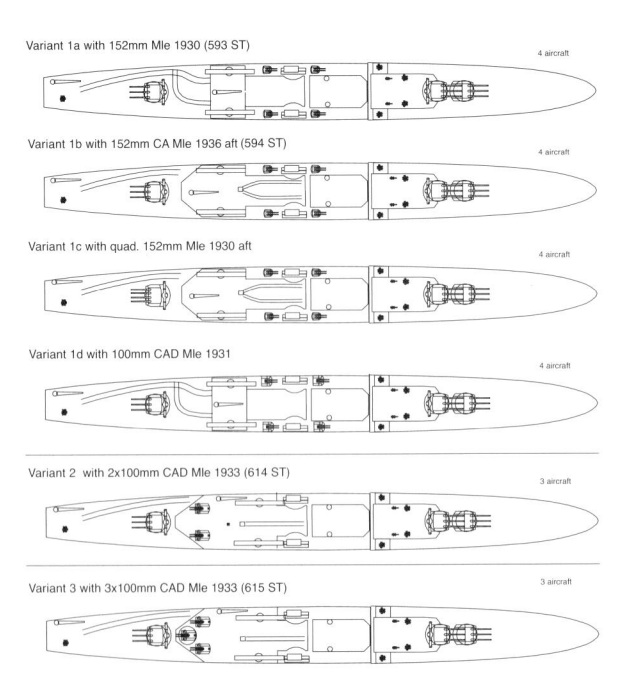

Preliminary Studies 1936 (Drawings by Bruno Gire)

In summary the STCN pointed out that even assuming that armament and protection remained unchanged the above modifications would leave 170 tonnes available, of which only 120 tonnes was usable![4] It must therefore have already been clear that dramatic improvements in speed, armament and protection would not be forthcoming, and that any further modifications to the existing design would have to be subject to the usual process of compromise inherent in ship design. Despite this, the STCN note went on to suggest possibilities which in due course would result in a distinctive cruiser design.

Suggested Modifications

First the STCN looked at possible changes in the main armament of the ships. There were three possibilities:–

– To retain the current turret (albeit with loading at 45°) but to increase the number of guns to ten, the after turret becoming a quad. (Two twins and two triples as in the *Abruzzis* were considered, but this would have had too great an impact on length and displacement.)
– To adopt the new Model 1936 DP turret of the *Richelieu* class, in which the guns could elevate to 90°.
– To adopt a modified *Richelieu* turret with elevation restricted to 70°.

Option i) had the advantage of superior distribution of the main armament (six guns forward, four aft), but a new quad turret would have to be developed. There would also be training and fire control issues, and access to the aircraft hangar (if fitted) from the quarterdeck would be impossible due to the greater width of the turret.

Option ii) was found to be only partially realisable. The

THE CRUISER DE GRASSE

Richelieu turret was 70 tonnes heavier even without allowing for munitions (magazine stowage would necessarily be greater for a DP gun). Installation of such a turret would have to be restricted to the after gun mounting; this would greatly complicate fire control and would again preclude access to the hangar because of the greater width of the turret.

Option iii) was much more promising. Each turret would be 22 tonnes heavier – ie three could be had for the weight cost of a single *Richelieu* turret – and this would still leave 50 tonnes available for improvements to the anti-aircraft weaponry. This option was therefore the one favoured by the STCN.

Attention then turned to AA capabilities. It was not possible to increase the number of 90mm twin mountings beyond the four provided in the 7600-ton type, as even these four mountings had proved difficult to accommodate. It was possible to increase gun calibre by adopting the 100mm CAD Mle 1931 mounting installed in the 10,000-ton cruiser *Algérie* in their place, and this would still leave 70 tonnes available for the favoured 70° option for the main guns. However, this failed to meet two concerns regarding the existing arrangements: the relatively poor arcs of the side-mounted 90mm mountings, which on forward bearings were constrained by the superstructures and on after bearings by the tall aircraft hangar; and the distance of the mountings from their magazines, which effectively limited them to rapid bursts of AA fire using the ready-use munitions available.

The STCN now proposed its most radical solution: the adoption of the new fully-enclosed 100mm CAD Mle 1933 to be installed in the new series of *avisos-dragueurs*. This promised to be a much more effective weapon in the anti-aircraft role than either the 90mm Mle 1926 or the 100mm Mle 1931. Being an enclosed mounting it was significantly heavier (30 tonnes as opposed to 13.5 tonnes for the open mountings) and had to be replenished from a magazine located directly beneath with hoists on the axis of the mounting, but it provided much-enhanced protection for the gun crews and could be fitted with RPC, thereby facilitating centralised fire control. Installation of either two or three of these mountings (see preliminary study drawings) would mean abandoning the aircraft hangar so that the guns could be placed directly above their magazines, which would be adjacent to the after 152mm magazine. However, this location offered infinitely superior AA arcs, as all mountings could be fired on after bearings and the centre-line mounting, which was raised on its own deckhouse, was capable of firing even on forward bearings against aerial targets at altitude.

Two alternative plans (614/615 ST – see drawings) were provided to illustrate this option. In both cases the catapults were moved farther forward and the number of aircraft was reduced from four to three, the third being stowed, wings folded, between the catapults. Adoption of either of these proposals in conjunction with the 70° option for the main guns would give the following munitions stowage: 1602 rounds of 152mm, and either 1280 rounds (two mountings) or 1920 rounds (three) of

Table 2: WEIGHTS

	La Galissonnière	De Grasse
Hull:	2524t	2887t
Wooden deck:	–	50t
Protection:[1]	1505t	1519t
Armament (incl protection):	1155t	1383t
Munitions:	239t	264t
Torpedoes + TT:	33t	46t
Aviation facilities:	118t	164t
Propulsion:	1238t	1366t
Fittings:	1041t	1269t
Margin:	–	–
Weight equivalent to **Light Displacement:**	**7795t**	**8948t**
Fuel/provisions[2]	1850t	2483t
Full load Displacement:	**9645t**	**11,431t**

Note: Trials displacement = light displacement + one half fuel and provisions, thus:
Trials Displacement: 8720t 10,190t

1 Breakdown of protection weights:

Belt	520t	501t
Deck	500t	542t
Transverse b/hds	74t	75t
Splinter b/hds	192t	187t
Steering gear	18t	19t
CT	58t	67t
Nav Brdge, etc.	–	10t
Funnel uptakes, cabling	85t	118t

2 Breakdown of fuel and provision weights:

fuel oil	1530t	2080t
diesel	55t	54t
petrol	4.5t	5.3t
reserve oil	20t	22t
feed water	120t	165t
drinking water	10t	14t
washing water	40t	55t
food and provisions	34t	41t
meat	2.8t	6.9t
wine	10t	14t
consumables	23t	25t

100mm. Both types of munitions would include percussive and time-fuzed rounds.

The STCN study also investigated the possibility of investing the additional 120 tonnes available in protection. Variant 4 had increases in horizontal protection only, Variant 5 increases in vertical protection only, and Variant 6 a mix; all three variants assumed that the original armament – ie that of the 7600-ton type – was unchanged. Detailed tables of thicknesses and weights were drawn up for comparison with Variants 1-3, but although there was seen to be some benefit in increasing the protection over the steering gear, the overall increase in protection was found to be insignificant, and would certainly have added less to the ship's capabilities than the

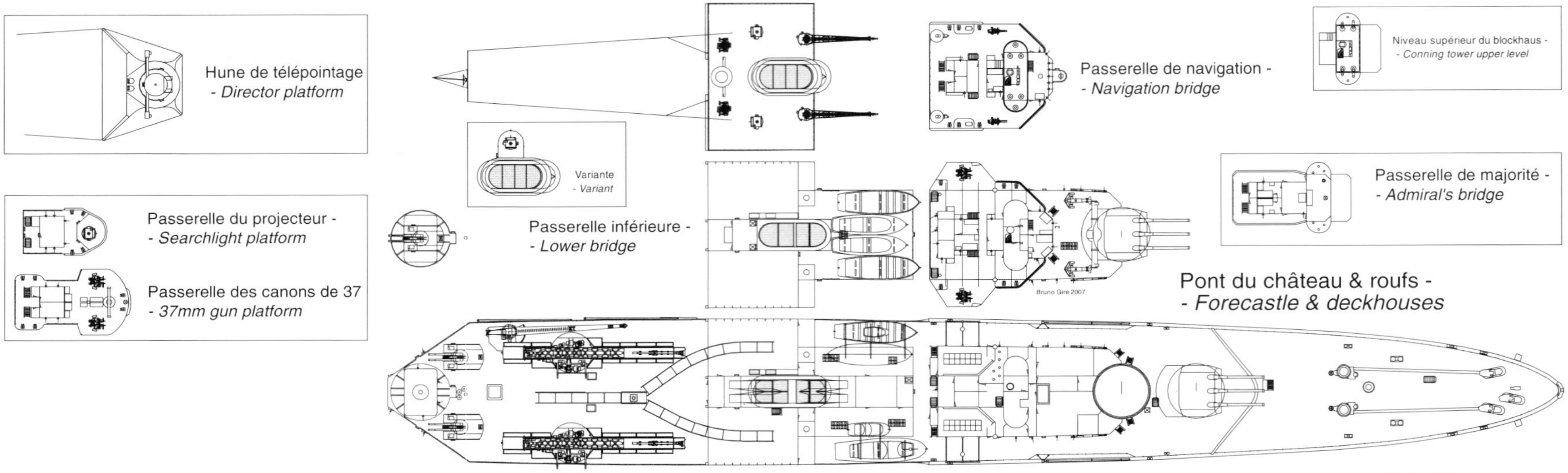

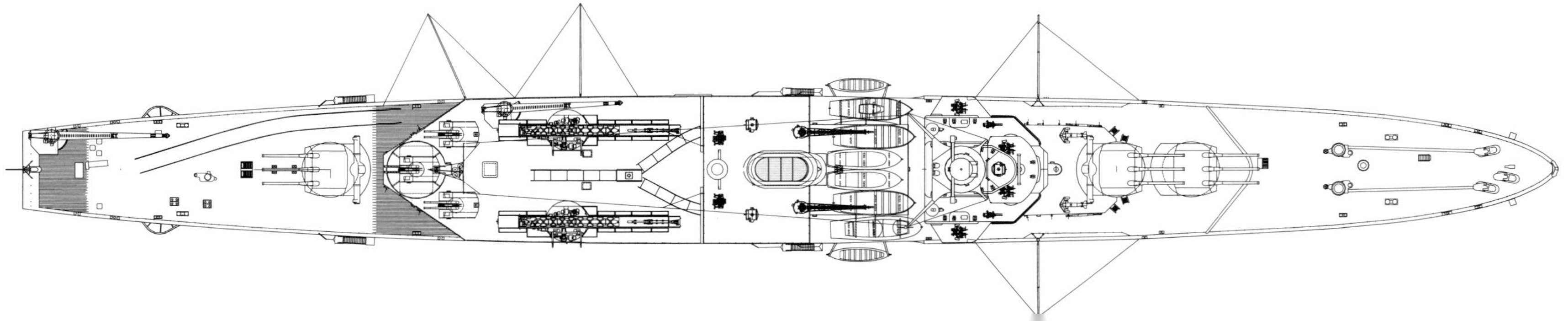

WARSHIP 2008

Niveau supérieur du blockhaus -
- Conning tower upper level

Passerelle de majorité -
- Admiral's bridge

Passerelle de navigation -
- Navigation bridge

Pont du château & roufs -
- Forecastle & deckhouses

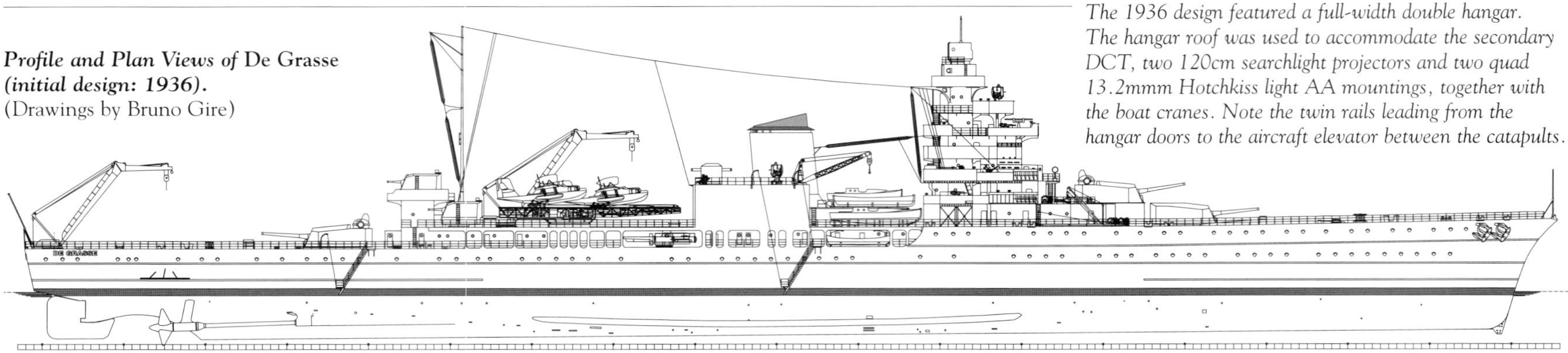

The 1936 design featured a full-width double hangar. The hangar roof was used to accommodate the secondary DCT, two 120cm searchlight projectors and two quad 13.2mm Hotchkiss light AA mountings, together with the boat cranes. Note the twin rails leading from the hangar doors to the aircraft elevator between the catapults.

Passerelle inférieure -
- Lower bridge

Variante
- Variant

Hune de télépointage
- Director platform

Passerelle du projecteur -
- Searchlight platform

Passerelle des canons de 37
- 37mm gun platform

Profile and Plan Views of De Grasse (initial design: 1936).
(Drawings by Bruno Gire)

118

possible modifications to the main and secondary guns.

Having considered all the possible options the STCN therefore expressed a strong preference for a ship with the 70° main gun mounting, two or three 100mm *type avisos-dragueurs*, twin catapults on the shelter deck and three aircraft, with protection similar to the *La Galissonnière*. This was accepted by the Naval General Staff.

The 1936 Design

By late 1936 detailed drawings for the new ship had been produced. There was one important modification: by adopting a broad single funnel in place of the twin funnels of the 7600-ton type sufficient space was created for twin hangars, Royal Navy-style, abeam the funnel. As with the British ships the roofs of the hangars were used to accommodate HA fire control directors and light AA guns (see 1936 drawing), and there were tracks leading from each hangar to the centre-line, where they crossed a powered elevating platform similar to that of the new battleships, the function of which was to raise the aircraft to the level of the catapults; they could then be transferred manually without use of the crane.

There was, however, a cost to the new arrangements. Space for the catapults was squeezed to such an extent that the port-side catapult had to be moved inboard in order to accommodate the handling crane. An athwartships catapult similar to that fitted in the latest British battleships and cruisers would have provided a far superior arrangement, but no such model had been developed for the Marine Nationale.

The second problem was that there was a substantial increase in topweight, and the Marine Nationale became concerned that standard displacement might now exceeed the 8000-ton treaty maximum. By 1938 the double hangar had again been suppressed, and the reserve aircraft had to be stowed on the centre-line rail between the catapults (see 1938 drawing). The layout of the fire control directors and the light AA needed to be revised in consequence. In part compensation, Vice-Admiral Darlan requested at the last moment that the original twin torpedo tubes become triples. This change was implemented, but it is clear from a note from the Chief of Naval Staff that although officially the new cruiser displaced precisely 8127 tonnes this figure was likely to be exceeded on completion.[5]

The 1938 Design

By January 1938 the official specifications of the *De Grasse* were as follows:-

– main armament: as *La Galissonnière* but with triple mountings derived from the dual-purpose mounts developed for the battleships of the *Richelieu* class; maximum elevation 70°;
– secondary armament: three twin 100mm Mle 1933 dual-purpose guns in pseudo-turrets *type avisos-dragueurs*;
– close-range AA: four twin 37mm Mle 1933 semi-automatic mountings, with one quad and two twin 13.2mm Hotchkiss MG;
– fire control: two director control towers superimposed (as in the battleships) atop the forward tower, of which the lower was for control of the main and secondary guns against surface targets and the upper for HA fire control (100mm); there was also an after auxiliary DCT for emergency control of the 100mm guns;
– torpedo tubes: two triple banks of tubes;
– aviation: two aircraft (one reconnaissance, one fighter) accommodated either on the catapult or on rails on the centre-line;
– protection: armour broadly comparable to *La Galissonnière*, but with additional light splinter protection for the command spaces and the directors;
– speed and endurance: a maximum speed of 33.5 knots was specified; endurance was to be 8000nm at 15 knots with a full load of fuel; both these figures were an improvement on the *La Galissonnière* (31kts/5000nm at 15kts).

Hull

Length between perpendiculars was increased by 8.5m over the 7600-ton type and beam by just over a metre. Trial displacement, projected at 10,190 tonnes, was almost 1500 tonnes in excess of the 7600-ton cruisers and broadly comparable to that of the latest Italian cruisers of the *Abruzzi* type.

The hull-form was derived from the *La Galissonnière* class, but in order to secure the high speed required it was finer forward with greater flare, and the stem was less curved at the waterline. There were 60-metre bilge keels 0.7m wide. High-tensile 60kg steel was used for construction of the hull – 50kg standard construction steel had been used for the earlier ships. Overall hull weight as a proportion of light displacement remained at just over 32% (see Table 2).

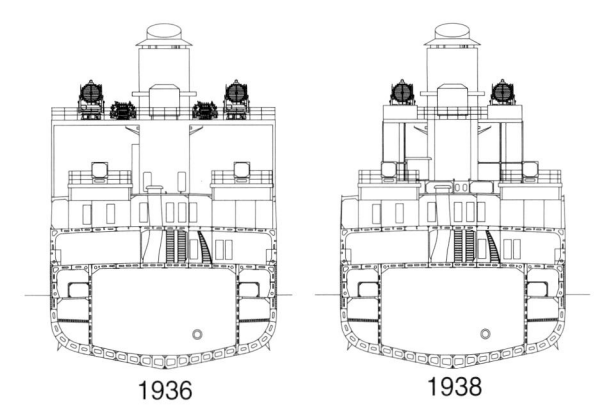

Sectional Views of 1936 and 1938 Designs
These sectional views at Frame 66 highlight the key differences between the 1936 and 1938 designs. The upper part of the 1936 section is dominated by the full-width double aircraft hangar; in the 1938 view the secondary DCT and the 120cm searchlight projectors have been relocated. (Drawings by Bruno Gire)

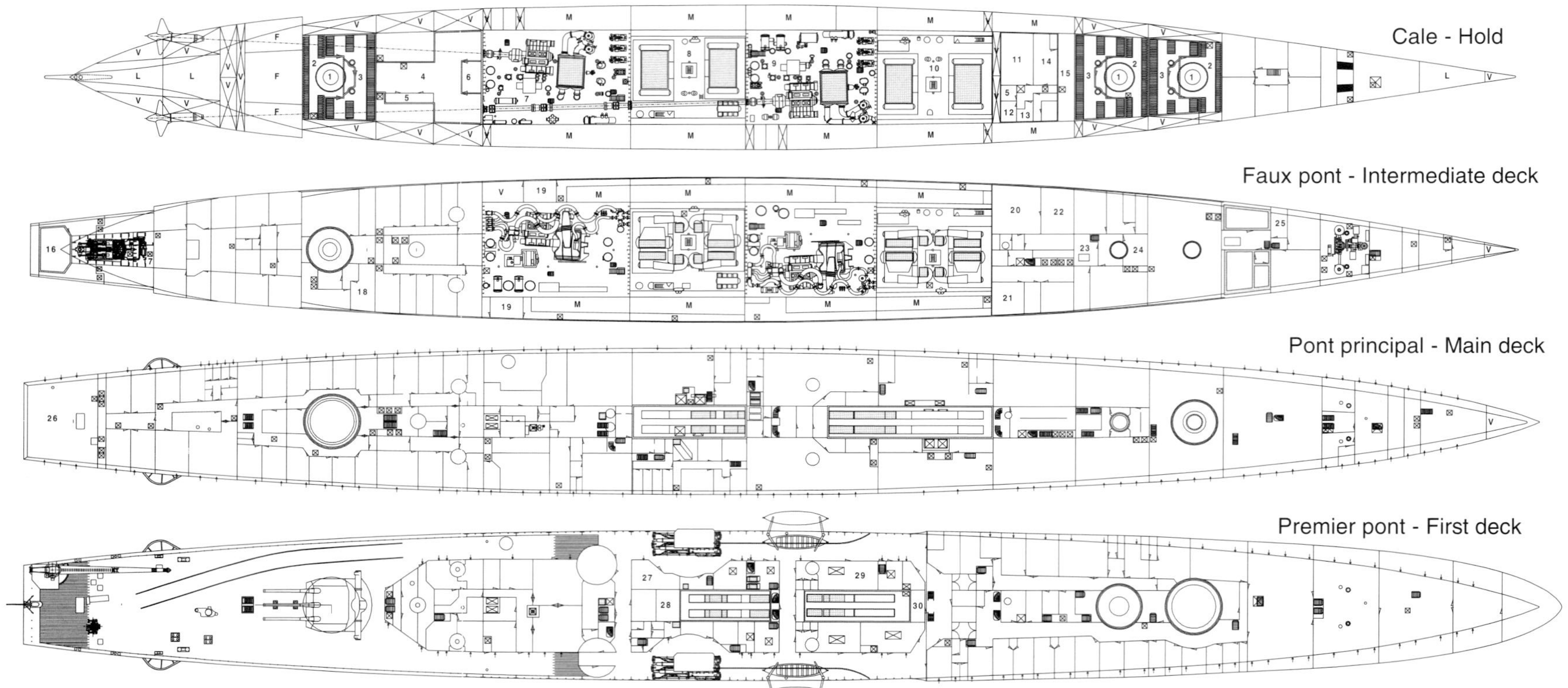

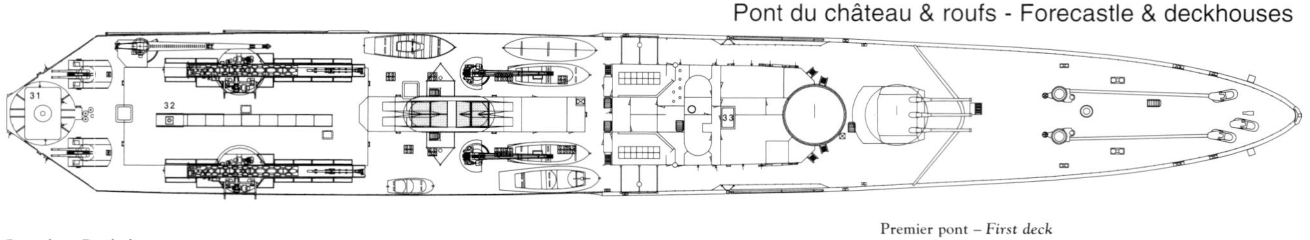

WARSHIP 2008

Cale - Hold
Faux pont - Intermediate deck
Pont principal - Main deck
Premier pont - First deck
Pont du château & roufs - Forecastle & deckhouses

De Grasse 1938: Emménagements – Internal arrangements

Compartiments communs – Common to all decks
V – Vide – Void
M – Soute à mazout – Fuel oil
L – Lest liquide – Water ballast
W – WC
A – Ventilation – Vent

Cale – Hold
1. Tourelle de 152 chambre de distribution – 152mm handing room
2. Soute à obus – 152mm shell room
3. Soute à poudre – 152mm magazine
4. Soute à munition de 100 – 100mm magazine
5. Fusées – Fuzes
6. 100mm éclairants – Illuminating shell
7. Machine bâbord – Aft engine room (port shaft)
8. Chaufferie arrière – Aft boiler room
9. Machine tribord – Fwd engine room (std shaft)
10. Chaufferie avant – Forward boiler room
11. Munitions de 37 – 37mm munitions
12. Bombes – Bombs

13. Grenades – Depth charges
14. Soute pour armes légères – Small arms magazine
15. Appareil d'écoute sous-marine – Underwater sound device

Faux pont – Platform deck
16. Soute à essence – Petrol tank
17. Appareil à gouverner – Steering compartment
18. Poste secondaire de sécurité arrière – After damage control station
19. Poste de TSF protégé – W/T office (under armour)
20. Poste de combat artillerie – Transmitting station

21. Poste central radio – W/T Office
22. Central C.A. – AA plot
23. Salle d'opération – Operations room
24. Salle des tableaux – Plot room
25. Poste secondaire de sécurité avant – Forward damage control station

Pont principal – Main deck
26. Treuil de la rampe d'amerrissage – Winch for recovery mat

Premier pont – First deck
27. Atelier torpilles – Torpedo workshop
28. T.S.F. – W/T office
29. Local du diesel de secours – Emergency diesel room
30. Poste sécurité – Damage control centre

Pont du château et roufs – Forecastle and deckhouses
31. Poste de repos pour les servants des tourelles – Gun crews' shelter
32. Élévateur d'aviation – Aircraft elevator
33. Poste radio-goniométrique – Radio-goniometry (HF/DF) room

120

THE CRUISER DE GRASSE

Profile and Plan Views of De Grasse (final design: 1938)

In the 1938 design the double hangar was suppressed in order to save weight. This meant accommodating the secondary DCT atop its own pedestal, and the searchlights on platforms projecting from the sides of the funnel. There were now goose-neck cranes for the boats. The rails between the catapults provided a rest position for a third aircraft. (Drawings by Bruno Gire)

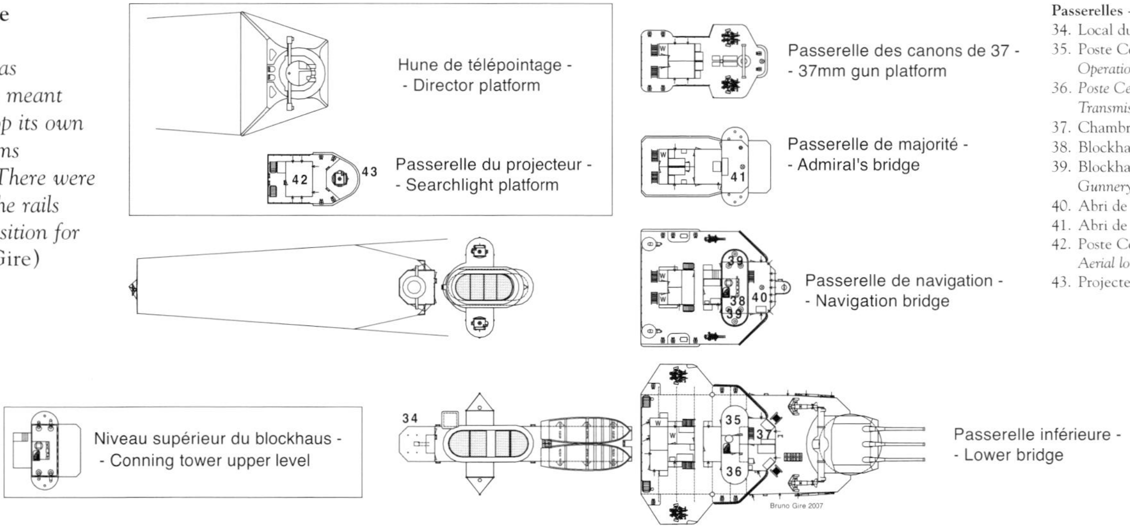

Passerelles – Bridges and platforms
34. Local du conjugateur – Computer room
35. Poste Central Opérations – Operations centre
36. Poste Central Transmissions – Transmissions centre
37. Chambre des cartes – Chart house
38. Blockhaus de manoeuvre – Conning tower
39. Blockhaus de tir – Gunnery officer's position
40. Abri de navigation – Wheelhouse
41. Abri de majorité – Admiral's bridge
42. Poste Central veille haut – Aerial lookout centre
43. Projecteur de 1200 – 1200mm searchlight

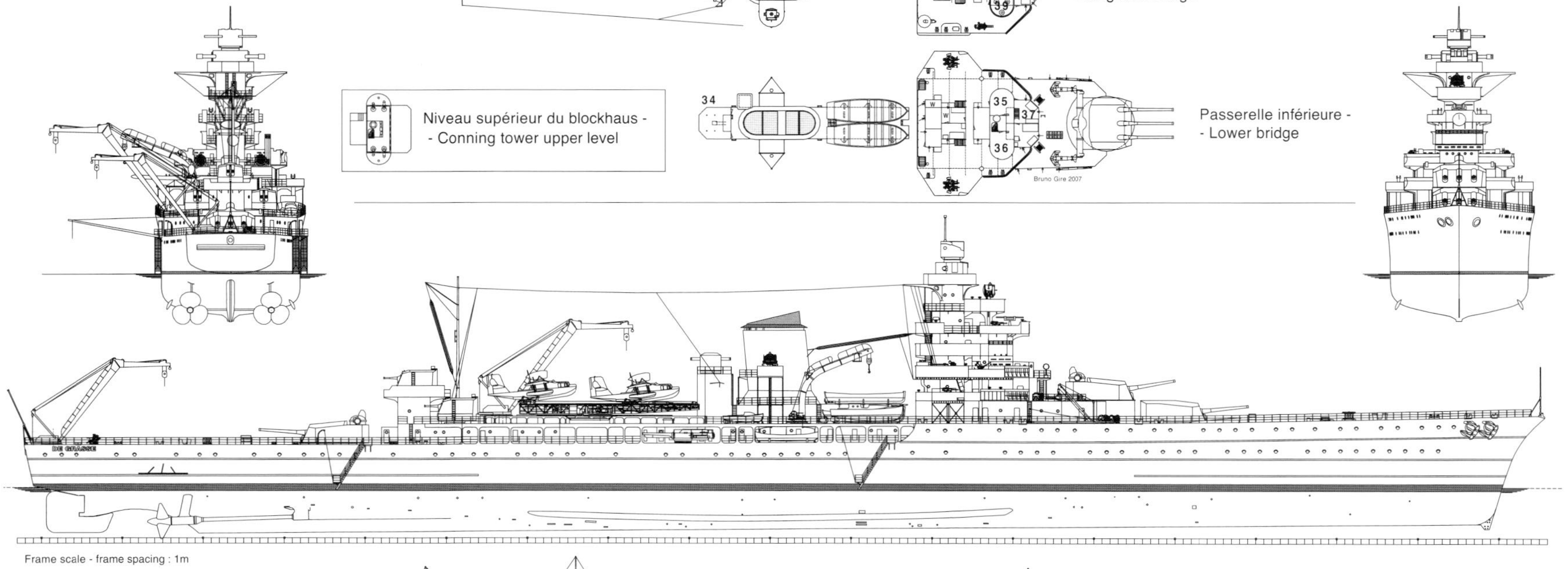

- Passerelle des canons de 37 - 37mm gun platform
- Passerelle de majorité - Admiral's bridge
- Passerelle de navigation - Navigation bridge
- Passerelle inférieure - Lower bridge
- Hune de télépointage - Director platform
- Passerelle du projecteur - Searchlight platform
- Niveau supérieur du blockhaus - Conning tower upper level

Frame scale - frame spacing : 1m

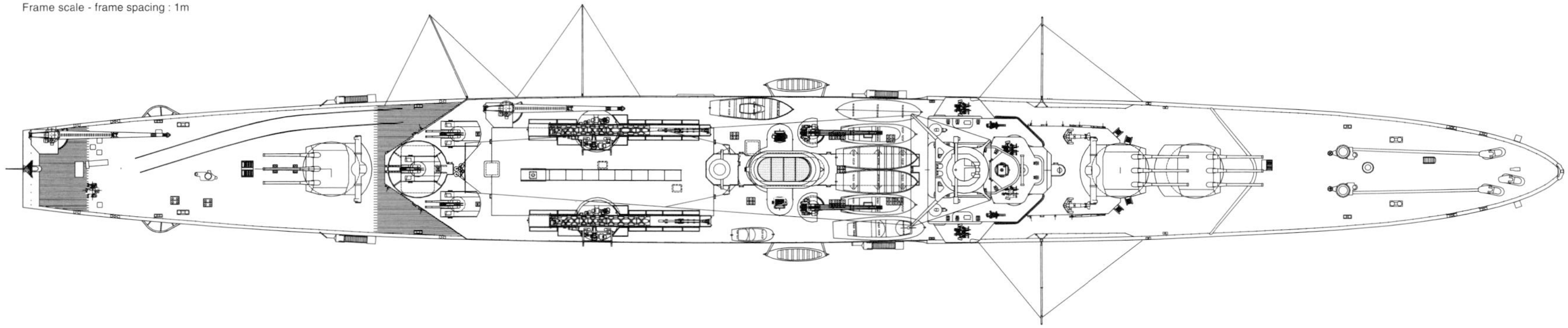

121

Protection (1938)
(Drawings by Bruno Gire)

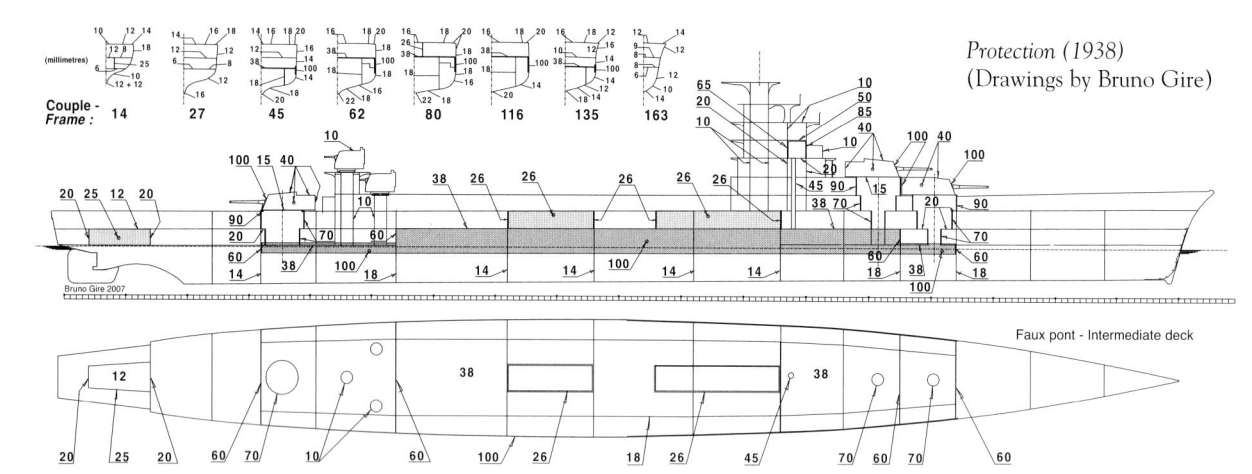

Faux pont - Intermediate deck

Construction was on the longitudinal principle. There was some welding of joints and decks but riveting continued to be employed for the hull plating. Topweight was reduced, as in other contemporary light French surface units, by the extensive use of duralumin for internal partitions, ladders and other fittings. The upper deck had wood planking from the stern to the catapult pivots. The forecastle was to have a linoleum or rubberised covering as far as turret no.1, and the same covering was to be applied to the after part of the boat deck. All other exposed parts of decks were to have a special paint being trialled on the *Mogador* class. There was more attention to corrosion issues than in earlier ships; all metal sheets of 5mm thickness or less were to be galvanised, and other parts of the hull were to receive two coats of lead paint or special paint.

Protection

The protection system of the *De Grasse* class was similar in conception to that of the *La Galissonnière*. The midships section was protected by a 100mm vertical belt of special steel 3.5m high, which extended from the main deck to one metre below the waterline and covered the machinery, transmitting station and other main control spaces, together with the magazines for no.2 152mm turret and the 37mm AA. This belt was continued aft at a reduced height of 1.6m to protect the after 152mm and 100mm magazines and shell rooms (Frames 32-54), and forward to cover the magazine for no.1 152mm turret (Frames 135-144). There were 60mm transverse bulkheads at frames 32, 54, 135 and 144 to enclose the armoured citadel, and these bulkheads were reinforced to 18mm between the lower edge of the armour and the ship's bottom. 80kg special steel was preferred to cemented armour because the technology of the period was insufficiently advanced to manufacture plates of the required length, and the number of vertical joints in the armour would have weakened the integrity of the bulkheads. Nevertheless a few plates of cemented armour were ordered for possible installation in these cruisers.

Outboard of the machinery, at a distance of 5.8m from the centre-line, there was a longitudinal bulkhead of 18mm 80kg special steel, and there was a similar bulkhead alongside the magazines up to the level of the magazine crowns. The uptakes for the broad single funnel were protected by longitudinal and transverse bulkheads 26mm thick between the armoured deck and the upper deck.

Horizontal protection was on a par with the *La Galissonnière* class: the main deck above the machinery was reinforced to 38mm in special steel to protect the machinery and main control spaces, and the crowns of the 152mm and 100mm magazines were given the same protection. All penetrations of the armoured deck (funnel uptakes, ventilation trunking, etc.) were covered by fixed

Table 3: EFFECTIVENESS OF ARMOUR

Values for penetration at normal angles. Armour effective:

	BEYOND		
Vertical armour	130 Mle 1932	138 Mle 1927	152mm Mle 1930
(100mm special steel)	7400m	10,200m	13,900m

	UP TO		
Armoured deck	130 Mle 1932	138 Mle 1927	152mm Mle 1930
(38mm special steel)	15,700m	16,200m	17,500m

Note: These figures do not take into account:
the 18mm splinter bulkhead behind the vertical belt;
the upper deck above the armoured deck.

Table 4: TURRET AND CONNING TOWER ARMOUR

Turrets:

fwd faces:	100mm
sides:	40mm
roofs:	40mm
coamings:	90mm
seatings:	70mm

Conning Tower:

walls:	95mm at sides, 85mm fwd/after faces
roof:	50mm
floor:	20mm
comms. tube	45mm

or removable grilles of special steel. The steering gear, as in *La Galissonnière*, was protected by an armoured box with 26mm sides, 20mm end bulkheads and an 18mm roof. The estimated effectiveness of the main vertical and horizontal plates is tabulated in Table 3.

The turret and the conning tower armour was again similar to the *La Galissonnière* (for details see Table 4). In addition, the operations/transmission centre directly beneath the conning tower was protected by 20mm splinter plating. Plating of 10mm 80kg steel was applied to the gunhouses of the 100mm DP guns, the forward tower and some of its internal partitions, and the gun director housings. This was intended to provide protection against strafing and shell splinters.

Compartmentation was so arranged that all sections of the ship were as far as possible autonomous. The ship was divided into 16 compartments by 15 main watertight bulkheads, and the propulsion machinery, as in the *La Galissonnière* class, was arranged as two independent units, each with its own pumps and other auxiliary machinery, in order to minimise the effects of flooding of the machinery spaces.

As in the *La Galissonnière* class there was to be an elaborate gas protection system. The alert system comprised three klaxons plus a network of green lights. There were gas masks for individual protection, all ventilation machinery for the machinery, the magazines and the command spaces could be shut down from the bridge, and there were also remote-controlled gas-tight covers for the ventilation trunking.

Armament

The triple 152mm mountings to be installed in the *De Grasse* were essentially of the same model as the one designed for the battleships of the *Richelieu* class, but with a number of important modifications. Like those of the battleships – and unlike those of the *La Galissonnière* class – they were dual-purpose mountings intended to engage aircraft as well as surface targets. However, whereas the mountings in *Richelieu* had a theoretical angle of elevation of 90°, with loading at all angles of elevation, this was reduced to 70° for the mountings in *De Grasse*. This reduced the depth of the gun wells. Moreover, the three hoists which served each of the three guns – one for charges, one for percussive shells, the other for time-fuzed anti-aircraft shells – were disposed longitudinally. This meant that the distance between the guns could be reduced, resulting in a turret ring of smaller diameter, with a consequent saving in armour protection. The all-angle reloading mechanism was virtually identical to that of the *Richelieu*, and given that the battleship mountings were to give trouble at angles of elevation in excess of 75°, the arrangements adopted for the *De Grasse* would probably have been more satisfactory and just as effective.

There was magazine space for an impressive 1980 rounds (including exercise rounds). However, dual-purpose capability came at a cost. Only 900 rounds (100 per gun) were SAP; the remainder were fuzed HE rounds primarily for anti-aircraft use.

The lower of the two DCTs atop the forward tower, which was equipped with an 8-metre stereo rangefinder, was specially fitted to control the main guns, director fire against surface targets being conducted from the armoured conning tower. The transmitting station was located forward beneath the armoured deck. As in the *Richelieu* full remote power control (RPC) in both elevation and azimuth were to be provided. Turrets nos.2 and 3 were also equipped with 8-metre stereo rangefinders and could act as secondary fire control positions, and turret no.3 was to be fitted for this purpose with a mechanical computer *type Aviso* Mle 1936.

The 100mm Mle 1933 was a 45-calibre weapon which fired a 14.9kg shell at a muzzle velocity of 760m/s. The twin base-ring mounting, a lighter version of which was also to have been fitted in the *avisos-dragueurs* of the *Elan* and *Chamois* classes, had a protective shell of 10mm thickness, and therefore required more powerful servomotors. The guns, which were in individual cradles, could elevate from -10° to +90° and were supplied by pusher hoists with mechanical loading. Total provision was 1840 rounds, of which 600 were percussive rounds for use against surface targets and 280 were illuminating shell.

The principal fire control director for the 100mm guns was the upper DCT on the forward tower, although these guns could also be controlled by the lower DCT when firing against surface targets. There was an auxiliary DCT on the after tower directly abaft the funnel for emergency use. The upper DCT on the forward tower was fitted with a 6-metre stereoscopic rangefinder and the after DCT with a 5-metre stereo model.

Much attention was given to the protection of the 152mm and 100mm magazines fore and aft. The magazines were isolated from the hull by two protective 'walls': the 100mm outer armour belt and the 18mm internal 'splinter' bulkhead. There were the customary provisions for ventilation, refrigeration and flooding the magazines, and the space between the magazines and the bulkheads was to be filled with an inert substance called Alfol, which replaced the rockwool favoured in earlier ships. The 152mm shells stowed in the magazine were protected by aluminium plates and the 100mm fixed ammunition by aluminium sheaths.

The three 100mm mountings were grouped around the after tower, which gave them excellent arcs on after bearings but restricted coverage forward of the beam, particularly at low angles of elevation. In order to compensate for this four 37mm Mle 1933 twin AA mountings[6] were mounted forward, two at the level of the forecastle deckhouse abeam turret no.2, and two at the level of the Admiral's Bridge. The light AA outfit was completed by two twin 13.2mm Hotchkiss MG in the bridge wings and a quadruple 13.2mm Hotchkiss on the quarterdeck; the latter was offset to starboard to clear the aircraft rails. No form of external direction (other than visual spotting by lookouts) was provided for any of the light AA guns, which relied on their on-mount gunsights.

The two triple 550mm torpedo mountings were located on the upper deck amidships, as in the *La Galissonnière* class, and training arcs were 50° either side of the beam. As in the earlier cruisers no reloads were provided. The six

Type D5 torpedoes were embarked using the boat cranes.

There were three 120cm searchlight projectors for night action: one on the face of the forward tower, the other two on platforms projecting from the sides of the funnel. Full RPC was provided; all projectors could be controlled from positions port and starboard in the bridge wings, and the forward projector could also be controlled from the main 152mm DCT.

Aviation

The twin catapults were located amidships on either side of the shelter deck abaft the single funnel. It was planned to accommodate a single reconnaissance floatplane with a maximum take-off weight of 3300kg (the latest Loire 130 model) and a single float fighter (the Loire 210, due to enter service in 1939). Between the catapults was a lift with a rotating platform, similar to that installed in the *Dunkerque* class, which raised the aircraft to the level of the catapult. The aircraft could be transferred directly onto the latter with the lift in the raised position.

A canvas recovery mat similar to that fitted in the earlier cruisers and the seaplane carrier *Commandant Teste* (see *Warship 2002-03*) was to be installed in the transom stern. This was served by a 4-tonne crane with a 13.5-metre reach located on the port corner of the stern. Once the aircraft was safely on the mat it was lifted aboard by this crane and placed on rails which ran forward along the quarterdeck to port of the after 152mm turret. A second 4-tonne crane, located on the shelter deck close to the port catapult and with a 16-metre reach, then lifted the aircraft onto the centre-line platform. There were 12-metre booms abeam the after turret to handle the aircraft when alongside. The cranes were to be used for recovery only; all aircraft manoeuvres prior to launch were carried out without use of the forward crane, which was normally stowed fully deployed on the shelter deck so as not to obstruct the port catapult.

As in the *La Galissonnière* class the aviation fuel – 5000 litres for the planes and 1800 litres for the boats – was stowed in special tanks located in the stern and isolated from all surrounding bulkheads; the tanks had a heat-resistant coating. The fuel was pumped to the aircraft station amidships using CO_2 under pressure.

Propulsion

Although the layout of the propulsion machinery of the *De Grasse* was identical to that of the *La Galissonnière* class, with two independent propulsion units each comprising a boiler room with two boilers side by side and a set of geared turbines, power was increased significantly in order to secure the higher speed of 33.5kts stipulated in the staff requirements. Whereas both the *La Galissonnière* type and the 203mm cruiser *Algérie* had a total horsepower (designed) of 84,000shp, in the *De Grasse* class this figure was to be increased to 110,000shp (121,000shp with forcing), which was close to that of France's first Treaty cruisers of the *Duquesne* class.

The four identical Indret small-tube boilers, which featured four collectors, superheating and air reheating, were similar in principle to those developed for the *contre-torpilleurs* of the *Mogador* class (see *Warship 2007*); they were rated at $35kg/cm^2$ (385°C) – equivalent to 500psi and 725°F. Each boiler was enclosed in its own housing and had its own auxiliary ventilators, emergency feed pumps, and lub oil pumps.

Each of the two Rateau-AC Bretagne turbine groups comprised main HP, MP and LP turbines with single-reduction gearing. A cruise turbine, with single reduction gearing and a Vulcan coupling, was located in the housing of the MP turbine. It was decoupled above 15,000shp, equivalent to a speed of 20 knots. The reverse turbines were incorporated in the LP turbine housing. Together the reverse turbines were rated at 23,000shp, and were to be capable of stopping the ship when she was making 18 knots in only two and a half ship lengths. As with the boilers, each of the turbine groups was provided with its own independent auxiliaries. For estimated performance figures for power and endurance see Table 5.

The number of high-performance systems to be fitted in these ships necessitated a major increase in electrical generating power. The *La Galissonnière* class had been fitted with four paired 200kW turbo-generators located in the two engine rooms; the *De Grasse* class would have the same arrangement, but each of the four turbo-generators was rated at 300kW. The two dynamos in the same group

Table 5: POWER AND ENDURANCE (ESTIMATED)

Power vs speed

Basin trials suggested the following figures (trial displacement):

5710shp	= 15kts
15 290shp	= 20kts
33 320shp	= 25kts
60 170shp	= 30kts
110 000shp	= 34kts
127 460shp	= 35kts

The contract stipulated 33.5kts to be attained on trials.

Endurance

Practical consumption at various speeds (increase of 30% over theoretical consumption to take account of operational conditions):

33kts	1179kg/nm
25kts	593kg/nm
20kts	417kg/nm
15kts	241kg/nm

Bunker capacity 2080t fuel oil, so practical endurance estimated as follows:

33kts	1760nm
25kts	3500nm
20kts	5000nm
15kts	8600nm

[Order for emptying fuel bunkers established: lateral bunkers fwd and abeam turbines first, lateral abeam boiler rooms last.]

could be coupled together in parallel. The provision for spare capacity was such that three dynamos were sufficient to power all service on board, even for night action; this permitted one dynamo to be closed down for maintenance. When alongside electrical power was provided by one or more of the three 150kW diesel generators, each of which was capable of a 180kW overload for one hour. One diesel generator was normally sufficient, but two or three needed to be on-line in order to train all turrets without the boilers being lit. Two of these three generators were located on the main deck above the forward boiler room; the third – considered to be the 'emergency' generator in the event of major flooding below – was housed in the forward deckhouse on the First Deck.

Complement and Command Spaces

Accommodation was to be provided for an admiral and his staff together with the ship's crew: a total of 691 officers and men. The Admiral's rooms, together with those of the Captain and the First Officer, were located in the after deckhouse. All furnishings were made of light alloy, as in the *Mogador* class. The Chief Petty Officers' accommodation was in the forecastle, with the other POs accommodated one deck below at main deck level. All officers and senior petty officers had bunks; junior petty officers and lower rates had hammocks. The galleys were located in the forward deckhouse at the level of the First Deck, while shops and other services, including an 8-bed infirmary, were at the same level further forward, in the forecastle. There were sufficient provisions for 30 days – wine stowage was sufficient for 90 days! The workshops and offices were on the main deck amidships with the exception of the torpedo maintenance workshop, which was located in the midships deckhouse.

The main purpose of the forward tower was to support the two superimposed fire control directors for the main and secondary guns. Each level of the tower was to have day cabins or rest rooms for the personnel on watch.

The bridge structure was on three levels. The lower level housed the Admiral's office, the chart room, the Captain's day cabin plus one other, the main operations centre, and the telephone switchboard and battery room. There were six stations for (low-level) lookouts at this level, together with two twin 37mm AA mountings. The intermediate level housed the navigation bridge, the Conning Tower, a day cabin and a signal room. The navigation bridge was protected by 10mm splinter plating and had five turning scuttles on its front face plus fixed scuttles at the sides. There were stations at this level for the port and starboard chiefs of the watch and two twin 13.2mm MG mountings. The upper level housed the Admiral's bridge, which was fully enclosed, the Admiral's operations/transmissions room, and two day cabins (one for the Admiral, the other for his Chief of Staff).

Above the Admiral's bridge there was an open platform for two twin 37mm AA mountings, a gyro-compass, a navigation rangefinder with a 3-metre base, a day cabin and rest room, and four (aerial) lookout positions. Both the navigation bridge and the Admiral's bridge were arranged to permit sky views, and from the navigation bridge there was direct access to the conning tower via an armoured door. The main operations centre could be accessed from the conning tower via holes in its sides which were closed by armoured covers.

Authorisation and Construction

The first of the three cruisers, *De Grasse*, was authorised on 31 Dec 1936 under the 1937 Estimates. The order was placed with the Lorient Naval Dockyard, and the ship was laid down on 28 August 1939, a few days before the outbeak of the Second World War; she was due to enter service in September 1942. The second ship, *Châteaurenault*, was authorised 31 Dec 1937 under the 1938 Estimates and ordered from the private shipyard Forges et Chantiers de la Méditerranée; her entry into service was projected for 1944. A third ship, *Guichen*, was authorised 2 May 1938 under the supplementary 1938 *bis* Estimates, and was to have been built by Forges et Chantiers de la Gironde at Bordeaux.

When war was declared on 3 Sept 1939, construction of the *De Grasse* was suspended (the orders for her two sisters would be cancelled). Work was resumed on 28 September with the workforce available, but was again suspended on 10 June 1940. The ship was only 28% complete at this time; the boilers and machinery had yet to be installed. On 22 June the Germans occupied Lorient and envisaged continuing construction with a view to clearing the slipway. Work on the hull proceeded slowly, and in August 1942 it was proposed to complete the ship as an aircraft carrier of 11,000 tons, with a complement of 33 aircraft. More than a year elapsed before work on this project commenced; there were delays in the delivery of equipment, and little enthusiasm or urgency was displayed by the dockyard workers. Work was further delayed when the ship was struck by two Allied bombs. When Lorient was liberated on 9 May 1945 the Commissariat de la Marine found that a large quantity of material had been concealed in the double bottom of the ship! Construction was again resumed, and the hull was finally launched on 11 Sept 1946. The hull would now remain alongside while new plans for the ship's completion were considered.

Revised Plans

In late 1946 it was still envisaged that *De Grasse* could be completed quickly without major redesign. It was felt that the 1938 design had been sufficiently advanced in conceptual terms to be still relevant to the postwar era. Both major Allied navies, Britain and the USA, seemed convinced of the value of the 6in dual-purpose gun. The US Navy had laid down the two cruisers of the *Worcester* class, armed with twelve 6in/47 Mark 16 guns in a new high-elevation (78°) twin mounting, in early 1945. The Royal Navy cruisers of the *Neptune* class, initially proposed under the 1944 Programme, would have had four triple Mk XXVI mountings in which the guns could elevate to 80° – a two-gun version of this turret would later

The hull of the De Grasse *is towed from Lorient to Brest in February 1951 for completion. Note the reconfigured stern.* (Musée de la Marine)

enter service in the three cruisers of the *Tiger* class, launched 1944-45 (see p.147) but completed only 1959-61.[7] Both these navies appear to have subscribed to the view that pending the development of effective surface-to-air missiles only a gun of this size and range firing proximity-fuzed shells would be capable of defending a surface group against large air-to-surface missiles launched at long range.

The 100mm calibre of the projected secondary battery guns was still considered effective against aircraft, being intermediate between the 4.5in secondary guns of the British *Neptune* and the 3in weapon adopted postwar by the Americans for their cruisers and destroyers. Although the twin 45-calibre Mle 1933 under development during the 1930s had never entered service, the Marine Nationale had in 1945 begun the development of a new weapon with even better performance (20-25rpm), the 100mm/55 Mle 1945, which would equip the rebuilt battleship *Jean Bart* from 1952. A much heavier secondary battery was now envisaged, the aviation facilities being landed in compensation. The original 100mm wing mountings were to be retained, but were to be moved slightly farther forward so that two superimposed mountings could be accommodated on the centre-line aft, firing above the after 152mm turret. A further two twin mountings were to be installed abeam the single funnel, for a total of twelve 100mm Mle 1945 guns in six twin mountings.

The original light AA was now considered hopelessly inadequate by the Marine Nationale, which had been very impressed by the performance of the 40mm Bofors quad mountings installed in the *Richelieu* and the modern cruisers and *contre-torpilleurs* refitted in the USA during 1943-44. It was therefore proposed to fit seven quad Bofors mountings in place of the original 37mm and 13.2mm AA. There were to be two mountings abeam the bridge in place of the lower 37mm mountings, four on the shelter deck amidships in place of the catapults, and a seventh mounting on the quarterdeck aft. Coverage of forward arcs was now arguably even less impressive than in the original design, but the postwar gun mountings would have undoubtedly proved more effective.

Had it not been for a chronic shortage of funds and the chaotic state of France's naval dockyards and their associated industries during the late 1940s there can be little doubt that *De Grasse* would have been completed to the revised plans outlined above. The French naval plan of January 1946 called for three (subsequently two) 'sea-going combat groups' (*groupes de combat de haute mer*) based around the four surviving 152mm cruisers (*Emile Bertin* + the three 7600-ton cruisers *Gloire*, *Montcalm* and *Georges Leygues*) and the two ex-Italian cruisers of the *Attilio Regolo* class. A revised long-term plan (*Marine Future*) promulgated in November 1947 called for six 152mm cruisers (the three 7600-*tonnes* plus three new-build) and six smaller AA cruisers. Under this plan the completion of *De Grasse* was to be authorised in 1950, with two new cruisers authorised in 1954 and 1956 respectively. The first five of the AA cruisers, studies for which were to begin immediately, would be authorised in 1949, 1950, 1952, 1954 and 1956.

On 30 January 1948 the Naval General Staff duly requested a formal study of an AA cruiser of 5/6000 tons standard. The displacement clearly suggested that the Navy was at this stage contemplating a ship similar in size and conception to the Royal Navy's *Dido* and US Navy's *Atlanta* classes. The British ships were armed with four/five twin 5.25in gun mountings, their larger American counterparts with six twin 5in mounts, and it was envisaged that the new French AA cruisers would be armed with the twin 130mm mounting under development postwar, which as a result of a decision 6 June 1947 would now be modified to accommodate a 127mm/54 gun designed to use US Navy 5in munitions. However, a new 152mm dual-purpose weapon using proximity-fuzed shells was not excluded from consideration.

The constructors of the STCN experienced considerable difficulty in designing an effective ship on such a limited displacement, and came up with two basic designs:

– CA1: 6150tW (6968 tonnes trials), six twin 127mm, six twin 57mm.
– CA2: 6600tW approx. (7400 tonnes trials), two triple 152mm DP, four twin 100mm, four twin 57mm.

Plan 50, adopted 9 April 1948, envisaged the completion of *De Grasse* alongside the first of the AA cruisers in 1952. Three months later the CA1 design was adopted, but with some modifications to allow more space for machinery and accommodation. There were to be three twin 127mm mountings forward but only two aft, the twin 57mm mountings being paired abeam the forward superstructure, amidships and on the quarterdeck. The first was to be ordered 1951 or 1952 for completion 1956, and the second 1955 for completion 1959.

Conversion of De Grasse to AA cruiser

The *Projet de statut naval* of 29 August 1949 still envisaged six 7000t AA cruisers – a figure subsequently amended to five cruisers of 8000t. However, the projects draw up by the Marine Nationale postwar were becoming increasingly detached from the hard financial realities which faced the French Government of the period. The military ports of Cherbourg, Brest, Lorient and Toulon were littered with wrecks, and many key facilities had been sabotaged or damaged by Allied bombing. The large prewar naval dockyard workforce had been run down on mobilisation, and the suspension of construction on ships already laid down and the cancellation of these orders during the period of the Vichy Government meant that there was no reason to restore it to its prewar size; private shipyards had been similarly affected. Few of the advanced weapons under development prewar had materialised, and the progress of the war had highlighted the importance of electronic sensors such as radar and Asdic/Sonar, an area which the prewar Marine Nationale had conspicuously neglected and in which it had acquired expertise only through its acquaintance with equipment of British or American design. Worst of all, France was all but bankrupt.

French priorities in the early postwar years were reconstruction, the consolidation of existing force structures and the integration of ex-German and ex-Italian war prizes, together with the development of a new generation of weapons and sensors of French design and manufacture; new construction would have to wait. However, the prevailing world political situation would ensure that the wait was of limited duration. French membership of NATO in 1949 was to be followed by a massive injection of American funding from the early 1950s in the form of the Mutual Defense Assistance Program (MDAP). In January 1951 it was decided that *De Grasse* would be completed as an anti-aircraft cruiser, with 55% of the funding coming from MDAP. At the same time it was decided to modernise the two ex-Italian cruisers *Guichen* and *Châteaurenault* (see *Warship 2005*) to complement the new 'fleet escorts' of the *Surcouf* class. The latter were to be armed with a combination of the new 127mm Mle 1948 DP gun and the 57mm Mle 1951 AA gun, together with the new generation of air surveillance, target designation and fire control radars of French design and manufacture, and these would also be the main weapons and sensors fitted in the *De Grasse*.

General Configuration

When launched on 11 September 1946 at Lorient the hull was complete to the upper deck, and the propulsion machinery and hull protection were in place. It remained to build new superstructures and instal the new armament. This would involve some modifications to the existing structure: in particular, the magazine arrangements would need to be drastically revised, and new munitions hoists accommodated in place of the barbettes for the original three triple 152mm.

The reduction in topweight resulting from the elimination of the 152mm turrets and conning tower with their heavy armour permitted much more built-up superstructures, which where possible were constructed of light alloy. The forecastle was extended to the quarterdeck, and a broad deckhouse built out to the ship's sides amidships to accommodate the powerful battery of AA guns. There was now a massive bridge block for the command spaces with a heavy pole mast at its after end. The funnel was more upright than in the original design, and was topped

An early view of De Grasse *at Brest before her entry into service; the radar antennae have yet to be fitted.* (Marine Nationale, courtesy of Robert Dumas)

by a prominent cowling designed to take the exhaust gases clear of the enlarged bridge structure (see inboard profiles). The after superstructure was kept to a minimum, as in the original design – just sufficient to accommodate the after guns and their fire control directors. Abaft the funnel was a simple pole mast for the ESM antennae and radio communications aerials.

The anti-aircraft battery was disposed symetrically at either end of the ship. There were two superimposed twin 127mm/54 Mle 1948 mountings on the centre-line fore and aft, with two wing mountings at the corners of the deck above, making for a 'lozenge' arrangement. The ten twin 57mm/60 Mle 1951 mountings were grouped around the forward and after superstructures one or two decks above, with one mounting of each group on the centre-line and the remaining four paired at the sides. The four fire control directors for the main armament, which were of the same model installed in the fleet escorts of the *Surcouf* class, were disposed in a 'lozenge' arrangement which reflected the layout of the turrets, the side-mounted directors being mounted directly abaft the forward 57mm guns on either side of the funnel. They were complemented by four smaller fire control directors for the 57mm guns, two of which were on the centre-line fore and aft, and the other two in the bridge wings above the forward group of gun mountings. This layout was intended to optimise all-round coverage for the AA battery at all angles of elevation, with up to eight aerial targets able to be engaged simultaneously.

Armament

The 127mm/54 Mle 48 was a semi-automatic weapon with a practical range of 15,000m against surface targets and 10,000m in the anti-aircraft role. It fired a shell weighing 32kg with a separate C1 charge weighing 19kg. Each gun was served by twin hoists – one for shells, the other for cartridges – with two loaders in the turret and two replenishing the hoists from the handing room below. There was a trayworker and a gunlayer for each gun, and a sightsetter, a supervisor and a turret commander for each mounting, for a total manning requirement of eleven in the mounting and four in the handing room below. The shell rooms and magazines were on two levels fore and aft of the machinery spaces. They housed a total of 4800 shells and charges, based on a provision of 300 rounds per gun. Each twin 127mm mounting had a total weight of 48 tonnes, of which the elevating mass accounted for 14 tonnes.

The 127mm gun mountings had full remote power control (RPC) when controlled by the directors, which were fully stabilised in azimuth and elevation; however, this weapon was considered effective only against aircraft with a speed below 300m/s. In normal practice one director controlled two mountings, but there was provision both for independent manual control and for control by the 57mm directors when firing against aerial targets. Each of the directors for the main guns incorporated a rangefinder with a 6-metre base, primarily for fire support against targets ashore. On the starboard face of the director was

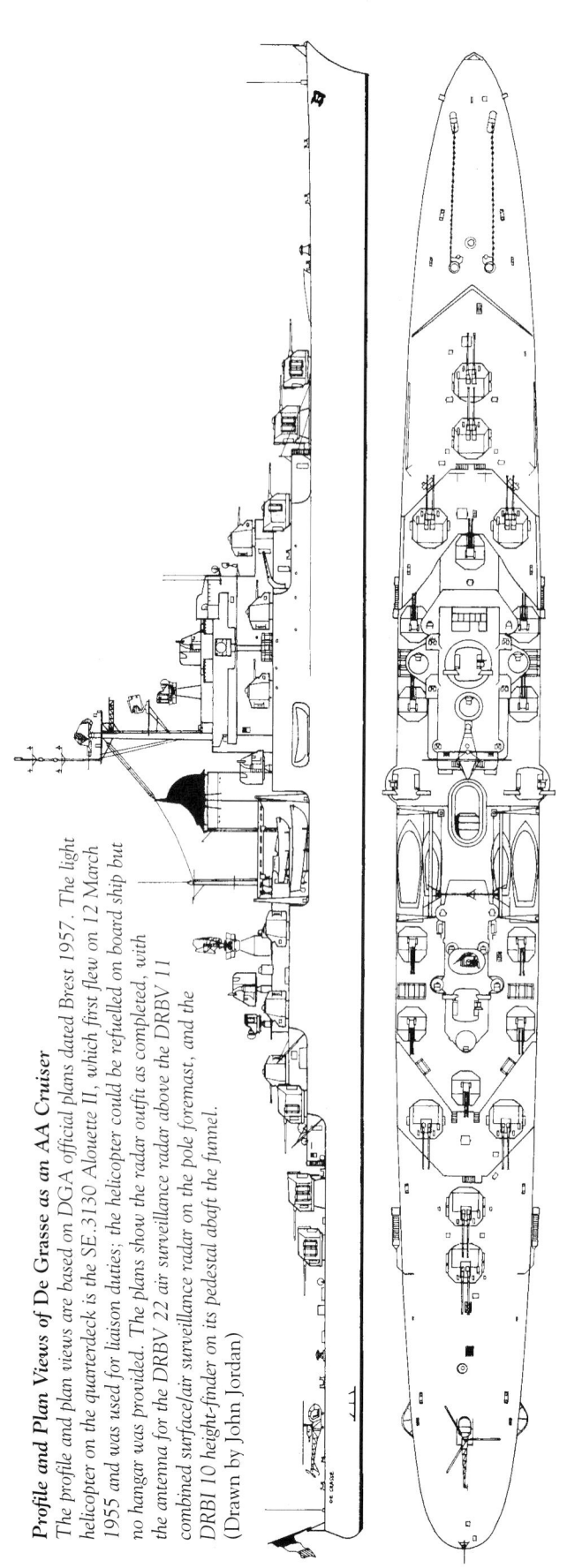

Profile and Plan Views of De Grasse as an AA Cruiser
The profile and plan views are based on DGA official plans dated Brest 1957. The light helicopter on the quarterdeck is the SE.3130 Alouette II, which first flew on 12 March 1955 and was used for liaison duties; the helicopter could be refuelled on board ship but no hangar was provided. The plans show the radar outfit as completed, with the antenna for the DRBV 22 air surveillance radar above the DRBV 11 combined surface/air surveillance radar on the pole foremast, and the DRBI 10 height-finder on its pedestal abaft the funnel.
(Drawn by John Jordan)

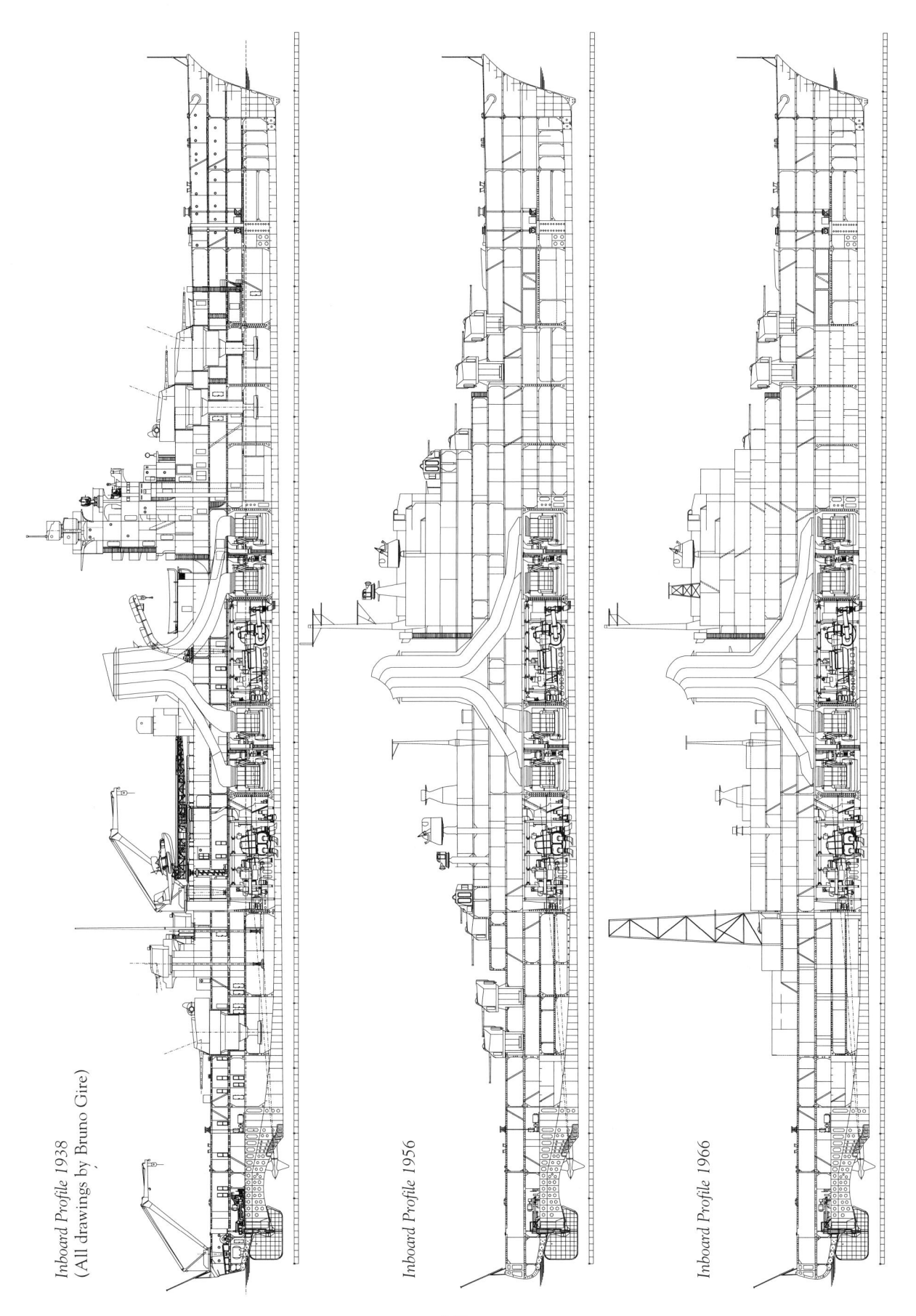

Inboard Profile 1938
(All drawings by Bruno Gire)

Inboard Profile 1956

Inboard Profile 1966

A photo taken from the quarter-deck, with the larger 127mm guns mountings bracketing the after 57mm centre-line mounting. (Collection Landais, courtesy of Robert Dumas)

mounted the small parabolic antenna for the DRBC 11 'S'-Band fire control radar, one of the first examples of the new generation of radars of French design and manufacture. There was a single *poste central* for surface fire and four PC for anti-aircraft fire, two for the 127mm guns and two for the 57mm guns distributed fore and aft.

The 57mm/60 gun was a Bofors model designed postwar as a scaled-up version of the wartime 40mm/60, but the mounting was of French design and manufacture. The Mle 1951 was an improved variant of the Mle 1948 mount which equipped the rebuilt battleship *Jean Bart*. Performance data for the two mountings was broadly similar, but the later model had higher speeds of elevation and training. The gun, which retained the standard Bofors 'fan-feed' system for supplying ammunition, fired fixed ammunition of French design with a total weight of 6.4kg; projectile weight was 2.96kg, with a 0.94kg BM4 charge. The fan feed (quadrant-shaped hoppers mounted at the trunnions) was joined at the trunnion axis by an inverted-'U' feed hoist which extended down to an automatic-feed ready-service box on the floor of the mounting. The ready-service box was refilled by hand at a rate of 40 rounds per minute from a hoist turning with the mount and extending down to the distribution room below. Between them the box, the feeder hoist and the fan feed had a capacity of 80 rounds per gun. Munitions were stowed in four-round cases in magazines adjacent to the 127mm magazines fore and aft; 30,000 57mm rounds (1500 per gun) were provided. There were two loaders on the mounting and two munition handlers below; the gun crew for each mounting was completed by two gunlayers, a sightsetter and the gun commander, for a total of six on the mounting and two below. Each 57mm mounting had a total weight of 18 tonnes, of which the elevating mass accounted for 3.9 tonnes.

Like the 127mm guns the 57mm AA had full RPC in azimuth and elevation, and employed a tachymetric system of control against aerial targets. Each of the four directors incorporated a rangefinder with a 2.1m base, and was fitted with a DRBC 30 'X'-Band fire control radar. Director control could be exercised either from the after director or from an emergency optical position aft. There was an anti-aircraft *poste central* between decks which could be used for either surface or AA fire. The mountings could also fire independently in local control.

The weight and manning implications of this powerful anti-aircraft battery were considerable. The total weight of the gun mountings alone came to 1,128 tonnes (768t for the 127mm, 360t for the 57mm), and they required a total of 400 men to man them (240 + 160); the total weight of munitions was 463 tonnes. Moreover, these figures do not take into account the weight and manning requirements

Table 6: GUNS MOUNTED IN DE GRASSE AS AA CRUISER

	127mm/54 Mle 1948	57mm/60 Mle 1951
Gun data		
munitions	separate	fixed
projectiles:	OEA Mle 1948 BF	
	OEA Mle 1948 CA	OEA Mle 1950
projectile weight:	32kg	2.96kg
charge:	C1: 8.5kg	BM4: 0.94kg
muzzle velocity:	810m/s	865m/s
max. range at 40°:	21,800m	13,000m
practical range:		
surface targets	15,000m	–
aerial targets	10,000m	5600m*
Mounting data		
weight of mounting:	48 tonnes	18 tonnes
turret shield:	10mm face/sides	10mm face
	7mm roof/rear	7mm sides/roof
elevation of guns:	–5° / +70°	–10° / +90°
training speed:	25°/sec	40°/sec
elevation speed:	25°/sec	40°/sec
firing cycle:	14-15rpg/min	50-60rpg/min
gun crew:	11 in gunhouse + 4	6 on mount + 2

* the 57mm shells were designed to auto-destruct after 10 secs.

Note: BF = but flottant (anti-surface)
CA = contre avions (anti-aircraft)

of the four main and four secondary fire control directors, the surveillance, target designation and height-finding radars, and the radar/FC control spaces. The weight allocated to armament (including protection) in the original prewar design was 1,383 tonnes, and further savings of around 280 tonnes were made by dispensing with the conning tower, torpedo tubes and aviation facilities, so accommodating the weight of the new armament was (just!) feasible. However, the original complement of 690 rose to 950 in the AA conversion, and this naturally had major implications for the provision of accommodation – hence the much-enlarged superstructures.

Electronics Outfit

As originally completed *De Grasse* carried virtually a full complement of the new surveillance and target designation radars developed postwar for the Marine Nationale. The pole foremast carried the DRBV 11 air/surface surveillance radar and, above it, the DRBV 22A medium-range air surveillance radar. The latter was a D-Band model developed from the US Navy's SPS-6, and had a similar parabolic antenna of open lattice construction with a prominent feed-horn below.

The radar outfit was completed by the DRBI 10 3-D height-finding radar, similar in conception and configuration to the contemporary US Navy SPS-8, mounted atop a cone-shaped pedestal on the after deckhouse. The DRBI

Table 7: RADARS MOUNTED IN DE GRASSE AS AA CRUISER

Model	Function	In service	Performance
DRBV 20A	air surveillance	1954	A (P)* Band: 250km
DRBV 22A	air surveillance	1956	D (L) Band: 130-220km
DRBV 11	target indication	1954	E/F (S) Band: 60km (surf.) 120km (aerial)
DRBI 10A	height-finder	1957	E/F (S) Band: 185km
DRBC 11	127mm FC (4)	1954	E/F (S) Band: 60?km
DRBC 30	57mm FC (4)	1954	I (X) Band: 40km

* US equivalent radar bands in brackets

10 was to be installed, together with the DRBV 22A air surveillance radar, in the second series of fleet escorts of the T53 *Duperré* type, which were designed as escorts for the new carriers and were equipped for picket and fighter direction duties. Both *De Grasse* and her purpose-built half-sister *Colbert* would be fitted with three fighter direction centres. However, although these capabilities were a major advance on anything previously attempted by the Marine Nationale, manual plotting continued to be used to monitor the air situation around the ships, and 15 aerial contacts was considered to be the maximum number which could be successfully handled. Further improvements would have to await the computer-based and highly-automated SENIT data processing systems introduced during the 1960s.

In addition to being fitted with the new generation of French radars, *De Grasse* had the latest ESM equipment and the DSBV 1 torpedo detection sonar. The latter, a passive model operating over the 5-40 kHz range, was housed in a retractable dome just forward of the magazines, while the ARBR 10 and ARBR 20 antennae, for the detection of radar and radio emissions respectively, were fitted atop the pole mast abaft the funnel. There was also a standard NATO IFF interrogator Mk 10 to identify 'friendly' radar emissions.

Completion and Early Service

Completion of *De Grasse* as an anti-aircraft cruiser was protracted. She was towed from Lorient to Brest Naval Dockyard on 14 February 1951, and reconstruction began immediately but was delayed by the late delivery of equipment, much of which was still under development when work began. *De Grasse* was to have begun her trials in August 1954, but these were again delayed, this time by an accident: when she was floated out of dry dock a water inlet was accidentally left open, a major compartment was flooded and the ship settled on the bottom. She finally ran her speed trials in April 1955.

In late August 1956 *De Grasse* left Brest for Toulon, officially entering service on 10 September. She subsequently became flagship of the *Escadre de la Méditerranée*, flying the flag first of Admiral Barjot and then of Vice-

Admiral Jozan. In March 1957 she took part in manoeuvres in the Mediterranean which simulated the defence of a convoy against aerial attack.

When her half-sister *Colbert* entered service in 1959 (becoming flagship in her turn) *De Grasse* returned to Brest for her first major refit, which took place from 22 December 1959 until February 1961. The refit focused on improving accommodation. The four inboard 57mm mountings, which had relatively restricted arcs, were removed, together with the two side-mounted fire control directors for the 127mm guns. The hull opening for the whalers beneath the bridge was plated in, and at the after end of the bridge structure, in place of the 57mm mountings and directors which had been removed, new 'side pods' were built out to further increase internal volume.

Left: An aerial view of De Grasse *taken in 1959, shortly before her first major refit.* (Marine Nationale, courtesy of Robert Dumas)

Below: A close-up of the after port side of the ship. The flag is that of a vice-admiral. (Marine Nationale, courtesy of Robert Dumas)

THE CRUISER DE GRASSE

A stern quarter view of De Grasse *taken during the late 1950s. She retains all of her original guns and FC directors.* (Courtesy of Robert Dumas)

De Grasse *leaving Toulon in 1962, following her first major refit. The original DRBV 11 dual-function radar has been superseded by the DRBV 20A (lower foremast platform), and four of the 57mm mountings have been removed, together with the two side-mounted fire control directors for the 127mm guns. There are new accommodation pods abeam the after end of the bridge structure.* (Collection Landais, courtesy of Robert Dumas)

De Grasse after modification to a command ship 1965-66. (Collection Landais, courtesy of Robert Dumas)

The radar outfit was also upgraded, the major change to the ship's external appearance resulting from the replacement of the original DRBV 11 dual-function radar (lower foremast platform) by the more successful DRBV 20A, which had a maximum range against aerial targets of about 250km.

Following this refit *De Grasse* again served with the Mediterranean Squadron, replacing *Colbert* as flagship (VAE Jubelin) from the end of 1962 until mid-1963. She left Toulon for the last time on 4 May 1964, arriving back in Brest in early 1965 for conversion to her new role of command ship for the French nuclear tests in the Pacific.

Polynesia and the CEP

The first French atomic tests took place in the Algerian Sahara in 1960. During the early 1960s, with the independence of Algeria, it was decided to create a new trials centre in French Polynesia, which would become the *Centre d'Expérimentation du Pacifique* (CEP). A naval command ship was required to coordinate operations off the Mururoa atoll, and *De Grasse* was duly taken in hand at Brest in early 1965 to perform this role. Only six of the original eight twin 127mm mountings were retained – the two quarterdeck mountings were removed – and all 57mm mountings were landed. Only a single 127mm director (atop the bridge) and a single secondary director (centreline aft) were retained.

The bridge structure was extended forward and to the sides to provide sufficient volume for new command and control spaces which included a meteorological office, and the existing DRBV 20 and DRBV 22 air surveillance radars were replaced by a single more advanced model, the DRBV 23. The pole foremast now carried an ANUR 3 Tacan beacon to facilitate air operations; the DRBI 10 height-finding radar was retained. A computer to predict fall-out after firings was installed, and there was now a giant quadripod lattice mainmast aft, carrying communications equipment which enabled the ship to act as a relay between Paris and the control centre ashore (*Poste Central des Tirs* or PCT). In place of the after 127mm mountings a hangar was built on the quarterdeck to accommodate meteorological balloons for atmospheric testing.

The ship's complement was now reduced to 595, but there was additional accommodation for 120-160 civilian technicians and VIPs. The superstructures were made gas-tight and there was an elaborate Nuclear/Biological/Chemical (NBC) washdown system. The firing of the nuclear devices tested was initiated from the control centre ashore, but *De Grasse* had a supervisory role and could interrupt the firing sequence. The ship was used as DIRCEN (*Direction des Centres d'Expérimentations Nucléaires*) and as flagship of GOEN (*Groupe Opérationnel d'Expérimentation Nucléaire*) under the command of the vice-admiral responsible for firings and forces in the area.

De Grasse was overall command ship for all six of the nuclear testing 'campaigns' which took place between 1966 and 1972,[8] and hosted President Charles de Gaulle during the 1966 series of tests. She made her final entry into Brest 9 November 1972 after a 'farewell' world tour. The tall quadripod mainmast had to be dismantled to enable her to make her way up the River Penfeld into the inner reaches of the dockyard. She hauled down her colours for the last time on 28 February 1973, after which she was placed in the Special Reserve B category, becoming Q 521. She would be sold in January 1975 and subsequently towed to the breakers at La Spezia, Italy, after a roller-coaster of a career which must surely rank as one of the most extraordinary in the annals of any navy.

A close-up of the stern, showing the small hangar for meteorological balloons at the base of the tall lattice radio mast. (Collection Landais, courtesy of Robert Dumas)

Sources:

C3-1 Spécifications for 'croiseur protégé "De Grasse"', Centre des Archives de l'Armement; various other associated notes and updates.

Table 8: The cruisers of the De Grasse class

Name	Builder	Laid down	Launched	In service
1937 Programme				
De Grasse	Arsenal de Lorient	28.08.39	11.09.46	03.09.56
1938 Programme				
Châteaurenault	F.C. Méditerranée	Cancelled		
1938 bis Programme				
Guichen	F.C. Gironde	Cancelled		

Characteristics (1938)

Displacement:	8000 tons standard, 8948 tonnes light, 10,190 tonnes trial, 11,431 tonnes deep load
Dimensions:	length 180.4m pp, 188.0m oa; beam (wl) 18.6m; draught 5.5m
Machinery:	four Indret boilers, 35kg/cm^2 (385°C); two-shaft Rateau A.C.B. geared steam turbines; 110,000shp for 33.5kts
Oil fuel:	2080 tonnes; radius 1760nm at 33kts, 5000nm at 20kts, 8600nm at 15kts
Armament:	nine 152mm/55 Mle 1930 in triple mountings Mle 1936 (1980 rounds)
	six 100mm/45 Mle 1933 DP in three twin mountings Mle 1937 (1840 rounds)
	eight 37mm/50 in four twin mountings Mle 1933 (6000 rounds)
	eight 13.2mm Hotchkiss MG in two twin mountings and one quad mountings Mle 1931 (2000 rpg)
	six tubes for 550mm torpedoes Mle 1923D in two triple mountings Mle 1928T
Aircraft:	two catapults; two aircraft (1 Loire 130 recce; 1 Loire 210 float fighter)
Protection:	belt 100mm; deck 38mm; turrets 100mm faces, 40mm sides; conning tower 95mm sides, 50mm roof
Complement:	691

The anti-aircraft cruiser *De Grasse*: characteristics (as completed)

Displacement:	9380 tons standard; 11,350 tonnes trials; 12,520 tonnes full load
Dimensions:	length 180.4m pp, 188.0m oa; beam (wl) 18.6m; draught 5.5m, 6.3m max.
Machinery:	four Indret boilers, 35kg/cm^2 (385°C); two-shaft Rateau A.C.B. geared steam turbines; 105,000shp for 33kts
Oil fuel:	1850 tonnes; radius 6000nm at 18kts, 2000nm at 21kts
Armament:	sixteen 127mm/54 DP Mle 1948 in twin mountings Mle 1948 (4800 rounds)
	twenty 57mm/60 Model 1947 in twin mountings Mle 1951 (30,000 rounds)
Electronics:	surveillance radars: DRBV 22A, DRBV 11, DRBI 10B, DRBN 31
	FC radars: four DRBC 11, four DRBC 30
	ESM: ARBR 10, ARBR 20
	sonar: DSBV 1
Protection:	belt 76-100mm; deck 38-68mm
Complement:	950 (980 as flagship)

René Bail & Jean Moulin, *Les croiseurs De Grasse et Colbert*, Charles-Lavauzelle (Paris 1984)

Jean Moulin, *Le croiseur Colbert*, Marines (Bourg-en-Bresse 1996).

Official plans of *De Grasse* (1936, 1938, 1956 and 1966), Centre des Archives de l'Armement.

Footnotes:

1. For a full description of these ships see the author's 'The 7600-ton cruisers', *Warship 1995*
2. The earlier London Treaty of 1930 had succeeded in limiting the gun calibre of future cruisers to 6in, but the US Navy had insisted on retaining the 10,000-ton maximum displacement figure.
3. The NGS request is in Note 477 EMG.3 of 25 May; the STCN response is Note No.29888 C.N.4
4. Perceptive readers familiar with the 'staff requirements'/'constructors advice' process, will see in this a polite but firm 'put-down' to a General Staff slavering over the prospect of the improvements in performance which might be bought with an additional '400 tonnes'.
5. Note 100 EMG.3 dated 29 January 1938.
6. The Directeur Général de l'Artillerie Navale had pressed for the new axially-fed 37mm automatic mounting then under development (Mle 1935), but finding locations where the magazine could be located directly beneath the mounting seems to have proved difficult; the Mle 1935 would in any case fail to materialise before the Armistice of 1940.
7. See George Moore, 'Post War Cruiser Designs for the Royal Navy 1946-56', *Warship 2006*.
8. Lack of space precludes publication of details of these campaigns in this annual; we will be publishing a brief note in *Warship 2009* with a table outlining the campaigns and the ships which participated.

FIRST CLASS CRUISERS
Part Three

In this long-awaited final part of a trilogy of articles, **Chris Ware** examines the development of the Royal Navy's First Class cruisers from the turn of the century and concludes with a study of operations in the First World War.

The Devonshires

The *Devonshires* were to be similar to the *Monmouths* and *Suffolks* in overall size and armament. The major change would be the inclusion of 7.5in guns fore and aft. In fact the design of this class went through a number of changes, some of them after the early units of the class were launched. They were initially referred to as the 'New Monmouths'. As sketched out they would have been 450ft long between perpendiculars; length overall would have been 465ft, beam 67ft and displacement 10,200 tons. The horsepower of this class would have been some 22,000ihp for a designed speed of 23 knots. The major difference between the New Monmouths and the preceding classes was the substitution of single 7.5in guns fore and aft for the twin 6in of the *Monmouth* and *Suffolk* classes. They would have carried ten 6in guns on the broadside to be placed in double casemates fore and aft and a single casemate amidships.

This sketch design was eventually rejected and a modified version of it took shape, resulting in the *Devonshires*. The new design was to have the same length overall as the New Monmouths; however, there was to be an increase in beam from 67ft to 68ft 6in, and the displacement was increased by 650 tons to 10,850 tons. As designed and tendered for the new ships were still to carry just the two single 7.5in guns fore and aft and have the 6in guns as proposed for the New Monmouths. It was in the area of the anti-torpedo-boat armament that the *Devonshires* were falling behind; as designed and built they were to carry twenty-five 3pdr guns which would be inadequate to the task. As Keith Macbride pointed out in his article in *Warship* nearly twenty years ago[1] the then Director of Naval Ordnance had misread the situation. Torpedoes were coming into service with longer range because of the gyros which helped to keep them on their set course and heater units which gave them more propulsive power. The 12pdr would not be fitted in First Class Cruisers until the *Minotaur* class, even though they were a feature of the battleships building at the time.

The armour protection of the new class was to comprise a 4in belt, a similar thickness on the barbettes, turrets and casemates, and 1.25in on the main deck.

The most radical change to the *Devonshires* came after the tendering process had been completed and construction of the class was underway. This was the replacement of the forward double casemates with a single turret-mounted 7.5in port and starboard; this was as carried out from January 1904. There would be no saving in weight from this arrangement, which would leave the new ships with a mixed broadside of three 7.5in and three 6in guns.

The other area in which significant changes were made was the power plant. The *Devonshires* would figure prominently in the debate within the Royal Navy over what type of boiler should be adopted: cylindrical or water.[2] Despite opposition from the Engineer in Chief

HMS Roxburgh in Plymouth Sound. The 7.5in turreted mountings mark the Devonshires out from their predecessors of the Monmouth *class.* (CPL)

HMS Antrim *at Antwerp in July 1906. Note how close to the water are the lower casemated 6in guns. (Leo van Ginderen collection)*

this class was to have a set of cylindrical and a larger number of watertube boilers. His view was overruled despite the fact that the mixed installation would lead to an overly complex arrangement which would require two sets of stokers trained to operate the different boilers. In the end the *Devonshires* were fitted with six cylindrical and between fifteen and seventeen watertube boilers. The battle of the boilers would not be settled until the last of the armoured cruisers.

Duke of Edinburgh *class*

The next class would see a change both in overall size and armament over the *Devonshires*. With this would come a return to vessels which were designed to be part of the battle fleet as well as hunting down the armoured cruisers of foreign powers. They were to be built under the new Director of Naval Construction (DNC) Sir Phillip Watts. Their length was to be some 480ft, an increase of 15ft over the *Devonshire* and her sisters; there was to be an increase in beam from 67ft to 73ft 6in, and draught at legend design would be 26ft. All of this would serve to increase their displacement to 13,965 tons.

It was in the size and disposition of their main armament that the *Duke of Edinburgh* and her proposed sisters would differ from the *Devonshire* class. They were to carry six 9.2in in single turrets: one forward, one aft, and two on each broadside. They would also carry ten 6in guns: five on each broadside in the waist of the ship. Alongside the main armament there would be twenty-two 3pdr guns as anti-torpedo-boat armament. Whilst the disposition of the 9.2in guns was supposed to allow for three of them to be able to fire ahead or astern, the effects of blast meant that they could be trained only within 30 degrees of the ship's axis. The other issue, and one which bedevilled other designs of the period, was the siting of the 6in guns low down in the waist of the ship, where the guns could not be fought in any kind of seaway. This arrangement would attract considerable criticism, and it is interesting

A view of HMS Carnarvon under way. With their mix of medium-calibre guns in turrets and 6in QF guns in casemates the Devonshires *were the classic armoured cruisers of the period. (Leo van Ginderen collection)*

In HMS Duke of Edinburgh *and her sister* Black Prince *the main gun calibre was upped from 7.5in to 9.2in, and there were six main guns to enable four guns to fire on the broadside and three guns close to the ship's axis fore and aft. Despite the 'Abrahams & Sons, Devonport' label, this photo was taken in the Medway.* (World Ship Society, Abrahams Collection)

to note that as early as 1907 Brassey's Naval Annual was highlighting this potential weakness (see p.9); in the manoeuvres of the same year one of the class had been put out of action by the *Leviathan*. This problem was addressed in 1916 when the 6in guns were mounted behind shields on the upper deck.

In engineering terms they would carry not only coal but oil fuel, and part of the double bottom was converted to carry the 600 tons allowed for in the design. They were also designed with short funnels, something which would cause them problems when they first entered service. These had to be raised by some 6ft above the level of the charthouse to keep the smoke clear, and this modification was made to both ships four years after they were launched.

HMS Black Prince. *The photo illustrates clearly just how close to the ship's waterline the 6in casemate guns were located. This made it difficult to bring them into action in any sort of seaway.* (Leo van Ginderen collection)

FIRST CLASS CRUISERS

HMS Warrior. All four ships of the class were completed with short funnels to reduce their otherwise distinctive silhouette. However, this proved impractical and the funnels had to be raised by 15ft. In this later view Warrior has had her fore-funnel further raised in an effort to keep smoke clear of the bridge. (David K Brown collection)

Eventually only two ships were built to this design: *Black Prince* and *Duke of Edinburgh*; the design was then modified to become the *Warrior* class. In terms of armour protection this class was a marked improvement on the previous two. They would have a 6in belt of Krupp cemented plate which would be carried 14ft 6in above the nominal waterline and which was continued to 4ft 10in below. Turret faces were to be 7.5in; the shallow barbettes had 6in armour. The broadside guns were to have a shallow screen between them, something which could have been a weakness in action.

Warrior Class

The *Duke of Edinburgh* design was altered after the first two ships of the class. Length of the modified ships would remain at 480ft and they would have the same beam of 73ft 6in as their half sisters. They would also have the same legend displacement.

The major change was in the main armament. The *Warriors* would retain the six 9.2in disposed as in the earlier ships. However they would have four 7.5in turret-mounted guns in place of the 6in secondary battery: two

HMS Natal alongside at Vickers, Barrow, in 1907 with the Peruvian scout cruiser Almirante Grau alongside. The photo was probably taken during final fitting out. Note the black balls rigged from the ships' mainmasts, denoting that they are not under power. (CPL)

HMS Cochrane in 1914. In the Warrior *class the ten 6in casemated guns of the* Duke of Edinburgh *class were replaced by four 7.5in guns in turrets mounted between the 9.2in guns on the upper deck. This was to prove a far more satisfactory arrangement.* (Imperial War Museum, Q21094)

port and two starboard in the waist of the ship. These were to be mounted so that at designed displacement they would be some 24ft above the waterline, as against the 14ft for the 6in broadside battery in the *Duke of Edinburgh* class. The change in armament, especially the position of the guns, altered the metacentric height of the *Warriors*, making them much more stable gun platforms than some of their predecessors; so much so that two of the class came top in consecutive years in the annual gunnery shoots of the Atlantic Fleet.[3] As with the battleships of the *King Edward VII* and *Lord Nelson* classes, the increase in calibre of the secondary battery was in theory a good idea, as the true range of the weapons, both 9.2in and 7.5in, could be used with the introduction of range finders and other fire control equipment. The difficulties in spotting the fall of shot would, however, be exacerbated by the similarity in the splash size of the 9.2in and 7.5in guns. The *Warriors* also retained the 3pdr anti-torpedo-boat weapon, even though by this time it must have been apparent that the gun was too lightweight to cope with the latest British and German TBDs.

As with the preceding class all four ships, *Achilles*, *Cochrane*, *Natal* and *Warrior*, were designed with short funnels, which some two years after the class had been

HMS Minotaur, the name-ship of her class. These ships had twin 9.2in turrets fore and aft with ten sided 7.5in single turrets. Despite the additional 10ft in length they were considered overgunned and cramped. (CPL)

FIRST CLASS CRUISERS

This early photograph of Minotaur *is a clear illustration of the smoke problem associated with the original short funnels. They would subsequently be raised as in the* Duke of Edinburgh *and* Warrior *classes. (Imperial War Museum, Q39612)*

launched had to be raised (in this case by 15ft) to stop smoke inference. The *Warriors* seem to have been popular, both at the time and in subsequent reviews of armoured cruisers.[4] They were by all accounts good sea boats, and with a balanced main armament and armour protection on the same scale as their half-sisters they were seen as powerful additions to the fleet. However, even as they and the last armoured cruisers were under construction, a new type of ship was being designed and built. Although initially typed 'armoured cruisers', these would subsequently be reclassified as 'battle cruisers'.

Minotaur Class

This would be the last class of armoured cruisers to be able to trace its lineage back to the *Orlandos* and the protected cruisers of the late Victorian era. The new class was to be longer than the *Warrior* class by some 10ft (490ft) and beam was increased to 74ft 6in, an increase of one foot over the previous class. Displacement would also increase to 14,600 tons as designed, and over 16,000 tons at deep load.

Consonant with the increase in dimensions was a rethink on the armament that this new class would carry. There was to be no increase in the calibre of the main armament. However, the *Minotaur* class were to have twin 9.2in guns fore and aft mounted in turrets, and the secondary armament would be ten 7.5in carried, as with the *Warriors*, on the broadside in turrets. They would also, at last, receive the 12pdr anti-torpedo-boat guns which the Director of Naval Ordnance had been arguing for since the *Devonshire* class was conceived.

The armour belt of the new class would be 6in tapering to 3in, which was the same as for the *Warrior* class. Like the *Warriors* they would have shallow barbettes with 7in armour, and the hoists for the turrets would have 3in armour. There would be a slight increase in the turret armour: this would be 8in, as against 7.5in for the previous class. With this class sanity also prevailed with all the boilers being of the watertube type. The design IHP for the engines would be 27,000, and their speed was to be 23 knots. Of the three vessels of the class, *Defence* and *Minotaur* shared the same lines, but *Shannon* had one foot less draught and did not make her designed speed on trials. As with both the *Duke of Edinburgh* and *Warrior* classes the funnels as designed were too short and had to raised after completion. By the time the *Minotaurs* were completed the new armoured cruisers of the *Invincible* class were on the stocks.

With this class the armoured cruiser returned to ships which were as large in tonnage terms as contemporary battleships, their battleship counterparts being *Lord Nelson* and *Agamemnon*. Their role was being undermined by Fisher's new ships; with turbines supplanting triple expansion engines the new 'Dreadnought' battleships and in particular the *Invincible* were designed for speed and long range action, although the theoretical long range of their guns was not matched by their fire control arrangements – but that is a different story for another occasion. The *Minotaur* class was not as popular as the preceding class, being seen as over-gunned and to some extent under-armoured. They were, like *Lord Nelson* and *Agamemnon*, the last representatives of a series of classes of ship, each of which was an outgrowth of the last, which dated back to the late 19th Century, and for all their fire power, which should not be lightly dismissed, the rules of the game had changed. Jacky Fisher's reforms reset the clock at zero and all of the armoured cruisers, be they just off the slipways or older, found their role and their potential opponents to be radically different from what had been envisaged when they were designed. How they fared when war broke out in 1914 is the subject of the next section.

Operations in the First World War

First Class cruisers have had a bad press as far as their operations during the First World War are concerned. Because of this, and in keeping with Jacky Fisher's oft-quoted dictum that they 'could neither fight nor run away',[5] the entire concept has been written off. How far is this a fair assessment of the type? As is so often the case when war breaks out, the First Class cruisers were pressed into a variety of roles, most of which they had not been designed for.

One good example of this is the operations of 7th Cruiser Squadron, 'Cruiser Force C', in the southern North Sea in the opening months of the War. The squadron comprised the *Cressy* and her sisters the *Aboukir*, *Bacchante*, *Euryalus* and *Hogue*. Their intended role was to act as part of a screening force to stop German encroachment into the Channel. As outlined in Part Two of this series these vessels had been designed either to operate on foreign stations and hunt down enemy commerce raiders, or to act in the van of the battle fleet if required. Patrolling as distant cover for light forces had not been part of the thinking behind their design.

With their heavy 9.2in chase pieces and double-casemated 6in guns, they were designed to run down their opponents and overwhelm them. Such forces as they were likely to meet in the southern North Sea, be they light cruisers or destroyers, would most likely have been able in all except the most adverse weather conditions either to have outrun them or, as was the case with the *Kent* at the Battle of the Falkland Islands (see below), to outrange them. Churchill, as First Lord of the Admiralty, had had some qualms about their being stationed in this area; he minuted on 18 September that they were in an exposed position and should be withdrawn;[6] they were, he thought, too close to the enemy, and should be deployed to the Channel to carry out escort work, leaving patrol work to newer light vessels covered by battle cruisers. This minute is dated just four days before the ships were lost. However, there were at this early stage of the War too few new light cruisers, so the older vessels remained on station. What occurred on 22 September has been much discussed and analysed in the 93 years since. All three vessels lie within 1,000 yards of one another on the sea bed.[7] Whilst a close examination of the wrecks might show what damage the torpedoes from *U 9* did, it is difficult not to agree with the findings of the Board of Enquiry that the losses on that fateful day were the result of human error, not material failure.

The Battle of Coronel

Coronel is one of only two action in which armoured cruisers fought as originally envisaged. A detailed description of the prelude to the battle is perhaps not necessary for these purposes; what is of interest is the tactical choic-

HMS Shannon as completed with short funnels. (World Ship Society, Abrahams Collection)

es of Rear Admiral Craddock, and how the two armoured cruisers, *Good Hope* and *Monmouth*, stood up to a gunnery action against near-contemporary German vessels.

The *Scharnhorst* and *Gneisenau* had one major advantage over the British vessels, this being their 8.2in gun armament; not just in terms of calibre but also in terms of how it was arranged, with twin turrets fore and aft, as well as two single guns on each beam on the main deck. All of these could be worked in the heavy Pacific swells, unlike the lower 6in casemate guns of *Good Hope* and the *Monmouth*, which suffered from lack of freeboard in any kind of seaway. They could also outrange, in practice, the 9.2in guns mounted aboard the *Good Hope* as chase pieces. Craddock's need to close the range to allow him, in theory at least, to smother the German vessels with 6in fire was obvious. His misjudgement placed him silhouetted against the setting sun, in heavy seas, and some 300 hundred miles away from his slowest and heaviest support, the pre-dreadnought battleship *Canopus*. It would seem that Craddock wished to close the range to 5,000 yards or under. At this range rate of fire might have counted for something; however the heaver batteries of *Scharnhorst* and *Gneisenau* were even more telling at this range.

Such evidence as there is suggests that the armour on *Good Hope's* fore turret was a weakness which would become apparent in other armoured cruisers later in the war. There was also a major fire after the hit on the fore turret. In fact it would seem, again from third party testimony, that it was fire reaching one or more of the *Good Hope's* magazines which caused her to sink. *Monmouth*, on the other hand, seems to have gone down through sheer weight of fire, the *Nürnberg* closing to as little as 600 yards as the *Monmouth*, which was listing to port, tried to turn end on to the heavy beam seas. She too had a number of major fires caused by what seems to have been hits on her main battery. The uncomfortable conclusion is that, not withstanding their lack of gunnery practice before November 1914, ships of the *Good Hope* and *Suffolk* classes would have been at a severe disadvantage had they met their opposite numbers closer to home in the North Sea, albeit in the pre-deadnought era.

The Battle of the Falkland Islands

At the Battle of the Falkland Islands in December 1914 two British armoured cruisers were present: the *Cornwall* and the *Kent*. Both vessels were of the same class as the unfortunate *Monmouth*; on this occasion, however, they were tactically in the superior position. While the battle cruisers dealt with Von Spee's heavy units, it was down to the light cruiser *Glasgow*, a survivor of the Battle of Coronel, and the *Cornwall* and *Kent* to deal with the German light cruisers, *Dresden*, *Leipzig* and *Nürnberg*. *Dresden* eventually got away, while the *Glasgow* and *Cornwall* ran down the *Leipzig*. The action between *Kent* and the *Nürnberg* became a protracted chase in which the *Kent* had to exceed her best speed by 1.5 knots. According to some accounts, aboard the *Kent* they began to burn all non-essential wood work as well as the coal, a top speed of 25 knots being achieved. There is even a story, possibly apocryphal, that a number of the crew were ordered aft to keep her stern down, as her propellers were broaching as she pitched during the chase.

When action was joined the range was approximately 11,500 yards. The *Nürnberg's* 4.1in guns comfortably matched the range of *Kent's* older 6in battery, and it is of interest in the context of this article to note that *Kent* was hit no fewer than 36 times by her opponent. One event of note which illustrates the vulnerability to flash of these ships was when a shell hit a casemate, exploded and caused a cordite fire and flash into the magazine, the danger of a magazine explosion being averted by the swift action of a Royal Marine sergeant. What is evident from this is the ease with which the flash passed down the hoist, perhaps giving some clue as to what happened aboard *Monmouth* in the previous month.

As the range closed the *Kent* began to get the better of the action, her 6in main armament disabling the *Nürnberg's* steering. Eventually the range closed to 3,000 yards, at which range *Kent's* superior firepower overwhelmed the German ship. The Battle of the Falklands was the only action in which a ship of this class in British service came close to fulfilling its original purpose, albeit as part of a larger action.

Jutland

The Battle of Jutland is seen by some as the vindication of Jacky Fisher's dictum quoted above, with the lumbering behemoths either fouling the range for parts of the fleet while trying to get into position, or blundering into the head of the German line prior to being shot out of the water. First it should be stated that the reason why the armoured cruisers were still with the Grand Fleet in 1916 was numbers; even allowing for the building programme currently underway there were still too few of the newer cruisers for all the demands made on them. Moreover, without that perfect vision given by hindsight, at the time the later armoured cruisers were still seen as a powerful adjunct to the fleet.

The *Defence* came under heavy fire at very short range, 7,000 yards from the High Seas Fleet. Dives on the wreck[8] confirm eyewitness accounts that she was hit aft, and that the explosion travelled along her 7.5in broadside battery. Although the wreck, which was found in 2001, is remarkably intact, the deflagration of her cordite sank her with the same chilling effect as it did the battle cruisers lost on 31 May 1916. Ironically it was the same mixture of lack of flash-tight precautions, unstable British cordite, exacerbated by the poor discipline in closing up working spaces responsible for the loss of her newer sisters of the battle cruiser type, which caused her catastrophic end.

The other vessels in Arbuthnot's squadron also had a torrid time at the hands of the German battleships at the head of the line. The *Warrior* received approximately fifteen 12in shell hits. She was engaged at between 8,000 and 10,000 yards, and there was no catastrophic cordite fire aboard her; there were, however, a number of fires, accumulated smoke from which may have helped to shield her from further attention. Such damage as there was causing flooding, particularly in the engine rooms, which meant that although she could leave the line under her own power she was unable to keep steam up. Taken in tow by the *Engadine*, *Warrior* had to be abandoned with a rising sea on 1st June due to an inability to check the flooding.

The *Black Prince* appears to have received some damage during the action which saw the loss of the *Defence* and the severe damage to *Warrior*. She took station astern of the Grand Fleet, and according to German accounts a vessel of the *Black Prince* class was spotted around midnight and taken under fire by the *Thüringen* at between 750 and 1100 yards. Other ships of the German line joined in, including the *Friedrich der Grosse*, at ranges between 900 and 1300 yards with both 12in and 5.9in guns. After 40 seconds there were observed explosions forward and aft and the *Black Prince* sank. The acount from German sources fits fairly closely with what occurred aboard the *Defence* earlier in the day: explosions in one or more of the main turrets, followed by cordite deflagration and rapid sinking of the vessel.

Conclusion

All of the above would seem to support Fisher's ideas concerning older vessels and their potential vulnerability in a 'modern' war. However, few of these ships, with the exception of the *Kent* at the Battle of the Falkland Islands, saw action which approximated to their original design concept of running down enemy surface raiders.

It would take far too long to give a detailed service history of the various classes during the First World War. Many of the ships, such as *Edgars* (10th Cruiser Squadron), were demonstrably too old to perform blockade duties off the north of Scotland, where their sea-keeping and engine rooms were tested beyond endurance. It would be easy to say that they were not designed for these duties; many of the classes described in Parts One and Two of this article had as their rationale independent operation on distant stations or in some cases, as with the *Cressy* class, also operating as an adjunct to the fleet. However, neither of these duties would, under normal circumstances in the Victorian or Edwardian navies, have exposed ships such as the *Edgars* or their successors to prolonged periods at sea throughout the winter months. Despite legend designs which give an impressive radius of action for most of the armoured cruisers, these ships were designed with the implicit understanding that they would in practice hop from one coaling station or dockyard to the next. The more modern battleships of the Grand Fleet found squadron patrols equally taxing on their machinery during the Great War.

Lack of endurance and mechanical reliability are not the only features which the armoured cruisers shared with the new battleships or battle cruisers. Their vulnerability to loss through cordite explosion was mirrored by their newer half-sisters, the battle cruisers. Poor discipline in keeping open flash-tight doors was something that the battle cruisers suffered from; the wreck of the *Defence*, as already alluded to, shows similar signs of hatches and doors unsecured. This reveals a systemic failure within the Royal Navy in training and shipboard operation across the fleet rather than a weakness in the design of the armoured cruisers *per se*. Arbuthnot's headlong rush to engage the crippled *Wiesbaden* could be seen as emblematic of a perceived need to overwhelm an

A splendid photo of HMS Defence *underway, possibly taken shortly before the outbreak of war. The funnels have now been raised, modifying the silhouette considerably.* (David K Brown collection)

A late war photo of HMS Minotaur, *showing the many modifications undergone by these ships. (Compare with* Defence, *opposite.) The foremast is now a sturdy tripod and has lost its topmast altogether. The torpedo nets have been removed, and a camouflage pattern applied. (David K Brown collection)*

opponent at close range, a position which inherently placed the armoured cruisers at a disadvantage in a fleet action. Arbuthnot does not appear to have recognised that his ships were not designed to stand in the line against modern dreadnought battleships.

The plain fact is that with the coming of war the Royal Navy used all of the ships it had; it was a question of cold hard numbers, as there would always be more tasks than ships available to fulfil them. Armoured cruisers required large crews, and were in some cases slow and in others vulnerable when exposed to more modern opponents. However, they had one advantage: they were available in numbers. Too few of the newer cruisers were available, hence armoured cruisers of the two latest classes were attached to the Grand Fleet. The loss of at least two of them was down to a failure of command as well as an obsession within some quarters of the fleet with high rates of fire.

In theory the *Cressy* and her sisters were more powerful than their likely surface opponents in the Broad Fourteens; however the Royal Navy – or more properly many of its senior officers – had taken insufficient account of the submarine threat. If the record of the armoured cruisers is decidedly mixed, it is perhaps as much down to the exigencies of war and the frailty of those whom commanded them, at all levels, as to any weakness in their design.

Sources:
NMM ADM 138 Ships' Covers: *Devonshire, Duke of Edinburgh, Minotaur.*
Arthur J Marder, *From Dreadnought to Scapa Flow*, Vol.2, OUP 1965.
Geoffrey Bennett, *Coronel and the Falklands*, Batsford 1963.
Geoffrey Bennett, *The Battle of Jutland*, Batsford 1964.
Alan Coles, *Three Before Breakfast*, Kenneth Mason 1979.
John Campbell, *Jutland: an Analysis of the Fighting*, Conway Maritime Press 1986.
Nicholas Lambert, *Sir John Fisher's Naval Revolution*, University of Yale Press 1999.

Footnotes:
[1] Keith McBride, 'The First County Class Cruisers of the Royal Navy, Part II: The Devonshires', *Warship* Vol.47 (Conway Maritime Press, July 1988).
[2] See Part Two of this series, *Warship 2001-2002* (Conway Maritime Press 2001).
[3] *Brassey's Naval Annual* 1908, p.10; *Brassey's* 1909, p.12.
[4] *Brassey's Naval Annual* 1908, p.10.
[5] Arthur J Marder, *Fisher papers*, Vol.2, 1955.
[6] J Corbett, *Official History of the War at Sea*, Vol.1, p.234 (London 1920).
[7] See divenet.com, accessed on 22 August 2007.
[8] See deepblue.net, accessed 23 August 2007.

Shannon *laid up after the end of the war. Deemed obsolete and expensive in manpower, none of these ships was retained in active service into the 1920s. (Imperial War Museum, SP1548)*

WARSHIP NOTES

This section comprises a number of shorter articles and notes, generally highlighting lesser known aspects of warship history.

HMS FURIOUS

Warship's Assistant Editor presents two unusual photographs of the famous aircraft carrier.

With the confirmation in the summer of 2007 of the orders for the two new aircraft carriers for the Royal Navy, *Queen Elizabeth* and *Prince of Wales*, the British government ended a great deal of concerned speculation about such matters as whether the expertise and industrial capacity to create ships of this size and complexity still existed in the country, as well as about the future of Portsmouth as a naval base. However the decision also ended a certain amount of discussion about the names, there having been the suggestion that one of the ships should be called *Furious*, in honour of the vessel which at the moment remains the last British warship of that name, the aircraft carrier that served with distinction during the two World Wars and played such a major part in the development of naval aviation. *Furious*' career would undoubtedly be worthy of a major book on its own, but for now *Warship* presents two unusual photographs of the ship at very different stages of her long and eventful life.

The first photograph shows Leading Aircraftsman (or Sgt. Pilot)[1] Lloyd Bennett – later Squadron Leader Lloyd Bennett, DFC & bar – and was taken on board HMS *Glorious* on a fine sunny day in the spring of 1934, using his Pocket Kodak camera. In the background are HM Ships *Furious* and *Courageous*. It is difficult to be precise in dating the photograph, or the location. However *Furious* had only emerged from refit in May 1931, then serving with the Atlantic Fleet until February 1932 after which she was with the re-named Home Fleet up to the outbreak of war, except for a temporary six month attachment to the Mediterranean Fleet between May and October 1934.

HM aircraft carriers Furious *(left) and* Courageous, *seen from* Glorious, *spring 1934. (Photograph courtesy of Al Fox)*

Glorious meanwhile was with the Mediterranean Fleet throughout this period, except from July 1934 until the start of the following year, when she was undergoing a refit at Devonport (*Furious* taking her place in the Mediterranean fleet for much of this time). *Courageous* was with the Mediterranean Fleet until June 1930, and then after a two month refit joined *Furious* with the Atlantic and (after March 1932) Home Fleets until the end of 1938.

This was a significant time in the development of British naval aviation: although the three carriers had first operated together in 1929, it was in 1933, during joint exercises in the Mediterranean involving the Atlantic and Mediterranean fleets, that the three carried out successful large scale aerial torpedo 'attacks' on the combined fleets. At around the same time a solution began to be found to one of the main problems of operating aircraft from carriers with the installation of the first truly satisfactory arrester gear, in the shape of hydraulic cylinders attached to cross-deck wires, on board *Courageous* and *Furious*.

Lloyd Bennett, born in 1911, had first flown with the RAF in 1930, and made his first deck landing on HMS *Glorious* on 28 November 1933. On this occasion he was a passenger in Osprey S1686,[2] flying from RAF Hal Far in Malta, which had been used as an embarkation and landing airfield for carrier aircraft since the 1920s. The landing on *Glorious* was to collect mail and stationery for Hal Far. Although it appears that Bennett enjoyed shipboard life, this seems to have been the only time that he actually flew to or from a carrier, and he instead continued to operate out of Hal Far, flying in a mixture of Ospreys, DH Moths, Fairey IIIFs & Ripon IIs, practising formation flying, dual flying, low flying, landings and forced landings, until the end of February 1934. (He didn't fly again until October of that year, from RAF Hornchurch in Essex.) However the date of the photograph, and the fact that he clearly isn't wearing flying gear, suggests that during this time he may have taken passage home on board *Glorious*. The page in his Log Book covering this period is signed off by Cdr. Abel-Smith[3] (S.Ldr, RAF),[4] HMS *Glorious*, Gibraltar, 31 March 1934.

The second picture, also undated, was taken in around 1948, when *Furious* was being scrapped by Arnott Young & Co. shipbreakers at Dalmuir on the Clyde. The photograph was discovered by Ian Johnston in the archives of John Brown & Co. while he was in the process of researching for his book 'Ships for a Nation' (Argyll Publishing, 2000). It shows *Furious* lying in what had originally been the fitting out basin for William Beardmore's Naval Construction Works, but which had been taken over by John Brown & Co. after Beardmore's became a

Furious *being scrapped at Dalmuir. To the left is the incomplete cruiser HMS* Tiger. *(Photograph courtesy of Ian Johnston)*

victim of the recession in the 1930s. The site of Beardmore's shipyard and engine works was taken over in 1939 to become a Royal Ordnance factory, while the basin went on to see extensive use during the wartime construction programme, in particular for the fitting out of mass produced convoy escorts such as 'Loch' class frigates, for which the capacity of John Brown's original basin was not sufficient by itself. With the defeat of the U-boats the constructon programme began to be reduced, and the basin was relinquished in 1945, being taken over by Arnott Young & Co. and subsequently used for the breaking up of many units of the wartime Royal Navy.[5]

One of the ships visible to the left of the photograph is the cruiser *Tiger* (ex-*Bellerophon*), launched by John Brown on 25 October 1945 but then moved the short distance to Dalmuir where she was laid up unfinished while deliberations took place over her future. She was eventually only completed – to a much modified design – over a decade later. Comparing the *Tiger*, no small ship herself and riding high in the water, with *Furious* gives a clear indication of just what a huge vessel the old carrier was. The photograph is quite possibly part of a series being taken as record shots of *Tiger*, the photographer being unable to resist the impressive bulk of *Furious*. After a long and distinguished career *Furious* had spent much of the time since the war's end in the ignominious role of being used as a target in various trials – it may well be that some of the damage visible in the photograph is the result of these, rather than being the work of the shipbreakers.

Notes:
[1] A number of the more successful adult entrants who had joined the RAF to train as clerks (as in Bennett's case), cooks, ground crew, medical orderlies and suchlike were permitted to learn to fly. Since only officers and NCOs were allowed to become aircrew, these therefore became Sergeant Pilots.
[2] Aircraft with S registrations were all allocated to the FAA.
[3] E.M.C. Abel-Smith commanded 408 Flt, equipped with Hawker Osprey and Nimrod biplane fighters, embarked on *Glorious* from the autumn of 1932, becoming part of 802 Squadron in April 1933, with Abel-Smith as CO. Surviving the sinking of *Courageous* in 1939, he went on to have a successful wartime and post-war career in naval aviation, including commanding HMS *Biter*, ending up as Vice-Admiral Sir Connolly Abel-Smith.
[4] At this time Fleet Air Arm pilots also held a commission in the RAF – they were actually serving in the Fleet Air Arm of the Royal Air Force.
[5] The basin was filled in during 1989-90, and the site is now occupied by a hospital.

Sources:
Beaver, Paul, *The British Aircraft Carrier* (Patrick Stephens Ltd, Wellingborough, 1982)
Bennett, Squadron Leader Lloyd, DFC & bar, Pilot's Flying Log Book, 1930-57 (courtesy of Al Fox)
Burt, R. A, *British Battleships, 1919-1939* (Arms & Armour Press, London, 1993)
Jenkins, Cdr. C. A, *HMS Furious; Aircraft Carrier 1917-1948*, pt.II: 1925-1948 (Profile Publications, Windsor, 1972)
Johnston, Ian, *Beardmore Built: the Rise and Fall of a Clydeside Shipyard* (Clydebank District Libraries and Museums Department, 1993)
Moore, George, 'Cruisers for the Royal Navy: the 1932-42 Programmes', in *Warship 1997-98* (Conway Maritime Press, London, 1997)
Nesbit, Roy Conyers, *RAF: An Illustrated History from 1918* (Sutton Publishing, Stroud, in association with the RAF Museum, 1998)

Thanks to David K Brown, Ian Johnston, Chris Savill and Al Fox for help with this note. *Warship* would be interested to hear from any readers who can offer any additional information relating to these two photographs.

THE MYSTERY OF THE SS CASTOR

Jean Hood writes about an unresolved mystery involving the Italian submarine Enrico Tazzoli *during the Second World War, which she came across while researching her new book 'Submarine' (Conway, 2007).*

When the Second World War ended, both sides had long lists of vessels, both naval and mercantile, which had simply failed to reach their destination, and log books or patrol reports claiming unverified sinkings. Sixty years of combing through the archives has answered many questions, but the following incident remains something of a mystery to a man who was there at the time:

> When I was exec. of the *Enrico Tazzoli* we undertook a long patrol of some three months in the Caribbean. During daylight on 1 August 1942 we torpedoed and sank a small Dutch steamer of 1638 tons, the *Castor*, registered in Amsterdam. There's nothing unusual about that, but what is strange is that every post-war publication has reported the same alternate (sic) version: the *Tazzoli* is supposed to have sunk, on that occasion, the Greek steamer *Kastor* of 5497 tons. I don't know from where the various authors, starting from J Rohwehr in his very detailed *Axis Submarine Successes 1939-1945*, have found the information regarding the *Kastor*, and I don't know who sank it, given that nobody has admitted responsibility for so doing; I don't know where and when the *Kastor* may have been sunk, but it certainly wasn't sunk at the spot where we sank the *Castor* – a position which is documented in Comandante di Cossato's patrol report. What I do know for a fact is that Comandante di Cossato, myself and several members of the crew saw the *Castor*, a Dutch ship, sink, and her identity was confirmed by the survivors with whom we spoke. So what is unusual is that not only is there no trace of the sinking, there is no evidence of the existence of a Dutch ship named *Castor* which in July 1942 happened to be sailing not far from the island of Trinidad.

That account is by Comandante Mario Rossetto, former 1st Officer of the *Enrico Tazzoli*, one of the Regia Marina's submarines operating out of Bordeaux in the Atlantic, and his memory of the incident is confirmed by both the patrol report and a book written by one of the *Tazzoli*'s crew shortly after the war.

Di Cossato's patrol report (which uses Rome time) states:

> 1 August 1942. Proceeding normally until 1616 when in Lat 11°10' N, Long 59°10' W with 140 revs we saw smoke bearing 20°. At 1820 in Lat 10°40', Long 58°40' W going at 200 revs a tanker was located on alpha bearing 350°. I attempted to pursue it, but this vessel was faster than mine. Broke off chase and turned to pursue the steamer. At 2259 … submerged for attack. At 2358 ready to fire. At 0016 with a firing angle of 11° I fired tubes 2 and 4 which hit after 50 and 52 seconds respectively. At 0023 I surfaced. The steamer, which according to information received from the survivors turned out to be the Dutch 'Castor' 1880 tons, had sunk.

In 1951, crew member Antonio Maronari published *Un Sommergibile Non è Rientro al Base*. Of that August day he wrote: 'with difficulty we read the name of the ship on a life-jacket: Castor. Poor little Castor!… the Castor belonged to the H/Kon. St. Mt. di Amsterdam and was in the service of the British and displaced 1683 tons.

The *Tazzoli* radioed her success to Betasom, which in turn informed Mariscom by telegram specifying the tonnage of the Castor as 1830 tons. That report, presumably, became the source of the contemporary entry in the unpublished Wreck Book for 1942 compiled by Lloyd's Register of Shipping. However, within days the name of the ship was amended to that of the Greek ship *Kastor*, at 5497 tons a much larger vessel. No source was given, but the logical source for such a report has to be the survivors, and two genealogical websites shed some light on this:

http://archiver.rootsweb.com/th/read/USNAVY/2002-07/1026399831

> My uncle was serving as a 3rd Engineer on the KASTOR, a Greek freighter, en route from Bombay and Table Bay laden with 9202 tons of general cargo and was headed for Trinidad and St. Johns, N.B. She was torpedoed at 22:59 hours on August 1 1942 by the Italian sub. ENRICO TAZZOLI (Fecia di Cossato).The KASTOR sank in about 3 minutes at the position 11.06 N, 59.05 W, (about 250 miles off the coast of Brazil) with 4 crew members lost and 31 survivors…

Attempts to contact the poster, Mary Helen Chrisman, have so far failed, so it is impossible to establish how much her uncle knew of the submarine that sank his ship and how much of her information was gleaned from post-war publications such as Rohwer's.

http://scarisbrick.name/NamesB-D.htm

> Cecil Juan Scarisbrick… On the List or Manifest of Alien Passengers as Member of the Crew on the S.S. 'George Washington', which arrived in Baltimore, Maryland on 9 Aug 1942 and Port Everglades, Florida, on 25 Aug 1942, from Port of Spain, Trinidad, British West Indies. Survivor of ex-S.S. 'Kastor'.

Lloyds War Losses, subsequently compiled by Lloyd's of London, states: 'Kastor 1.8.42. Torpedoed by subm Enrico Tazzoli (Ita), sunk, 11 06 N, 59 05 W (4+, 25 surv).'

The *Castor* of 1683 tons was a Norwegian vessel which survived the war. There was a Dutch Castor, lost 27/11/1942 in the East Indies, and another, 1830 tons, which was surveyed by Lloyd's Register in 1943 and survived the war. That particular ship, belonging to the Kon. Nederl. Stoomb. Maats., Amsterdam, certainly operated in the right area: she rescued survivors of the Swedish merchant ship *Amerikaland*, torpedoed by *U-106*, and landed them at Curaçao in February 1942. Those were the owners mentioned by Maronari in his book, but such information may have been gleaned later? Research this year at the Dutch Archives in the Hague (file reference 2.16.56.10/6), however, shows that no Dutch ship was lost on the day when the *Castor* was supposedly sunk.

So, an Italian ship sank a Dutch ship that did not exist;

a Greek ship was sunk by an unknown submarine. After Rossetto was given his own command, the *Tazzoli* was lost in 1943 with all hands; her former captain, who had also left her, committed suicide in 1944. Now 92, Rossetto remains adamant about the ship they sank on 1 August 1942, not only maintaining that they had the information from the survivors but stressing the size of the ship. Given the predilection of commanders in general for exaggerating the size of their victims, it is odd that an experienced and successful C/O and his executive officer would mistake a vessel of under 2,000grt for one of almost 5,500grt.

Warship would be pleased from any readers who can shed any light on this mystery.

THE BOMBING OF HMS *IRON DUKE*

William J Crawford supplies photographs, which it is believed have never been published before, from a series taken by Sub-Lt. J R McCosh RNVR, showing the bombing of HMS Iron Duke *in Scapa Flow on 17 October 1939.*

Having been an Uppingham Cadet Officer five years previously, the outbreak of war had meant that for Jimmy McCosh the 1939 grouse season was exchanged for something very different: priority for call up without undergoing the usual basic training. He had enrolled in the Royal Naval Volunteer Reserve in mid-May, was mobilised as a Probationary Sub-Lieutenant three months later, and under the Reserved Auxiliary Forces Act was ordered on 25 August to report to the King's Harbourmaster at Invergordon.

Driving up to Cromarty in his red Triumph sports car, he discovered that his first ship was to be HMS *Hood*: the spectacular battle-cruiser that was the heaviest, longest and most powerfully engined ship in the Royal Navy. Her massive profile and long sweeping sheer added to her reputation and proud position as Queen of the world's battle fleets, and for the past two decades this one ship had symbolised Britain's naval might and imperial grandeur. Displacing 42,100 tons and 860 feet long, she was powered by four-shaft Parsons steam turbines rated at 144,000hp, which gave her a trials speed of 32 knots. In August 1939, the *Hood* had just completed a brief refit at Portsmouth, and was commanded by Captain I G Glennie, referred to as 'Skips'. The *Hood* was on her way up to 'Port A' (the censor's designation for Scapa Flow), where Vice-Admiral Sir W J Whitworth broke his flag at her truck as Second-in-Command, Home Fleet.

Just one week after McCosh joined the ship, the C-in-C Home Fleet, Admiral Sir Charles Forbes, sent out the message:

> 'War having been declared against Germany, I am confident that the conduct of every officer and man will ensure it being brought TO A SPEEDY AND SUCCESSFUL END'.

The 'phoney war' period was one of great activity and hard work as far as the Home Fleet was concerned, and Admiral Forbes took the heavy ships deep into the North Sea on deployments that were christened 'Forbes legs'. On 25 September, the fleet sailed out to cover the withdrawal of the damaged submarine HMS *Spearfish* from the Skagerrak, and was discovered the next morning by German Dornier flying boats, which inevitably resulted in a full-scale bombing later in the day by Heinkel He.111 medium bombers. Despite the best efforts of the anti aircraft gunners, disaster was only just averted: the aircraft carrier *Ark Royal* was near missed, and one heavy bomb actually struck the *Hood* a glancing blow on the quarterdeck before falling into the sea. Although there were no casualties, the episode demonstrated that the *Hood*'s anti-aircraft battery was neither sufficiently numerous nor sufficiently well directed to provide adequate protection from a serious air attack. Jimmy McCosh's Action Station was in the Air Defence Post, so he was very much part of this action.

Once back in Scapa Flow, he was initially dismayed to find himself seconded temporarily to a rather less glamourous ship, HM Tug *St. Martin*, but in the event this turned into a very rewarding interlude. The captain was a cheery RNR Lieutenant called Bill Smith and the No.1 was Sub-Lt. Ronaldson, also RNR. The tug was kept constantly occupied with the many movements of the heavy ships, and when these were out at sea, there was time to examine the capsized hulk of the German battlecruiser *Derfflinger*, formerly part of the scuttled High Seas Fleet and now lying upside down on the Flow's surface with the salvage company's tall air locks and pumping houses still in place. Most of the other scuttled German warships had already been raised and towed down to Rosyth for scrapping in the Admiralty dry dock there, but *Derfflinger*, brought to the surface just before the outbreak of war, was destined to remain at Scapa until 1946, the pumps being run intermittently to maintain sufficient buoyancy. Then she was finally towed down the west coast to be dismantled in the Admiralty floating dock stationed at Faslane, the last ship of the former *Hochseeflotte* to be scrapped. The Flow teemed with fish, and it took just a hand line off the tug's broad strake to catch a bucket load. There were sections of boom, made up at the fleet base at Lyness, to be towed into position and handed over to the boom defence vessel. There was target towing work, during which the Admiralty Pattern VI floating target had to be streamed astern at high speed (12 knots!) while the many ships working up at Scapa improved their gunnery. In between all this activity Jimmy found time to visit an old friend, Pat Scott, who had been given the command of one of the 4.7in anti-aircraft guns defending the fleet base.

But the real excitement for the *St. Martin* came on the morning of 17 October, when the *Luftwaffe* staged an air raid, during which a stick of bombs straddled the old battleship HMS *Iron Duke*. Completed just prior to the outbreak of the First World War, the *Iron Duke* had been the flagship of the British Grand Fleet for much of the conflict, including the Battle of Jutland in 1916. During 1931-2, under the terms of the London Naval Treaty, she was converted into a gunnery training ship, losing much of her original armament, armour protection and boilers, and acquiring various new weapons and associated fire control equipment. She served in this capacity until the spring of 1939 when, with the prospect of a war in Europe

WARSHIP 2008

looming, the Royal Navy's apparent shortage of capital ships led to the proposal to re-equip her as a front-line battleship. The sheer cost of this, and the dubious fighting value of the resulting vessel, meant the proposal was never acted upon. (At much the same time it was also proposed to re-purchase the equally venerable *Almirante Latorre*, ex-HMS *Canada*, from Chile!)

As it was, *Iron Duke* was destined to have a most thoroughly inactive war. Used for a while as a boys' training ship, she was then moved to Scapa Flow for use as the fleet's headquarters depot ship, with many of her remaining guns being landed to improve the base's defences. On 17 October 1939, with hostilities just six weeks old, the base was raided by twelve Junkers 88 bombers.[1] Four attacked *Iron Duke*, and while all four missed, two or three of the bombs exploded sufficiently close to the old ship's side to open up her seams. Rapid flooding of C boiler room and the magazines under Q and Y turrets resulted, made worse by the fact that main deck scuttles were open, and she was soon listing at an angle of 20-25°. Worst of all, dozens of mail bags were lying on the port quarter-deck ready for distribution to the ships of the fleet by the base MFVs, and as the heel worsened, it looked as if they were all going to go overboard. With panic spreading amongst the battleship's crew, *St. Martin* bustled up and put a boat across to the buoy that held the sinking battleship. Unshackled from the buoy in a hurry while a towing hawser was secured, the *Iron Duke* was towed by the St

Taken from St. Martin *as the tug was approaching the stricken* Iron Duke *(note the sailor in the foreground clutching a lifebuoy); visible on the battleship's port-side quarterdeck are the dozens of mail bags, which were there ready for distribution to the ships of the fleet by the base MFV's, one of which is also shown.*

As the heel worsens, the towing hawser stretches from the tug to the Iron Duke, *after a boat had been put across to unshackle her from the buoy.* (Photographs courtesy of William J Crawford.)

Martin across to the shallows of Ore Bay and beached on the mud, later being dragged further inshore at high tide.

Thus the fleet's mail was saved, and a few days later the *St. Martin* was back at the scene with a naval diving party, who sent their diver down to examine the damage. But as the old lady was not going anywhere, did it matter that she no longer floated? Apparently not: *Iron Duke* stayed for the rest of the war, immobile and serving as a base and tender ship for Scapa Flow. Her cells (along with those of the depot ship HMS *Tyne*) were used to hold offenders from ships of the fleet, prior to the twice-weekly transportation south. The story grew up that such was the volume of rubbish that was discarded overboard during these years that she ended up aground not on sand, mud and shingle but on a vast submerged mountain of old tin cans and other junk. In 1946 she was refloated and towed away for scrapping. Lt. Jimmy McCosh was killed on 12 April 1942 while commanding *MTB.44* operating from Dover.

[1.] The Home Fleet was not in the base at the time because Admiral Forbes had taken the modern ships to Loch Ewe with the very object of putting them beyond the range of the Luftwaffe, after HMS *Guardian* had laid nets at the entrance to keep out any U-boats. What happened to *Iron Duke* clearly demonstrated the good sense of this move, although in the event U-boats proved the greater threat, as shown by the loss of the *Royal Oak*.

[This Note is an edited and expanded version of an excerpt from the forthcoming book *A Naval Odyssey* by William J Crawford: a history of the seven generations of the author's family who served in the Royal Navy between 1746 and 1946. Additional information comes from *British Battleships, 1919-1939* by R.A. Burt (Arms & Armour Press, London, 1993) and from 'Home Fleet Destroyer Orders', 15 April 1943, reprinted in *The Royal Navy Officer's Pocket Book, 1944*, edited by Brian Lavery (Conway, 2007). Thanks also to David K Brown and Geoffrey Hudson for additional help. © 2007 W.J. Crawford, extra material by Stephen Dent.]

THE FONDS POTSDAM

Important documentation about the interwar Marine Nationale seized by the Germans in 1940 is only now becoming available. John Jordan tells the story behind the article on the cruiser De Grasse *(see p.115).*

Shortly after the fall of the Berlin Wall, the colonel in charge of the Postdam military archives of the German Democratic Republic informed the French Ambassador in Berlin that the archives included a large batch of documents of French origin, and that he thought that these should now be repatriated.

The embassy sent lorries carrying young soldiers on National Service to Potsdam; the archives of French origin were recovered, and those concerning the Marine Nationale arrived at the Service historique de la Marine at Vincennes in June 1990. It would be subsequently christened the 'Fonds Potsdam'.

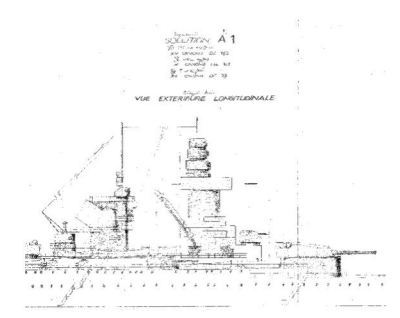

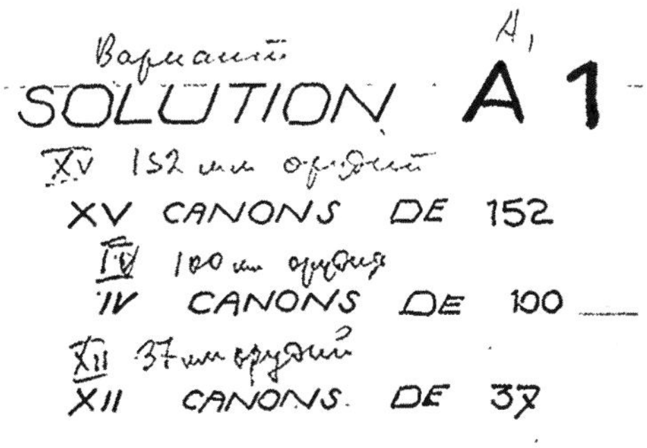

Plan showing the midships profile of the battleship Gascogne. *The close-up of the writing at the top detailing the ship's armament has annotations in Russian above each line. (Courtesy of Bruno Gire)*

Plan P.N.279 (battleship Gascogne*). The official German stamp reads: 'Amt für Kriegsschiffbau – Archiv u. Plant. K1'. Some of the handwriting is Russian. (Courtesy of Bruno Gire)*

The archives were accompanied by two inventories, the first of which (*Anlage Nr.1*) established the broad categories, and the second (*Anlage Nr.2*) the origin of the items. The first inventory stated that 143.4 metres of shelving were required to store the archive!

In its original form the archive comprised packages of documents, carefully tied up with string, each about 15cm thick; the documents on the top and bottom of each package had classification stamps, and it was initially thought that these would make sorting an easy matter. However, when the packages were opened it was found that the documents they contained were totally unrelated. They therefore had to be reclassified by examining all the documents and putting them into newly-defined categories.

The documents had originally been taken by the Kriegsmarine following the Armistice of 1940, and had been archived by the *Amt für Kriegsschiffbau* (lit. Warship Building Office/Bureau). They were subsequently seized by the Russian military services and archived by two services of the Soviet Navy. The German designations which appeared on the classification form accompanying the documents were frequently corrected and annotated in cyrillic script.

The second of the two inventories reveals that many of the documents originated from the French Naval Dockyards or contracted suppliers. Some of the documents relating to submarines were taken from DCN Cherbourg (which was responsible for coordinating submarine construction) but are copies of plans drawn up by Brest and Toulon. There are also documents relating to the Polish Navy, but it is not clear whether these were taken from Warsaw or from Paris.

The documents of the *Fonds Potsdam* relate primarily to ships built from the 1922 Programme up to 1940, as well as the older battleships of the *Bretagne* class. They are currently being stored in boxes, each with a red mark and an inventory of contents, as a separate archive. Electronic and paper copies of these inventories are grouped together and archived for the convenience of archivists and researchers. All the documents concerning a particular ship or submarine are grouped under the name of the vessel.

The classification process was initiated by Admiral Kessler, who at that time was Head of the Service historique de la Marine. The documents were sorted and inventories drawn up by Ing. Gén. du Génie maritime Maurice Brunet in accordance with instructions from the archivists responsible for the naval archives; he was assisted by students on National Service. Their hard work has only recently begun to bear fruit, and specifications and plans of the warships planned during the late 1930s but not completed, including the cruisers of the *De Grasse* class and the battleships of the *Gascogne* class, are only now becoming available to naval historians.

THE MIHOGASEKI INCIDENT

Hans Lengerer recounts one of the hard lessons of the IJN's Night Battle Training programme, and questions the Japanese belief in the overwhelming importance of 'spiritual power'.

Among the measures the Imperial Japanese Navy pursued in order to compensate for the quantitative inferiority established with the signing of the Washington Treaty in 1922, the night battle of the fleet played a role of particular importance. It was recognised that such tactics might favour a numerically inferior fleet against a superior enemy. By rigorous and realistic training under actual battle conditious technical and tactical problems were to be resolved, and night battle techniques developed and perfected. An evolution which began with the night attack of the small torpedo-boats on the superior Chinese forces at Weihaiwei (February 1895) was to be developed to perfection, and a level of proficiency attained which would secure this objective. Exceptional training under difficult conditions naturally had its price in terms of setbacks, sacrifices and lives. However, nothing oould discourage the IJN's leaders, and their belief in the effectiveness of the night battle strategy emerged as both doctrine and tradition.

The destroyers were at the centre of the attacking forces, and it would be these ships which would suffer the most. One of the biggest incidents was the result of night battle training of the Combined Fleet on 24 August 1927 in the Sea of Japan near Mihogaseki. On that day *Otsu Butai* (the destroyers and light cruisers) was to attack *Ko Butai* (the battleships and their escorts). 'Force B', made up of light forces, sortied from Miho Bay at 1930 and steamed at high speed and without lights into the dark night. The 26th Destroyer Division (*Kaki, Nire, Kuri, Tsuga* – all 2nd class destroyers of the *Momi* class) was in line ahead on a course of NE followed by the four ships of the 27th Destroyer Division (also *Momi* class). There was 300m between the ships and 400m between the divisions. Steaming at 20 knots on an almost parallel course and at a distance of 2500m to port of the 26th Division were the light cruisers *Jintsu* and *Naka* (both of the 5500-ton *Naka* type), which were to provide support. It was known that 'Force A' (with the heavy ships) would be approaching from the NW, and *Jintsu* and the other ships changed course to N 25°E 7.5km east of the Jirozaki Lighthouse, arriving in the reconnaissance area at 2222 ready for a high-speed run to the battle area. From 2230 the wind became stronger, the state of the sea moderate and visibility worsened, but still the lights remained dowsed. At 2306 *Jintsu* made out a black silhouette at 30° to port. Assuming this to be an 'enemy' vessel the light cruiser prepared for a torpedo attack and the 27th Division, seeing *Jintsu*'s signal light indicating that she had sighted enemy forces, also made ready. When *Jintsu* delivered her torpedo attack at 2312 the 'target' responded by illuminating her with searchlights. Despite the rapid closing of the two forces the torpedoes were released, and the captain of *Jintsu* then ordered a hard turn away and reloading of the torpedo tubes, but the umpires ruled that she had lost the chance of a further attack because she had been caught in the searchlights. She was therefore compelled to turn away to avoid being taken under fire by the secondary guns of the battleships *Ise* and *Hyuga* of 'Force A'. On the starboard quarter of the light cruiser the four destroyers of the 26th Division were following closely, and *Jintsu* circled to starboard to allow them an opportunity to attack.

The searchlight continued to hold the ship in its beam and at 2314 *Jintsu* turned NE, then ENE, and from 2316 she turned again to the SE. At 2318 the glare of the searchlight ceased, and Captain Mizuki, *Jintsu*'s CO, oould see nothing. He ordered speed to be increased first to 24 knots, then to 28 knots (2nd and 3rd Battle Speeds respectively), and during this time a darkened silhouette – presumed to be the light cruiser *Yubari*, flagship of the destroyer squadron – was reported 20° to starboard at a distance of about 2,000m passing from right to left. If this ship was indeed the *Yubari* it could be assumed that her destroyers were following close behind. When *Jintsu* turned to port a blacked-out destroyer crossed her bows, which were currently pointed SW, from left to right at a distance of only 400m. This was *Hishi*, the leading ship of the 27th Division, followed by the second ship *Warabi*. Both COs recognised the danger and ordered evasive manoeuvres, but *Jintsu* was closing so quickly on the destroyer that these had little effect. The light cruiser struck *Warabi* from 45° off the starboard bow in the for-

These two photos show the extent of the damage to the bows of Jintsu *(left) and* Naka *(right). The destroyers* Warabi *and* Ashi *fared even worse, with the former being sunk with heavy loss of life and the latter losing her stern.*

ward boiler room just abaft the bridge. The boiler casing was breached, resulting in an explosion like that of a magazine. Fierce fires broke out which reached as far as *Jintsu's* bridge, and *Warabi* broke in two, with the fore part sinking instantly and the after part following. *Hishi* returned to the point of collision and *Sumire* also hove to. Both ships switched on their searchlights, lowered cutters and motor boats and rescued survivors but could not find a any trace of the destroyer. 104 men of *Warabi's* crew were either dead or wounded – the final death toll was 92.

Even before the rescue began *Naka*, which was running about 500m in the wake of *Jintsu* and had followed her turn to port, collided with the 3rd ship of the 27th Division, *Ashi*. Her CO, Lt-Cdr. Suga, had seen *Jintsu* approaching the destroyer in line ahead at speed and, sensing the danger, ordered 'Starboard 15°'. When he saw the big colunm of flame leap from *Warabi* he tried to avoid a collision by ordering full speed and and rudder hard over to starboard to pass *Naka's* bow. However, *Naka* continued turning to port and before *Ashi* reached her full battle speed the light cruiser collided with her port side at an angle of about 80°. It was 13 seconds since *Naka's* red port lamp had disappeared and her green starboard light had been recognised (after *Jintsu's* collision *Naka* had switched on side lights) and in this time the combined speed of the ships had reduced the distance between the two ships from 400m to zero. Time was 2321, one minute after the *Jintsu/Warabi* collision. *Naka's* bow cut into the stern of *Ashi* in front of no.3 main gun, and 27 men working on the upper deck were thrown overboard and lost. *Ashi's* stern sank but the larger part of the ship remained afloat. The bows of both light cruisers were cut off below the upper deck level, with *Jintsu* the more severely damaged of the two. *Naka* entered Maizuru N.Y. at 1800 on 25 August under her own power; *Jintsu*, towed by the battleship *Kongo*, arrived at 1300 on the following day followed at 1930 by *Ashi*, under tow from the light cruiser *Abukuma*. After temporary repairs, the light cruisers were moved to Kure N.Y. for a complete reconstruction.

This night battle training ended with 119 dead and more than 50 injured, the loss of one destroyer and the stern of another, and severe damage to two light cruisers requiring repairs which took roughly two and five months respectively. However, instead of discouraging further such exercises it effectively spurred the IJN on to even greater efforts.

The most ardent advocate of the off-setting of quantitative inferiority by technical, tactical and strategical superiority combined with 'spiritual power' – factors which could not be limited by treaties – was Vice-Admiral Katô Kanji. The latter had been antagonistic to the Navy Minister Admiral Katô Tomosaburô at the Washington Conference, and had resolutely opposed the 5:3 ratio because of what he considered to be its adverse effects on Japan's security. When he became C-in-C of the Combined fleet on 10 December 1926 for a period of two years he emphasised the importance of the night battle, and stressed the need for incessant training by banishing weekends from the naval calendar – the calendar ran from 'Monday Monday...to Friday Friday'. On the day following the Mihogaseki incident he delivered an address to his commanders outlining his views with regard to 'exceptional forces'. After deploring the loss of 150 skilled and brave comrades who, unlike ships, could not be replaced, he made an appeal that: 'no one should be demoralised by the accident; on the contrary all should do their utmost to carry out the severe and hard battle training which is absolute necessary...'. He continued: 'manoeuvres like those of yesterday... have to be carried out, and our navy is compelled to concentrate upon them because of the inferior 5:3 ratio...'. After stressing that 'the lives of the crews should not be risked carelessly...' and arguing that 'this dangerous training must be embarked upon to make the crews at one with their ships', he pointed out spiritual power and psychological factors as 'exceptional forces which must be used both in training and manoeuvres' in order to 'secure the victory in the 5:3 battle'. His address went on: 'One always has to search for problems over and above the usual ones, and to overcome them without accident and loss. Only then will the will to win and the necessary skills be as one'.

While this rigorous night training would bring about the IJN's early successes around the Solomons, beginning with the Battle of Savo Island, and in subsequent night battles even when the American ships were fitted with radar, these 'exceptional forces' were undoubtedly (much) over-stressed and did not fully compensate for material disadvantages. In making them the central element in its strategy the IJN made a fateful decision.

THE VICTORIAN GUNBOAT *HANDY*

Stephen Dent, Warship's Assistant Editor, and Ian Sturton provide a pictorial feature on the Victorian 'flat-iron' gunboat Handy

Lying in a creek at the back of Portsmouth Harbour is a remarkable survival of the Victorian navy: the 'flat-iron' gunboat *Handy*. The gradually decaying hulk of the gunboat, originally built in 1882-3, has for some years rested on the mud at Pound's Yard, surrounded by many more recent naval vessels being broken up for scrap at the end of their active lives. In 2006, with the yard due to be redeveloped, *Warship*'s Assistant Editor, together with a photographer, received permission from owner Harry Pound to visit the yard while working on the new edition of the book *Send a Gunboat* (see review on p.195) by Antony Preston (*Warship*'s founding editor) and John Major.

Handy was originally built by W G Armstrong, Mitchell & Co Ltd. of Newcastle upon Tyne, for the purpose of testing guns and mountings produced by Armstrongs at Elswick.[1] Completed in 1883, at 115ft long, 37ft wide and 8ft draught, she displaced 523 tons and was similar to, but rather larger than, the numerous 'flat-iron' gunboats of the *Ant*, *Gadfly* and *Bouncer* classes. Her Ross & Duncan compound engine powered a single screw and gave her a speed of 9 knots. Bought by the Admiralty the following year, *Handy* was used for the same purpose as for which she had been built, serving as tender to the gunnery school HMS *Excellent*, whose name she took in 1891. She carried a wide variety of guns and mountings during her career, from 13.5in down to 4in, and during the First World War served off the coast of Belgium as part of Rear-Admiral Hood's bombardment force after it had become apparent that heavier guns were needed than those which were currently being used. At the time she mounted a 9.2in gun on an open platform – the 9.2in she carried prior to the war was a Mk. X in a Mk. VS mounting, the same as those on the battleships of the *King Edward VII* class (see *Warship* 2002-2003) and the armoured cruisers of the *Black Prince* and *Achilles* classes (see pp.137-140).

Renamed *Calcutta* (Dec. 1916) and then *Snapper* (Aug. 1917), she was sold in April 1922 to Dover Harbour Board, which converted her for use as a floating crane. At

Excellent, ex-Handy, *mounting a 12in gun, leaving Portsmouth Harbour in about 1895.* (From 'The Navy & Army Illustrated', Peter Brook collection)

this time she acquired another new name; *Demon*.[2]

Pounds acquired the old vessel in the early 1970s, demolishing the crane but retaining the hull and machinery. However since then the deckhouses have been removed and stacked on the fore-deck, and the machinery taken out and placed on the quayside in the yard. Although *Handy* no longer floats, much of her hull and many of her fitting still survive, testament to the toughness of her iron construction. In store at the Explosion! Museum of Naval Firepower across the harbour in Gosport are two mountings thought to possibly date from her time as a trials vessel.

Pound's Yard occupies the site of the former Tipner Naval Ordnance Depot, which had been taken over from the Ministry of Defence at around the same time as *Handy/Demon* was acquired. The yard, which contains a number of Grade II Listed Buildings, including the late eighteenth century powder magazines, the cooperage, shifting room and perimeter wall, is to be redeveloped, possibly as a new football stadium for Portsmouth FC. In the light of this the gunboat's future must lie in the balance: surely it would be a tragedy if the will – and the funds – cannot be found from somewhere to preserve this vessel which, while small and unspectacular, has survived for over 120 years and been part of the histories of Tyneside, Portsmouth, Dover and the Western Front.

Excellent, *ex-*Handy, *as she appeared during the First World War, mounting a 9.2in gun.* (Imperial War Museum, SP 210)

WARSHIP NOTES

The original caption to this illustration, from The Illustrated War News, *28 April, 1915, is titled 'The old Navy and the new Navy, off Belgium: HMS 'Excellent' (dating from the 'seventies) and a naval seaplane'. (A more precise identification of the seaplane has not been possible – it could be a Short, Wright or Farman – though the fact that the tip of the starboard upper wing appears to be missing could be significant in explaining the actual incident depicted.* Warship *would be interested to hear from any readers who can provide any more information.)* Excellent *was one of a number of vessels, including the old battleship HMS* Venerable *and several old cruisers, sloops and other gunboats, that arrived to operate off Belgium after the Scouts had returned to England, their guns having proven not to be heavy enough. (© The Illustrated London News Picture Library)*

Notes:

1. The gunboat *Drudge*, often listed with *Handy*, was in fact not a sister ship at all, but was built for Armstrongs as a substitute after *Handy* had been sold to the Royal Navy. Completed in 1887, she was also considerably larger, displacing 890 tons and measuring 125ft x 35ft2in x 12ft5in, enabling her to carry trainable gun mountings for trials work. As well as these she was fitted with a 4,900ft^3 slag hopper on each side to allow her to carry waste from the iron works out to sea for dumping – concern for the marine environment not being something that was on too many people's minds in the late nineteenth century. In 1901 *Drudge* too was taken over by the Royal Navy, also going on to serve as tender to – and taking the name of (subsequent to *Handy*) – *Excellent*. Later she was a floating workshop for HMS *Dryad*, before again fetching up in commercial service in Dover, apparently finally being scrapped in France in the 1960s.

2. Although almost certainly the longest lasting of all of the 'flat-irons', *Handy* was hardly unique in having a lengthy and varied career. Part of this may be attributed to their extremely stout construction, which as well as being necessitated by their carrying unusually heavy guns for vessels of their size was also a feature of many warships of that era (for example the battleship *Sultan*, completed at Chatham in 1871, survived as a hulk until 1946 – and this after having sunk in 1889 after striking an uncharted rock off Malta, subsequently being raised). The 'flat-irons' also owed their longevity, ironically, to the fact that they had quickly been made obsolete by the development of mines, torpedoes, and torpedo boats, which had taken away

This port side view of Demon (ex-Handy) *as she is today makes a good comparison with the pictures above and opposite. Note the line of the breastwork on the deck forward, and the deckhouses placed on the deck. (Geoffrey Dennison)*

An annotated sketch plan based on the original plans shows the internal arrangements of Handy, *with the officers' and crew's quarters forward, both accessed from the upper deck, with the first to port and the second to starboard; then the magazine and shell rooms (to port and starboard respectively); then their respective handling rooms with hatches to the upper deck; and then the boiler and engine, in one compartment with coal bunkers to each side. The sketch plan includes the following handwritten data in the margin:*

Class at Lloyds	*[illegible, might be A one]*
Gross Tonnage	*256*
Under Deck tonnage	*256*
Nett Register "	*110*
Draft of Water Loaded	*7ft 8ins*
Deadweight at Load Draft	*147*
Total Cargo Capacity	*nil*
Capacity of Coal Bunkers	*437 [somethings – illegible, might be 437 cu ft at 45 cu ft per ton?]*
Total Water Ballast	*nil*
Engines	*[abbreviated, illegible, might be 'Com. Sur. Con. Toms'?]*
Diameter of cylinders	*21ins and 38ins*
Length of Stroke	*24ins*
Pitch of screw	*9ft 0ins*
IHP	*315*
Speed on Trial	*9kts*
Draft on Trial	*[?] 6ft 7.5ins*
Displacement	*412 tons*
Midship Area	*215 sq ft*
Deadweight on Trial	*109 [or 100]*
$\frac{D^{2/3}V^3}{P}$	*128**
$\frac{MV^3}{P}$	*499 [or 497]**

Handy, *like* Drudge, *was originally registered as a merchant vessel, since she was built for a private concern and not for a navy, hence some of the figures given above.*

* The first formula is what is known as the Admiralty Co-efficient, and is used to estimate the power for a new ship by comparison with a similar predecessor. D = displacement in tons; ⅔ = raised to the power two-thirds; V3 = speed in knots, cubed; P = indicated horse power. The second formula is similar but with $D^{2/3}$ replaced by M, which is the immersed midships sectional area in square feet. It was common practice to try both and usually choose the higher value of P.

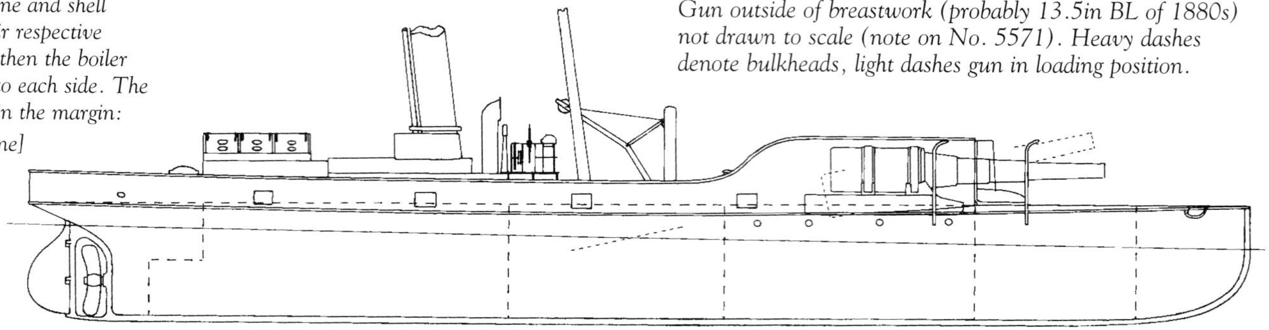

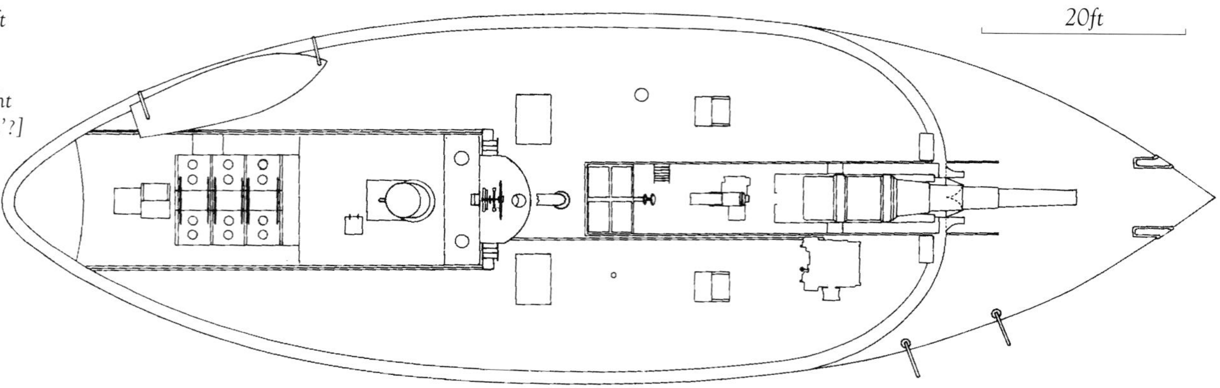

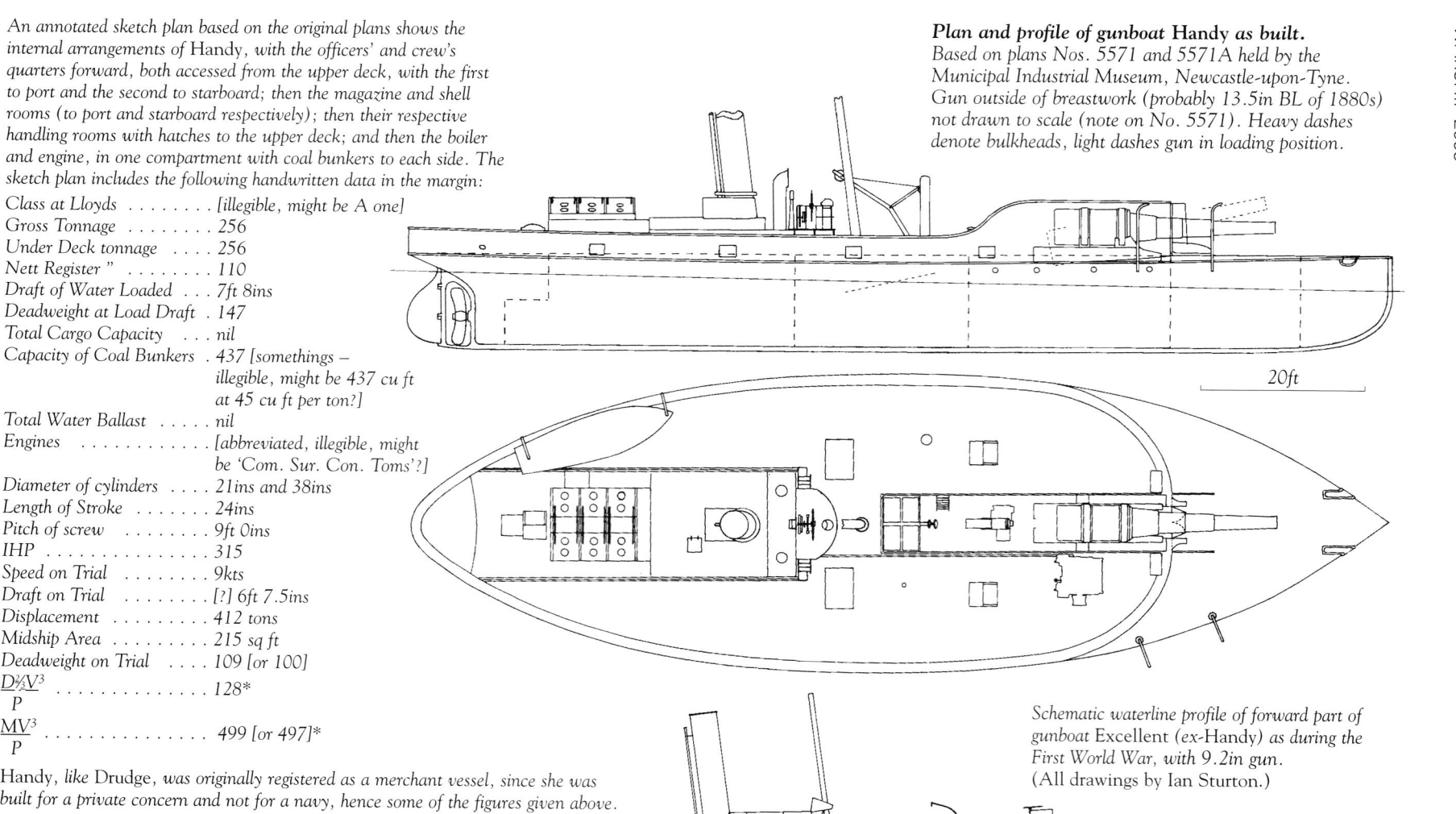

Plan and profile of gunboat* Handy *as built.
Based on plans Nos. 5571 and 5571A held by the Municipal Industrial Museum, Newcastle-upon-Tyne. Gun outside of breastwork (probably 13.5in BL of 1880s) not drawn to scale (note on No. 5571). Heavy dashes denote bulkheads, light dashes gun in loading position.

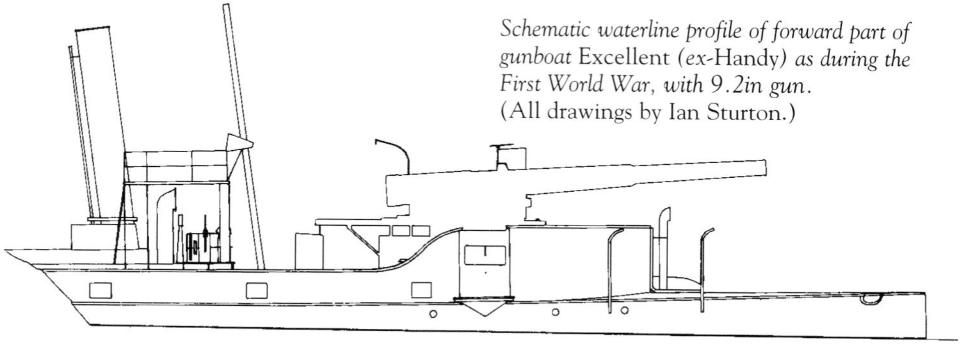

Schematic waterline profile of forward part of gunboat Excellent *(ex-*Handy*) as during the First World War, with 9.2in gun.*
(All drawings by Ian Sturton.)

WARSHIP NOTES

General view of Demon *(ex-*Handy*) from the port quarter, showing details of the hull, rudder and surviving bulwarks at the stern.* (Geoffrey Dennison)

their original coast defence role and meant that many were soon relegated to assorted subsidiary duties or sold into commercial service. For these their shallow draught, their great manoeuverability (the original twin-screw 'flat-irons' could turn in their own length, thanks to their screws being able to be reversed against one another) and stability resulting from their hull form, as well as their inherent sturdiness, meant that they were ideally suited. While some fell victim to the 'Fisher Axe' in the early years of the twentieth century, many survived in some form or another into the 1920s and beyond.

Sources:

Anderson, Richard M, 'Flatirons: the Rendel Gunboats', in *Warship International* Vol 13 no.1 (INRO, Virginia, 1976)

Brook, Peter, *Warships for Export: Armstrong Warships 1867-1927* (World Ship Society, Gravesend, 1999)

Campbell, NJM, 'British Naval Guns 1880-1945', no.7, in *Warship* no.24, (ed. R. Gardiner) (Conway Maritime Press, London, 1982)

Evans, David, *Arming the Fleet: the Development of the Royal Ordnance Yards, 1770-1945* (Explosion! Museum of Naval Firepower, Gosport, in association with English Heritage, 2006)

Gardiner, Robert (ed.), *All the World's Fighting Ships, 1860-1905* (Conway Maritime Press, London, 1979)

Hepper, David, *British Warship Losses in the Ironclad Era* (Chatham Publishing, London, 2006)

Preston, Antony, & Major, John, *Send a Gunboat* (Longman, Green & Co. Ltd, 1967, revised edition published by Conway Maritime Press, London, 2007)

Warlow, Lt. Cdr. B, *Shore Establishments of the Royal Navy* (Maritime Books, Liskeard, Cornwall, 2000)

National Historic Ships Register: http://www.nhsc.org.uk

The Illustrated War News, 28 April 1915

Thanks to DK Brown, Wyn Davies, the Discovery Museum, Newcastle, and Hannah Armstrong at *The Illustrated London News*

A view of the starboard bow. Note the name 'Demon' painted on. In the background is the M275 into Portsmouth (Stephen Dent)

Detail of the hull aft, showing the scuttles. (Geoffrey Dennison)

WARSHIP 2008

Detail of the surviving pieces of the superstructure. (Stephen Dent)

Detail of the stern, showing the rudder and propeller. (Geoffrey Dennison)

Two views of the remains of the vessel's machinery, now removed and resting on the quayside. (Stephen Dent)

View from aft, showing how the deck houses have been removed and placed on the deck forward. (Stephen Dent)

Looking aft, showing the interior of the boiler and engine compartment. (Geoffrey Dennison)

A's & A's

ARMED MERCHANT SHIPS 1885

In his article on Nathaniel Barnaby (*Warship* 2007, p.43) David K Brown stated that he was uncertain how many merchant ships completed conversion into cruisers in the war scare of 1885. Colin Jones has written in about two such vessels requisitioned in Australia:

Among the liners taken up for service as auxiliary cruisers during the Russian war scare of 1885, two were completed for sea in Australia. The *Massilia* and *Lusitania* were requisitioned at Sydney by Admiral Tryon on 17 April.

The *Massilia* was dealt with first and completed on 6 May and ran gunnery trials on 8 May. Only one gun was fired at a time to preserve the marble fittings in the public rooms. Her engines were protected by 12 feet of coal stowed in cabins and adjacent spaces and she mounted six 64-pounders and three 40-pounders (one for chase), drawn from other ships of the squadron. She also drew 120 men from the squadron.

The *Lusitania* followed on and was completed on 16 May. She had similar coal protection and mounted eight 64-pounders (two for chase) and two 40-pounders, two of the broadside guns being able to be traversed to the engaged side. She drew 150 men from the squadron and carried out gunnery trials on 22 May. The two ships were provisioned for six months. The crews of the regular warships were to be completed by men arriving as replacements.

IJN KANA SCRIPTS

Regular *Warship* reader Björn Rehnfeldt from Stockholm, Sweden, has written in about a caption to one of the photos published with Hans Lengerer's article on the Japanese Destroyers of the *Hatsuharu* class (*Warship* 2007, p.91):

The caption to the picture on page 93 of the IJN destroyer *Hatsuharu* reads: 'The name, in Hiragana script, is written on the hull amidships, ...'. This statement is incorrect, as the syllabary used is not Hiragana but Katakana, the characters of which are rather more angular than those of Hiragana. The Hiragana script was used for the names on the stern of all IJN warships, but the names used for recognition purposes on the hull sides of the destroyers were painted in Katakana. Both scripts read from right to left.

The accompanying table shows the full Hiragana and Katakana alphabets, both of which are syllabic, together with their Romaji (Latin) transcription. The photo of the destroyer *Ayanami* shows the ship's name in Hiragana on the stern, and in Katakana on the starboard side.

Editor's note: *Björn and I entered into a lengthy correspondence on this one, and each of us competed to produce the most complete table to illustrate the Hiragana and Katakana scripts (Björn won, as you can see from the accompanying table). I should also point out that the caption error was not the author's but mine. In a further caption error on p.70, for which the editor was also responsible, the liner* Roma *became the 'battleship* Roma'. *Apologies for these errors both to the authors of the articles and to the readers.*

YUGOSLAV DESTROYER SPLIT

Following the publication of the article 'The Star-Crossed Split' by Vincent O'Hara and Enrico Cernuschi in *Warship* 2005, we have received this correction from Dr. Zvonimir Freivogel:

The article on the Yugoslav destroyer *Split* contains an error concerning the AA weaponry of the ship. The secondary (anti-aircraft) battery, as envisaged, was indeed to comprise ten 40mm guns but these, like the main 140mm guns, were ordered from Skoda, while the 15mm anti-aircraft machine guns were ordered from Czeska Zbrojowka at Brno. It was originally assumed that the 40mm guns

This early photo of the 'Special Type' destroyer Ayanami *has the ship's name in Hiragana on the stern and in Katakana on the side amidships.*

The table shows the two kana syllabaries, Katakana and Hiragana, with their 'Romaji' transcription. Both scripts read from right to left. (Björn Rehnfeldt)

were a Bofors model of Swedish origin, but following the recent opening of the Skoda archives it has become clear that they were designed and manufactured by Skoda. No Bofors guns were ever ordered, and we now have complete data for the Skoda weapons, which were also carried by the Royal Yugoslav destroyers of the *Beograd* class. The 15mm machine guns were also originally thought to be of Swedish origin, but it has now been established that this gun too was a Czech model, built under licence and used under the name of 'Besa' by the British armed forces.

BRENNAN TORPEDO

The following letter has been received from *Warship* reader Douglas Thompson:

I recently read *Warship 2006* and noted David K Brown's short article on the Brennan Torpedo in the Warship Notes section of the annual (p.147). At the end of the article he states that there may have been a launching site in Hong Kong. I can confirm that this was indeed the case and enclose some photographs I took of the installation in 2003. The site is at the northeastern end of Hong Kong Island and guarded the narrow eastern approach to the harbour. It is now the home of the Hong Kong Museum of Coastal Defence and well worth a visit. As the photos show, two additional Brennan torpedoes survive in addition the the one in Gillingham that is illustrated in the article.

David K Brown adds: *There seem to be very few differences between the two torpedoes though there are slight changes in the way the wires passes the propeller. Hong Kong was the last Brennan instal-*

Photos of the two Brennan torpedoes which survive at Hong Kong. Panels have been cut into the sides for display purposes. (Douglas Thompson)

lation to be built. The launchway was hewn out of the rocks at Lei Yue Mun.

MYSTERY GUNBOATS

In *Warship 2007* (p.180 'Name a Gunboat') we published three photos of unidentified Victorian gunboats from the collection of the late Antony Preston. We have received the following letter from R G Todd, Key Specialist Curator at the National Maritime Museum Historic Photographs & Ship Plans Section:

The top photograph is of the composite gunboat *Wasp* (1886) moored off Sheerness on 4 May 1887 (NMM Neg. G10299). The middle photograph is of the survey vessel, former composite gunboat *Stork* (1882) at Chatham alongside the hulk of the floating battery *Thunderbolt* (1856), which became a pierhead in 1873 and was broken up in 1949 (NMM Neg. G10296). The third photograph is of the composite gunboat *Lizard* (1886) moored at Devonport soon after completion (NMM Neg. G10289). All three of these prints are from original 15" x 12" glass plates held in the National Maritime Museum's Historic Photographs Collection and this is, no doubt, the source from which Antony Preston acquired them. As an aside, Antony Preston was the subject specialist on the interview board that I attended in November 1979 when applying for the job I am still doing after 27 years (and enjoying every minute of it).

On another matter, on p.188, bottom left column, Wyn Davies incorrectly states that the old Brass Foundry at Woolwich is the Imperial War Museum's drawing repository. It is of course the repository for the National Maritime Museum's Historic Photographs and Ship Plans & Technical Records collections. I have worked in the Brass Foundry for the past 17 years!

WORLD NAVIES IN REVIEW 2007

Conrad Waters provides *Warship* readers with his annual overview of naval developments, construction and procurement.

Introduction

An observer of global maritime affairs over the past twelve months might be forgiven for feeling a sense of déjà vu. A distinct chill has entered the post Cold War environment and the appearance of Russian long-range reconnaissance aircraft to eavesdrop on the regular Exercise Neptune Warrior off Scotland in May was just one of a series of developments that reflected a more assertive military stance by Moscow. Such headline-grabbing initiatives – which also included a symbolic claim to the Arctic's vast mineral resources through the use of a Mir submersible to plant a flag on the seabed close to the North Pole – do little to change the overall balance of power. However, it is clear that Russia intends to use its resurgent economic strength to become a more influential player on the world's oceans. Speaking before the annual Navy Day celebration, the then naval commander-in-chief, Admiral Vladimir Masorin, outlined ambitious long-term expansion plans. These include the construction of six aircraft carriers in the 2015-2030 timeframe to restore the fleet to its previous second-place ranking behind the US Navy. Whilst increased funding is being provided to support these aspirations, the run-down and fragmented state of the Russian Federation's shipyards could be a serious hindrance to their consummation. It is therefore unsurprising that much emphasis is being placed on industrial restructuring. A new United Shipbuilding Corporation has been formed to consolidate the state's interests into a cohesive framework. Efforts are also underway to re-establish indigenous manufacturing capabilities lost in the break-up of the former Soviet Union.

The Russian Federation is not alone in facing problems with its shipbuilding industry. The United States' ambitions to rebuild fleet numbers look vulnerable to a series of cost overruns that are most apparent in the two prototypes for the key Littoral Combat Ship (LCS) programme. A second Lockheed Martin ship was cancelled in April after failure to agree a fixed-price contract, whilst deletion of General Dynamics' follow-on vessel, LCS-4, was confirmed on 1 November. Quality is also an issue, most evidently in respect of the first and much delayed LPD-17 class vessel, *San Antonio*, which has been plagued with construction defects. In both cases, much of the problem appears to have been caused by starting assembly before the technology used in a design has been properly matured. Already squeezed by the global demands of the 'war on terror' and China's emergence as a major regional naval power, the USN's maritime supremacy appears increasingly under threat as it struggles to translate its ongoing technological leadership into a balanced, cost-effective fleet.

European Navies

The efficiency of Europe's maritime sector has also been under scrutiny in recent years, with many commentators doubting whether the industry's highly fragmented structure could be sustained in an era of much depleted order books. Whilst the anticipated process of consolidation has taken time to evolve, 2007 saw important developments. In France, the long-mooted alliance between DCN and Thales was finally brought to a successful conclusion. The state-controlled naval shipbuilder has acquired the latter's French naval businesses in

RFS Admiral Panteleyev *& USS* Lassen *conduct a replenishment exercise. Relations between the Russian Federation & the West are becoming chillier. (US Navy)*

return for surrendering a 25% stake in the enlarged group – renamed DCNS – which might be increased to 35% over time. Across the Channel rationalisation of the remaining British shipyards was achieved through an agreement to merge VT Group's and BAe Systems' surface facilities in Portsmouth and Glasgow into a joint venture. A similar simplification of submarine activities has been brought closer by Babcock's acquisition of the Devonport naval dockyard, which will now be run in association with the company's existing facilities at Rosyth and Faslane. However, cross-border consolidation looks more difficult to achieve in the light of the increased potential for both political and commercial disagreement. For example, the investment made by Thyssen Krupp Marine Systems in revitalising its Greek Hellenic Shipyards subsidiary has been called into question by a protracted dispute with the Hellenic Navy over acceptance of the new Type 214 submarine, *Papanikolis*.

There also seems to be a growing acceptance amongst the leading European maritime nations that the post Cold War drawdown of force levels has now run its course. Although this might be more a reflection of a desire to secure shipyard votes than any conversion to the merits of maritime influence, recent commitments to expensive new programmes (such as the French 'Barracuda' class nuclear powered attack submarines, German F-125 frigates and British CVF aircraft carriers) represent major investments in the future. Meanwhile, an increasing flow of long-awaited equipment is starting to compensate for previous withdrawals of so-called 'legacy assets', in many cases producing a quantum leap in capabilities, narrowing the gap with the US Navy and providing a welcome boost to inter-operability. As always, however, budgets remain tight with some fleets doing better than others. The Netherlands, in particular, continues to experience a difficult environment in the light of the high cost of the country's involvement in international operations. Table 1 sets out the numerical strength of the larger European navies towards the end of 2007.

A computer generated image of France's deuxième porte-avions (PA2). Sacrifices might be required if she is to be ordered in 2008. (DCN)

The major European Navies

France: The run-up to the French 2007 presidential election saw confirmation of several orders for new defence equipment. The most significant of these was the long-awaited announcement on 22 December 2006 of an initial contract worth more than €1bn for the design, development and production of the prototype 'Barracuda' attack submarine. Now scheduled to be delivered later than initially planned in 2016, first of class *Suffren* will be followed by five sister boats at roughly two yearly intervals under a total €8bn programme designed to replace the existing *Rubis* vessels on a one-for-one basis. Displacing 4,765 tonnes in submerged condition, the 99m long *Suffren* will be powered by a derivative of the K-15 nuclear reactor already installed in the *Le Triomphant* class SSBN and is likely to be capable of considerably more than her official design speed of c.25 knots. Armament will be a mixture of up to 20 torpedoes, Exocet anti-ship and Scalp land attack cruise missiles. A contract for the development and manufacture of up to 250 of the naval version of Scalp, which will first enter service in 2013 on the new FREMM frigates, was signed at the end of 2006.

However in the post-election environment there is insufficient money in the current procurement budget to meet all desired programmes, result-

Table 1: MAJOR EUROPEAN NAVIES – NUMERICAL STRENGTH (END 2007)

Country	France	Germany	Greece	Italy	Netherlands	Spain	Turkey	UK
Aircraft Carrier (CVN)	1	–	–	–	–	–	–	–
Support/Helicopter Carrier (CVS/CVH)	1	–	–	2	–	1	–	3
Strategic Missile Submarine (SSBN)	4	–	–	–	–	–	–	4
Attack Submarine (SSN)	6	–	–	–	–	–	–	9
Patrol Submarine (SSK)	–	12	9	7	4	4	14	–
Fleet Escort (DDG/FFG)	17	15	14	14	9	10	18	25
Patrol Escort/Corvette (FFG/FSG/FS)	15	2	3	8	–	–	6	–
Missile Armed Attack Craft (PGG/PTG)	–	10	19	–	–	–	25	–
Mine Countermeasures Vessel (MCMV)	16	20	10	12	10	6	18	16
Major Amphibious (LHD/LPD/LPH/LSD)	4	–	–	3	2	2	–	7

ing in some uncertainty over the future of the planned second aircraft carrier – *deuxième porte-avions* (PA2) – modelled on the British CVF. Design work on the c.75,000-tonne vessel, which will be adapted for conventional take off and landing operations, is now well advanced. However, an order has been delayed until the first half of 2008 pending a review of defence commitments which will lead to publication of a new White Paper on defence and national security. Whilst it seems likely that PA2 will eventually be approved, not least because of the considerable sums already invested in the project, other purchases might be scaled back in compensation. For example, there is speculation that the surface fleet will shrink from its current level of 32 escorts due to cuts in the planned total of 17 multi-mission FREMM frigates. Eight of the class are already on order in both anti-submarine and land attack variants. Construction work on the first, to be named *Aquitaine*, commenced at DCNS' Lorient yard in February.

Lorient is also involved in completing France's pair of the four Franco-Italian 'Horizon' air defence frigates. The first of these, *Forbin*, spent much of the year continuing a series of sea trials that started back in June 2006. Delivery is scheduled for mid-2008, thereby allowing the 37-year old veteran *Duquesne* to be retired from the air defence role. Work on *Forbin*'s sister, *Chevalier Paul*, is now well advanced and she commenced her own trials on 13 November.

Following rectification of defects involving the flooring of her accommodation areas, the second new LHD, *Tonnerre*, was delivered in February and subsequently embarked on an extended cruise to American waters. This included a series of exercises with US Marine Corps that were intended to test the design's compatibility with American amphibious equipment such as the landing craft air cushion (LCAC) and a range of helicopters. She was subsequently declared fully operational on 1 August. Sister ship *Mistral* had achieved similar status the previous December but returned to her builders Brest over the summer for completion of post-trials remediation work. The two vessels have already been well received in service and are intended to be a key element of France's future contribution to the rapid-reaction NATO Response Force (NRF).

Italy: The *Marina Militare* spent much of 2007 eagerly awaiting delivery of the aircraft carrier *Cavour*, which made her first voyage from Fincantieri's Muggiano shipyard in December 2006. Of c.27,000 tonnes full load displacement, *Cavour* is the largest Italian warship built since the Second World War and the most powerful of a number of 'mini-flat-tops' currently entering service with European and Asian fleets (see Table 2 for further details). Originally intended to have a primary orientation towards amphibious operations, the final design ordered in November 2000 emerged as more of a traditional STOVL (short take-off/vertical landing) aircraft carrier with a secondary helicopter assault capability. A typical air group will comprise eight AV-8B Plus Harrier fixed wing aircraft and twelve EH-101 helicopters. *Cavour* is also equipped with a comprehensive command and control system derived from that fitted in Italy's 'Horizon' class air defence frigates, with which she shares a number of other systems such as the EMPAR SPY-790 multifunction radar and Aster 15 surface-to-air missile. *Andrea Doria*, the first Italian 'Horizon', was handed over in December following an extensive series of trials that commenced on 20 September 2006. Construction of sister ship *Caio Duilio* has been protracted, although her launch took place at Riva Trigoso on 23 October.

Future building will be dominated by plans for ten Italian variants of the Franco-Italian FREMM frigate, of which four will be completed in anti-submarine and six in general purpose configurations. Only two prototype ships – to be named *Carlo Bergamini* and *Carlo Margottini* – were ordered when the project was launched. However, a modest improvement in the budgetary situation during 2007 and significant political support for the project makes it increasingly likely that further orders will be forthcoming by the end of the decade so as to maintain the surface fleet at twelve vessels. It is envisaged that the first ship will now commission in 2012, more than three years later than first expected.

Both Type 212A class submarines are now in service following the commissioning of *Scirè* in February. First of class, *Salvatore Todaro*, departed on a well-publicised deployment in support of NATO's Operation Active Endeavour during the same month. The *Marina Militare* remains keen to order a second batch in the near term but this will be contingent on future budget decisions. The profile of the fleet's amphibious units has also been raised following successful involvement in peacekeeping operations off

Italy's aircraft carrier NMM Cavour started sea trials in December 2006. (Maurizio Brescia, via Vincent O'Hara)

WORLD NAVIES IN REVIEW 2007

Table 2: Recent Mini 'Flattops'

Class:	Mistral	Cavour	Juan Carlos I	Hyuga	Dokdo
Country:	France	Italy	Spain	Japan	South Korea
Type:	LHD	CVS	LHD	DDH	LHD
First Operational:	2006	2008	2009	2009	2007
Number:	2	1	1[1]	2	1[2]
Displacement (FL):	21,500t	27,100t	27,800t	18,000t	19,000t
Dimensions:	199m x 32m	236m x 39m	231m x 32m	197m x 33m	200m x 32m
Speed:	19 knots	28 knots	21 knots	30 knots	22 knots
Complement:[3]	160	528	243	322	300
Air Group:[4]	Nil jets 16 helicopters	8 jets 12 helicopters	11 jets 12 helicopters	Nil jets 11 helicopters	Nil jets 10 helicopters
Armament:	2 x twin Simbad PDMS 2 x 30mm guns	32-cell Sylver launcher for Aster 15 SAM 2 x 76mm & 2 x 25mm guns	4 x 20mm guns	16-cell Mk 41 launcher for Sea Sparrow SAM/ASROC 2 x Phalanx CIWS 2 x 20mm guns 2 x triple TT	1x Sea RAM PDMS 2 x Goalkeeper CIWS
Lift:[4]	450 (900 austerity) 60 armoured vehicles 4 x LCU/2 x LCAC	325 (415 austerity) 60 armoured vehicles	900 100 armoured vehicles 4 x LCU/1 x LCAC	Not Applicable	700 70 armoured vehicles 2 x LCAC

Notes:
[1] Two additional units ordered by Australia.   [2] Up to two further units projected.   [3] Excluding air group and embarked troops.
[4] Specimen maximum capacity – trade-off required between air group and lift potential.

Lebanon. Further investment in enhancing these capabilities by acquiring a vessel larger than the existing *San Giorgios* is envisaged. However, even with the recent improvement in funding, it seems that hard choices will be inevitable and the project will possibly be linked to the replacement of the carrier *Giuseppe Garibaldi* in the middle of the next decade.

Spain: The *Armada Española* has benefited from a strong flow of orders in recent years, meaning there has recently been something of a pause in new announcements while previously authorised construction progresses. Prominent amongst these is the LHD-type strategic protection ship, *Juan Carlos I*, which makes an interesting contrast with the Italian *Cavour*. While capable of deploying a similarly-sized air group, she incorporates many amphibious capabilities – most notably a stern well dock – deleted from *Cavour*'s original design, but still retains features – such as a ski-jump – needed to support STOVL aircraft operations. Against this, her top speed is considerably slower and she lacks many of *Cavour*'s sophisticated control and defensive systems. She should be launched by early 2008, with delivery scheduled for around the end of the year. The design has already found favour overseas, with Australia ordering two variants for its own LHD project in preference to a modified French *Mistral*.

Other new construction moved ahead during 2007. The keel of the new fleet replenishment vessel *Cantabria* was laid on 18 July and floating out is expected during February 2008 prior to end of year completion. Looking further ahead, she will be joined by the first four BAM offshore patrol vessels, a fifth F-100 air defence frigate, and four S-80 patrol submarines, for which the UK's BAe Systems has been contracted to supply pressure domes in a move that can be seen as a further weaken-

SPS Juan Carlos I, the new LHD-type strategic projection ship under construction for Spain, will soon be ready for launch. (Navantia)

ing of the alliance between Navantia and DCNS. Reports in the Spanish press suggest that the Navy has longer term ambitions to rebuild its submarine force to as many as eight vessels through an order for up to four further S-80s. Confirmation of a sixth F-100 – for an escort fleet of twelve frigates – and further patrol vessels are the other priorities.

Operationally, the fleet has continued the recent trend of being increasingly visible in support of NATO and other activities. Most notably, the lead F-100 frigate, *Álvaro de Bazán*, visited Australia early in the year to support Navantia's successful bid to supply the design as the basis of the new air warfare destroyer programme. Her world export promotion tour involved a circumnavigation of the globe, reportedly the first time this feat had been accomplished by a Spanish warship in 142 years.

United Kingdom: 2007 started badly for the Royal Navy. The strain of ongoing military operations in Afghanistan and Iraq resulted in widespread speculation about further naval cutbacks, including immediate reduction to reserve status of as many as six of the 25 strong escort fleet and potential cancellation of the flagship future aircraft carrier (CVF) project. Although both rumours ultimately proved unfounded, March brought more personal tragedy when an explosion of an oxygen generation candle on the submarine *Tireless*, participating in an Anglo-American exercise under the Arctic ice cap, killed two crew members and injured a third. The same month saw the capture and detention by Iranian Revolutionary Guards of fifteen sailors and Royal Marines from the frigate *Cornwall* whilst they were involved in routine boarding operations in the Persian Gulf. Although the personnel involved were eventually released unharmed, the subsequent decision to allow some of those involved to sell their stories to the press probably marked a nadir in the Royal Navy's recent public relations effort.

More positively, however, 2007 saw significant progress with hitherto protracted modernisation plans. The first new generation SSN, *Astute*, was rolled out for naming and launch at BAE Systems' Barrow yard on 8 June, marking the successful turnaround of a much-troubled project that commenced with an order for the first three boats as far back as March 1997. Authorisation for a fourth unit of the class, to be named *Audacious*, was confirmed on 21 May. *Astute* herself was left stranded due to a fault on the synchrolift following roll out and did not actually enter the water until a week later. She will commence sea trials early in 2008 prior to entering operational service the following year. Also due to join the active fleet in 2009 is the first Type 45 destroyer, *Daring*, which departed the Clyde for a month's preliminary testing on 18 July. Intended to check the smooth operation of the ship 'platform', including key propulsion and engineering equipment, the process reportedly exceeded all expectations. Of particular note was the performance of the revolutionary all-electric power and propulsion system, which produced a maximum speed of 31.5 knots against the 28 knots contracted.

Whilst *Daring* was at sea, a flurry of announcements at the end of the British parliamentary year did much to clarify the structure of the Royal Navy in the decades ahead. On 25 July, the long awaited 'main gate' authorisation for construction of two new CVF future aircraft carriers was finally confirmed in a series of statements that also endorsed the retention of all three UK naval bases following the conclusion of a ten month-long strategic review. The two 65,000-tonne ships – to be named *Queen Elizabeth* and *Prince of Wales* – will be built in a series of blocks in yards around the country by the previously established Aircraft Carrier Alliance under a contract worth around £3.9bn. Construction will start in 2008, with final assembly taking place at Babcock's Rosyth facility prior to delivery in 2014 and 2016 – roughly two years later than originally planned. Confirmation of the programme – and of the future naval base structure – also resulted in a green light for the merger of BAe Systems and VT Group's surface shipbuilding and maintenance interests. It was reported that the deal is associated with a 15-year agreement guaranteeing a minimum workload of approximately one major escort vessel per year for the relevant yards.

In the short term, this future surface construction programme will be dominated by completion of further Type 45 destroyers. Second of class, *Dauntless*, was launched on 23 January, with *Diamond* following on 27 November. Financial arrangements for completion of a further three vessels – all of which are already under construction – were agreed during August and plans for a further two remain under consideration. Looking further ahead, the Future Surface Combatant (FSC) project has undergone several changes in direction since studies began in late 1990s, and the latest thinking involves three different classes: a high end anti-submarine warfare escort (designated C1), a less capable

The first British Type 45 destroyer, HMS Daring, *departs on initial sea trials on 18 July 2007.* (Conrad Waters)

WORLD NAVIES IN REVIEW 2007

The modified 'River' class offshore patrol vessel, HMS Clyde, entered service as Falkland Islands guardship during 2007. (Conrad Waters)

The Astute *class submarine programme is back on track. Here HMS Astute herself is pictured after roll out. (BAe Systems)*

stabilisation combatant (C2) and a multi-role ocean patrol vessel that can be configured for mine-countermeasures and other operations (C3). This apparent willingness to use some resources to obtain a larger number of less sophisticated vessels marks a major departure for the Royal Navy, reflecting the views of the current First Sea Lord, Sir Jonathon Band, that the fleet has shrunk too far to meet all current tasking.

The only addition to the front-line fleet in 2007 was the new offshore patrol vessel *Clyde*, which replaced *Dumbarton Castle* as Falkland Islands guardship. The handover of *Lyme Bay* to the Royal Fleet Auxiliary on 2 August marked completion of the four-strong auxiliary LSD project and provided partial compensation for the accelerated run down of the 'Leaf' class support tankers.

The Medium-sized European Navies

Germany: The *Deutsche Marine* continued its process of re-orientation towards global maritime operations during 2007. The most notable development was the announcement of the formal go-ahead for the F-125 frigate programme, with an order for four ships placed with the ARGE F-125 consortium of Thyssen Krupp and Lürssen on 26 June. Of c.6,800 tonnes full load displacement, the new frigates are designed for despatch on potentially lengthy, medium intensity stabilisation operations at some distance from their home base and will incorporate features such as extensive duplication – including adoption of a twin island superstructure – and a combined diesel-electric and gas turbine propulsion system which will both reduce maintenance and facilitate survivability. A system of crew rotation is intended to allow them to remain for up to two years in the operational area. Deployments in support of Operation Enduring Freedom off the Horn of Africa and Germany's ongoing leadership of the maritime element of the United Nations Interim Force in Lebanon (UNIFIL) have put the current 15-strong escort fleet under some pressure over the last year, so this capability is certainly needed. However, it will not be until 2014 that the first ship is completed.

In the meantime, good progress is being made with the K-130 corvette programme and the fifth and final ship, *Ludwigshafen am Rhein*, was christened at Lürssen's Bremen yard on 27 September. First of class *Braunschweig* commenced sea trials in December 2006 and, along with sister *Magdeburg* was scheduled for delivery around the end of 2007. The fourth and last of the initial batch of Type 212A patrol submarines, *U-34*, was delivered on 3 May 2007, her arrival compensating for previous withdrawals of elderly Type 206A boats

Good progress is being made with Germany's K-130 corvette programme. Here first of class FGS Braunschweig is seen on sea trials. (Thyssen Krupp Marine Systems)

167

and maintaining a twelve-strong submarine flotilla. Construction work on the second batch of two vessels started on 21 August.

The *Deutsche Marine's* next priority is to secure a commitment to a third Type 702 *Berlin* class replenishment tanker, for which it is hoped that an order will be placed by the end of 2008 for commissioning in 2012. In the longer term, plans to acquire a more extensive logistical support and military deployment capability through investment in joint support ships, presumably of a similar configuration to those planned for the Royal Canadian Navy, have been reported. However, previous ambitions of this nature have not secured funding and this is likely to remain a serious obstacle to future progress.

Greece: The Hellenic Navy's modernisation plans are currently being constrained by tight controls on defence funding that aim to keep overall expenditure to around 1% of GDP or about half that seen at the start of the decade. As a result, it is not surprising that the bulk of the procurement budget is being devoted to completing previously authorised projects. So far as the surface fleet is concerned, the most prominent of these are construction of the five *Roussen* fast attack craft being built by the Elefsis shipyard in conjunction with VT Group and the upgrade by Thales and Hellenic Shipyards of six of the ten former *Kortenaer* class frigates previously acquired from The Netherlands. Both programmes are progressing well. Frigate modernisation has now reached the approximate half way mark, whilst *Ritsos* – the fifth *Roussen* – was launched on 9 October 2006. VT remains optimistic that an option for a further two vessels will be taken up in the near future. In the meantime, mine countermeasures capabilities have received a boost with the transfer of the former US Navy *Osprey* class *Heron* and *Pelican* at a ceremony at Ingleside, Texas, on 16 March.

Renewal of the submarine force is proving more problematic. The Hellenic Navy has refused to take delivery of its first Type 214 boat, the German-built *Papanikolis*, due to complaints that include surface instability, propulsion deficiencies and periscope vibration. *Lloyds List* reported in August that payments amounting to as much as €450m had been withheld on the total €2bn four-vessel contract with Thyssen Krupp Marine Systems. As a result, the production schedule for the remaining three boats, being completed at the group's Hellenic Shipyards subsidiary, has been threatened. The dispute appears to have soured a lengthy and hitherto successful partnership with the German shipbuilding sector, with potential implications for the planned six-strong multi-mission frigate contract for which France and Spain are also competing.

The Netherlands: The Royal Netherlands Navy continues to experience a seemingly relentless flow of cutbacks in the face of financial austerity. Previously announced plans to reduce the surface fleet to just six frontline escorts have been confirmed with news of an agreement to transfer the 'M' class frigates *Van Nes* and *Van Galen* to Portugal during 2008-09. In addition, lack of funding has forced abandonment of the purchase of Tomahawk cruise missiles for the *De Zeven Provincien* LCF air defence frigates, which will likely have to make do with cheaper but less effective Vulcano extended range munitions being developed by Oto Melara for the 127mm gun. Lack of trained personnel is also having an impact, resulting in the reported enforced withdrawal from operations of the submarine *Bruinvis* for at least a year due to a lack of suitably qualified crew.

The delivery of the modified *Rotterdam* class LPD, *Johan de Witt*, following extended trials resulting from problems with her podded propulsion system, left the Dutch shipbuilding industry bereft of substantial domestic work prior to confirmation of an order for four new ocean patrol vessels on 20 December. Of around 3,750 tonnes full load displacement, these ships are intended to supplement the escort fleet in lower intensity roles and will therefore have a light armament built around a 76mm gun and facilities for a NFH-90 size helicopter. A diesel-electric propulsion system will provide a modest maximum speed of c.22 knots. The most distinctive design feature is undoubtedly a new Thales pyramid-like integrated sensor mast that is intended to point the way ahead for ships of this size. It is expected that construction will be split between Damen group's Schelde Naval Shipyard at Vlissingen and its Galati facility in Romania, with the first ship scheduled for delivery by the end of 2010.

Turkey: The Turkish Navy is now at a transitional stage in its renewal programme, with a number of longstanding projects drawing to a close. The final *Preveze* Type 209/1400 patrol submarine, *Birinci Inönü*, commissioned during the course of the year, whilst construction of *Kiliç* fast attack craft and 'Aydin' mine-countermeasures vessels is also close to completion. *Amasra*, the first Turkish-built unit of the latter class was accepted on 24 January, with *Ayvalik* following on 22 June. As a result, attention is turning to a new round of projects.

The most of advanced of these is the US$1.5bn 'MilGem' national corvette programme, with *Heybeliada* – the prototype of up to twelve planned ships – currently scheduled for launch in 2008. A number of key systems were contracted during 2007, most notably an agreement for supply of the main propulsion system by the local subsidiary of MTU. With surface fleet numbers falling due to the progressive withdrawal of elderly second-hand escorts – particularly the remaining *Knox* class frigates – the new class is urgently required if this trend is to be halted.

Another priority is commencement of a programme to maintain the 14-strong submarine flotilla, with plans for modernisation of the ageing Type 209/1200 *Atilay* class abandoned in favour of a series of air independent propulsion (AIP) equipped boats. Proposals were sought by the middle of November, with yards in France, Germany, Italy and Spain all reported as being interested in supplying a design and technology for local build. If all goes well, the first boat will be delivered from the local Gölcük Naval Shipyard in 2015. Preliminary exploration of the acquisition of a new LPD and associated landing craft

WORLD NAVIES IN REVIEW 2007

is also underway, marking a further expansion of Turkey's growing naval ambitions.

Other European Navies

Balkans: Modernisation of the region's naval forces continues at a slow pace, with much of the available cash going to other branches of the armed forces. However, Bulgaria started final negotiations for a c.€800m order for four DCNS 'Gowind' type corvettes in October, whilst transfer of further surplus vessels from Belgium remains on the agenda. Romania is currently focused on the ongoing upgrade of the former Type 22 frigates purchased from the UK but has also announced plans to acquire four multi-mission corvettes, as well as four minesweepers, around the turn of the decade. Both fleets are faring better than the rump of the former Yugoslavian Navy now controlled by Montenegro. The country's main naval base has been surrendered for commercial redevelopment and most of the fleet sold, with only two *Kotor* class light frigates and a handful of fast attack craft retained for essentially coastguard type duties.

Baltic Republics: The Baltic navies have been more fortunate in the post Cold War environment, with Estonia and Latvia starting to take delivery of, respectively, surplus UK *Sandown* and Dutch 'Tripartite' minehunters during 2007 and Lithuania concluding a deal to purchase up to three 'Stanflex 300' multi-role patrol ships from Denmark by 2009.

Belgium: The former Netherlands 'M' class frigate *Leopold I* entered service on schedule on 29 March. Successful completion of subsequent work-up allowed decommissioning of the last operational *Wielingen* class vessel, *Westdiep*, on 5 October. The second 'M' class, *Louise Marie*, will be delivered in March 2008 and four NFH-90 helicopters have been ordered for the new ships.

Ireland: The Irish Naval Service has invited bids for two offshore patrol vessels and one extended patrol vessel to replace its existing P21 class. An order should be placed by the end of 2008.

Poland: Work continues to move ahead slowly on the protracted MEKO A-100 light frigate programme. Italy's Avio has been contracted to supply a LM-2500 gas turbine propulsion system for the first of class, which should enter service around the end of the decade.

Portugal: The *Marinha Portuguesa*'s agreement to purchase a pair of surplus Netherlands 'M' class frigates in replacement for the two remaining *João Belo* class ships will stabilise the frontline escort fleet at five ships. *Van Nes* will be transferred at the end of 2008 and *Van Galen* a year later. The remaining light frigates will be progressively replaced by the *Viana do Castelo* ocean patrol vessels, with the first two scheduled for delivery imminently. Construction of the two new Type 209PN AIP-equipped submarines is also well advanced and the first will be launched during 2008.

Scandinavia: Ironically the transition of Scandinavia's fleets from their former regional Cold War orientation towards more global interventionist capabilities is coming to fruition as the environment with Russia is starting to feel a little chilly. However, regular sightings of the region's ships in the warmer climate of the Mediterranean in support of NATO and UN operations are a clear demonstration of the flexibility of maritime forces and their ability to meet a range of threats.

The Royal Danish Navy has possibly changed most in recent years, and there was further evidence of this in 2007. Technical completion of *Absalon* – the first combat support ship first delivered back in 2005 – was finally achieved after installation of radar, command and other systems. Sister *Esbern Snare* should be finished in 2008. Work is underway on three similar frigate-like 'patrol ships' following signature of a contract with Odense Steel Shipyard on 20 December 2006. Norwegian fleet renewal is also advancing well. The new frigate *Fridtjof Nansen* completed successful Aegis combat system ship qualification trials (CSSQT) in conjunction with Spain's F-100 class *Méndez Núñez* and the American *Arleigh Burke* class *Gridley* (DDG-101) in June, taking some of the heat out of discussions with Navantia over cost and quality control issues. Second of class, *Roald Amundsen*, was delivered on 21 May, whilst the fourth of the five vessels, *Helge Ingstad*, was launched on 23 November. 2008 will start to see the arrival of *Skjold* class fast attack craft from series production following launch at the end of 2006 of the second of class *Storm*.

In the Baltic, Sweden is busy

FNS Tornio. *The four-strong flotilla of* Hamina *class fast attack craft is now ready for deployment.* (Aker Yards)

upgrading the *Visby* class to full operational specification following arrival of the fifth and final ship, *Karlstad*. However, equipment-fit is being reduced due to funding issues and further defence cuts are in the offing. The Swedish Defence Minister, Mikael Odenburg, resigned in September following reports of a c.US$600m reduction in the country's procurement budget. Whilst there still appears to be a desire to proceed with the A-26 submarine that has emerged from the ashes of the earlier 'Viking' project, other purchases will suffer. Meanwhile, in Finland, the four-strong flotilla of *Hamina* class fast attack craft is ready for operational deployment following delivery of the final ship, *Pori*, in June 2006. A €245m order for three new minehunters derived from Intermarine's *Lerici* design was placed under the MCMV 2010 programme in November 2006.

The Russian Federation

Recent media attention on the Russian Federation Navy has tended to focus on the fleet's longer term ambitions to re-establish a blue water presence on the world's oceans. Russian warships have certainly become more visible in recent years in support both of national 'flag waving' objectives and international exercises. However, these deployments have been almost exclusively in the hands of elderly Soviet-era warships benefiting from varying degrees of refurbishment and modernisation. Current investment on new construction is directed towards the key priority of renewing the submarine-based nuclear arsenal and the linked aim of improving the security of coastal waters.

Only mixed success is being achieved with this primary objective. The trials of the new 'Bulava' missile, being undertaken by the refurbished Project 941 'Typhoon' class SSBN *Dmitriy Donskoy*, hit serious problems towards the end of 2006, with three consecutive test failures being experienced on 7 September, 25 October and 24 December. It was therefore with some relief that a further trial firing from the White Sea on 28 June concluded with the test missile successfully impacting the Kura range on the Kamchatka Peninsula. In spite of this, the announcement in August that the new missile would go into mass production was something of a surprise, as further tests are still planned to ensure its reliability. It would appear that much of the haste is driven by the need to ensure the new Project 955 'Borey' class submarines that the missile is intended to equip are not left without their primary armament. First of class *Yuri Dolgorukiy* was launched from the Sevmash plant at Severodvinsk on 15 April and is expected to be delivered in 2008 after completion of sea trials. A further two boats are currently under construction and it is reported that as many as eight are scheduled for completion by 2017 to replace the ageing 'Delta III' and 'Typhoon' classes.

The other main nuclear-powered submarine programme is focused on completing the sole Project 885/855 'Yasen' submarine *Severodvinsk*, first laid down as long ago as 1993 but with sea trials reported to commence by the start of 2009. In the absence of orders for further attack submarines, the fleet will become increasingly reliant on the SSK-type boats of the Project 677 'Lada' class. Lead boat *St. Petersburg* completed an extensive series of tests with deep water dives in the Baltic during 2007. Two further boats of modified design are under construction following the start of work on *Sevastopol* on 10 November 2006. Additional orders are planned.

Expenditure on new surface vessels has been relatively modest in comparison, with the available money largely channelled into construction of the Project 2038.0 *Steregushchy* stealth corvettes, the first of which spent much of 2007 on sea trials prior to commissioning in November. These 2,200-tonne multi-role vessels are primarily intended to operate in coastal waters to protect the sea lanes transited by the strategic missile carrying submarines on their journeys to and from the open sea. Design features includes an all-composite superstructure, enclosed radar mast and topside shaping to reduce radar cross-section to a minimum, whilst a powerful armament and sonar suite is shipped given the modest size of the hull. As of the autumn of 2007, four additional ships were under construction for the Russian Navy following start of work on *Stoiky* on 10 November 2006. All are planned to be in service around the end of the decade. Rather lower priority appears to be accorded to the first Project 2235.0 frigate, *Admiral Gorshkov*, which was laid down in 2006. However, the replacement of Commander-in-Chief Vladimir Masorin by former Northern Fleet C-in-C, Vladimir Vysotsky, in September 2007 might herald a change in emphasis, as Vysotsky is reported to be sympathetic to devoting more resources to blue water naval forces.

Numbers of active units have changed little year-on-year, although precise information is difficult to compile. The surface fleet includes c.30 front-line escorts, the carrier *Kuznetsov* which returned to operational service during the year after refit, 15 strategic missile submarines, c.15-20 nuclear attack boats and c.15-20 patrol submarines.

The Middle East, Indian Ocean and Africa

Tensions remained high in the Middle East during 2007, accounting for considerable maritime activity. United Nations forces continued peacekeeping operations off Lebanon throughout the year under the auspices of the German-commanded UNIFIL maritime component. The mission is seen as being broadly successful in curbing arms smuggling to the local Islamic militias and Germany's leadership has been extended into 2008. Meanwhile, the fallout from Israel's excursion into Lebanon in the summer of 2006 claimed the scalp of naval commander, Vice-Admiral David Ben-Bashat, who tended his resignation on 26 July. The Admiral effectively took responsibility for operational failures that facilitated Hezbollah's attack on the 'Sa'ar 5' class corvette *Hanit* on 14 July 2006 with C-802 surface-to-surface missiles thought to have been supplied by Iran. Iranian provocations – most notably the seizure of British Royal Navy crew from the frigate

Cornwall – also elevated ongoing friction in the waters of the Persian Gulf. The dangers of all-out conflict appear to be fuelling an uplift in defence spending that will doubtless feed through to new naval construction.

Elsewhere in the region, NATO's willingness to operate over a wider geographical arena was seen in the deployment of Standing NATO Maritime Group 1 on a two-month circumnavigation of Africa, providing the opportunity for training with units of the newly modernised South African Navy, which is rapidly extending its influence in the Continent's southern waters. International maritime cooperation was also evident in the Indian Ocean. September's Malabar 2007-02 exercise saw Australian, Japanese, Indian, Singapore and United States warships combine in what was probably the largest demonstration of regional maritime collaboration to date. Whilst assertions that the war games were designed to counter potential Chinese ambitions were strenuously denied, the exercise does point to a growing partnership between the Indian Ocean's emergent superpower and the United States and its Asian allies.

Table 3 sets out current fleet strengths.

The Middle Eastern Navies

Egypt: Egypt's current priority appears to be modernisation of fast attack craft forces. Surplus Project 205 'Osa' vessels have recently been bought from Finland and Montenegro to replace or supplement units of the class already in Egyptian service in what seems to be an interim move pending completion of the 'Ambassador Mk III' new-build project. Long lead items for these three new-build ships to be constructed by America's VT Halter Marine under the US Foreign Military Sales programme were ordered in November 2006. Egypt has also acquired the *Osprey* class mine-hunters *Cardinal* and *Raven,* which were handed over following completion of US Navy service in January 2007.

Israel: Modernisation of the other branches of the armed forces to make good deficiencies identified during the 2006 Lebanon campaign are likely to constrain further investment in Israel's naval arm. However, it has been reported that the TEFEN 2012 5-year military plan makes provision for acquisition of the first of two new multi-mission surface combatants, which are likely to be based on the Lockheed Martin version of the littoral combat ship. The programme will complement the substantial investment made in the submarine fleet as a result of the order for two additional AIP-equipped versions of the *Dolphin* class placed with Germany's Thyssen Krupp Marine Systems.

Oman: The protracted acquisition process for three new ocean-capable patrol ships finally reached its conclusion on 16 January with the announcement that Britain's VT Group had been awarded a £400m contract to supply the vessels. Construction work on the 2,500-tonne, 98.5m long corvette-like ships started in October, with the first scheduled for delivery early in 2010. Armament includes MDBA Exocet surface-to surface and MICA surface-to air missile systems, as well as an Oto Melara 76mm gun. Further flexibility is gained through provision of a flight deck and hangar, which will doubtless be used by the Super Lynx helicopters recently supplied to Oman's air force.

Saudi Arabia: The Royal Saudi Naval Forces also appear to be interested in British naval technology and there have been ongoing rumours in the potential acquisition of between two and four Type 45 *Daring* class destroyers. If the deal goes ahead, it is likely they will be used to reinforce the Eastern Fleet based on Al Jubail.

United Arab Emirates: With the lead ship of the 'Baynunah' class corvette programme due for launch by France's CMN during 2008, progress is also being made with the follow-on ships being built by Abu Dhabi Ship Building, which laid the keel of the third unit on 22 June. Work on the fourth of six vessels started on the same date.

Indian Ocean Navies

India: The last few years have seen India embarking on a significant upgrade of fleet capabilities on the back of the stronger funding position provided by the country's healthy economic growth. The path towards creating an effective 'blue water' navy is, however, not proving altogether straightforward, with both domestic and overseas building programmes suffering from delays and cost overruns.

Perhaps the most pressing requirement is for renewal of the fleet's naval air component. India's sole aircraft carrier *Viraat* – the former British *Hermes* – is nearly fifty years old and the Sea Harrier FRS.51 fighters which form her core air group are also facing obsolescence. Although new

Table 3: MAJOR NAVIES IN AFRICA, THE MIDDLE EAST & THE INDIAN OCEAN – NUMERICAL STRENGTH (END 2007)

Country	Algeria	Egypt	India	Iran	Israel	Pakistan	Saudi Arabia	South Africa
Support/Helicopter Carrier (CVS/CVH)	–	–	1	–	–	–	–	–
Patrol Submarine (SSK/SS)	2	4	16	3	3	5	–	2
Fleet Escort (DDG/FFG)	–	6	21	–	–	6	7	4
Patrol Escort/Corvette (FFG/FSG/FS)	6	4	8	5	3	–	4	–
Missile Armed Attack Craft (PGG/PTG)	12	25	12	22	10	4	9	2
Mine Countermeasures Vessel (MCMV)	–	12	14	–	–	3	7	4
Major Amphibious (LPD)	–	–	1	–	–	–	–	–

aircraft in the form of Russian-built MiG-29K jets are now starting to be delivered, the refurbishment of the former Russian Project 1143.4 carrier *Vikramaditya* (ex-*Admiral Gorshkov*) that they are to fly from has been prolonged by structural and cabling problems and her projected 2008 delivery looks increasingly unlikely. To make matters worse, delays in India's indigenous aircraft carrier project mean the planned 2012 commissioning date is set to go back by approximately two years. As a result, *Viraat* will probably remain in service so that long-held ambitions to operate separate carrier groups on both the east and west coasts can be achieved.

Surface fleet modernisation is also proving to be frustratingly slow. Of the three Project 17 frigates derived from the Russian-built *Talwar* design building at Mumbai's Mazagon Dock, the first, *Shivalik*, was launched back in April 2003 but has still to join the operational fleet. With construction of the Project 15A *Kolkata* destroyers also proving somewhat protracted, it is not surprising that increased emphasis is being placed on collaboration with overseas yards, with a number of foreign shipbuilders being approached for proposals to assist with the design and construction of follow-on Project 17A frigates. Current plans envisage the first ship being built overseas, with up to six vessels following in India.

Rejuvenation of the submarine flotilla is a little more advanced. The rolling modernisation of the eight earlier units of the ten-strong Project 877EKM 'Kilo' class is drawing to a close, with all but *Sindhudhvaj* having now entered refit. Fabrication of the first of the six 'Scorpène' type boats ordered from DCNS in 2005 commenced at Mazagon on 23 May. Further orders are planned in the medium term to achieve a force level of 24 submarines, with Russia and Germany also said to be interested in securing a contract for their 'Amur' and Type 214 designs. It is likely, however, that part of this total will be made up of nuclear-powered boats, with the first of India's secretive 'advanced technology vessels' reputedly due for launch in 2008. There are continuing reports that one or two former Soviet 'Akula' class SSNs will

'Malabar 2007-02' was one of the largest international exercises in the Indian Ocean to date. Here RSS Formidable is seen operating with INS Brahmaputra. (US Navy)

be transferred on lease as an interim measure. In the meantime, a further addition to the fleet's capabilities was made on 22 June when the former US Navy LPD *Trenton* was commissioned as *Jalashwa* at Norfolk naval base. Along with the ongoing construction of the 5,600 tonne *Shardul* class tank landing ships – the first of which entered service on 4 January – she provides a range of new amphibious, surveillance and humanitarian options that will greatly enhance India's regional maritime potential.

Pakistan: Significant reductions in fleet strength over the past decade have left Pakistan with only modest naval capabilities compared with her Indian neighbour. Her most potent force is the submarine arm, which will be the first in the region with AIP when the MESMA equipped 'Agosta 90B' *Hamza* commissions in 2007. France's DCNS has received an order for additional systems to equip the two earlier units of the class, which will be installed by means of a 9m hull plug. Pakistan is in the market for three to four additional patrol submarines, with local construction of Germany's Type 214 design rumoured to be the preferred option.

Renewal of the surface fleet will be achieved by construction of four new Chinese F-22P frigates, with the keel laying ceremony for the first taking place at the Hudong Shipyard, Shanghai, on 31 July. Named *Zulfiqar*, she should be in service by 2009. Medium term plans envisage the purchase of another batch of new-built escorts but, in the interim, the acquisition of second-hand tonnage remains on the agenda with reports that the United States has been approached regarding the transfer of up to six surplus FFG-7 class frigates.

African Navies

Nigeria: The pressing need to improve the security of Nigeria's economically crucial coastal oil fields appears to have resulted in the provision of funds to improve the fleet's operational availability. The surprise appearance of the MEKO 360 frigate *Aradu* at the 2005 British fleet review has been followed by the re-emergence of several additional warships from dockyard hands, including the Vosper Mk 9 corvette *Enymiri* and a number of previously laid up 'Combattante III' fast attack craft.

South Africa: 2007 marked the completion of the MEKO A-200SAN 'Valour' class programme, with third of class *Spioenkop* commissioned on 16 February and the fourth and final ship *Mendi* following on 20 March. An option, as yet unexercised, remains for a further vessel. First of class *Amatola* attended Flag Officer

Sea Training (FOST) in the UK during the summer and emerged with a creditable 'satisfactory' rating.

The second of three Type 209/1400 patrol submarines, *S102 Charlotte Maxette*, arrived in Simon's Town on 26 April. The final boat was named *Queen Modjadji* in Germany on 14 March and she will be delivered in the first half of 2008.

Australasia and the Far East

The re-emergence of Russian sabre rattling and continued friction in the Middle East has meant that the Asia-Pacific has appeared less frequently in defence press headlines over the past year. However, the underlying picture is little changed, with the combination of strong economic growth and intra-regional mistrust continuing to fuel defence spending. The fruits of previously announced projects were seen in launches of Korea's first KDX-3 Aegis destroyer, *Sejongdaewang Ham* and Japan's new 'DDH' helicopter carrier, *Hyuga*, whilst a number of new programmes – most notably Australia's acquisition of new amphibious and air defence ships – achieved the final green light.

As always, the centre of attention is the expansion of the Chinese People's Liberation Army Navy (PLAN). More details of the second generation Type 093 'Shang' SSN and Type 094 'Jin' SSBN class submarine designs emerged during the year as they moved closer to joining the operational fleet. Initial analysis suggests that they will be considerably more capable and stealthy than previous designs and their arrival will certainly complicate life for the US Navy's planners. The most recent diesel-powered SSKs also appear to be effective vessels. This was graphically demonstrated by the reported surfacing of a Type 039 'Song' class boat within five miles of the US carrier *Kitty Hawk* (CV-63) on 26 October 2006 having allegedly shadowed the carrier battle group undetected – an incident that did much to raise the profile of currently unfashionable ant-submarine warfare skills and may also have an influence on future spending priorities.

Table 4 provides a summary of current force levels.

Australia: The most significant news in 2007 was the 20 June statement that designs from Spain's Navantia had been selected for both the new generation air warfare destroyer and the amphibious assault ship projects. The big surprise was the choice of an 'Australianised' version of Navantia's F-100 over an 'evolved design' developed from the US *Arleigh Burkes* by Gibbs & Cox for the destroyer contract, as the Royal Australian Navy reportedly favoured the latter's greater helicopter carrying and missile capacity. Three ships of the so-called *Hobart* class will be delivered from Australia's ASC between 2014 and 2017 under an AU$8bn contract. The two *Canberra* class LHDs will be similar to Spain's *Juan Carlos I*. Their hulls will be built by Navantia prior to final outfitting by Tenix in Australia. Completion is expected between 2013 and 2015 at a total cost of c.AU$3bn.

The decommissioning of *Adelaide* in early 2008 will reduce the the surface fleet to twelve frigates: the four remaining units of the FGG-7 class and the eight more recent *Anzacs*. Modernisation of the former is now well-advanced, with *Sydney* carrying out firing trials of the newly-fitted Evolved Sea Sparrow Missile in August and *Melbourne* being provi-

South Africa's 'Valour' class frigate SAS Amatola visited the UK for FOST training over the summer. (Conrad Waters)

Table 4: Major Navies in Asia & Australasia – Numerical Strength (End 2007)

Country	Australia	China	Indonesia	Japan	Korea S	Singapore	Taiwan	Thailand
Support/Helicopter Carrier (CVS/CVH)	–	–	–	–	–	–	–	1
Strategic Missile Submarine (SSBN)	–	2	–	–	–	–	–	–
Attack Submarine (SSN)	–	5	–	–	–	–	–	–
Patrol Submarine (SSK/SS)	6	55	2	16	10	4	4	–
Fleet Escort (DDG/FFG)	12	45	6	44	17	2	26	8
Patrol Escort/Corvette (FFG/FSG/FS)	–	30	22	9	28	6	–	9
Missile Armed Attack Craft (PGG/PTG)	–	55	4	9	–	6	50	6
Mine Countermeasures Vessel (MCMV)	6	20	11	29	9	4	12	6
Major Amphibious Unit (LHD/LPD/LSD)	–	1	3	3	1	4	1	–

Note: Chinese numbers approximate.

sionally accepted from Thales Australia on 8 October. The next major surface programme will be the planned upgrade of the Anzacs' self defence capabilities, including an improved command and control system, and installation of CEA Technologies' CEAFAR phased array radar. At the lower end of the technological spectrum, the replacement of the old Fremantle patrol boats by the new Armidale class was completed during the year, with Townsville and Ipswich withdrawn on 11 May. While the Armidales have been hit by fuel contamination problems, all of the original batch of twelve were in service following the commissioning of Launceston on 22 September. The two follow-on boats ordered in June 2006 to improve surveillance of Australia's north-west continental shelf should follow by early 2008.

Longer term planning is starting to turn to replacements for Australia's existing six Collins class submarines, as well as the likely retirement of the Anzacs from 2020 onwards. It is probable that there will be considerable interest in the General Dynamics version of the US Navy's LCS for the latter's successor given local firm Austal's involvement in this innovative trimaran.

Brunei: The protracted disagreement over acceptance of the three Nakhoda Ragam corvettes was settled in builder BAe Systems' favour during 2007. However, Brunei no longer seems to have a need for such sophisticated ships and has appointed Germany's Lürssen to broker a sale to another country. Resolution of the dispute resulted in various spurious newspaper reports about the difficulties of finding a new home for warships designed to accommodate 5ft 6in Brunei sailors, tall stories that were firmly refuted by the firm's surface shipbuilding division's 6ft 1in Head of Communications, who claimed to have experienced no difficulty with the vessels' operating environment.

China: 2007 brought a degree of clarity over modernisation of China's often enigmatic submarine force. Satellite pictures indicated that the first Type 094 'Jin' SSBN had commenced sea trials and that at least one additional boat was in an advanced stage of construction. Equipped with around twelve of the 8,000km ranged Julang-2 ballistic missiles, these boats represent a quantum leap in technology over the sole existing Type 092 'Xia' strategic missile submarine and, when operational, will make it easier for the PLAN to target the continental United States. Further information has also come to light with the release of the first images of the Type 093 'Shang' class SSN, which is likely to replace the five noisy, obsolescent 1980s vintage Type 091 'Han' class boats. Of around 7,000 tonnes dived displacement, the new submarine has a tear-drop shaped hull and is equipped with both bow and flank mounted sonar, as well as six torpedo tubes. Whilst these nuclear-powered boats have attracted most attention, the underwater forces will continue to be dominated by diesel-powered designs. The most effective of these are the twelve 'Kilo' class vessels purchased from Russia, as well as the indigenous Type 039 'Song' and Type 041 'Yuan' classes.

Delivery of the 7,100 tonne Type 051C class destroyer Shenyang towards the end of 2006 was followed by the second of class Shijiazhuang in March 2007. Armed with the sophisticated but bulky SA-N-20 'Rif M' improved naval export variant of the Russian 'Grumble' surface-to-air missile, these ships are otherwise throwbacks to the sole Type 051B Shenzen and do not represent latest Chinese design practice. With ten new destroyers built or purchased since the turn of the millennium, current construction has turned to renewal of the frigate fleet with the Type 054A 'Jiangkai II' variant of the original 'Jiangkai' class apparently now in series production. Approaching recent European frigates in size and stealth capability, key features include a 32-cell vertical launch system

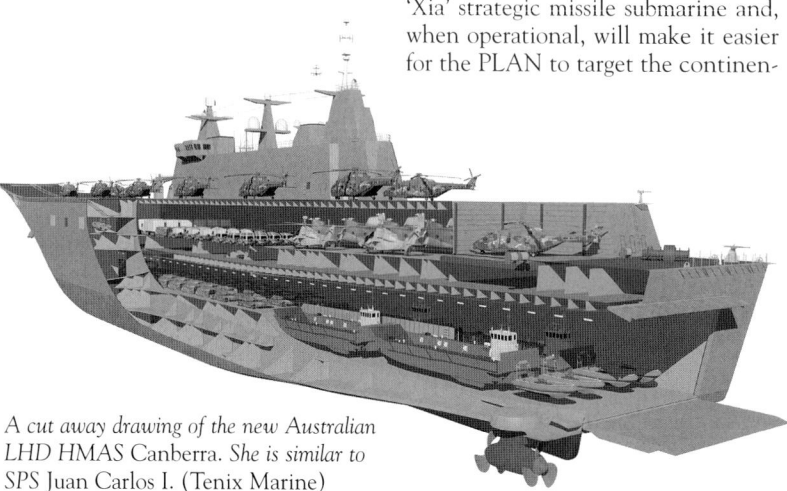

PLAN Guangzhou *seen on a visit to the UK. China has commissioned ten destroyers since the new millennium.* (Conrad Waters)

A cut away drawing of the new Australian LHD HMAS Canberra. *She is similar to SPS* Juan Carlos I. (Tenix Marine)

(VLS) forward of the bridge, a full outfit of Russian radars and a combined diesel and diesel (CODAD) power plant based on that used in the French *La Fayettes*.

Rumours persisted about the likely development of carrier-based aviation, in particular the possible return to service – at least in a training role – of the former Soviet Project 1143.5/6 *Kuznetsov* class carrier *Varyag* after completion of refurbishment work. Meanwhile, amphibious capabilities will be boosted by delivery of the initial Type 071 LPD, incorporating both a large helicopter deck and a well docking facility at the ship's stern. Of around 15,000 tonnes full load displacement, the lead ship was launched at Shanghai's Hudong Zonghua shipyard on 22 December 2006 and carried out trials during the course of 2007.

Indonesia: The Indonesian Navy has turned to Russia for help with speeding up its modernisation programme. The signature in September of a reported US$1.2bn line of credit is said to make provision for the immediate purchase of two 'Kilo' class patrol submarines, with the possibility of more surface and sub-surface vessels to follow. In the interim, the first of the Dutch-built SIGMA corvettes, *Diponegoro*, was handed over on 2 July, with delivery of second-of-class, *Hanasudin*, due in November. Of 1,700 tonnes full load displacement, these sleek 91m diesel-powered vessels can reach 28 knots and have a 76mm gun, a hull-mounted sonar, helicopter landing facilities and provision for surface-to-surface and surface-to-air missiles. They appear well-suited for improving coastal security within the vast Indonesian archipelago, and more may supplement the second batch of two now under construction.

Japan: The JMSDF has significantly expanded the scope of its activities in recent years, most notably in the Indian Ocean. Whilst a changed domestic political situation may curtail this mission, recent procurement is shifting the fleet's emphasis away from its previous regional anti-submarine orientation and towards a structure which facilitates such long-distance operations. The most tangible sign of this was the launch of the new helicopter-carrying 'destroyer' *Hyuga* on 23 August. Essentially a light aircraft carrier of 18,000 tonnes full load displacement, *Hyuga* is the lead ship of a pair of sisters intended to replace the elderly *Haruna* class and, like their predecessors, intended to be the focal point of an anti-submarine task group. However, a capacity to embark at least eleven aircraft, coupled with installation of a Mk 41 VLS for Sea Sparrow and ASROC missiles, a sophisticated command system and the domestic FCS-3 phased array radar derived from Thales' APAR, make them far more effective and flexible ships. The launch has certainly attracted the attention of Japan's neighbours, who remain nervous of any move towards a more interventionist foreign policy.

When *Hyuga* is delivered, she is most likely to operate within the air defence umbrella provided by the Aegis-equipped destroyers of the *Kongou* and *Atago* classes. The first of the two latter ships was commissioned on 15 March. Her sister should follow in 2008. Meanwhile, the *Kongous* are being equipped with the SM-3 version of the Standard missile and upgrades to their radar system at the rate of one ship per year between 2007 and 2010 to fit them for their planned theatre ballistic missile defence (TBMD) role. *Kongou* herself is the first of the class to undergo the necessary modifications and she carried out a successful first firing against a ballistic missile target on 17 December.

Malaysia: Development of the Royal Malaysian Navy's new submarine force continued during 2007. The fore and aft hulls of the first of class were joined together at DCNS' Cherbourg facility on 14 March prior to a planned October launch. Similar 'closure' took place on the second boat on 24 July at Navantia in Cartagena. Both vessels, reportedly to be named *Tunku Abdul Rahman* and *Tun Razak* after former Prime Ministers, will commission in 2009.

Additional funding has been made available to complete the four remaining *Kedah* class 'MEKO 100' corvettes following financial restructuring at the Penang yard contracted to build them. All should be in service by the end of 2009. Progress has also been made in discussions with the UK's BAe Systems for the domestic construction of two modified *Lekiu* class frigates.

New Zealand: An important stage in the Project Protector modernisation programme was achieved on 31 May when the 9,000 ton, Dutch-built multi-role vessel *Canterbury* was formally handed over following completion of fitting out by Tenix in Melbourne. Essentially an adaptation of a commercial ferry design to act as a second-line amphibious vessel, she is capable of carrying up to 250 troops and their equipment for deployment

The Royal New Zealand Navy's new multi-role vessel, HMNZS Canterbury, *seen here at Sydney in September 2007.* (Leo van Ginderen collection)

by up to four embarked helicopters or by means of two 59-tonne landing craft accessed via a stern door ramp. Although the overall project is now running late, delivery of both the initial offshore patrol ship, *Otago*, and the first inshore patrol vessel, *Rotoiti*, were expected early in 2008. An additional offshore patrol ship, *Wellington*, and three further inshore vessels should enter service later in the year.

Singapore: Expansion of the Republic of Singapore Navy's capabilities passed another major milestone on 5 May (the fortieth anniversary of the RSN's establishment) when the first *Formidable* class stealth frigate was formally commissioned. The new frigate subsequently demonstrated Singapore's enhanced ability to participate in regional security operations when she joined the five nation Malabar 2007-02 exercises in the Indian Ocean. Her five sisters should join her in the active fleet during 2008, where they will replace the aging *Sea Wolf* fast attack craft.

Modernisation work on two former Swedish *Västergötland* A-17 class submarines *Västergötland* and *Hälsingland* is currently underway prior to planned transfer around 2010. There are also ongoing rumours that Singapore is considering participation in the new A-26 submarine programme, which Sweden is attempting to resurrect from the ruins of the previous regional 'Viking' project.

South Korea: The Republic of Korea Navy continues to make steady progress towards achieving its blue water naval ambitions. The most notable development in 2007 was the acceptance into service on 3 July of the new 13,000-tonne standard displacement LHD, *Dokdo*. Capable of deploying 720 marines from up to ten helicopters and two LCAC hovercraft, she is intended to form the focal point of the first of a series of new rapid response squadrons that will also include the more recent KDX destroyers. Two sister ships are planned for the next decade.

Equally important will be the KDX-3 Aegis-equipped destroyers. The first, *Sejongdaewang-Ham*, was launched by Hyundai Heavy Industries on 25 May accompanied by

The first of South Korea's KDX-3 Aegis equipped destroyers, ROKS Sejongdaewang-Ham, has now been launched. (Hyundai Heavy Industries)

local press reports comparing her favourably with the Japanese *Atago*. Of 7,600 tonnes standard displacement, she is an enlarged version of the American Flight IIA *Arleigh Burke* class and will be followed by at least two sisters. In the meantime, completion of the preceding KDX-2 destroyers is almost complete with the delivery of the fifth ship, *Gang Gam-Chan*, on 1 October, while the sixth and final unit, *Choi Yeong*, will follow early in 2008.

Beneath the waves the first locally-produced Type 214 submarine, *Son Won Il*, spent much of the year undergoing trials. The second of the initial batch of three boats, *Jung Ji*, was launched in June and work is well underway on the third. A further six are planned before work starts on the indigenous KSS-3 class. Also launched in June was the prototype PKX fast attack craft, *Yoon Young-ha*. Of 450 tonnes standard displacement and capable of more than 40 knots, she is powerfully armed with 76mm and 40mm guns, as well as surface-to-surface missiles. If she is successful, the design will enter series production to replace the obsolescent 'Sea Dolphin' and 'Wildcat' class patrol boats.

Taiwan: The Republic of China's defence efforts remain feeble compared with developments across the Taiwan Strait. The arrival of the second pair of *Kidd* destroyers in November 2006 has not been followed by tangible progress with the long-mooted enhancement of the submarine fleet. However, transfer of twelve PC-3 Orion anti-submarine aircraft does look set to go ahead after several years of discussion, and it has been reported that an order has been placed for diesel engines to allow series production of the new KH-6 guided missile patrol craft. The transfer of two retired *Osprey* type minehunters remains a possibility.

The Americas

Developments in the region are inevitably dominated by the United States, which released its first formal maritime strategy since the late 1980s at an international seapower conference in Newport, Rhode Island on 17 October. Entitled 'A Cooperative Strategy for 21st Century Seapower', the document is regarded as being the brainchild of former Chief of Naval Operations (CNO) Admiral Mike Mullen, who was elevated to chairmanship of the Joint Chiefs of Staff shortly before the new policy was released. Presented jointly by the new CNO, Admiral Gary Roughead, and the Commandants of the US Marine Corps and Coast Guard, the plan retains focus on what it describes as the core capabilities of forward presence, deterrence, sea control and power projection. However, it also adds the maintenance of maritime security and the provision of humanitarian and disaster response to these key competencies. The main underlying emphasis appears to be on improving the Navy's ability to utilise international maritime cooperation as a means of conflict prevention, whilst retaining the option of responding more forcefully should the circumstances require.

Stabilising force levels will be key to the new strategy's success. Despite a recent pause in the rate of decline, this remains a major problem. Table 5 gives an overview of current regional fleet numbers.

Argentina: The collapse of the deal to acquire the former French *Ouragan* class LPDs due to concerns over asbestos contamination means Argentina remains without an effective amphibious fleet. Still worse, a serious fire onboard the veteran icebreaker *Almirante Irizar* on 10 April, while fortunately contained without loss of life, destroyed both embarked Sea King helicopters and has left a serious gap in the fleet's ability to maintain Antarctic patrols. Consideration is being given to chartering the Russian *Vassily Golovnin* while extensive repairs are completed.

Brazil: The *Marinha do Brasil* has suffered from financial austerity in recent years and fleet numbers and availability have declined as a result. However, the situation appears to be changing, with modernisation of the submarine force being given priority. Lockheed Martin has been approached to provide new combat systems for the existing Type 209 boats, whilst a non AIP-equipped version of Thyssen Krupp Marine Systems' Type 214 has been selected for future construction. In the longer term, additional funding equivalent to US$500m over the next eight years will be provided to kick-start previously stalled plans for a nuclear-powered submarine.

Meanwhile the carrier *São Paulo* has undergone a lengthy and expensive refit to remedy a long list of deficiencies arising largely from her increasing age. The corvette *Barroso* was expected to start trials around the end of the year to meet a planned December 2008 commissioning date.

Canada: The recent ramp-up in Canadian defence expenditure was evident in the commitment to modernisation of the twelve *Halifax* class frigates, which currently comprise the core of the escort fleet. Starting in 2010 – a little later than first planned – this US$3.2bn upgrade will focus on improved command, control and radar systems. A similar amount will be spent on procurement of between six and eight ice-strengthened patrol ships which are primarily intended to reinforce Canada's sovereignty of its Arctic waters under a decision announced on 9 July. With a contract for construction of three 28,000-ton JSS joint support ships likely to be awarded in 2008, the medium term structure of the surface fleet is starting to take shape.

Work to bring the four former *Upholder* class submarines into service continues but there are signs that Canada might be running out of patience with the troubled boats. Press reports have suggested that preliminary investigations are being undertaken on the potential acquisition of a new AIP-equipped design that would be better suited to Arctic deployment. There are also suggestions that the operational fleet might be reduced in the short term to help finance the ambitious renewal agenda, with the two *Protecteur* support ships and more *Iroquois* class destroyers in line for early retirement. The decommissioned *Huron* of the latter class was despatched in a SINKEX on 14 May 2007.

Chile: Revitalisation of Chile's surface fleet is nearly complete. All four 'L' and 'M' class frigates acquired from

Chile's Almirante Cochrane (ex HMS Norfolk). Modernisation of the surface fleet is nearly complete. (Conrad Waters)

Table 5: MAJOR NAVIES IN THE AMERICAS (END 2007)

Country	Argentina	Brazil	Canada	Chile	Ecuador	Peru	USA	Venezuela
Aircraft Carrier (CVN/CV)	–	1	–	–	–	–	11	–
Strategic Missile Submarine (SSBN)	–	–	–	–	–	–	14	–
Attack Submarine (SSN/SSGN)	–	–	–	–	–	–	57	–
Patrol Submarine (SSK)	3	5	4	4	2	6	–	2
Fleet Escort (CG/DDG/FFG)	4	10	15	8	1	9	104	6
Patrol Escort/Corvette (FFG/FSG/FS)	9	4	–	–	6	–	–	–
Missile Armed Attack Craft (PGG/PTG)	2	–	–	7	3	6	–	6
Mine Countermeasures Vessel (MCMV)	–	6	12	–	–	–	14	–
Major Amphibious (LHD/LPD/LPH/LSD)	–	2	–	–	–	–	33	–

the Netherlands are operational, whilst the first of the three Type 23 frigates purchased from Britain to arrive in Chile – the *Almirante Lynch* (ex-*Grafton*) – docked at Valparaíso on 14 September. The transfer process will end with the commissioning of the former *Marlborough* as *Almirante Condell* early in 2008. Along with the Type 22 *Almirante Williams* (ex-*Sheffield*) delivered earlier, this provides Chile with a force of eight modern front-line escorts.

Peru: *Quiñones*, the final second-hand *Lupo* class frigate bought from Italy, arrived at Callao on 22 January. The future escort fleet will be standardised around eight vessels of this type, allowing the withdrawal of the veteran British-built *Daring* class destroyer *Ferré* on 13 July. *Almirante Grau* – the world's last conventionally armed cruiser – remains in service but her days are now numbered.

Trinidad & Tobago: A £150m contract was signed with the UK's VT Group on 5 April for three 90m offshore patrol vessels. Scheduled for delivery from 2009, the new ships are capable of 25 knots and incorporate a flight deck for helicopter operations.

United States: The USN faces the pressing challenges of the need to devise and implement a new construction programme capable of at least sta-

The third Virginia *class submarine, USS* Hawaii *(SSN-776), was commissioned on 5 May 2007. (US Navy)*

bilising numbers in the operational fleet whilst remaining within likely available funding. The release of a long-range shipbuilding plan in 2006 provided a broad indication of how this might be realised and an updated fiscal year (FY) 2008 version was published in February. Although continuing to target an average fleet of 313 vessels, the revised document envisages an uplift in the number of units procured due to increased purchases of surface vessels whilst containing total costs to around US$15bn a year over a 30-year timescale. Given that recent inflationary trends point in the opposite direction (see Table 6), it is perhaps not surprising that the Navy's financial assumptions have been treated with considerable scepticism by independent commentators. For example, the Congressional Budget Office has reported that spending on new construction will have to rise from the US$9.6bn annual average seen during 2002-07 to a total of no less than US$21.6bn p.a. if the programme is to be achieved.

The greatest difficulty will be maintaining a modern surface fleet. Escort numbers have recently been increasing slightly to just over 100 vessels as a result of the steady arrival of new Flight IIA *Arleigh Burke* class destroyers. However, commencement of work on the 62nd and final ship, the yet-to-be-named DDG-112, at General Dynamics' Bath Iron Works on 7 September, heralds a period of greater uncertainty. In the short term, construction will be dominated by commencement of work on the two lead DDG-1000 *Zumwalt* units, the first of which will now also be built at Bath to retain continuity of production. The design has attracted considerable controversy given the simultaneous introduction of several new technologies (e.g. the advanced gun system, dual band radar, integrated electric propulsion) and its cost is such that no more than seven ships are planned. With plans for follow-on CG(X) air defence cruisers likely to be equally expensive – a return to nuclear power is even

The UK's VT Group has been awarded a contract to build three offshore patrol vessels for Trinidad & Tobago's Coast Guard. (VT Group Plc)

being examined for some variants – there is significant reliance on production of smaller and cheaper littoral combat ships to make up the difference. However cost overruns on the first vessels have thrown the whole programme into disarray (one of the factors believed to be behind the resignation of the USN's senior acquisition official, Delores Etter, on 5 October), with further orders effectively suspended until the prototype ships commence trials and realistic project costs can be ascertained. Meanwhile, the *Arleigh Burkes* themselves are not enjoying a trouble-free press, with reports that many of the class will require strengthening of main traverse bulkhead beams at the bow due to higher than expected stresses.

Modernisation of the amphibious force has also been proving somewhat problematic, as evidenced by the poor construction quality seen in the first LPD-17 class *San Antonio* and reports of similar defects in her sister *New Orleans* (LPD-18). However, shipbuilder Northrop Grumman appears to be getting to grips with the problems it inherited with its acquisition of the Avondale business which was originally lead contractor for the class. The third ship, *Masa Verde* (LPD-19), has performed significantly better on sea trials. Work also appears to be going well on the new LHD-8, *Makin Island*, and she is on schedule for delivery in mid 2008. By that time construction will be underway on the first unit of the new LHA-6 type, which is essentially a slightly larger variant of the earlier ship but optimised for air operations, surrendering her traditional well deck for an enlarged hangar able to stow 31 aircraft, including a considerable number of the new JSF joint strike fighters. This additional flexibility will doubtless be welcome following the reduction in the strike carrier force to eleven vessels following the decommissioning of *John F Kennedy* (CV-67) on 23 March.

USCGC Matagorda, one of eight modernised '123' class cutters withdrawn due to structural defects. (US Coast Guard)

The submarine flotilla had a mixed year. On the one hand, the *Virginia* (SSN-774) programme is now delivering boats at annual intervals, with third of class *Hawaii* (SSN-776) commissioned on 5 May and the fourth, *North Carolina* (SSN-777) christened on 21 April. It also appears that funding will be made available to accelerate the transition to a two submarine p.a. procurement strategy before the currently planned 2012 so as to maintain force levels at around the 50 mark. In the meantime, the return of the *Ohio* (SSGN-726) boats to the fleet following conversion to specialised cruise missile carriers is boosting capabilities, with *Ohio* herself deploying on the modified class's first operational patrol in October. However, the series of accidents experienced in recent years continued with the deaths of two crew members from the *Minneapolis-Saint Paul* (SSN-708) on 29 December 2006 after they were swept into the sea whilst departing Devonport naval base, and a collision between *Newport News* (SSN-750) and a Japanese tanker in the Straits of Hormuz on 8 January. The incidents saw both captains relieved of their commands and a short operational stand-down imposed to increase focus on the basics of submarine operations.

The US Coast Guard has seen similar shipbuilding problems to the USN. The Integrated Deepwater System programme intended to recapitalise its assets has encountered difficulties, notably the emergence of structural problems in both the new-build *Bertholf* (WMSL-750) national security cutters and the lengthened 123ft 'Island' patrol boats, in the latter case so serious that eight modified vessels have been withdrawn for scrap. Procurement of the replacement Fast Response Cutter is being restructured to avoid repetition of past mistakes, with selection decisions being removed from the programme's lead contractors to be made 'in house'.

Table 6: *RISING USN ACQUISITION COSTS*

Cost growth in budgets for ships under construction during 2007

Class:	Number of Ships	Initial Budget	Latest Estimate (FY-08)	Total Cost Growth	Percentage Cost Growth
CVN 77:	1	$4,975m	$5,822m	$847m	17%
DDG 100-112:	13	$14,309m	$14,679m	$370m	3%
LCS 1-2:	2	$472m	$1,075m	$603m	128%
LHD 8:	1	$1,893m	$2,196m	$393m	16%
LPD 18-23:	6	$6,194m	$7,742m	$1,548m	25%
SSN 775-783:	9	$20,744m	$21,678m	$934m	5%
T-AKE 1-9:	9	$3,354m	$3,386m	$32m	1%
Total:	41	$51,941m	$56,578m	$4,637m	9%

Source: US Government Accountability Office.

NAVAL BOOKS OF THE YEAR

Brian Lavery
Churchill's Navy: the Ships, Men and Organisation 1939-1945
Conway Maritime Press, 2006:
hardback, 287 pages,
heavily illustrated; price £40.00.
ISBN 1-84486-035-3

Readers familiar with Brian Lavery's 1989 classic Nelson's Navy will immediately understand the concept behind this new stable mate: a book containing the answers to all those nagging little questions of detail, along with a wonderful portrait of the naval corporation, and a mass of evidence on facts and figures for the Royal Navy during the Second World War, as well as a generous collection of images, from across the full range of art forms, and all in an attractive large format package (including intermittent desert sand and sea-green pages!).

There is a vast body of literature examining the operational and technical aspects of the Royal Navy during the war. But sadly the number of those with first hand recollections is diminishing, leaving a serious gap in our understanding of the mundane, the everyday and the routine. Earlier generations had a shared history, a common knowledge of the period, and hence wrote from that perspective, but that is no longer the case. Therefore, by contextualising the operational and the material with the human dimension, this is a timely volume for it shows not just what the Navy did but how it worked.

Utilising the same logical structure and careful analysis that characterised Nelson's Navy Lavery has divided this book into twelve sections. The first half examines the Navy in 1939, British society and the naval war, the organisation of the service, from Admiralty Board to new recruits, by way of the peculiar demands of naval service, from seamanship and navigation to logistics and support afloat. The Navy's ships and weapons, enemy and allied fleets, the other British armed forces and the merchant navy are all considered.

Throughout it is the human element that emerges most strongly. During the war the Royal Navy went from 131,000 men, with 73,000 reserves in 1939 to 783,000 men and 72,000 women in June 1945. What was it like to serve in this organisation? The arrival of so many volunteers, conscripts and the revival of the Wrens changed naval society beyond recognition. This was inevitable, essential and, of course, problematic. The Navy was still characterised by an outdated class based recruitment system, one which could not survive the egalitarian challenge of waging a total war in an age of universal suffrage. Yet any system that could produce Andrew Cunningham and Philip Vian, Max Horton and Bertram Ramsay, cannot have been entirely faulty.

Some branches of the service quickly assumed a new character, with many anti-submarine escorts and almost all coastal forces being hostilities-only or volunteer officers and men, while the main fleets and units retained more regular personnel. Ample attention is paid to the Royal Marines, who entered the war in transition, and ended it with a new role in amphibious warfare and special operations. The massive development of the Fleet Air Arm added a new type of officer, one without any knowledge of ships! While the expansion of the Navy was nothing like that of the Army it was not far short of the RAF. Although some of the new people remained civilians in uniform, the unique culture of the service rubbed off on many more. From bell bottom trousers to crossing the line, the Navy was different and it seems that the girls still loved a sailor.

The second half covers the major components of naval power: the battlefleet, naval aviation, the submarine service, escorts, coastal forces, and amphibious warfare. Each looks at the ships, people and systems, their peculiar roles and characteristics, and how the human experience of each branch differed from the others. The old, homogenous pre-war navy did not survive the conflict, many and various new forms of service emerged, and each is covered. Battleships remained stiff and formal, while submarines and coastal forces developed a more relaxed command style. Four pages of appendices contain sketch details of all the main ship and aircraft types, membership of the Board of the Admiralty and the major commands.

In view of the enormous field that it surveys and the considerable addition that it makes to the extant literature it is but small criticism to mention a few issues that need attention in time for a second edition. Bruce Fraser might have been interested to find his name omitted from the list of Commanders in Chief Home Fleet. In two instances the pagination breaks down completely, with sections of text repeated or missing entirely. The 'Admiralty Fire Control Clock' on page 92 is the AFC Table, which entered service in the 1920s, controlling the heavy guns of all major warships built or rebuilt thereafter. More importantly, the claim that intelligence failure probably cost the Germans the Battle of the Atlantic is well wide of the mark. It was a campaign the Germans could not win; the Allies could only lose it.

In concluding Lavery reminds us of the Navy's remarkable achievement in the six long years of war, from shooting down the first German aircraft in 1939 to rightly representing Britain at the surrender of Japan in 1945. With unparalleled skill, commitment and dedication, combined with Nelsonian confidence and initiative that had been missing in the First World War, Churchill's Navy was a key component of allied victory. Brian Lavery has given us a study worthy both of his subject, and of a place on the bookshelf alongside its predecessor.

Andrew Lambert

William F Trimble
Attack from the Sea: a History of the U.S. Navy's Seaplane Strike Force
US Naval Institute Press 2005; hardback, 196 pages, 30 B&W photos; price $29.95.
ISBN 1 59114 878 2

The Seaplane Strike Force (SSF) was a concept developed for the US Navy during the early 1950s, when it was struggling for funding for its conventional surface forces against the USAF and its newly-created fleet of large inter-continental strategic bombers. The new generation of aircraft carriers was under the threat of extinction because of the perceived vulnerability of these costly ships and their escorts to atomic bombs and also because they were unable to operate large numbers of strategic strike aircraft with sufficient range to threaten the interior of the Soviet Union. Encouraged by breakthroughs in seaplane performance and the promise of the turbojet-powered Convair Sea Dart fighter and the Martin SeaMaster attack flying boat, the Navy believed it could challenge the Air Force in the strategic role.

The SSF as a 'weapon system' comprised a number of co-dependent and closely-integrated elements. The concept envisaged the rapid deployment in time of crisis of squadrons of SeaMaster flying boats, capable of delivering nuclear bombs and mines, to sheltered anchorages in Scandinavia or the Eastern Mediterranean. These anchorages would be protected from attack by high-performance Sea Dart fighters, and both aircraft types would be supported by a variety of specially-modified surface ships and submarines which would provide maintenance, ordnance and aviation fuel. Such improvised forward bases would not be known to the enemy and would therefore be invulnerable to a 'first strike' – unlike the large, fixed strategic bomber bases of the USAF. As the concept developed it became clear that the SSF would be a particularly valuable asset against the increasingly threatening Soviet submarine force by targeting bases and exit points.

However, the initial optimism about the potential of the new seaplane technology was rocked on its heels by the failure of the hydro-ski fitted to the Convair Sea Dart and the aerial break-up of the first two of the SeaMaster prototypes in December 1955 and November 1956 respectively. Despite extensive modification the SeaMaster would continue to suffer from serious vibration at high sub-sonic speeds, and with costs escalating and increasing doubts concerning the military value of the programme it was cancelled in August 1959, by which time almost half a billion dollars had been invested in it.

William Trimble's account of the SSF programme from conception to demise is both well-researched and well-written. The author has the ability to explain often complex principles of hydrodynamics and aerodynamics in a way that makes the technical problems experienced by the Sea Dart and the SeaMaster accessible to the lay reader. He also has a strong grasp of the strategic thinking of the period and of the nature of the inter-service – and even intra-service – rivalry which was at the heart of weapon system procurement during the 1950s.

The author's account of the SSF programme is prefaced by a look at prewar strategic thinking, in which both the US Navy and the IJN contemplated using large flying boats for long-range 'strategic' bombing missions, employing tenders or modified submarines for forward support and refuelling at sheltered anchorages in the vast 'no-man's-land' of the Pacific Ocean. Trimble also looks at the technological developments by the British RAE and the German DVL which from 1935 promised to break through the barrier preventing seaplanes from emulating the performance of land-based aircraft; the work of these establishments, using scale models in combination with wind-tunnel and tank testing, would lead indirectly to the advanced postwar American designs. Most fascinating of all is the author's account, well-illustrated with photos, of the specialised equipment developed to handle the Sea Darts and the SeaMasters at their forward anchorages; the reviewer was reminded of the technical ingenuity of the equipment devised to support the Normandy Landings barely years earlier.

This is an excellent and very readable book which contributes to a better understanding of naval strategy and procurement in the postwar USA.

John Jordan

Peter Haining
The Banzai Hunters
Robson Books, 2006; 192 pages, 34 illustrations and 3 maps; price £16.99
ISBN 1-86105-941-8

This is the story of a remarkable assortment of army and navy men in motor launches, landing craft, small boats, canoes and even frogman suits who operated in the Japanese-held the rivers and islands along the coast of Burma during the British 14th Army's assault in 1944-45. The missions that these men undertook in the thick, dense jungle of the Arakan required them to combat, in addition to the entrenched and ferocious Japanese, some of the deadliest animals, insects and diseases to be found on the planet.

The first chapter describes the vessels used and the bases from which they operated, as well as the aims of General 'Bill' Slim and his Japanese counterpart Major General Tokutaro Sakurai. The second chapter contains a graphic account of the terrain, climate, animal and plant life in an area, rightly described as 'the worst place on earth' (for human habitation), made even more inhospitable by the presence of the Japanese Army. Thereafter this interesting volume is made up of well-researched and detailed accounts of the personal stories by the men who served in this dangerous but 'forgotten' theatre of war and draws on documents and information from naval and army records to flesh out these accounts.

There are detailed descriptions of how Fairmile B motor launches and various types of landing craft were used to transport and support reconnaissance, intelligence-gathering and assault parties along the coast from Cox's Bazaar as far as Cheduba Island, accounts of the exploits of the Special Boat Service in their fragile canoes hunting Japanese units in the Arakan and of the demolition work carried out by frogmen. Such activities were often large enough to be given code names such as Operations 'Screwdriver', 'Attempt' and 'Turret'. Operation 'Block' was an all-arms attempt to prevent Japanese forces escaping from Ramree Island. The Japanese response to these repeated assaults along the coast and rivers is described in detail.

The book concludes with an account of the role played by this motley collection of seamen, marines and army personnel in Operation 'Dracula' – the recapture of Rangoon in May 1945. The well-chosen illustrations show the equipment used and the conditions encountered in this story of heroism in the face of considerable adversity and occasional cock-ups. All in all this is an interesting and well-written account of a little known naval aspect of the Second World War.

Richard Osborne

Roxanne Houston
Changing Course: the wartime experiences of a member of the Women's Royal Naval Service, 1939-1945
Grub Street, 2005; paperback, illustrated; price £8.99.
ISBN 1-904943-10-1

Based on the author's diaries, *Changing Course* is a memoir that evokes the family feeling of serving in the Navy in wartime. This time of course it is the WRNS and the book is an autobiography of someone who, determined to 'do their bit', managed to see a bit more of the world than the average Wren Officer, from Cornwall to what is now Sri Lanka. Along the way she experiences the privations, shortages, exhaustion and pain typical of the period, although the telling is from time to time tinged with just a touch of 'jolly hockey sticks', successfully lifting it above the maudlin. This does have the unintentional side effect of making the pain and shock she must have felt over the loss of a much loved younger brother a bit 'third party' in the telling, although the remoteness of time might also have some bearing on this. The author's style may lack the gritty humour of Nancy Spain's *Thank You, Nelson*, whose period her opening chapters parallel nicely in timescale, but she covers the same events from a different, but equally insightful viewpoint.

The primary source for the book means that the writing is necessarily episodic, and while it is understandable that Houston had few personal photos she could draw on it would perhaps have been good to have a few more illustrations to give a sense of place, particularly for the overseas locations. That said, a thoroughly engrossing tale, which makes me wish I had been able to get more details about her wartime career in the Wrens out of my mother before she died.

Wyn Davies

David K Brown RCNC
The Way of the Ship in the Midst of the Sea: the Life and Work of William Froude
Periscope Publishing, 2006; A4 hardback, 300 pages, extensively illustrated. Price £60.
ISBN 1-90438-1405

In 1870, the Admiralty agreed, at the instigation of William Froude, to build at Torquay the world's first ship model testing tank. As soon as it came into use, Phillip Watts became the first of a succession of promising young naval constructors who were appointed to work as assistants at Torquay or at its successor, the Admiralty Experiment Works, Haslar. In this tradition, David K Brown also worked at Haslar early in his career, so there is a direct historical link between the author of this biography and its subject.

William Froude made seminal contributions to giving ship design a sound scientific basis, and his testing methods remain, in their essentials, in use to the present day. Froude and his extended and gifted family were also closely involved in some of the most important intellectual and religious movements of the day, and his life yields many insights into mid-Victorian society. Brown has organised his fifteen chapters around these principal themes. This, he admits, sometimes makes it difficult to recognise when events were or were not occurring simultaneously, as well as for a certain amount of repetition (probably unavoidable in such a complex narrative).

William Froude was the fourth son of the wealthy Archdeacon of Totnes. After gaining a First in Mathematics at Oriel College, Oxford, he became a railway engineer, his second employer being Isambard Kingdom Brunel. He devised a new method for constructing skew bridges and, surprisingly in view of his later reputation for diffidence, earned Brunel's approval as a manager of large projects. Yet in 1846 William abandoned this career, partly to look after his slowly ailing father, though he also had ample time for other gentlemanly pursuits and for some research.

In 1857, Brunel asked William to make a theoretical study of rolling. Building on his own observations of the behaviour of a pendulum mounted on a small float, William, in conjunction with William Bell, developed a correct mathematical description of the behaviour of a ship in a seaway. Although difficult and sometimes misunderstood, the theory introduced the concept of metacentric height, and showed how rolling could be moderated by mass redistribution and the use of bilge keels.

In 1863, he also began an extended series of tests using a launch to tow models of different sizes and forms. He demonstrated that, contrary to the generally held view at that time, the results from models could predict the resistance of full sized hulls. He then obtained the support of Sir Edward Reed, the Chief Constructor of the Navy, for the building of a towing tank with himself as unpaid superintendent. After no more than a year's delay while funding was obtained, construction began in 1870 close to William's house. With his third son Edmund as his assistant, he designed the tank; the towing, measuring and recording equipment; and also the machines for moulding and cutting large numbers of wax models. As soon as it was completed, William's model-based predictions were triumphantly verified against results from towing experiments with HMS *Greyhound*. And systematic measurements of frictional resistance provided the data that allowed him to differentiate clearly between wave-making and frictional resistance and to refine the different scaling rules applicable to each. Then, having created this unique research tool, William went on to investigate propeller performance, displaying, as Brown says, his 'usual ability to break down a complicated problem into soluble parts'.

After the death of his wife Catherine in 1878 a distraught William was persuaded to take an extended holiday in South Africa, but there he contracted dysentery and died in the following year. In the penultimate chapter of the book Brown outlines son Edmund's career as he took over from his father as superintendent and supervised the move from the temporary buildings at Torquay to the new tank at Haslar. He then continued as superintendent until 1919, in his time making his own important contributions to naval architecture, especially in the development of more efficient hull forms.

The chapter on the history of ship hydrodynamics will be most accessible to those (unlike your reviewer) already versed in this complex subject. However, in the main, this is an account from which technical and non-technical readers alike can gain much, and it is well worth its rather high price. This review was written from a proof copy; it is to be hoped that in the published version the typographical and reference errors will have been eliminated, and that the many illustrations are reproduced in sizes appropriate to the detail that they contain.

John Brooks

Ewen Southby-Tailyour
HMS *Fearless*. The Mighty Lion. 1965-2002: A Biography of a Warship and Her Ship's Company.
Pen & Sword Maritime, 2006; 352 pages, well-illustrated; price £25
ISBN: 1-84415-054-2 and 978-1-84415-054-0

The First Lord of the Admiralty's Explanatory Statement on the Navy Estimates 1961-62 announced the ordering of two 10,000-ton assault ships of a new design to replace the ships of the Royal Navy's ageing Amphibious Warfare Squadron. The cost was to be £8 million each. 'Their Lordships were aghast at the price' writes Lord Carrington, the First Lord who ordered the ships, in the foreword to this splendid warship biography. Seldom has The Queen had better value for her money. *Fearless* was always better known than her sister ship *Intrepid* but the book may be seen as a literary tribute to them both.

Launched by Harland and Wolff on 19 December 1963, *Fearless* was to serve the Royal Navy for 37 years and 'can justifiably claim to be the most famous and influential ship of her era.' Completed in November 1965, in the middle of the Cold War, she was at the forefront of Britain's NATO order of battle and was omnipresent in national overseas interventions, conflicts and withdrawals from Africa and the Middle East. She landed a force in Saudi Arabia, the 'tanks' into Northern Ireland and played a leading role in the Falklands invasion in 1982. She served as the Dartmouth Training Ship, showed the flag throughout the world and served to the very end of British colonial history, standing-off in the South China Sea in 1997 during the handover of Hong Kong. Her operational career ended supporting the NATO deployment in Afghanistan.

Dedicated to the five-man crew of LCU Foxtrot Four from *Fearless* commanded by Colour-Sergeant B.R. Johnston QGM who were killed in action in Choiseul Sound on 8 June 1982, the book has introductory chapters on amphibious warfare and the LPD concept, on staff requirements and specifications, but the primary aim of the author, who served in the ship under every one of her Captains, was 'to give an overall impression of what life was like in the last third of the twentieth century (and for two years of this century) in the Royal Navy in general but in this extraordinary class of ship in particular'. He invited all survivors of the twenty Commanding Officers (in some cases the XO) to contribute, and the result is a fascinating and authoritative anthology (if a bit wardroom-heavy).

Most of her people looked back at their time in 'The Mighty Lion' (an allusion to her ship's badge) with pride but 'not everyone in the twenty-first century enjoyed serving in a ship conceived in the 1940s, designed in the 1950s and built in the 1960s'. She was of unlovely but distinctive appearance, with her funnels *en echelon* with two machinery spaces having one set of turbines and one set of boilers in each, making the port shaft longer than the starboard one. Her mechanical state was legendary and defects started early and followed her through life. ('Two of my marine engineers came to see me – always in pairs when there's bad news' – Captain Malcolm Williams). But in 37 years service, before decommissioning in March 2002, she steamed 749,000 nautical miles and took part in 140 operational exercises.

Lawrence Phillips

Admiral James L Holloway III, USN (Ret.)
Aircraft Carriers at War: a personal retrospective of Korea, Vietnam and the Soviet Confrontation
Naval Institute Press, 2007; hardback, 352 pages, illustrated; price £20.00.
ISBN 978-1-59114-391-8

This memoir of one of the US Navy's most senior admirals is set out along the lines of a formal report, interspersed with personal anecdotes and illuminating stories. Once one overcomes a slight bemusement at the author's chosen format, which at times makes the narrative seem a little impersonal and 'detached', the text is found to be very readable and the anecdotes are genuinely interesting.

The author's apparently genuine surprise at finding himself eventually in the top job of Chief of Naval Operations and a member of the Joint Chiefs of Staff is quite refreshing. His description of life at or near the top in the US Navy up to the close of the Cold War is punctuated by his need to reorganise parts of the Navy along lines which at this remove seem to be mainly blinding glimpses of the obvious. Holloway is either being politely reticent about his own skills, despite having ably managed several high profile postings during his career, or equally politely generous to those who caused each mess in the first place. In either case he comes across as a gentlemen, and as someone well versed in matters naval and political. As just one example, he could have been very much more critical of those who allowed the armed forces to forget all they had learned in the Second World War in the short period leading up to the Korean War, but he simply treats it as a lesson to be re-learned and gets on with the task in hand.

The reader is left with the feeling that if the author could see things so clearly – his description of Donald Rumsfeld's change of character on assuming office is possibly more insightful than he intended – then why couldn't others? Although clearly from the 'hawk' camp Holloway has little sympathy with the 'neo-con' world view or the mess they seem to have got the US into today. He is after all an advocate of a system that can be said to have won the Cold War; it is his successors who seem to have lost the subsequent peace!

This book would have benefited from more illustrations – the photographs here are largely personal, with no attempt to depict the major historical events. This represents something of a lost opportunity, as the mark of this book, at once tactful and erudite, is to evoke some of the most important conflicts in the latter part of the Twentieth Century.

Wyn Davies

Graham Smith
HMS Endurance, the Red Plum
Coach House Publications
Limited, 2006; softback, 96 pages, illustrated with many photographs (mostly colour); price £12.95.
ISBN 1-899-392-467

This well illustrated softback provides a detailed but easily digestible description of the current HMS Endurance: the ship and her company, her work and her area of operations, plus a brief history of her predecessors. The high production values mean it looks and smells like a brochure for a luxury yacht; and in some respects, compared with a traditional warship, Endurance does resemble, if not a luxury yacht, then at least a cruise liner. And this was in part what she was designed as.

This reviewer can readily recall the day he was asked to carry out an 'on hire' survey on behalf of the owners when the Royal Navy first chartered the then Polar Circle. She had been built with a view to running cruises to the edge of the ice cap whilst carrying out supply runs for various clients. Unfortunately the market dipped just as she was completed and the Navy's interest was probably rather timely.

On a cold, grey Portsmouth morning a small party assembled on the quay side at Fountain Lake Jetty to watch her arrive. There were, as normal, two groups carrying out the survey, one for the charterer and one for the owner. At the end of the day the two surveys would be compared and agreed, and that would define the state in which the ship was to be handed back to the owner. In the event this never happened; the Navy was so pleased with her that they bought her outright and will presumably continue to use her for some time to come. It's probably just as well, as it might have come to light that I wrote both surveys, whilst the Navy representative took the photos as a *quid pro quo* – in those days it was practically impossible to get a camera into a Royal Dockyard unless it was an MoD camera!

Oddly enough, a few years later my company surveyed another ship from Reiber Shipping which was to become the British Antarctic Survey's RRS Ernest Shackleton, illustrated alongside the Endurance on p.13. Although she is not named in the caption, the similarity between the two ships is very clear from the photograph. Both were very well designed and clearly well thought out for cold weather operations.

I can recall the awe that the comparatively vast accommodation spaces struck in the minds of the Navy's representatives during that first visit to the Polar Circle, space which I suspect was a bit of a godsend after a few months rubbing shoulders with the same people day after day. This sense of space is expertly captured by the pictures in Graham Smith's offering, and it is the illustrations that the book is really about – the photos both of the ship and of the wonderful scenery around her would frequently stand comparison with those of Herbert Ponting from Captain Scott's expedition. The book is probably worth its asking price for the pictures alone. Notably, according to the text, many were taken by the ship's company.

Do I have any niggles? Well a few: the editor has allowed far too many split infinitives for my liking, and I lost count of the number of sentences which started with 'And…'! One might also quibble that it reads at times a bit like an authorised biography, but none the less this book, about a unique vessel, is well worth having.

Wyn Davies

Hans Lengerer &
Waldemar Trojca
Japanese Warships at War.
(Vols.1 & 2)
Model Hobby, al. Korfantego 8, 40-004 Katowice, Poland, 2006 & 2007 (Distributor: Air Connection, Unit 2, 428 Gibraltar Drive, Mississauga, ON L5T 2M9 Canada); 216 & 224 pages, hardback, illustrated with B&W and colour photographs and colour paintings; price €46 (plus postage if ordered direct from the publishers).
ISBNs 83-60041-14-8 & 978-83-60041-24-6

Of all the warships of the 20th Century, those of the Imperial Japanese Navy must be the least well covered photographically, at least in western publications. These new books, the first two in a series of five volumes from a publisher who has hitherto largely concentrated on the military hardware of the Wehrmacht – but more importantly from an author well known to Warship readers – will go a long way to rectifying this state of affairs.

Vol. 1 comprises some 260 black and white photographs, mostly reproduced to a high standard and at full page size – although it should born in mind that many wartime and prewar views of Japanese warships are not of the best quality – plus an end section with colour paintings of various vessels. Many of the latter have appeared on the box artwork for plastic model kits of the 'Waterline Series'; most are very good indeed, and they will also evoke happy memories in anyone – this reviewer included – whose first interest in the IJN was inspired as a youngster by discovering these kits in the local model shop. As for the photographs, whilst some are well-known views the majority are unusual, if not completely unknown, and clearly come from a wide variety of sources. Many are detail and onboard views, making the book of particular value to model makers.

Vol. 2, billed as a 'Yamato Special', contains many familiar views of the great battleship, some less well known shots from her trials, and later ones from attacking American aircraft, together with an extensive colour section. The latter comprises 22 full-page views of the stunning 1:10 scale model on display at the Kure Naval Museum, and half a dozen close-ups of the full-size replica of a large part of the ship that was built at Onomichi as a set for the film 'Otokotachi no Yamato' ('Men of Yamato', Junya Satô 2005). There are two further colour selections: twelve pages of views of parts of the marine-growth-covered wreck of the *Haguro* in the Malacca Strait, and eighteen of what are evidently stills from colour movie footage of *Ise*, *Hyûga*, *Haruna*, *Aoba* and *Amagi* taken after the war. The quality of these stills is not great – as is always the case with images that originate in this way – but it is what they show that matters, such as the camouflage schemes that the battleships were sporting by this time.

In both volumes the captions (in English and German) are minimal; most give little more than name, date and place. Even so, some of the photos are clearly mis-dated or mis-captioned: the date of the photo on p.23 of Vol. 1 is given as 'about 1927', yet the photo features a *Takao* class cruiser, none of which was completed until 1932; in another example, the photo on p.134 of the same volume looks remarkably like the one from two pages previously, only reversed! It would have been good to have had a little more detail, especially given Hans Lengerer's immense knowledge of his subject. Perhaps the books should best be taken in conjunction with the same writer's other two new series, the web-only 'Contributions…', also reviewed in this edition of *Warship*; and the German-language 'Technical and Operational History'. In the introduction to Vol. 1 of '…at War' Lengerer invites readers to write in with any comments or corrections, for example on photographs that have been mis-identified – a full list of corrections will be published in Volume 5 – and on whether they would welcome the publication of official IJN drawings in future volumes. This unusual approach, allowing a series to develop over time in response to readers' wishes, is something for which the authors are to be applauded.

Vessels covered in these two books include all the prewar battleships plus the *Yamato*, the heavy cruisers of the *Furutaka*, *Aoba*, *Haguro* and *Takao* classes, the carriers *Hosho*, *Akagi*, *Kaga*, *Ryujo*, *Junyo*, *Amagi* and *Katsuragi*, submarines *I-400* and *I-402*, *Sakawa*, and some of the earlier light cruisers. The sharp-eyed will notice straight away that this list includes a lot of the ships which survived the war – albeit in many cases resting on the bottom of various Japanese harbours and of value only as scrap metal – and for which there is still relatively good photographic coverage after the widespread destruction of the Japanese records (including official photographs) during 1945. There has to be a concern that with a lot of the more 'glamourous' vessels having already been dealt with in Vols. 1&2, later ones may struggle a little in comparison. However, that is unlikely to worry the dedicated IJN enthusiast (and especially the modeller), for whom this series promises to be most welcome, especially if taken in conjunction with 'Contributions…'.

Stephen Dent

Sadao Asada
From Mahan to Pearl Harbor
US Naval Institute Press 2006;
hardback, 385 pages, tables;
price $32.95.
ISBN 1 55750 042 8

In his Acknowledgements the author states: 'In accordance with the established convention in academic works, Japanese names are presented with the family name preceding the given name'. The captions for the cover images on the jacket include the name 'Adm. Isoroku Yamamoto' (followed, incidentally, by 'Japanese battleship *Yamamoto*'!). Clearly the publishers should have allowed Sadao Asada to write – or at least check! – the jacket, as these are the only two two disappointments in this outstanding book.

Using a wide variety of previously unpublished sources Professor Asada shows the extent of the influence on early Japanese naval thinking of Mahan's seminal work *The Influence of Sea Power upon History*, with its emphasis on concentration of forces, the importance of the offensive, the key role of the battleship and the 'decisive fleet engagement'. These concepts were validated by Tsushima, and when the United States replaced Russia as the primary threat it was Japan's unshakeable belief in the decisive battle, also scheduled to take place in the Western Pacific close to Japan, that led to the 70% calculation which would subsequently become an irrefutable maxim for the IJN.

The problem was that by 1921-22 the world had changed. The more far-sighted senior officers in the Navy, such as Kato Tomasaburo, understood that national security was not simply a matter of the size of the stick you carried, and that the Washington Treaty was not just about naval arms limitation but was an international security system which encouraged understanding, respect for the interests of other nations, and détente. Although the IJN was confined to a 10:6 ratio in capital ships and aircraft carriers the US Navy, much to the chagrin of its own officers, had to accept the non-fortification of Guam and the Philippines, which effectively made the latter islands indefensible and greatly complicated the task of sending a fleet into the Western Pacific.

However, there were senior officers on the Naval General Staff who refused to see any advantage in the Washington outcomes, and who clung to the unshakeable belief that the 10:6 ratio was a national humiliation and threatened the security of the Empire. Kato Kanji and Suetsugu Nobomasa spent the 1920s stoking the flames of dissent among middle-ranking officers. When the collapse of the London Treaty negotiations was narrowly averted by a compromise which restricted Japanese heavy cruiser construction to 60.2% by 1936, junior IJN officers of the delegation rounded on the chief delegate Wakatsuki at the farewell dinner at Grosvenor House to vent their rage. Asada describes the scene: 'some were so excited as to have nosebleeds, and others were drunk and began tussling'.

Worse was to follow when the delegation returned to Japan. Stirred up by Kato Kanji and Suetsugu young naval officers became involved in the assassination of moderate politicians, and in 1933-34 Navy Minister Osumi conducted a systematic purge of senior officers of the 'treaty faction' which was so thorough that when preliminary talks for the next London Conference took place in 1934 it was difficult to find a senior officer willing to head the delegation.

The blinkered views of the naval right wing would lead Japan to disaster in a way that they could not have imagined. With the end of the treaty system the United States was able to send B-17s to the Philippines, while the Stark Plan for a Two-Ocean Navy provided for a 70% increase in the size of the US Fleet. US naval construction plans by this time amounted to two million tons, almost four times the size of the IJN's 3rd and 4th Replenishment Programmes combined. Meanwhile Japan had now acquired enemy status by its aggressive actions in China, leading to comprehensive US sanctions. In the end Japan was 'bounced' into a declaration of war by a combination of its own 70% obsession – late 1941 was the last time the IJN would attain 70% of US Navy strength – and the US oil embargo.

The irony of this is not lost on Asada, who also points out that ultimately the IJN lost confidence in the Mahanian strategy on which the 70% ratio was based. Accepting that the US Navy would not necessarily conform to the IJN's traditional strategic thinking, which prescribed a decisive battle in Japanese waters within 75 days, Yamamoto opted to take out the US Battle Fleet from the outset with an audacious aerial strike on Pearl Harbor. This served only to reinforce the US 'long war' option, which the Japanese knew spelled ultimate defeat. The rest, as they say, is history.

This is an excellent, thought-provoking book which highlights the dangers of divorcing naval strength from foreign policy objectives, and military expenditure from industrial and economic realities.

John Jordan

Peter Elphick
Liberty: The Ships that Won the War
Chatham Publishing, 2006: paperback, 258 pages; price £15.99
ISBN 1-86176-276-3

In this book Peter Elphick has produced a fascinating work, well-researched and supported by a wealth of eyewitness accounts – the list of acknowledgements running to four pages of named individuals. It falls naturally into three parts covering the beginnings of the project, the Liberty Ships at war, and their post-war use and gradual disappearance from service.

The first part covers the design origins and the various committees, agencies and persona, particularly R C Thompson and his team of the British Shipbuilding Mission to whom the book is dedicated, who combined to produce what is still in terms of numbers the world's biggest shipbuilding project. The achievements of the various shipyards – not just those of the well known Kaiser yards, but of all eighteen involved – are well documented and still have the power to astonish the informed reader. From green field site to first launch in a matter of months is an achievement not since matched in the annals of shipbuilding!

If there is one criticism that could be levelled against this book it is in this area: with the reader's appetite whetted a few photographs or drawings of these yards would have helped cement the descriptions (although in fairness a brief search of the internet suggests that there isn't the usual thorough coverage of this that might be expected).

Coverage of the actual war service of the ships is divided between the various theatres, with additional chapters on specific operations such as 'Torch' and Normandy, on specific events of interest like the explosion at Bari and the on-going saga of the *Richard Montgomery*, and on the use of the ships by the other Allied nations. It is this section that contains some of the more graphic personal accounts from crew members and, in particular, from survivors of lost or damaged ships. Again, the depth of the research is particularly evident in that practically every torpedo incident described is accompanied by details of the submarine involved.

The final part of the book examines the impact on post-war shipping of these hundreds of ships and opens a window on some little-known but vitally important debates. Whilst it is clear that the US establishment did not wish to allow the British Empire to regain its pre-war dominance, it was equally clear that the US Merchant Marine was in no position to take over. Thus the initial refusal to sell surplus Liberties to the UK was eventually overturned and many vessels, each of them identified by the author in an appendix, enjoyed a long and fruitful career under the red ensign. Another fact that deserves to be better known outside shipping circles is the role the Liberties had in establishing the Greek shipping industry as a major player, a development which would give rise to Aristotle Onassis and the modern super tanker.

A book to be recommended.

Wyn Davies

David Hepper
British Warship Losses in the Ironclad Era, 1860-1919.
Chatham Publishing, London 2006; 168 pages, hardback, illustrated; price £25.00.
ISBN 1-86176-273-9

One of the last reference books to appear under the Chatham imprint, this title, with its striking cover image of the cruiser *Gladiator* capsized off Yarmouth, is by and large a fine piece of work. David Hepper provides, in chronological order, details of every (or nearly every – see below) British naval vessel lost between 1860 and the end of the withdrawal from the ill-starred intervention in post-revolutionary Russia: everything from mighty battleships and battlecruisers to the humblest of hired motor launches – losses that occurred in battle, as a result of foundering, collisions, accidents and scuttlings.

There are three sections, of which that covering the years of the First World War is unsurprisingly the largest, making up some 70% of the book. Within these the format is the same, with each entry starting with the date of loss, followed by the name of vessel, type, basic details, name of commanding officer, an account of the actual loss and the events surrounding it, and finally references to primary and secondary sources – these last being very useful starting points for anyone who wants to dig deeper. In addition there are brief accounts of some of the wartime actions and incidents where a number of vessels were lost. Unfortunately casualty figures are not always given. Although everything is clearly laid out, a bit more care could have been taken in places; sometimes entries run over the page by just one line, or even by one word!

The ongoing dilemma as to what name to use for the Public Record Office / National Archives (depending on your inclination) is neatly resolved here by either using both in full with one in brackets, or by 'TNA: PRO'. Perhaps this is the way to go to keep everybody happy, at least to some degree?

The selection of photographs includes some well-known images, such as the destruction of the three battlecruisers at Jutland, but these are more than balanced by some very unusual ones: for example that of *Audacious* sinking being a different view from that usually published.

It should be noted that the book is an odd size for a reference work of this kind, being more suitable for a large format illustrated volume. It is not clear what reasoning, if any, was behind this strange choice. There is a much more important criticism, however. On 4 October 1906 the old first class twin-screw gunvessel *Landrail* sank off Portland while under tow after having been used as a target. Most of the crew were rescued, but one signalman was lost. There is no mention of this incident in the book, and this inspires the inevitable question of whether there are other similar omissions, and therefore just how thorough, reliable and comprehensive it really is.

That said, overall this book contains a great deal of information presented in a most clear and easily accessible manner, and anyone interested in the Royal Navy in the nineteenth and early twentieth centuries should find it a quite invaluable addition to their library.

Stephen Dent

Hans Lengerer and Lars Ahlberg
Contributions to the History of Imperial Japanese Warships
For subscriptions contact lars.ahlberg@halmstad.mail.postnet.se; subscription rate U.S. $50.00 per issue

This not a book, but a subscription-only journal, delivered by email. The subscriber agrees to purchase at least the first three issues, and ten subscribers are needed to make publication viable. Each issue totals about 100 sides of single-spaced A4, with tables, and may include illustrations. The material is principally based on translations from referenced Japanese sources, with occasional additions from post-war U.S. reports. Each issue contains about six articles, either free standing or instalments of a part-work, with an addendum and reactions from readers. The first two issues, dated September 2005 and March 2006, and the contents pages of the next two were supplied for review. The presentation is good – although there were no illustrations – and there is a high degree of accuracy; much information is presented in tables.

Lengerer, an established expert on the Japanese Navy, has contributed many articles to *Warship*. To give an idea of the journal's scope and range, the first article in Issue 1 is a lengthy account of the origins of the *Ise* class battleships, including political and financial aspects ignored in the usual books; it is continued in Issue 2 as far as the changes made to the main armament during the major reconstructions of the 1930s. Other chapter headings listed include 'IJN's first warship order to a foreign country', 'Armoured frigate *Fuso* and belted corvettes *Kongo* and *Hiei*', 'CV *Shokaku* class', 'DD *Umikaze* and *Yamakaze*' and 'Torpedo boats'. Text and footnotes are frequently illuminating; the little known 1874 attempt to buy the Brazilian turret ship *Independencia*, then building on the Thames, is outlined, as is Japan's 1900s preference for Vickers over Armstrong battleship designs. Cruisers are very largely ignored, possibly because of the existence of the excellent book by Lacroix and Wells, and little is said about submarines.

This novel and authoritative journal, utilising much material only previously available in Japan, both fills a significant gap in the literature and makes an interesting contrast to other Japanese ship periodicals; it is almost at the opposite extreme to Akira Endo's fascinating *Senzen Senpaku* (Japanese Ships) 1853-1952, which publishes – untranslated – complete Japanese documents and articles on both warships and merchant ships, and contains an excellent selection of drawings and photos (an occasional Western article or book section concerned with Japanese ships may be included). The generalist monthly *Sekai no Kansen* (Ships of the World) takes an intermediate, lavishly illustrated approach.

The question of value for money will be raised; one issue is expensive compared to the annual *Warship* or a year's subscription to *Warship International*, and the total lack of illustrations in the issues reviewed is unfortunate. The IJN specialist will, however, find much of absorbing interest.

Ian Sturton

D K Brown
Nelson to Vanguard
Chatham Publishing 2006; paperback, 224 pages, 200 illustrations; price £16.99. ISBN 1 86176 189 5

First published as a hardback in 2000 (see review by Antony Preston in *Warship* 2001-02) as the third in David K Brown's series of books on warship design and development in the Royal Navy, *Nelson to Vanguard* has been very difficult to obtain for some time, and the publisher has now decided to reprint it in paperback form at a much-reduced price. The book is in a slightly smaller format than the original, but is printed on superior-quality paper and has suffered little in the process.

The first eight chapters detail the history of each of the major categories of warship from the Washington Treaty of 1922 to the end of the Second World War. These are followed by chapters on modernisation, wartime damage, production and repair, and one which asks the question: 'What is a good design?' The book concludes with appendices which support or develop points made earlier in the text.

David K Brown is well known to readers of *Warship* for his succinct, intelligent analysis and for his willingness to 'take on' entrenched historical dogma, and these qualities are admirably to the fore in this book. He makes the point that the effects of the interwar treaties on the Royal Navy have been much exaggerated, and that they at least had the benefit of setting an 'internationally agreed size of the fleet', whereas the Army and Air Force had no such basis for agreement and actually emerged worse off.

Other important issues pursued in the Appendices relate to aspects of design which the author feels the Navy got wrong. There is a detailed critique of the unit machinery arrangement adopted for the more modern British cruisers, in which wing spaces flanked the second the two boiler rooms, thereby threatening the ship's stability in the event of a torpedo hit amidships. Some British cruiser designs – notably the 'Town' class – also had their hull girder weakened by the break abaft the forecastle, a structural weakness exacerbated by the stepping down of the side armour at this point. Comparative studies of aspects of British and foreign (especially US Navy) ship design focus, to the detriment of the Royal Navy, on anti-aircraft capabilities and on the cost in terms of weight, maintainability and endurance of the Navy's resistance to high-pressure steam and lightweight turbines.

This is not a book for 'rivet counters'. If you want to know precisely how many 20mm Oerlikons were mounted on a particular destroyer in May 1943, look elsewhere. Its strength is in its understanding of the historical and technical context in which these ships were developed, the military rationale behind each individual design, and how the ships perfomed when tested – often to destruction – in the crucible of war. The new edition is excellent value for money, and is thoroughly recommended to anyone who does not already own the hardback version.

John Jordan

Bradley Peniston
No Higher Honor: Saving the USS *Samuel B. Roberts* in the Persian Gulf
Naval Institute Press, Annapolis, 2006; 275 pages, 18 b & w photographs, 1 map and 3 diagrams.
List Price $29.95
ISBN 1-59114-661-5

Roger Thompson
Lessons Not Learned: The U.S. Navy's Status Quo Culture
Naval Institute Press, Annapolis, 2007; 251 pages, 10 b & w photographs. List Price $34.95.
ISBN 978-1-59114-865-4

These two books from the U.S. Naval Institute Press offer contrasting views of the world's largest and most powerful navy. Essentially, Bradley Peniston's book concentrates on a single incident in 1988. However, in the process, he draws into his narrative a number of political, matériel and personnel issues. Roger Thompson, on the other hand, takes a broad sweep across several decades in a highly critical examination of the consequences of this current hegemony in naval power. Although there is little obvious common ground, both provide an insight into the workings of the US Navy, and the political hand that guides it, that can be in turn reassuring and disturbing.

It is a sobering thought that a large percentage of the population inhabiting the shores of the Arabian Gulf will have only experienced war and conflict during their lifetimes and never the stability that comes from lasting periods of peace. Such is the longevity of what is the most recent manifestation of unrest in this troubled region that it is easy to forget some of the less eye-catching events, such as the so-called 'Tanker War' of the 1980s which took place at the height of revolutionary fervour in Iran during that country's war with neighbouring Iraq.

The focal point of *No Higher Honor* comes during this conflict when the *Oliver Hazard Perry* Class frigate USS *Samuel B. Roberts* was nearly lost after striking an Iranian mine in the Gulf in April 1988. The immediate repercussions of the incident led to a far more active involvement by the United States in the region and directly to the largest surface action involving its navy since World War II.

Peniston's book, covering the entire career of the frigate from her construction at Bath Iron Works in Maine through to her later service after a $38 million refit following the mining incident, uses a wealth of eye-witness statements, interviews, media articles, government documents and extensive secondary sources to produce an extremely comprehensive account both of the ship and of the men who were serving in her at the time. It also provides an insight into how this event, amongst others, contributed to America's ever-deepening involvement in the region which, of course, lasts to this day. The author reveals his journalistic origins in his approach to the subject, with the story given 'an angle'. *Samuel B. Roberts* is a product of Admiral Zumwalt's 1970s 'High/Low' naval shipbuilding strategy: a mix of costly carriers, missile cruisers and nuclear submarines balanced by a large number of inexpensive escorts typified by the numerous *Perry* Class. *Roberts*' predecessor had been one of the 'tin-can heroes' of the Battle of Leyte Gulf and Peniston homes in on this theme in creating a portrait of the ship as a 'no-frills', unglamorous, workhorse of the fleet.

Linked to the above is his portrayal of the ship's C.O., Cdr. Paul Rinn. Raised in the Bronx; tough, focused and uncompromising, he drives his crew hard, concentrating on the basics of good seamanship and imbuing in them the traditions of their wartime forebears. His single-minded determination to make the *Roberts* the most efficient fighting unit in his squadron includes the repetitious, tedious but vital task of daily damage-control drills. This, of course, ultimately pays off. Peniston is an accomplished story-teller and the description of what happens in the minutes and hours after the mine detonated and the crew efficiently go about the business of saving the *Roberts* is riveting as the narrative switches between different eye-witnesses in various corners of the ship.

In the wider sense, *No Higher Honor* also provides a very interesting commentary on naval combat in the 1980s, including such incidents as the Iraqi Exocet missile attack on *Roberts*' sistership USS *Stark* in 1987, the mining of the US supertanker MV *Bridgeton* in the same year, and the ramifications of these, including the crippling by mines of two high-value warships, USS *Tripoli* (LPH10) and USS *Princeton* (CG10), during Operation Desert Storm.

Direct reprisal by the Americans for the mining of *Roberts* resulted in Operation 'Praying Mantis', which the author claims featured the first ever missile duel between surface warships. This is covered in some depth, likewise the earlier 'shadow-boxing' between the US warships escorting American-flagged tankers through the Gulf and some aggressively handled Iranian frigates seeking to disrupt the flow of commerce. A form of unofficial electronic warfare resulted, with each side 'painting' the other with their fire control radars until someone gave way.

Although the author tends to overplay his image of the *Roberts* as an unsung, ungainly hero of the US fleet, nevertheless, what stands out, is the dedication and skill of the crew in successfully accomplishing the task all sailors dread. One is left, therefore, with the impression that, if this ship is in any way representative, the most powerful navy in the world remains in capable hands.

No such reassurances can be garnered from *Lessons Not Learned: The US Navy's Status Quo Culture*. According to Roger Thompson, there have been serious shortcomings and weaknesses over the last fifty years in practically every aspect of the Navy's work and these have been cleverly disguised or ignored by politicians, writers and senior officers within the service. He commences what amounts to a polemic by discussing various international naval exercises during the Cold War and post-Cold War eras which have resulted in very poor performances and 'defeats' for the US Navy, particularly with respect to anti-submarine warfare. He claims that the 'nearly continuous neglect of ASW' has diminished the combat capability of the surface fleet through a fixation with 'supercarriers and nuclear submarines', and repeatedly cites how smaller navies using quiet, diesel-electric submarines have frequently outmanoeuvred and embarrassed the technologically superior but overrated American ships during exercises. The outcomes have been covered up, distorted or simply ignored by the USN's public relations network, by successive administrations, and by the media. In the latter case, the writer Tom Clancy comes under persistent fire from Thompson for simply misleading the public.

The handling of the nuclear carrier fleet and the capabilities of their 'elite' naval aviators are singled out for criticism, with examples of how Canadian and Israeli fighters have outperformed their American counterparts in training and how the latter were frequently embarrassed in dogfights during both the Korean and Vietnam Wars. Shortcomings in mine countermeasures are also aired; the incidents described by Peniston in *No Higher Honor* are of course highlighted.

Thompson moves on to expose the lack of training in fundamental warfighting skills, in tactics and in strategy and what amounts to a systemic failure in human resources management which has created a massive turnover in personnel. Extensive drug and alcohol abuse have had a serious effect on the fighting ability of individual ships and there are some depressing accounts provided of incidents ranging from sabotage to racism.

Thompson concludes by offering a twelve-point programme to address the situation, but in truth this really doesn't go into any detail. If one accepts that *Lessons Not Learned* is simply intended to be a provocative, 'wake-up call' for the USN to look critically at itself from its current position as the undisputed leading naval power, then the author has succeeded in his purpose. However, it is not only monotonously one-sided but quite blatantly biased, particularly towards the Canadian Armed Forces. Thompson is Canadian. Although his bibliography runs to a very impressive 27 pages, he has been highly selective with his evidence and one craves throughout for greater objectivity and for the counter-arguments he has chosen to omit.

Jon Wise

Norman Polmar
Aircraft Carriers: a History of Carrier Aviation and its Influence on World Events – Vol. 1 1909-1945
Potomac Books 2006; hardback, 576 pages, 389 B&W photos, maps, appendices; price $49.95. UK price £31.50.
ISBN 1 57488 663 0

This book was first published in 1969 and one reviewer described it as 'the bible for flattops and their operations for [the past] thirty-five years'. This is at once its strength and its weakness: encyclopaedic in its compass and still eminently readable, *Aircraft Carriers* was in many ways a ground-breaking book when it first appeared and for that reason alone it merits a second edition. The account of carrier operations during the Second World War is both thorough and sound; the narrative is enhanced by many new photographs, some of which are previously unpublished.

The downside is that some of the perspectives appear to have been set in stone, reflecting as they do much of the received wisdom regarding the development of carrier aviation that was prevalent in the 1960s. There are indications that Polmar has attempted to incorporate some more recent scholarship, but a more radical re-write might have avoided the errors and omissions which remain. In philosophical and operational terms the author's account of carrier aviation development during the interwar period is undeniably US Navy-centric, seeming to view USN developments as a yardstick by which to judge the other major navies rather than as a single philosophical strand among a number of divergent approaches each of which appeared at the time to have equal validity. He therefore fails to address in depth key issues such as why the Royal Navy considered and rejected the 'deck park' during the early 1930s, why both France and Italy decided during that decade that advances in land-based aircraft effectively precluded the operation of carriers in the Mediterranean – thinking which influenced the British 'armoured carrier' concept – and the extent to which IJN deck operating cycles continued to diverge from those developed in the US Navy. Whilst none would deny that by late 1943 the US Navy had developed carriers, aircraft and operational doctrines ideally suited to naval air operations in the wide expanses of the Pacific, it is still intriguing to speculate how well a *Yorktown* with an air complement of F2A Buffaloes, SB2U Vindicators and TBD Devastators (and a light AA armament of four quad 1.1in guns!) might have fared in the Mediterranean against *Fliegerkorps X* in early 1941.

There are also factual errors which remain uncorrected: *Akagi* as first completed had only two elevators, not three (p.64); and of the early British armoured carriers only *Indomitable* was redesigned with an additional half hangar (p.84). However, the author's overall grasp of his subject is such that these have to be considered minor blemishes in what is generally an accurate account of international carrier development, while he really comes into his own when recounting the various actions in which carriers were prominent during the Second World War.

Unfortunately the paper chosen for this new edition is too thin for the quality reproduction intended, leading to 'show through' from the reverse side. The print itself is also a little 'grey', and the overall look is rather dated. Whilst a heavier paper would undoubtedly have made for a thicker and more expensive book, the benefits would surely have outweighed the cost.

John Jordan

Jak Mallmann Showell
The U-Boat Century: German
Submarine Warfare 1906-2006
Chatham Publishing, 2006;
224 pages, 400+ photographs;
price £19.99
ISBN 1-86176-241-0

Writing a book to mark the centenary of submarines in the German Navy is no mean challenge, but Jak Mallmann Showell has risen to the occasion with a fascinating and comprehensive account that avoids the temptation of focusing on the Second World War.

The first seven chapters, just over half of the book, provide a chronological narrative of German submarine development, and the consequent operations of the U-boats in peace and war, illustrated by copious images, many of which will be new to the reader. Within the vast scope the author finds time to linger, for example, on the career of Otto Weddigen and on Hirschfeld's memories of the Schnorkel as fitted to the Type XB minelayer *U-234*. The book brings us right up to date with a detailed description and images of *U-31*, the first of four Type 212s.

Weapons systems, anti-submarine warfare, bases, builders, long distance voyages and flotilla organisation: each has its own chapter, avoiding over-complication earlier on, and the main narrative ends with a brief chapter on the recruitment and training of the submariner. A chronology provides an historical framework, while the extensive bibliography includes the author's opinion on the usefulness of each book, as in 'Contains a large number of letters which might be difficult for people unaccustomed to German handwriting'.

Mallmann Showell's real achievement lies in producing a highly readable and coherent narrative of a complex subject, which is deceptively and painlessly crammed full of facts and figures. He writes beautifully, driving the narrative forward and changing pace effortlessly, moving from résumé to close detail with something of a cameraman's eye, and his choice of words is a pleasure.

While this is a beautiful book – the jacket illustration (by Claus Friedrich Bergen) is particularly fine, and the four hundred B&W illustrations have reproduced sharply on the glossy paper. However a slightly larger format would allow these images to breathe more. For example, the double-page spread devoted to *U-23* (1975) has thirteen images, together with a column of captions; overlapping and allowing them to meet in the gutter gives a congested feel. The text also suffers from the format. Integrating the text and images is a bonus, but there are times when a few pages of uninterrupted text would have given a great deal of reading pleasure and aided digestion.

Nevertheless, overall a first rate, accessible overview by a respected expert of this most significant arm of the German Navy.

Jean Hood

Ian W Toll
Six Frigates: how piracy, war
and British supremacy at sea
shaped the birth of the world's
most powerful navy
Michael Joseph, 2006; 592 pages,
illustrated; price £25.00.
ISBN 0-718-14658-1

For a first book, the author has picked a challenging topic – an account of the formation of the US Navy demonstrated by the careers of the first six frigates authorised by Congress – but he has carried it off in some style. With 467 pages of text, 16 pages of colour illustrations and over 100 pages of introduction, notes, chronology, bibliography and index this is no light read, but despite its weight (both academic and avoirdupois) it reads well.

Although much of the technical side and some of the political issues will be familiar, they have been stitched together here into a tapestry of events that still has the power to amaze. Until the arrival of these big frigates, the Royal Navy had always won, and expected to win, single ship contests, so their defeats at the hands of a newcomer were doubly shocking.

Although the author notes that the US Navy ships were manned by paid volunteers whilst the Royal Navy ships had pressed men in their crews, he doesn't explore the implications of this quite as fully as he might have when analysing the reasons behind the Yankee victories. Nor does he dwell for long on the large superiority in armament enjoyed by the big frigates other than to point out the far-sightedness of their architect and chief proponent, Joshua Humphries.

Other references quote later Royal Navy assessments which point out that the big frigates' armament was often twice the weight of their RN opponent with gun crews at least as well drilled. It is then disappointing to learn in this context that the *Chesapeake* was one of the smaller frigates and her crew recently assembled and totally unpractised, taking some of the gloss off HMS *Shannon*'s victory.

Where this book differs from most are the lengths to which the author has gone to cover the political and economic situation of the newly fledged United States in detail, thus setting the various arguments for and against any sort of navy into a more understandable context, particularly when dealing with the problem of the Barbary pirates. Given his background as, amongst other things, a political aide and speech writer, he brings a degree of authority to this aspect of the history, with some very readable pen portraits of the chief protagonists of the time. He keeps this juxtaposition of politician and navy throughout the narrative and concludes with the thought-provoking statement that it was the performance of these six ships and their smaller consorts in the otherwise unsatisfactory war of 1812-13 that turned the United States from a plural entity to a singular one.

The sheer size of the author's bibliography is some indication of the depth of research behind the work, resulting in a history of the foundation of the US Navy that is unlikely to be surpassed for some time.

Wyn Davies

Robert J Cressman
USS *Ranger*: The Navy's First Flattop from Keel to Mast, 1934-46
Potomac Books 2005; softback, 451 pages, many B&W photos; price $26.95.
ISBN 1 57488 519 7

This book does exactly what it says on the tin: it is a full operational history of the USS *Ranger*, arguably the most neglected of the US Navy's prewar carriers. The world's first fleet carrier to be designed and built as such, *Ranger* introduced many of the key features of her more glamorous successors. She was the first carrier with an open hangar (originally to have been fitted with cross-deck catapults for the launch of reconnaissance and ASW patrol aircraft), the first with arrestor wires to permit landings over the bow, the first with cafeteria-style messing, and the first in which a ready room was provided for each air squadron. Unlike the battleship and battlecruiser conversions of the 1920s *Ranger* was designed 'from the inside out', her primary role as a mobile base for naval air squadrons taking precedence over 'ship' characteristics.

Ranger was completed in 1934, at a time when naval aviation was still in its infancy in terms of both technology and tactics. The author's detailed accounts of the flight deck crashes which regularly occurred brings home just what a dangerous practice flying from a carrier was during these early days. We also see how this painful learning process brought the required improvements in hardware, pilot training, and deck procedures.

From 1935 *Ranger* took part in all the major 'fleet problems' during which she conducted combined operations with *Lexington* and *Saratoga* which, while they did not resolve the question as to whether carriers should operate independently or with the battle fleet, did show that either option was a possibility.

Ironically it was the 'ship characteristics' sidelined during her design which were responsible for *Ranger*'s relegation first to the Atlantic and ultimately to the role of training carrier. Her flight deck was considered only just large enough to operate a full air group, and because she was so lightly built she pitched and rolled badly in the Pacific swell, resulting in an inordinately high number of crash landings. Although relatively well-equipped in terms of AA provision – *Ranger* was the first US carrier with the Mk 33 fire control system – she was completely unarmoured and had no anti-submarine protection system. During 1943, when a thorough modernisation was contemplated, it was estimated that in her currently overloaded state she would probably be sunk by a single torpedo. Considering that her operations in the North Atlantic exposed her to packs of German U-boats this was a major concern.

Arguably the most interesting action of *Ranger*'s brief career as a wartime carrier was her participation in the 'Torch' landings in North Africa in November 1942. The author gives a full account of her air operations against a variety of targets around Casablanca. She certainly impressed RN observers with her ability to conduct round-the-clock air operations against hostile shipping and in support of the landings ashore.

Although the detailed account of landing incidents and training flights can become repetitive, there can be no doubting the thoroughness of the author's research. This is a well-written and often very readable account, illustrated by a large number of carefully chosen B&W photos.

John Jordan

Vincent P. O'Hara
The US Navy against the Axis: Surface Combat 1941-45
Naval Institute Press 2007; hardback, 384 pages, 20 B&W photos, many tables and maps; price $36.95 (UK distributor: Greenhill Books, £25.00).
ISBN 1 57488 519 7

A follow-on from the author's previous *The German Fleet at War 1939-45* (reviewed in *Warship* 2005), this new book adopts a similar approach to the task of recounting the US Navy's surface operations during the Second World War. O'Hara rightly points out that although the Pacific theatre is mostly associated with the great carrier battles, for a long period, from the autumn of 1942 to the autumn of 1943, the US Navy was down to two fleet carriers and the Imperial Japanese Navy was attempting to rebuild its shattered air groups, so combat devolved onto the surface forces: battleships, cruisers and destroyers. The battle of attrition in the Solomons became the crucible in which the surface warfare doctrines of both navies were tested to destruction. This key theatre is very much at the centre of the book, as the author looks at how doctrine was modified in the light of experience, and in particular at how the tactics employed by the US Navy evolved to take account of radar, which in the early stages did not always confer the anticipated advantages in night fighting.

The first part of the book, which deals with the confused cruiser/destroyer battles around the

Dutch East Indies, provides in effect a 'warm-up' to the main show in the Solomons, while the later part deals with the 'Torch' and Normandy landings, and the battles for Leyte Gulf, by which time the US Navy's material superiority was matched by an increasingly effective doctrine, with disastrous consequences for the elite IJN surface forces thrown into this last desperate battle. The inclusion of Vichy France under the term 'Axis' is debatable – France was never a member and at the time of the landings in North Africa was strictly a neutral country – but this is a criticism of the 'catch-all' title not the coverage; the French surface forces at Casablanca actively opposed the landings and provided a fierce test for the US naval forces present.

As in the author's book on the Kriegsmarine each of the battles recounted here is accompanied by a table giving the composition and organisation of the forces present and data for each ship, and most are accompanied by clear maps drawn by the author to a consistent style and format. At the end of each account there is a brief analysis of failures and of lessons learned, and this is clear and balanced and mercifully free of the polemic which mars some accounts of the US Navy's actions. The black & white photographs, although not central to the book, are generally well-chosen and give a feel for the ships involved and for the nature of the conflict.

John Jordan

Tony Booth
Admiralty Salvage in Peace and War 1906-2006
Pen and Sword Maritime 2007; hardback, 224 pages, 16 B&W photos; price £19.99
ISBN 978-1-84415-565-1

During the 1820s, John and Charles Deane developed a helmet to enable firemen to enter a smoke-filled building. Surprisingly, perhaps, their invention was spurned, but a decade later it was taken up by an Admiralty desperate to deal with the hazardous wreck of HMS *Royal George* which had capsized back in 1782. This was the true beginning of the future Admiralty Salvage Service – and indeed of commercial diving – although it would take the loss of HMS *Montague* in 1906 before the Admiralty decided to create a special department to handle the salvage of warships. The First World War, however, soon found this organisation also salvaging damaged merchant vessels.

Booth deals very competently with the bureaucratic wrangling within the Admiralty and with the commercial salvage companies that bedevilled the organisation over the decades, as well as with the technical developments introduced by a succession of imaginative and practical salvage officers when faced with new challenges. He passionately champions the remarkable achievements of the Service, calculating that during the First World War it salvaged 90 Royal Navy vessels and 730 merchant ships (15% of the total attacked). Without that, he concludes, Britain might not have beaten the U-boats. During the Second World War the figures were no less striking, and in addition he records the work done to clear ports of scuttled ships, and how salvage personnel, some of them civilians, fought gallantly on the D-Day beaches.

Operations narrated in detail make riveting reading. The salvage of the *Coulmore* in 1943 rivals that celebrated post-war epic of the *Flying Enterprise*; and the recovery from the Mediterranean of wreckage from the BOAC Comet which crashed in January 1954 led to the discovery of the cause of the accident and a critical change to the design of aircraft windows. Perhaps the most fascinating story is that of John Pollard and the Phoenix Units in 1944. Part of the Mulberry Harbours, one had broken its tow and run aground, and while examining it Deputy Salvage Director Pollard discovered major structural problems that threatened the whole of the D-Day operation, so beginning a race against time to make the required modifications. The book brings us right up to date with the moving of three decommissioned Russian nuclear-powered submarines.

While a little more editorial sharpness would have been useful, the brevity of the bibliography as compared with the extensive list of primary sources reveals just how much original research has gone into this excellent book. Tony Booth has proved himself a true fairy godmother to this unjustly neglected cinderella of naval history.

Jean Hood

Howard D Grier
Hitler, Dönitz and the Baltic Sea
Naval Institute Press, 2007 (UK distributor: Greenhill books); hardback, 320 pages, 12 photos, 7 maps; price £20.
ISBN 1-59114-345-1

In support of the thesis that Hitler's determination to hold on to the Baltic coast from Leningrad to Courland was not sheer stubbornness but was out of determination to retain the use of the Baltic for training for the Type XXI U-boat which, prompted by Dönitz, he saw as the only war winning weapon, this book opens with seven chapters on the fighting along this coast. This campaign is little known and the book is worth reading for this aspect alone. Considerable attention is paid to the relationship between Hitler and his generals – a relationship all too often characterised by arguments over permission to withdraw. An unusual character is the little known Field Marshal Schörner who had an unusual skill in persuading Hitler to agree to a withdrawal and even, on occasion, withdrew without getting permission. Dönitz comes across as a dedicated Nazi, not the 'simple sailor' sometimes portrayed. He certainly argued hard for holding the Baltic front.

The difficult relationship with Sweden is covered, but Chapter 9 is the key to the argument, discussing the submarine war in general while concentrating on the Type XXI programme. The author covers most of the problems: the frequent delays due to the bombing of key factories making components, the problems with dimensional tolerances on hull sections, the complex hydraulic system, all of which proved difficult to rectify and which, exacerbated by the loss of skilled workers, caused major delays.

Two errors which might seem trivial but would have had a major effect on ASW operations. The submerged speed is given as 18 knots but 16½ for one hour was more realistic. Since the best ASW ships of the 'Loch' class had a top speed of 20 kts this is significant. Also, the diving depth is quoted as 376ft yet, on trial, U-2529 reached 220 metres. Fast submarines need a considerable safety margin, and postwar British studies suggest 500ft as a usable depth. However, by early 1945 much of the Baltic was within range of Allied bombers and U-boat losses were heavy particularly due to mines.

Certainly, Dönitz believed that the capability of the Type XXI would change the balance in the Atlantic and he tried to convince Hitler of that. Whether he accepted Dönitz's view we can never know. Readers must make up their own minds as to whether Grier has proved his thesis but the effort will be worthwhile. There is still much to be learnt about the last year of Nazi Germany.

The author might have looked at developments on the other side. By 1945 sonobuoys were in limited use, trials were in hand using helicopters from ships and plans were well advanced to fit Squid to the 'Captain' class. The XXIs would not have had it all their own way. Moreover it is questionable whether the Allies would have accepted defeat with a couple of atom bombs in store.

Eur Ing David K Brown RCNC

William N Still, Jr.
Crisis at Sea: the United States Navy in European Waters in World War I
University Press of Florida, 2007; 742 pages, seven maps, thirty B&W photographs; price $100.00
ISBN 0-81302987-2

The story of the US Navy in World War I is not one of great sea battles like Midway or Leyte Gulf. For those who associate the names Sims, Benson, and Fletcher with classes of destroyer there is much to learn in William N Still's monumental *Crisis at Sea*, a history of the US Navy in European waters and the effort involved in creating from scratch on foreign soil the administrative and physical infrastructure of an American fleet

Careful attention is required to follow the various topics and personalities that populate this closely written and meticulously researched work. The book's twenty chapters are organized thematically. The first eight deal with politics, command, administration, and logistics. Three chapters dissect social aspects while another covers material (warships and weapons). Operations are the major subject of the book's final third with chapters focused on convoys, escorts, mining, the North Sea, the Mediterranean, and patrolling. A concluding chapter describes reactions upon the war's end.

The strengths of *Crisis at Sea* are its research and its sheer variety. Still places great reliance on period letters and diaries and he quotes from these generously. There is a lot to like in some of the detail. For example, there was the submarine sailor who reported for duty with a pet baby skunk. 'You can't take it below,' his captain objected. 'Think of the smell.' 'He'll get used to it,' the sailor replied, 'same as I did.' (p.214) The Royal Navy's turret officers could not change a solenoid in a sub-calibre firing mechanism, although it 'could have been fixed in a minute by any turret officer in [the US] fleet.' (p.201). Scottish women had poor teeth, but, 'cripes . . . the English girls go them one worse.' (p.300) US floatplanes carried three or four pigeons for emergency communications, which were released 'by throwing them out away from the propellers...' (p.464)

The level of detail in *Crisis at Sea* can also get tedious, however, and at times it lacks focus. Six pages, full of insults, street fights, and rancour, are spent relating the difficult nature of Irish-American relations (p.289-294), but the excellent relations between the Americans and Scots are dismissed in one sentence. Some of the problem resides in the redundancy required by the book's structure. The US destroyers based at Queenstown, for example, are touached upon in the chapters on bases in Europe, on relationships with Great Britain, in the social chapters, and in the operational chapters on convoys, on escorts, and on patrolling. The author's fondness for contemporary points of view means he often quotes multiple period comments on a subject, such as US mines, both in praise and condemnation. However, lacking interpretation, it is not clear how bad (or good) the mines were, although this does become apparent several chapters later when he covers the North Sea mine barrage. The unqualified quotation of contemporary opinions is characteristic of *Crisis at Sea* and detracts from its clarity.

For all its structural idiosyncrasies, redundancies, and relentless detail, however, *Crisis at Sea* is clearly an important work. It provides an excellent foundation for the study of important aspects of the US Navy during the First World War and serves up a broad range of subjects not typically found together between the covers of a single history. The massive bibliography and extensive footnotes provide a valuable resource for anyone interested in a closer study of the book's many topics.

Vincent O'Hara

Jean Hood
Come Hell & High Water: Extraordinary Stories of Wreck, Terror and Triumph on the Sea
Conway Maritime Press, 2006; 400 pages, 19 plate illustrations, 15 text illustrations; price £20.00.
ISBN 1-84486-034-5

In this selection, Jean Hood presents seventeen true 'incidents', covering the years 1752-2005. As the title suggests, each of these narratives relates a different tale of adversity which generically serve to illustrate not only mankind's ignorance, incompetence and greed but also his heroism, selflessness and raw courage in the face of the sea's insurmountable indifference. The author has made a conscious effort to avoid some of the more familiar stories of this kind, although she makes an exception in the case of *Titanic* which she suggests is just too famous to omit. She insists that her choice is entirely personal and her intention with these 'maritime dramas' is 'to move, shock or amaze'.

Readers seeking incidents with a specifically naval flavour will be attracted by perhaps half a dozen of the chapters. The author's account of the lamentable aftermath of the sinking of the liner *Laconia* off the West African coast in 1942 leaves one with a mixture of sadness for the suffering caused by the inevitable consequences of total war but also with admiration for those who seek to rise above the resulting dilemmas, in this particular case the captain of U-156. Avoiding the more familiar accounts of submarine accidents Hood writes about the efforts to save the crew of USS Squalus in 1939 and brings things right up to date by including a chapter on two recent incidents involving Russian submarines: the Kursk in 2000 and Priz AS-28 five years later.

Several chapters require the author to familiarise the reader quickly with the details of a lesser-known period in history and, inevitably, this can mean that there is the problem of trying to encapsulate a very complex set of circumstances within the space of a few pages. The account of the fatal collision between HMS Victoria and HMS Camperdown in the Mediterranean in 1893, widely recognised as a pivotal moment which raised fundamental and far-reaching questions about command, communication, leadership and training in the Victorian Royal Navy (indeed its effect was discernable at Jutland over twenty years later), is concluded with a discussion about the shortcomings in the design of the two ships involved – an important matter, granted, but not the key issue involved.

However, the book is very thoroughly researched with a comprehensive set of endnotes plus lists of primary and secondary sources, many drawn from countries other than the UK. A great deal of attention has also been paid to giving it as wide an appeal as possible. The author has adopted a rather unusual stylistic approach: each incident is described with passages of fictionalised narrative mixed in with a more conventional recounting of the historical events supported by her own interpretations and comments. Whether or not this approach works will depend on the tastes of the individual reader.

Credit must be handed to Conway for producing such an attractive book at a comparatively inexpensive price. The illustrations complement the text very well; the maps are useful and clear and some of the Victorian etchings and line drawings induce a splendidly melodramatic atmosphere in keeping with some of the contemporary accounts that Hood utilises to good effect. It is therefore a pity that the text is spoiled in places by needless typographical errors and omissions.

Each of the short, self-contained chapters in Come Hell & High Water is an intelligent blend of drama, adventure and historical detail which should appeal to many readers. Despite the fact that roughly two thirds of the world's population lives within 400 kilometres of the sea there is little natural awareness, understanding or respect for this most potent force of Nature; an attempt to address this issue in a lively, accessible and novel format is therefore to be commended.

Jon Wise

Jon Sutherland, Diane Canwell
The Battle of Jutland
Pen and Sword Books, Barnsley 2007; hardback, 214 pages, 51 illustrations; price £19.99.
ISBN 1-84415-529-3

Another book about Jutland! The battle has led to so many books that new, serious works can be justified only in the light of new evidence such as diving on the wrecks. On the other hand, books aimed at attracting new, general readers are always welcome. Popular histories are not easy to write, as lengthy justifications must be avoided whilst still touching on the latest evidence.

The treatment is straightforward. The pre-war building race is outlined, with the Admiralty criticised for failing to adopt the Pollen fire control system. A description of the earlier actions of the battlefleets in the early years of the war follows. There could have been a little more on the failure of Beatty's signal team at Scarborough and Dogger Bank. The Battle of Jutland proper begins on page 81.

The main story follows the usual chronological order dealing with the battle cruiser action, the brief encounters of the battle fleets and the night action. A few track charts would have helped, particularly if traditional charts had been revised in the light of the position of the major wrecks, now surveyed. The authors make good use of eye witness accounts of which some, particularly the German ones, are little known.

Some aspects are less certain than suggested; for example, it is possible that Indefatigable was sunk by a shell penetrating the deck but there is no clear evidence to that effect. Marlborough may have been hit by a torpedo launched by V48 but Wiesbaden is also possible. The effect of the hit was less dramatic: an initial heel of 7-8°, soon reduced. The illustrations include portraits of the admirals involved, not just the overall Commanders seen so often but the lesser squadron flag officers, as well as a representative selection of ship pictures.

The book needed more careful proof reading as there are far too many errors. Though trivial in themselves, these are so numerous as to damage the credibility of the whole. A few examples: Dreadnought did not have 12-12in guns (p.8), Queen Elizabeth did not have 13.5in guns (p.10), Invincible did not have a speed of 27 knots (p.9) – although the correct figures are given on later pages. On page 90 we learn that the battle cruiser action opened at a range of 1,500 yards.

Eur Ing David K Brown, RCNC

Brian Lavery
River-class Frigates and the Battle of the Atlantic:
A Technical and Social History
National Maritime Museum, London, 2006; soft cover, 256 pages, many illustrations & diagrams; price £14.99.
ISBN 13 978 0948065 736

Written by a noted authority on the Royal Navy, this book started life as an attempt to provide a detailed overview of a single warship class from as many different angles as possible. Selecting the 'River' class frigates by virtue of their position as one of the most important British ocean-going warships both designed and built during the Second World War, Brian Lavery sets about his assigned task in comprehensive fashion. Commencing with an overview of the origins of the class, successive chapters describe the ships' structure and propulsion, weapons fit and equipment in impressive detail. Moreover, wider factors are not forgotten, with additional sections dedicated to personnel, their accommodation and the practicalities (including training, bases and organisation) of supporting the ships in operational service. This is rounded off with an overall assessment of the design, as well as its subsequent impact on modern surface escorts.

The book's key strength is Lavery's encyclopaedic knowledge of the Royal Navy's structure and organisation during the Second World War. This is often evidenced by the provision of a greater level of information than might strictly be required by the subject in hand, be it the development and initially troubled introduction of the Hedgehog anti-submarine mortar, or the recruitment of Royal Navy stokers in wartime conditions. This broad approach adds to overall readability of what could otherwise be quite a technical account, and leaves the reader with a wider insight into the Allied conduct of the Battle of the Atlantic than might initially be anticipated.

There is, however, some room for minor criticism. For example, whilst the book is not short of illustrations, there are few external photographs of the ships in service. When coupled with an almost complete lack of information on subjects such as camouflage or specific variations from ship to ship, this makes the volume of less value to potential purchasers such as ship modellers, who might otherwise be thought of as a natural readership. The book is also comparatively weak on the ships constructed for the Royal Canadian and Royal Australian Navies and the specific local factors governing their operation. Whilst the omission of the RAN is understandable given the focus on the Battle of the Atlantic, it does preclude detailed consideration of HMAS *Diamantina*, the only member of the class to have survived into preservation.

Nevertheless, this is a well-researched and well-written description of a previously little-covered escort class which re-introduced the term 'frigate' to modern warship classification. It is also worth noting that the publisher's courageous use of a high quality but soft cover format has resulted in an affordable book which may therefore appeal to a broader range of purchaser than the usual enthusiast.

Conrad Waters

Antony Preston & John Major
Send a Gunboat: the Victorian Navy and Supremacy at Sea, 1854-1904
Conway Maritime Press, 2007; 208 pages, many B&W photos, maps & drawings; price £25.00. ISBN 0-85177-923-9

First published in 1967, the much praised *Send a Gunboat* has now been republished with an additional Foreword by Professor Andrew Lambert of Kings College London and an Afterword by Professor Eric Grove of the University of Salford.

As Professor Lambert states, this was a pioneering book when first published, detailing not only the many small naval campaigns which the Royal Navy undertook in the Victorian era, but also giving the history of the ships most associated with these, the gunboats. From their conception as small, heavily armed vessels, able to fire into the defences of Cherbourg, to their use in the Baltic and Black Seas during the Crimean War, and thence to their role as 'imperial policemen', gunboats were an indispensable part of the Royal Navy, both as a part of the evolving grand strategy developing with France, Russia or the United States in mind, and as small, shallow draft vessels, able to act in the littorals against slave traders, pirates and recalcitrant rulers.

The book was written at a time when Great Britain's ability to act outside of the NATO area was seriously in doubt. Subsequent events have seen the Royal Navy reconnecting with its earlier role of projecting power from the sea, either alone, as in the case of the Falklands War of 1982 and Sierra Leone in 2000, or in concert with other navies, such as in the Bosnian conflict or the Gulf Wars. The Royal Navy has recently launched several new amphibious warfare ships and has reconfigured her small aircraft carriers to take on the role of supporting forces ashore, and other major navies, notably that of the United States, are now re-examining the worth of ships which are able to operate in the littorals and deliver a heavy punch far inland. In the words of Professor Lambert: '...The contemporary relevance of *Send a Gunboat* has never been greater...', a view echoed by Professor Grove in his Afterword.

Sandwiched between these two contributions is a gem of a book. Fifteen chapters take the reader from the early gunboats and their service in the Crimean War to China, fighting pirates and rebels, through crises and confrontations in American and Malaysian waters, to actions off Alexandria and up African rivers, and finally the 'Fisher Axe'. There is also a 'Genealogy of the Gunboat Navy' in a format familiar to readers of Conway's *All the World's Fighting Ships*, detailing the development and service lives of the ships, and four appendices, including a list of all the applications made to the Admiralty between 1857-1861 for warships to 'show the flag', protect British interests, or even '...preserve order among the shippers of guano...' (a request by the Colonial Office, in May 1857; HMS *Cordelia* duly obliged). Appendix D details the history and restoration of HMS *Gannet*, now preserved at The Historic Dockyard, Chatham.

In short, Conway deserve only praise for revising and reprinting this book, which is to be recommended not just to those with an interest in the Royal Navy and its gunboat diplomacy of the 19th century, but to anyone interested in the challenges faced by navies today and in the future.

Andy Field

Chris Thomas
Lamentable Intelligence from the Admiralty: the sinking of HMS *Vanguard* in 1875
Nonsuch Publishing, Dublin 2006; paperback, 192 pages, illustrated: price €21.99. ISBN 1-84588-544-9

The name *Vanguard*, despite its appropriately martial tone, has been something of an ill-starred one in the service of the Royal Navy. There have been ten *Vanguards* in all, from an Elizabethan galleon up to the present nuclear submarine; the latter had her maiden voyage disrupted by anti-nuclear campaigners, while her predecessor, Britain's last and mightiest battleship, ran aground at the mouth of Portsmouth harbour while being towed to the breakers. The second *Vanguard* was humiliatingly sunk during De Ruyter's raid on the Medway; while the seventh and eighth, both battleships, were lost as a result of accident, in the second case with terrible casualties. However it is the story of the earlier of these, the seventh *Vanguard*, that is the subject of Chris Thomas' book.

Thomas takes very much a family history approach, and therefore comes at the story from a slightly different angle to the one with which *Warship* readers are most familiar. Thus, although one of the early chapters covers development in warship design in the period in question, there is a great deal more detail about those who were serving on the ships, about what life was like for the officers and men, about the individual careers of various amongst these, and about the wider contemporary social, economic and political scene. A detailed picture is built up of service in the mid-Victorian Navy. One unintentional but entertaining consequence of this is that the reader is treated to a parade of some most splendid names, so typical of the period (perhaps the best being one Charity Truck, unfortunately not a central character in the story). One of the major pitfalls of family history research is also well illustrated by the fact that there were at least three men by the name of John Davis or John Davies on board *Vanguard* at the time of her sinking.

The actual ramming and sinking of *Vanguard* by her sister ship *Iron Duke* is but a small part of the narrative, but it is here that Thomas excels, brilliantly conveying the tension as the great ships blundered about in the fog off the Irish coast, and the drama during and after the collision. Not one man lost his life (though sadly the Captain's dog may have been drowned – sources disagree), especially remarkable considering that so thick was the fog that the remainder of the Squadron were unaware that anything had happened.

There then followed a Court Martial where, in an extraordinary turn of events, *Vanguard*, and specifically her captain, Richard Dawkins, were effectively made scapegoats. The press got into a right old lather over this, at which point the Admiralty dug their heels in, the whole business eventually becoming a political matter – this being the height of the Gladstone and Disraeli rivalry. None of this did any good for Dawkins who, while he may have made some mistakes, does not seem to have been any more culpable than a number of others, but who was made to carry the can. A major reason for Thomas' writing of the book has been to attempt to clear this unfortunate officer's name.

Although more rigorous structural editing would not have gone amiss, the story reads well. However, the author's habit of sometimes slipping into the first person is annoying, as is his tendency to digress during the narrative into thanking those who have helped him in his research, rather than leaving this for the chapter notes or the separate list of acknowledgments. There are various appendices and a bibliography, but unfortunately no index.

This is an unusual book, but a very good one, and thoroughly recommended to anyone interested in the Victorian Navy.

Stephen Dent

Steve Horn
The Second Attack on Pearl Harbor
Naval Institute Press 2005; hardback, 347 pages, tables; price $29.95.
ISBN 1 59114 388 8

The primary focus of this book is a detailed account of Operation K, the longest shore-based bombing mission of the Second World War, in which two Kawanishi H8K 'Emily' flying boats took off from Wotje in the Marshall Islands on 3 March 1942, were refuelled by specially-modified submarines at French Frigate Shoals, and subsequently dropped their eight 250kg bombs over Pearl Harbor. The mission lasted almost 36 hours and covered more than 4750 miles. Despite elaborate and detailed planning, extensive training of the aircraft and submarine crews, and impressive logistical feats, the mission itself was a failure. Low cloud over Pearl Harbor obscured the target, and the bombs were dropped harmlessly on the slopes of Mount Tantalus and into the sea in the harbour approaches. Meanwhile American Kittyhawk and Airacobra night-fighters, scrambled on the basis of radar contacts, blundered about in the dark without spotting the Japanese aircraft.

Unfortunately the book itself is also something of a damp squib. There is some fascinating material here, as the author also covers other Japanese plans to bomb the mainland United States and the Panama Canal using submarine-launched aircraft, balloons made by Japanese high-school girls out of tissue paper and paste, and the giant Project Z (or Fugaku) six-engined strategic bomber modelled on the American Superfortress. However, the organisation of the book is shambolic with a large chunk devoted to the first attack on Pearl Harbor – which has little relevance to the 'special operations' described in the rest of the book – as well as potted histories of the approach to the Pacific War and the war itself, which the author returns to whenever he runs out of interesting things to say. The historical commentary contains factual errors and some received opinions which have been all too readily accepted, and these cast a shadow over the quality of the new information provided. (His account of Japanese submarine aviation development is bizarre, to say the least.)

While at times being guilty of 'padding', Horn simultaneously fails to provide an analysis of the validity of Japan's special operations strategy or a detailed critique of the various initiatives and operations in the context of the progress of the war. Fascinating as they are, the accounts of the operations remain largely undeveloped. There are many missed opportunities: surely it is not unreasonable to expect an illustration of the impressive 'Emily' or the I-15 ('B' type) or I-400 (STo) submarine, while a map of the central Pacific area showing the Japanese bases in the Marshalls and their position relative to Pearl Harbor and French Frigate Shoals would help the reader to better understand the logistics of Operation K and to follow its progress. Instead, we get a relatively crude Glossary of Aircraft listing the aircraft which took part in the Pacific War, including well-known carrier planes such as the IJN 'Kate' and the Douglas Dauntless.

John Jordan

Wilfred Nunn
Tigris Gunboats: The Forgotten War in Iraq 1914-17
Chatham Publishing, London 2007; hard cover, 288 pages, 31 illustrations & 7 maps; price £19.99.
ISBN 978 1 86176 308 2

Tigris Gunboats is a personal account of naval operations during the First World War in the region then known as Mesopotamia. Written by Wilfred Nunn, the senior Royal Navy officer in the theatre for much of the campaign, it was first published in 1932 by Andrew Melrose Ltd. This new edition incorporates a short introduction by Sir Jeremy Greenstock, the UK's Special representative in Iraq during 2003-04, but is otherwise little changed from its original incarnation.

Vice-Admiral Nunn adopts a broadly chronological approach to his experiences. These commence with his receipt of orders whilst in command of the sloop *Espiègle* in the Persian Gulf in September 1914 to proceed up the Shatt el Arab waterway to protect local British interests in the event of a war with Turkey. Principal amongst these was the Anglo Persian Oil Company's refinery close to Abadan, which appears to have been remarkably lightly defended in view of the importance of its supplies to the new oil-fired capital ships being built for the Grand Fleet. The successful landing of a British Indian Army expeditionary force to secure the area was followed by a steady, often opportunistic expansion of this initial mission which ultimately resulted in the capture of Baghdad in March 1917. Throughout this period, the Royal Navy used a handful of gunboats to command the key communication channels of the Tigris and Euphrates Rivers.

The book's main strength – but also its weakness – is the eyewitness focus of much of the narrative, most notably of the events surrounding the first, unsuccessful advance on Baghdad in the autumn of 1915 which were to result in the prolonged siege and ultimate surrender of the force of Major General Charles Townshend at Kut. Townshend is portrayed during the retreat to Kut calmly sitting at a table studying books on Napoleon's campaigns. Juxtaposed with this to some effect are descriptions of the desperate rearguard action supported by the naval contingent which resulted in the capture of the gunboat *Firefly* following an unfortunate hit on her boiler. In spite of this, Nunn is careful to avoid criticism of any of the key participants in what was one of the most significant British military debacles of the Great War. This general lack of analysis – along with a seemingly ready acceptance of the official point of view – is frustrating, making it harder to place the account in a broader context.

To an extent, therefore, this new edition can be seen as something of a missed opportunity. It might have been more revealing to combine Nunn's text with the comments of at least one contemporary historian rather than rely on Sir Jeremy's pertinent but rather broad-brush comparisons with events in modern Iraq. In spite of this, Tigris Gunboats makes a valuable account of these lesser known operations available to a new generation.

Conrad Waters

Kenneth Rawson
Ever the Apprentice
The Memoir Club, Stanhope, 2006; softback, 237 pages, many illustrations; price £14.95.
ISBN 1 84104 155 6

This is the autobiography of Ken Rawson, naval architect and teacher. This reviewer served under him several times and benefited much from his wise guidance.

After a difficult childhood Rawson entered Portsmouth Dockyard as an apprentice in 1942. The education in the Dockyard Schools was intensely competitive, half the class being dropped at the end of each year so that even completing the four year course was a distinction. Rawson did more, coming out top of all Royal Dockyard apprentices nationwide. He was selected for training for the Royal Corps of Naval Constructors involving a year at the RN Engineering College, three years at Greenwich and a year at sea.

His first job was at the Naval Construction Research Establishment at Rosyth. He went on to work on frigate design leading to the 'Tribal' class while at the same time creating a new lecture course on structural design at the RN College. An exchange between Lloyds Register and the Naval Construction Department resulted in Rawson then working on merchant ships, followed by a move to Bath in charge of the refit of the carrier *Eagle*, a demanding task with little satisfaction. In 1965, together with a fellow constructor, Eric Tupper, he wrote a text book of naval architecture; this has now gone to five editions, selling 40,000 copies. In 1967 Rawson was promoted to Chief Constructor and moved to a small group studying the future of fleet maintenance, work which was transferred to Whitehall where he was able see the workings of senior Staff and Ministers at close quarters. In 1972 came a complete change when he became Professor of Warship Design at University College, London, (UCL). Next, an appointment as Assistant Director in charge of forward design of surface ships involved reading the Naval Staff's 'Wish List' and reconciling this with the resources available – money, manpower, shipyard capacity etc. In 1979 Rawson moved up to become Chief Naval Architect (CNA) at a difficult time – the era of the 'short fat' frigate controversy. As the Ministry's front man he was portrayed by the media as an ignorant reactionary. He felt that he did not get proper support from his masters. It is a complicated story which should be read by anyone concerned with Defence Procurement. The Ministry – and Rawson – were fully justified by an expensive independent enquiry. The Falklands War was sad in a different way with the loss of so many men and ships. With the 'short fat' lobby still active, there were more press reports suggesting that there were serious faults in Britain's ships but the Ship Department was fully supported by a Parliamentary enquiry. One of the main tasks of the CNA (and of his Deputy, this reviewer) was the safety of ships taken up from trade (STUFT). Horrified at the poor standard of the majority, both became active promoters of higher safety standards for RO-RO ferries.

Eur Ing David K Brown, RCNC

WARSHIP GALLERY: W J CONNORS

New Zealand's involvement with British forces in the First World War is generally seen in terms of the soldiers who fought and died at Gallipoli or in the trenches of the Western Front. There was, however, a little-known contribution to the Royal Navy which resulted from a drive in New Zealand to enlist personnel to help man the many coastal patrol vessels under construction by mid-point in the war. Ironically, the instigator of this scheme wore the khaki uniform of the Auckland Mounted Rifles when his unit sailed from Wellington in October 1914, part of the first contingent of 9000 New Zealanders to answer the call of King and Empire. He was Trooper W J Connors (WJC).

Although the NZ troops, and the Australians who crossed the Indian Ocean with them, were initially destined for Great Britain, by the time they reached Egypt planning was well underway for the landing on the Gallipoli Peninsula and these troops, later to become the famed Anzacs, were diverted to this campaign, WJC among them. In August 1915 he was wounded and later sent to Britain to recuperate.

His brother, Captain E J Connors RN, was on the staff of the Fourth Sea Lord and WJC discussed with him the possibility of recruiting experienced NZ yachtsmen and motor mechanics for the Naval Auxilliary Patrol. Captain Connors and another RN officer, a Commander Armstrong, were dubious that suitable men could be found there. WJC convinced them his scheme was practical, using as evidence, among other things, photographs from a NZ weekly paper showing that New Zealand had a strong off-shore yachting heritage and well-developed mechanical expertise. As a result Armstrong went to New Zealand in 1916 to select volunteers for the Patrol. In the meantime WJC was liaising long-distance with Major Charles Palmer of the New Zealand Army's Motor Service Corps, to find suitable recruits. (On the outbreak of war Palmer formed a Motor Boat Patrol Service. At that time had New Zealand had no official navy, although the RN maintained a presence there since the early 1800s).

The accompanying illustrations are from the collection of WJC, who was a keen photographer. As no written record exists, the sequence of his activities with the RN is difficult to establish. His first appointment as a naval officer appears to be as sub-lieutenant on the troopship *Demosthenes* on December 1916 – about the same time the first draft of yachties and mechanics left New Zealand. WJC was discharged from

The officer on the right of this photo of the flying navigation bridge of the Perlona *is thought to be Connors.*

Formerly a private yacht, the Perlona is listed in Dittmar & Colledge as a 'Motor Drifter'. An earlier photo in the collection shows her with the pennant number 118. According to Dittmar & Colledge this series of numbers was cancelled in 1918 and replaced by 4301-4319 from 9 May and 4320-4328 from 20 June to avoid confusion. This dates the photo from between the latter date and 14 December 1919, when she was released from service. Displacement is given as 57 tons and year of launch as 1895.

the NZ Army in May that year.

From his photographs it seems probable he was engaged on salvage work at some time. Two show him aboard a barge numbered U.C.2 with a forward mounted crane and a barge-like craft numbered A583 under tow. Other pictures show a broken-backed destroyer and damaged merchant ships. He appears to have served on the requisitioned steam yacht HMSY *Perlona* which bore the numbers 118 and 4320. Pictures in the collection show ML's at sea and close-up and on-board shots of the battered and shell-torn *Vindictive* after the April 1918 Zeebrugge raid, so it is possible that WJC was on one of the ML's involved in this operation. It is certain, however, that he was in the ML flotilla (pictured here) that travelled through the French/German canal system as part of the Allied occupation forces in Germany soon after the end of the Great War. Thus WJC, who left New Zealand with the first troops, returned well after most of his kiwi

A monitor, probably Terror, 'lets go' with her twin 15in guns during one of the many regular bombardments of Zeebrugge and Ostend.

brothers-in-arms were repatriated.

The NZ small boat recruitment scheme mustered 80 men for officer training, mainly yachtsmen with extensive experience, and 100 others who trained for duty in ML engine rooms as chief petty officers. However, WJC's associations with the Navy continued in the 1920s and '30s and throughout the Second World War when he served as Captain, Seatoun Barracks, Wellington. Between the wars he lobbied actively to form what ultimately became the strong Royal New Zealand Navy Volunteer Reserve, which was to provide many officers and men to serve in the Second World War.

At the end of his service, following the Second World War, WJC held the rank of Commander. He died while vising Australia from his home in Tauranga, New Zealand, in September 1970. He was 84. It is understood he emigrated to New Zealand from Devon as a young man.

Glenn Pettit

WARSHIP GALLERY

These remarkable photos were taken on the decks of the old cruiser Vindictive, between the Zeebrugge Raid of 23 April, when she was used to land 200 troops at the entrance to the Bruges Canal, and the Ostend Raid of 9 May, when she was used as a blockship. The photos were taken at Dover, probably during early May. Prior to the Zeebrugge operation a false deck (which is what the officers are standing on in the image above) was built about 12 feet over the main deck – this to raise the boarding ramps to the level of the Mole at Zeebrugge. Lewis guns, Stokes mortars, flame throwers, and whatever heavier machine guns were already aboard were fitted and sheltered with mattresses, sand-bags and whatever else came to mind. In these photos the decks have been tidied up and the blood from the Zeebrugge raid has been washed away.

The mattress padded fore-top to the left was the position from which Sgt Norman Finch, R.M.A., continued to fire the pom-poms and Lewis guns onto the Mole even after two German shells killed every other man in the top. Though severely wounded Sgt Finch maintained a continuous fire until yet another shell destroyed his remaining weapons. Sgt Finch was subsequently awarded the Victoria Cross for conspicuous gallantry.

Four ML's alongside the Watersports Clubhouse which served as the Flotilla's home base in Cologne. The presence of ML 576 indicates a date between late January 1919, when the second detachment of ML's arrived, and August of the same year, when five boats (including ML 576) were ordered home. The full dressing of the boats suggests that the event being celebrated was either 1) the change of command in mid-April, 1919 as General Sir Herbert Plumer returned to England, to be replaced by General Sir William Robertson (with a visit by Haig and numerous other dignitaries); or 2) a visit to Cologne by Marshall Foch and General Weygand on the 16th of May as they made a tour – the first since the Armistice – down the Rhine from Strasbourg to Cologne.

The Rhine Flotilla

Jeffrey Charles is a computer systems architect who has been conducting research into the Motor Launch Patrol of World War One, with an emphasis on the RNVR officers manning the ML's, for the past five years. Most recently he has been exploring the history of the post-Armistice Rhine Patrol Flotilla and is currently preparing a book on the subject to be published in late 2008. Further information about the history and deployment of the ML's is available on his website at www.motorlaunchpatrol.net.

In early 1915 Henry Sutphen, manager of the Electric Boat Company (Elco), met with Admiralty authorities visiting the United States to discuss the design of a 'mosquito' fleet of small, fast anti-submarine craft. An arrangement was made for the delivery of fifty 75ft motor launches (ML's). Under the leadership of Irwin Chase designs were completed in April and construction began in early May. The torpedoing of the *Lusitania* prompted the Admiralty to revise their order, adding 500 ships extended in length to 80ft. Incredibly, Elco delivered all 550 ML's within 488 days. Later, an additional 31 ships were delivered.

This lucrative contract, arranged among men with long-standing relationships, was not without controversy among English builders. Indeed, the story was followed and commented upon regularly within the pages of magazines such as *The Yachting Monthly*, acting during the war as the official publication of the R.N.V.R.

In any event, the ML's were delivered and quickly deployed within the Auxiliary Patrol about Great Britain and Ireland, the French coast, the length of the Mediterranean, and even the West Indies. Initial notions of using them for anti-submarine patrol work were tempered somewhat by experience when it became clear that the design did not lend itself well to extended duty at sea. Given her narrow beam and sharp bows, the ML was decidedly not a heavy-weather ship. The ML was quickly dubbed the 'Movie' by the R.N.V.R. officers commanding them, a comment on their heavy motion in a seaway. Indeed, motion aboard an ML was, for some, *the* defining characteristic of the ship.

With evolving experience, the ML flotillas were deployed for short-term patrol duties, monitoring civilian shipping, mine laying and clearing, laying smoke-screens to protect the monitors bombarding the French and Belgian coasts and, as the technology evolved, for underwater listening, usually working with larger craft more able to actually deal with the U-boats (though there were one or two confirmed kills attributed to the ML's).

Perhaps their most notable contribution came during the 23 April 1918 raids on Zeebrugge and Ostend when flotillas of ML's were detailed to provide smoke-screen cover for the blockships and the diversionary landing party ships. Certain ML's were also detailed to collect the crews of the block ships as they were scuttled. Among the eleven Victoria Crosses awarded after the raids that night and the follow-on raid on Ostend on 10 May 1918, three were awarded to ML commanders.

With the signing of the Armistice the Allied powers quickly moved to occupy the Rhineland. Control of the Allied bridgeheads on the eastern shore was obviously of importance, the bridgehead cities of Cologne (British), Coblenz (American) and Mayence (French) acting as headquarters for the respective powers.

Perhaps of lesser importance, but necessary for the overall strategy of controlling communications and commerce in the occupied territories, was control of traffic on rivers and canals. Within days of the Armistice the Field Navigation Commission, headquartered at Nancy, was established to regulate all navigable waterways within the occupied territories including rivers and canals in Belgium, the Rhine between Alsace-Lorraine and the Dutch frontier, the Moselle from Alsace-Lorraine to its junction with the Rhine, and the Saar from Alsace-Lorraine to its junction with the Moselle.

In support of this the British and French deployed ships to their respective headquarter cities. Both relied upon the ML (the French Navy having purchased forty ML's, or *Vedettes* as they termed them, from the Royal Navy during the war, plus an undetermined number directly from Elco).

Commander The Honorable P.G.E.C. Acheson, M.V.O., D.S.O., R.N., who had spent much of the war as the Executive Officer of HMS *Inflexible*, participating in the actions at the Dardenelles, the Falklands, Jutland, and the surrender of the German Fleet at Scapa Flow, was given a new command on 14 December 1918. He was to proceed to Cologne by way of the rivers and canals of France, departing on the 17th of the month with twelve ML's to comprise the Rhine Patrol Flotilla. Their course was an expedient imposed by the limitations of Dutch neutrality which prevented direct warship access via the Rhine.

The passage of the fledgling Rhine Flotilla from Portsmouth to Le Havre on 22 December 1918 was adventurous, with two of the ML's lost. The first, *ML 121*, Lieut. John Robinson, D.S.C., R.N.V.R., sank about fifteen miles down the coast from Le Havre on the Seine Bank. Robinson had been in command of the ML for all of eleven days, having come from *ML 424* aboard which he had participated in the St. George's Day raid on Zeebrugge – earning a D.S.C. for his actions. Later that day, *ML 566* (commander unknown) foundered off Cape Barfleur.

At Le Havre the flotilla appears to have picked up two more ML's, bringing it back to full complement. They

Three units of the French Rhine Patrol Flotilla, which was headquartered at Mayence (Mainz). The ML's themselves were sold to the French by the British in a batch of 40 ships. Additionally, the French contracted directly with Elco in the U.S. to purchase more ML's. Since they were already in full production it was a simple (and lucrative) matter for Elco to continue past the original order for 580 ships for the Royal Navy, eventually producing 701 ML's by war's end. These were sold to France, Italy and even Russia. In French service these boats were designated 'vedettes' (hence the 'V' pennant number). Note that the French ML's have the famous 75mm gun on the foredeck.

ML's of the Rhine Patrol Flotilla making their way to the Rhine. Due to Holland's neutrality they were unable to access the Rhine from the North Sea. Instead, they sailed to Le Havre, through Rouen, up the Seine to Paris, to the Marne all the way to Vitry-le-Françoise, through the Vosges by way of the Marne-Rhine Canal to Strasbourg, and then down the Rhine to Cologne.

An interesting aspect of this picture is the fact that each ML has been prepared for the trip. Once they passed through Paris and reached the Marne it became apparent that they would need to strike down their deckhouses to fit beneath the many bridges due to the high water levels. Acheson states in his diary that on occasion they had to wait for days for water levels to subside enough to make the passage. Masts would undoubtedly have come down earlier in the voyage – the ML's would never have made it through Paris with them stepped upright.

continued up the Seine, through Paris, crossing to the Marne and on to Vitry-le-Françoise. Here they entered the Marne-Rhine Canal, passing through Nancy before arriving at Strasbourg to enter the Rhine.

Meanwhile, on 3 January 1919, Lieut. R.G. Fife, R.N.V.R., received orders to proceed from Portsmouth with an additional four ML's (with at least one, ML 229, being commanded by Lieut. Robinson of the earlier, ill-fated ML 121). This second deployment was ordered to sail on 11 January 1919 following the same route as the main body of the Flotilla.

By the end of January the Rhine Flotilla was in Cologne with headquarters established at the appropriated facilities of the Cologne Watersports Club. This was built on a barge situated just to the south of the Hohenzollern Bridge along the Frankenwerft. Families soon joined those Flotilla officers able to live in rented housing

Life for the Flotilla included regular patrols of the Rhine within the British sector, duty as naval escort for visiting dignitaries (Foch, Weygand, the American General Allen, etc.) and formal visits to the headquarter cities of the other Allied powers during ceremonial events.

One such visit occurred in mid-April 1919 when Commander Acheson received orders from the Admiralty to proceed to Mayence for a review of the British and French Rhine Flotillas by General Mangin. Orders for the review were quite specific, detailing how many guns to fire in salute, where the Flotilla was to be on the river, how crews should be arrayed on deck, how many revolutions their engines were to turn, etc.

It is interesting to note that *Capitaine de Corvette* F. Darlan acted as the French liaison officer for the Flotilla. This was François Darlan, serving with the French Rhine Patrol Flotilla. In 1925 he was appointed liaison officer to the French Navy Minister, eventually rising through the ranks to Admiral and culminating in his appointment as Navy Minister under Petain in 1940. In December 1942 he was assassinated by a young French resistance fighter while visiting Algiers.

On 5 August 1919, Lieut. Stanley F. Laidlaw, R.N. received orders from Commander Acheson to proceed back to Portsmouth with five ML's. It appears the Admiralty wished to dispense with the Flotilla altogether. However, General Sir William Robert Robertson, in command of the British Occupation forces at this time, determined that the Flotilla could not be entirely dispensed with – to do so would appear to give the French, with their Flotilla, a free hand on all of the Rhine.

At some point in late 1919 ML 229, under Lieut. John Robinson, R.N.V.R., was extensively damaged in an explosion while fuelling at

WARSHIP GALLERY

ML 229 (Lt. John W Robinson) on the Rhine. Note the wireless aerial setup on the ship. Not all ML's were equipped with a wireless set. But it appears that many (if not all) of the Rhine Flotilla's craft were so equipped – probably seen as a necessity in communications while on patrol at a time when it was still not known for sure that the Armistice would hold or that a peace treaty would be signed.

As noted above, ML 576 joined the Rhine Patrol Flotilla as part of a second detachment of ML's in late January 1919. It is not clear who was in command of her at this point. In August of that year, five of the ML's, including 576, were ordered home under the command of Lieut. Stanley F. Laidlaw, R.N. Again, no commander is directly associated with this particular ship.

205

WARSHIP 2008

Three photos of ML 229 following the damage resulting from a petrol explosion which killed Motor Mechanic Lakey, RNVR, and injured Lt. Robinson and two other members of his crew. There was extensive damage to the hull; the explosion even knocked the caulking out of her seams!

In the view of the damaged hull note the large exhaust vent right above the water-line. The ML's carried two Standard Motor Construction Company six-cylinder petrol engines. They vented exhaust out each side – the ML's were not known for being the

WARSHIP GALLERY

Cologne. One member of the crew, Motor Mechanic Lakey, R.N.V.R., was killed and others, including Robinson, were wounded. The damage to the ship was extensive enough to make it a complete write-off.

In late August 1920, four ML's were ordered to Mayence on the occasion of the *Semaine Hippique* (Horse Week) of Wiesbaden. Arrangements were facilitated once again by the newly promoted *Capitaine de Frégate* Darlan, now Commander of the French Rhine Flotilla. As is often the lot of the common sailor or soldier, it was only Commander Acheson who was billeted in a hotel for the duration of the stay. The rest of the crews slept aboard their ships.

During the winter of 1920/1921 Commander Acheson's health began to fail. Though he would live until 1957 he determined that the time had come to retire from naval life. On 7 March 1921 Commander A.R.A. Macdonald, R.N., arrived to take over command of the Flotilla.

To date, little research has been done regarding the activities of the Flotilla and its men during its remaining years. We know that, at the end of 1921, the Flotilla was reduced to five ML's. The suppression of the Flotilla was again periodically suggested by the Admiralty; with local Occupation command arguing that the prestige value of having it in Cologne was more important than the cost savings. The last five ML's remained on station until 27 January 1926 when Cologne was evacuated by the British Army of Occupation. It is not yet known if the ML's were, at this point, able to take the more direct route home through the Netherlands and along the coast of Belgium and France or if they crossed France by way of the rivers and canals one last time.

These ML's were some of the very last to be decommissioned and sold out of the Royal Navy. All 581 were eliminated by 1927 – sold individually or in small lots for private yacht conversion or for use by other countries – thus bringing the story of the ML's of the Royal Navy to a close.

quietest craft on the water. Note also the large rubbing strake forward of the exhaust port. This was probably added as the ships were to make their way to the Rhine, knowing that they would encounter ice on the canals and rivers (and on the Rhine itself on occasion). Also of note is the wiring and plumbing. The engine room – where the explosion took place – was the mechanical heart of the ship. All wiring and most plumbing terminated in the engine room. Plumbing would have been for water (both for washing up and the w.c. and for fire-fighting) as well as fuel and compressed air (used to start the engines).

The two onboard photos give an excellent view of the six-cylinder petrol engines, which are largely intact following the explosion. Much of the plumbing and wiring, together with the auxiliary engine, had already been stripped out before the boat was brought to the yard. The four mounting points on the after bulkhead were for the electrical panel. For just such reasons as this explosion this bulkhead and the one at the forward end of the engine room were made of steel rather than wood.

In the first photo an RN (or RNR) lieutenant is overseeing repairs being conducted by the boatyard workforce. In the second we are looking at the chart house deck, which was located (vertically) about half-way down between the main deck and the engine room deck. Beneath the chart-house deck were the main port/stbd fuel tanks, which had a 790-gallon capacity – there were two more tanks aft in the lazarette with a 450-gallon capacity. The upper bulkhead between the engine room and the chart house was wood and was clearly carried away along with the chart house in the explosion.

WARSHIP 2008

This is almost certainly ML 542; her deck-house roof was of an unusual, and easily identified configuration. The photo was taken in Cologne alongside the Rheinauhafen looking north towards the Hindenburg and Hohenzollern bridges. While the ML's were based at the Watersports Club upstream of the Hohenzollern bridge the facilities there were not conducive to the loading and unloading of stores, fuel, etc; the dock facilities along the Rheinauhafen were clearly better for this. In this instance note the numerous small fuel cans - a dangerous way to fuel a boat as ML 229 would attest! At the end of this long pier was the customs house for the bonded section of the port facilities.

A sailor throws an empty petrol can (top left of photo) back onto the pier. Other cans are neatly stacked topsides.

A sailor gives gunnery instruction to three 'brown jobs'; the gun is the Hotchkiss 3pdr which replaced the old-model 13pdr fitted in early units. The photo is almost certainly of ML 291 (Commander Acheson's ship). The deckhouse configuration and the black cone atop the wireless aerial's lead into the charthouse/wireless cabin give her away. There is another picture, in the Robinson album (see website), of the ship underway with these same three Army officers aboard; they were probably on a tour in the vicinity of Cologne.